THE ART of SAFE CAVE DIVING

Dayton Saltsman, Editor

National Association for Cave Diving

Gainesville, Florida

The Art of Safe Cave Diving

Copyright ©1991, 1994, 1995 by the National Association for Cave Diving, Inc.
All Rights Reserved

No part of this book may be reproduced in any form
without the express written consent of the
National Association for Cave Diving.

Published in the United States of America
by the National Association for Cave Diving, Inc. (NACD)
P. O. Box 14492
Gainesville, Florida 32604

ISBN 0-938337-00-9

Library of Congress Catalog Card Number: 95-72414

First Printing November, 1995

DEDICATION IN MEMORY OF

Cuauhtemoc Gonzalez

Son of Carlos Hank Gonzalez

and to all those who died cave diving

teaching the rest of us how to cave dive more safely

ACKNOWLEDGEMENTS

Authors: Jeffrey E. Bozanic, Danny Brass, John Burge, Tom Cook, David Desautels, Rory Dickens, Mary Fahning, Richard Franz, Bill Gavin, Steve Gerrard, H. V. Grey, Paul Heinerth, Karl E. Huggins, Arthur Leitheuser, Mike McCaskill, Dale Malloy, Milledge Murphey, Ph.D., Dan Orr, Dayton Saltsman, Robert W. Smith, Parker A. Turner, Robert Tyson, Charles Vallance, and J. Billy Young.

Supplementary Authors: Danny Brass, Robert Millott, Ph.D. and Dayton Saltsman.

Illustrators: W. L. Adams, H. V. Grey, Karl E. Huggins, Cathy Murray, Robert Rutledge, Frank Rupert, Dayton Saltsman, and Carol Vilece.

Photographers: George Bortnyk, Jim Bowden, Jeffrey E. Bozanic, Larry Boucha, Nancy Boucha, Bryn-Alan Studios, Bill Carlson, Jim Coke, Diver's Alert Network (DAN), William Dooley, Lalo Fiorelli, Steve Gerrard, Lamar Hires/ Dive Rite Manufacturing, Steve Keene, Mark Kirby, Ann Kristovich, Mike Madden, Mario Mitchell, George Ryschkewitsch, Wes Skiles, Dennis Williams, and J. Billy Young.

Cover Design and Layout: Parker A. Turner.

Typesetting and Design: Maguire Printing & Design, Inc.

Editorial Assistance: Judy Hughes.

Text Coordinator: Steve Gerrard.

Editors / Reviewers: Jeffrey E. Bozanic, Danny Brass, Tim Brewton, David Desautels, Steve Gerrard, H. V. Grey, Jim Kasserman, Chris Muir, Machelle Muir, Milledge Murphey, Ph.D., Betty Orr, Robert Rutledge, Dayton Saltsman, Wes Skiles, Danny Wellner, and Oliver Wells.

Typist: Chris Bennett.

NACD Logo: Milledge Murphey, Ph.D.

All Rights Reserved.
No part of this book may be reproduced in any form
without the express written consent of the
National Association for Cave Diving.

The National Association for Cave Diving (NACD) hereby grants written permission to all contributors to *The Art of Safe Cave Diving* to publish their original works in the unedited form in which they were submitted.

All previously copyrighted material in *The Art of Safe Cave Diving* used with permission.

First and Last Things

The first thing is the title. It is the first thing you come to, and you might misunderstand it. It is not descriptive. There is no such thing as safe cave diving. There is *safer* and *less safe* cave diving, but no *safe* cave diving. The title was chosen for historical and literary reasons.

In 1973, the NACD published a comprehensive introduction to cave diving entitled *Safe Cave Diving.* It was edited by Tom Mount, the NACD's first Training Director, and met the needs of the cave diving training program for a suitable reference textbook.

The Art of Safe Cave Diving is the long-anticipated update. Three of the contributors to *Safe Cave Diving,* (Rory Dickens, Dale Malloy and Robert Smith) have also written chapters for *The Art of Safe Cave Diving.* Robert Smith's "Stress in Cave Diving" remains unchanged from the earlier publication. For these historical reasons, the title of this work contains and expands on the earlier title, just as the contents do.

The literary reasons for choosing the title are less straight-forward. It might be contrasted with one of the best known early scuba texts, *The Science of Skin and Scuba Diving.* One might wax philosophic about the choice of the word *art* rather than *science* or *practice* or *techniques.* Rather than defend the choice, consider some alternatives that were rejected. (Feel free to imagine additional titles: flattering or unflattering, serious or humorous, sacred or profane, according to your mood.) Titles not chosen include: *Son of Safe Cave Diving, Relatively Safe Cave Diving, The NACD's Big Book of Safe Cave Diving Practices and Principles,* and *You Might Think There's Such a Thing as Safe Cave Diving but Your Mama Knows There Ain't.*

Which brings us to the last thing. Your death. It is the last thing you will do in this life. It may be the last thing you do cave diving. I hope not. This book and all the efforts behind it are aimed at preventing that. Unfortunately, there is no way to guarantee a happy outcome for all dives. There is no recipe, no algorithm, no set of charms , rituals and talismans that can do that. And there's no guarantee against any of the lesser evils that may befall you when diving: DCS, air embolism, sinus squeeze, hypothermia, etc.

But while there are no guarantees in cave diving, or in life, there are strategies and practices that can help mitigate dangers and cope with problems. This book is full of them. Still, there are many things to learn beyond what's presented here: from instructors, from other cave divers, from other books and articles, and from your own experiences. The adventure, and the learning, never ends.

According to the philosopher Heraclitus, "You cannot step twice into the same river." Not only will you be different, so will the river æ or the cave. It will be changed just by your having been there. And if a lot of you go there, the cave æ or the river æ will be changed a lot. Usually, not for the better. Safety and conservation go hand-in-hand. Make your diving safe for yourself and for the cave. And recognize the subaquatic cave for what it is: a vast, subterranean wilderness that happens also to be the oldest, largest and best water filtration and distribution system ever devised. As well as one of the most fragile, delicate and strangely beautiful environments known. In this place, we are the outsiders, we are the aliens.

Sometimes the beauty, the fragility, and the other-worldliness can cause us to forget the danger. But it is always there. Some mistakes can be corrected, some difficulties can be overcome. In fact, with information from *The Art of Safe Cave Diving,* you should be able to anticipate or correct most mistakes and overcome most difficulties. But occasionally, one crucial mistake can mean death. At other times, otherwise small, insignificant little mistakes can accumulate until a critical mass is achieved, overwhelming the diver or dive team. There are some things that are still unknown about this alien world in the water beneath the ground. There are some people who will hesitate, even if only momentarily, at a critical point and miss the opportunity for timely action. And there are some things that, given the circumstances and the timing and the resources available, are inexorable.

But as auto racer Graham Hill said, "If you take the danger out of it, my grandmother can get in the car and go every bit as fast as I can." Cave diving isn't for everybody. It isn't for Graham Hill's grandmother. It isn't for Graham Hill. It isn't even for most scuba divers. As you read *The Art of Safe Cave Diving,* you will discover the qualities that are desirable for a cave diver. Although they will vary a bit from individual to individual, the fundamentals are universal. You must understand the risks realistically; assess objectively your ability to deal with them; and be willing to accept the consequences of your own actions and decisions, for yourself and for the entire dive team.

Cave diving is a risky business. The contributors to *The Art of Safe Cave Diving,* as well as the NACD, its Officers and Directors, make no claim that anything about cave diving is safe; no claim that anything in this book will prevent accident or injury; no claim that just because you picked up a copy of this book and read any part of it that you are better, safer, smarter, taller, or have in any way improved your chances of surviving the next ten minutes, much less your next dive; and no claim that anything in this book represents the current opinion of anyone, including the original author, about the best, safest, or most stylish way to cave dive. People who are accident-prone, claustrophobic, poor swimmers, egotistical, or harboring death-wishes are manifestly bad candidates for cave diving. Some other individuals are also bad candidates for cave diving, but the factors are not so obvious. It is up to you to be responsible and self-honest.

Considering all this, and the unfortunate number of individuals who die scuba diving in caves, as well as those few who die cave diving, you may be wondering why anyone would ever do it. It's a question frequently asked. I think the best answer was given by Tom Mount: "Either you're one of us and you understand it; or you aren't and you don't." Whichever group you fit into, you'll find *The Art of Safe Cave Diving* an interesting and informative book well worth your time, at least on an overcast Tuesday. By the end of the book, you should know whether you're one of us or not. You will probably also understand why *The Art of Safe Cave Diving* was chosen as the title.

The contributors bring quite a lot of experience and knowledge to the enterprise. Consequently, there is much information and a good deal of wisdom. There is also personal preference. Cave diving is a very individualized activity, and that individuality is preserved in this book. By the time you have finished *The Art of Safe Cave Diving,* and completed a thorough program of instruction, you will begin adapting and individualizing your cave diving choices, too.

Even if you are an experienced cave diver, you likely will find new and useful information. And if you find something safer, better or easier that is not in the book, write it down and send it to one of the cave diving periodicals to share with the rest of us.

If you meet one of the contributors, thank him for sharing his knowledge, even if you disagree. And before you criticize, check his current opinion. He may have revised it. Or perhaps the bone-headed editor altered the meaning or omitted critical information without realizing what he was doing. If so, the bone-headed editor now offers his sincere apology.

Live long and prosper!

Dayton Saltsman
St. Petersburg, FL
Fall, 1994

TABLE OF CONTENTS

EXPANDED TABLE OF CONTENTS

THE NEED FOR SPECIALIZED TRAINING

by Dale R. Malloy

The overhead environment encountered in cave diving is the centr-al factor around which all other aspects of diving in submerged caves must be planned. The fact that direct access to the surface at any time during the progress of the dive is impossible is still not obvious to the uninformed; hence, we continue to have the uninformed needlessly drown while attempting this new experience they have heard so much about.

In view of other conditions related to the overhead environment, most of which are not dangerous when encountered in open water, the cave diver must master the use of a variety of new techniques, equipment and an intense level of awareness of the dive as it progresses. This complex burden of equipment, techniques and behaviors is best learned under controlled circumstances, in much the same manner as the open water diver first masters a new, unfamiliar piece of equipment in a swimming pool or other sheltered dive site. As the diver develops the ability to confidently meet these demands, he or she then begins to venture forth and fully enjoy the sport.

Diver safety and comfort leading to enjoyment of the dive are major reasons for the diver acquiring additional knowledge and training about this special environment. Tangential to these reasons are:

1. the opportunity to help others safely enjoy the sport;
2. the opportunity to knowledgeably inform the public about cave diving training and safety;
3. the opportunity to perform biological and environmental research.

Some dive sites are accessible only to certified cave divers. That cave diving is not legally prohibited may be due to the cave diving community's response to a number of drownings in the mid 1970's, with a variety of programs to inform and educate divers, the public and public officials.

Knowledge of the need for special training and education for cave diving is essential to control the accident rate. Furthermore, it is not surprising that the person who masters the "art of safe cave diving" finds that his ability to enjoy open-water diving is enhanced by the respect and confidence gained from the advanced review and application of basic principles of diving and from the development of new talents which may be effectively used in all diving environments.

***Figure 1-1** Proper technique begins in the "classroom." Here, Ron Menke and Steve Gerrard teach line technique.*

In 1973, the National Association for Cave Diving (NACD) published the first edition of *Safe Cave Diving*. It was the first comprehensive text to detail state of the art considerations for cave diving safety. The NACD continues to lead the way in its emphasis on cave diving education and safety considerations for the novice. This second textbook, titled *The Art of Safe Cave Diving*, is intended to be a thoroughly updated resource, based upon an additional twenty years of experience by many people who have contributed to the development of the "art of safe cave diving." The contributors sincerely hope that you will consider the information in this text and use it toward your cave diving safety and enjoyment!

Chapter 1

A PHILOSOPHICAL APPROACH TO CAVE DIVING

by Dale R. Malloy

As with any textbook, *The Art of Safe Cave Diving* aims to provide knowledge about its chosen subject. But the book is not intended to be simply an accumulation of facts, it is also designed to help cave divers establish their own philosophy of safe cave diving. The knowledge in these pages represents practical wisdom, gained through the authors' direct experience and through the experiences of others. This book is intended to provide a basis for learning which will grow with continued experience. The purpose of this chapter is to stimulate consideration of each diver's need to develop a personal philosophy of cave diving. In some chapters of this text, the author explicitly states certain ideas related to philosophy. In other chapters, the philosophical statements of the author are only implied.

DEVELOPMENT OF A PERSONAL PHILOSOPHY

This task begins with consideration of the reason(s) why an individual decides to undertake cave diving. Different motivations for cave diving include curiosity, variety of diving experiences, enjoyment of the unique beauty of the underwater cave environment, research, challenges in developing technical diving skills, and more.

Regardless of motivation, whether for sport or occupation, most cave diving is done for enjoyment. A personal cave diving philosophy that overlooks or sublimates the fun is depriving the diver of a more fulfilling experience. However, the basis for creating enjoyable cave dives lies in safety.

The National Association of Cave Diving is an educational association which emphasizes cave diving safety. Personal and team safety should always be a basic operational premise for each dive. The concept of personal safety implies that each diver has a realistic perspective of her ability, and a grasp of her mental and physical capacities on a given day.

***Figure 1-1** The cave diver's most important piece of equipment is carried inside the hood.*

Mature judgment is an integral part of a safe cave diving philosophy. A diver must be able to face personal disappointment and peer pressure from missing or shortening a dive when uncomfortable, rather than risk her own and other members' safety by diving when too tired, irritable, preoccupied, or otherwise uneasy about diving at that time. A diver who proceeds with a dive while having these feelings has not mastered good judgment.

The development of a personal philosophy of cave diving must encompass responsibilities related to the diver and those who dive with her. On every dive, a diver has responsibilities to the diving community as a whole.

Although cave diving is a team activity, a diver must always be capable of self-support under all conditions which she chooses to dive. A breakdown in communications with other team members, or selection of team members who do not have a team support philosophy, has contributed to fatalities when the victim was not personally prepared for all eventualities.

Responsibilities toward others can be as simple as being considerate. Looking for opportunities to practice the Golden Rule can be a major contribution to cave diving safety and enjoyment. Being helpful, even when other team members can do for themselves, may make the difference between a comfortable, relaxing dive, and one that is marred by an unpleasant incident. To help someone else or to receive help from someone, just for comfort's sake, is not tantamount to becoming dependent on others.

Figure 1-2 (L-R) Bill Gavin, Parker Turner, Bill Main and Lamar English shortly after the connection of Sullivan Sink with Cheryl Sink, making it the longest surveyed subaquatic cave system in the world at the time. During subsequent explorations in the same area, Parker Turner drowned at Indian Springs as a result of an unprecedented hydrologic event which filled a section of tunnel with debris while a dive was in progress.

Cave divers have responsibilities to people outside of the dive team. The need to take care of the property of others, such as the landowner where the dive site is located, is obvious. Equally obvious is the responsibility to other cave divers towards preserving caves, maintaining permanent lines, sharing information, and avoiding unsafe dives. Unsafe dives not only put a dive team at risk, they also reflect poorly on the cave diving community and could lead to the closure of dive sites.

Cave diving can be quite expensive in terms of equipment, time, and skill development. It is logical, therefore, that one's personal reasons for cave diving will deeply affect the level of commitment the individual makes as a participant. Casual interest can be safe if personal goals are recognized and personal limits are respected. When these limits have not been respected, casual interest has resulted in fatal diving accidents. If this text dissuades someone from attempting cave diving by pointing out the complexity of doing it safely, then one purpose in addressing cave diving safety will have been realized.

On the other hand, a person who acquires the skills and judgment necessary for safe cave diving receives an additional bonus. The special levels of diver awareness, buoyancy control, body positioning, dive planning, and swim techniques which must be mastered for safe cave diving are very useful in open-water diving. They add greatly to increased diver comfort and enjoyment of open-water dives.

An experienced cave diver should have achieved a mastery of skills, mature judgment, and an awareness of useful techniques. Although a diver may have formed her own personal philosophy of cave diving, her opinions may change over time. Hopefully, there are new ideas in this textbook that the experienced diver is willing to consider and make part of her approach to cave diving. For the beginning diver, this textbook will help her form her cave diving philosophy. Drawing from the accumulated experience of the authors, this information should help eliminate mistakes commonly made by inexperienced divers and provide answers to many questions about the sport.

Chapter 2

A HISTORY OF CAVE DIVING: The Early Years

by David Desautels

INTRODUCTION

Since time began, the fear of the unknown has limited human exploration of caves. Through the ages, only the adventuresome have explored environments such as caves. These physical barriers to the unknown create a mystique beyond reality. George Benjamin summed it up well when he compared mountaineering and caving: "The mountaineer always has his target before him. The sight of the summit helps generate strength for the final assault. The caver can only grope in the dark. What keeps him going is the hope that one day he will break through into unexplored territory." This is more profound with diving, where the cave explorer descends into a water-filled cave, which compounds psychological fears. Limited by the amount of air that can be carried, the cave diver limits exploration or meets a swift death. In studies conducted by Dr. Robert Millott, it is well documented that cave divers differ from other divers (see Table 2-1). These adventurers are to be commended for their spirit, which folklore and curses could not inhibit.

19TH CENTURY BEGINNINGS

The first recorded cave dive with a hard hat breathing apparatus was on March 27, 1878, when a diver named Ottonelli dropped to the floor of the basin in the Fountain de Vaucluse in France. He was diving from a zinc boat that sunk during diving operations. From his account of the dive, he settled to the bottom of the basin at 45 feet before he descended to a maximal depth of 90 feet.

A visit to the caves of Adelsbury in 1888 led the famous French speleologist, E.A. Martel, to begin his numerous ladder descents between 1888 and 1913. From these descents, he recorded meticulous observations and was given the title of "Founder of French Speleology." Methods of çave exploration were rather primitive in that day. There is an account of an attempt to trace the flow of the Malham Tarn area in northwest Yorkshire in 1899 by placing three tons of salt into the sinks and tracing the outlet to Airhead Springs 3.4 kilometers away and 190 meters lower.

EARLY 20TH CENTURY

In 1909 Edward Thompson, the American Consulate to Mexico, began the first underwater archaeologic excavation in the western hemisphere. So that he might dedicate his life to the excavation of the ruins of Chichen Itza, Thompson purchased the land with monies acquired while he served as the American consulate. He was later funded by the American Antiquarian Society and the Peabody Museum of Harvard University. He knew he had discovered the ruins described by Bishop Diego de Landa in 1566 as a place of religious sacrifices.

Thompson learned to dive with a hard hat apparatus. After significant excavation with a diver-operated suction device, Thompson resorted to a dredging device before he began to see the fruits of his labor. He found arrowheads, copper chisels, human bones, and about $800,000 worth of gold bells, figurines and discs. All of these relics remained on display at the Peabody Museum while Thompson was considered a criminal in Mexico for removing the treasures. After a treaty was signed with Mexico, all the artifacts were returned andThompson was exonerated by the Mexican government.

As a boy, Norbert Casteret was only interested in climbing and exploring the Pyrenees near his home in France and often passed caves without much thought. One day, while exploring above St. Gaudens, he was driven into a cave by a torrential rain. Years later he explained his thoughts as he looked around inside his first cave. "It was the first time I had entered a grotto, but it was huge enough and rugged enough to satisfy the longings of an alpinist." After that experience, he began exploring caves in earnest, joining a caving group through which he met Count Begouen, a paleontologist who had found caveman statues in dry caves. Encouraged by Begouen, Casteret set out to explore all the uncharted caves he could find.

In one such cave near Montespan, a paleontologist by the name of Jeannel had come upon a pool of water. Casteret pedalled his bike to the cave and, leaving his clothes outside, went into the cave alone and waded about 185 feet into the pool from the entrance, where the cave roof came down to the water and made the stream impassible. Pondering the situation for some time, he thought of the Ice Age and how a glacier had possibly formed a passageway through the cliffs. Leaving his candle burning outside, he entered the water and after only a short distance, came up on the other side of a sump into an air-filled cave. Frightened that he might become disoriented in the darkness he quickly returned to his candle. The next day, August 19, 1922, Casteret returned to the cave and reentered the cave with matches sealed tightly in a bathing cap. Retracing his path, he returned to the unexplored cave and lit the special matches. He could see a shore about 400 feet ahead, where he was able to explore further. He found a huge passageway, with a 30 foot high roof and stalagmites across the floor. Encountering another sump some distance further, he plunged ahead without hesitation but found it to be a longer sump than the first. Finally, some

MBTI Preference	Cave Divers N=28	Student Divers* N=28	X²	College Freshmen N=2514	X²	High School Seniors N=306	X²	Engineers N=2188	X²
Extraversion (E)	5	9	3.05	1351	14.3*	166	13.6*	1066	10.5*
Introversion (I)	23	19		1163		140		1122	
Sensing (S)	11	13	.64	1372	4.3	218	12.2*	770	0.19
Intuition (N)	17	15		946		88		1418	
Thinking (T)	18	23	4.55	1566	8.3*	86	12.2	1470	0.1
Feeling (F)	10	5		1218		220		718	
Judging (J)	20	19	0.18	1296	9.8*	134	17.7*	1417	0.54
Perceiving (P)	8	9		1351		172		771	

*Divers participating in NACD classes
*P>.01

Table 2-1 χ^2 Values for Myers-Briggs Type Indicator Preferences of Cave Divers and Three Non-Cave Diving Populations

two miles inside the cave, the ceiling dropped to the floor with only small openings. Casteret squeezed his arm in as far as it would go — at the full extent of his reach he could feel branches and tadpoles. Knowing that tadpoles do not venture far inside caves, Casteret was convinced he had found an exit from the cave. Returning to the surface, he found he had been in the cave for five hours.

On his exit from the cave, Casteret picked up a tooth, which was later identified as belonging to an ordinary cow. Since cattle do not voluntarily enter caves, Casteret was encouraged to return to the cave to search for evidence of humans. After finding flint, Casteret almost stumbled across a statue of a crouching bear four feet long and two feet tall. He also discovered statues and drawings of horses, tigers, and lions. These were reported to be 20,000 years old. Casteret continued to explore caves for thirty years, using only breath-holding, as he could hold his breath for longer than two minutes.

1930 THROUGH 1950

In the United States, divers from the Smithsonian Institute made a hard hat descent into Wakulla Springs near Tallahassee, Florida in 1930 and discovered an almost complete skeleton of a Pleistocene mastodon. Unfortunately, it is uncertain whether these divers entered the cave entrance or if they remained outside in the basin. Based on the topography of the cave basin, it is doubtful they could have recovered an entire mastodon without entering the cave. It is only fitting that the frontier of cave diving was established in the Florida area, which would become an international center for cave diving.

In the early 1930's, Graham Balcombe and Jack Sheppard built a diving apparatus using a tee-connector cut from an old bicycle frame and 40 feet of garden hose. They used this in 1934 at Swildon's hole in Somersetshire, England, to dive 2,000 feet back in a cave. Diving with goggles, nose clip, and flashlight, Balcombe discovered that as he dived deeper his light went out. The mystery was explained upon ascent when he exited the silt and his light was still on.

In 1935, Balcombe and Sheppard entered Wookey Hole Cave, also in Somersetshire, this time equipped with traditional naval "hard hat" equipment, including copper helmets. Along on this dive was Penelope Powell, the first female cave diver. Powell wrote,

> Leaving the surface and the dazzling glare
> of the powerful lites and slipping down from

> the enveloping brown atmosphere, we suddenly entered an utterly different world, a world of green where the water was clear as crystal. So still, so silent, unmarked by the foot of man since the river came into being, awe-inspiring though not terrifying, it was like being in some mighty and invisible presence, whose indication was this saturating greenness.

Balcombe was to use a closed circuit oxygen apparatus in 1936, which became known as the "WHODBA" — Wookey Hole Divers Breathing Apparatus. This Breathing apparatus was used by cave divers in England and France for the next 15 years. (Not until 1955 was oxygen replaced with air as the depth of the Wookey Hole exploration exceeded 30 feet.) Balcombe and Sheppard were perhaps the most creative and prolific divers of their time; their techniques were to set the pace for Britain for many years to come. In England, the cave divers considered swimming unsafe so they carried heavy weights for bottom walking. In the spring of 1946, Balcombe and Sheppard founded the Cave Diving Group of Great Britain, the oldest cave diving organization in existence.

On September 27, 1938, Señor Negri, a salvage contractor from Marseilles, dived into the Fountain de Vauclause in France with full hard hat apparatus to seek the source of the annual surge from the Fountain. He stated that he found Ottonelli's zinc boat, which had been sunk some 60 years before in Ottonelli's own attempt to find the source of the flood. Some years later, Jacques Cousteau expressed doubts that Negri did anything more than dive out of sight of the spectators and broadcast fictitious commentaries from his underwater site slightly inside the cave. In fact, Cousteau was bitter that Negri had refused to discuss his dive while the Cousteau group were researching their dive into the infamous Fountain de Vauclause. Cousteau claimed that a near fatal accident could have been avoided had Negri shared his experiences.

On August 24, 1946, the flow of water from the Fountain de Vauclause near Avignon was especially quiet as Cousteau's group ventured to the spring to explore the source of its flooding, as Ottonelli and Negri had done years before. The spring, at the base of 600 foot cliffs, swells and floods the Sargue each year for five weeks in March. Hydrologists had investigated the spring for years, but poets had almost as reasonable an explanation for the flooding as the hydrologists. The poet Mistal's explanation was:

> One day the fairy of the Fountain changed herself into a beautiful woman and took an old strolling minstrel by the hand and led him down through Vauclause's waters to an underground prairie, where seven huge diamonds plugged seven holes. "See those diamonds?" said the fairy. "When I lift the seventh, the fountain rises to the roots of the fig tree that drinks only once a year."

The entire town, including the mayor, turned out to assist and watch Cousteau's group. Cousteau and Dumas dived first from a Canadian canoe from which they dropped a large pig iron weight with a line. They followed the line down to the weight and then gradually moved the weight down the slope until they reached a depth which Cousteau estimated to be 200 feet. Both divers were anxious about being in the cave. In fact, they felt that because of the environment their ears cleared more slowly, narcosis was more intense, and that the dive was the worst they had experienced in 5,000 dives. It was determined later that they were affected more by narcosis because carbon monoxide had gotten into their air and, at the depth to which they dived, the effects were compounded. At that depth, Dumas became semiconscious and Cousteau tried to get him to the surface quickly by signalling to Fargues, the line tender. Fargues misunderstood the signals and gave them more slack instead. After many anxious moments, Cousteau was able to get the proper signal to Fargues and they were pulled up to safety.

Cousteau's next group also had problems. Talliez walked wildly out of the water and was holding his knife by the blade, which cut his hand to the bone. Needing to be pulled up, he had cut the line at depth after it had coiled into a loop. Because he was unsure which end of the line to cut, he wound the rope around his arm and cut the rope without knowing which side of the line went to the surface.

The Cousteau group also explored the caves of Chatreux, Estramar. In Vitarelles on October 29, 1948, Jean Alinat succeeded in traversing a sump to emerge into a dry, air-filled cave where no one had ever gone before.

In 1949, Gordon Marriott had the misfortune to be the first recorded fatality in cave diving when he drowned in Wookey Hole, England, on April 9, 1949. In the April 13, 1949, newsletter of the CDG, Graham Balcombe described Marriott as follows.

> He was a diver and swimmer of exceptional skill and achievement; ex-Royal Marines, one of the first Frogmen, hero of the D-Day beaches, since when he has dived as leading demonstrator in the Butlin displays at their camps and in other demonstrations. All told a dazzling record of some five-hundred hours underwater.

The analysis of the accident, from the same issue of the CDG newsletter, includes this assessment.

> ...(T)he base organization treated Marriott as a guest and expert in his own right, and therefore did not press CDG normal requirements on him. We think it true to say the Controller of Operations and the attendants were dazzled by the brilliant record of the newcomer....
>
> ...At the inquest the jury returned a verdict that "death was due to anoxeamia, accidentally sustained during diving operations

when his oxygen supply became exhausted due to a fault in the test pressure gauge" and added a rider that "all divers,including guest divers, should be subjected to the same equipment tests as the members of the Diving Group " (Wells Journal, 22.4.49).

THE FIFTIES

In June of 1950, Walter S. Chamberlain entered the warm waters of Devil's Hole in Nevada and dived to a depth of 75 feet with a penetration of 75 feet. Also in 1950, Henri Lombard became the second recorded cave diving fatality when he drowned in Lirou Cave, France, on October 8.

On a more pleasant note, North Central Florida was continuing to establish its foothold in cave diving when an unnamed diver dived to the bottom of Jug Hole near Ft. White, Florida, in 1951 and recovered two crocodillian skulls. Then in January of 1953, Charles McNabb and Bill Ray began their exploratory work in Silver Springs near Ocala, Florida. After several dives in the basin of the beautifully clear waters of Silver Springs, even then a commercial attraction for tourists in Florida, the divers managed to enter the cave. This was no small task because the flow coming from the cave is adequate to provide the entire water supply of a fair sized city. After entering the cave, they were able to recover bones from prehistoric animals such as mastodon and mammoth.

John Lindbergh (son of Charles Lindbergh) equipped with little more than a flashlight and small nylon line connecting him to the surface descended into Bower Cave, California, on a solo dive in May of 1953. He swam at a depth of 25 feet and penetrated 150 feet into the cave, emerging into a huge, dry cave crowded with stalactites. A raft was inflated to use as a base of operations but the raft became over inflated which caused him to break his mask and fill his suit with water. Hurriedly taking what pictures he could, he returned to the surface holding his nose. On his second dive, he descended to 120 feet looking for the bottom, which he did not find. Later that year, in nearby Devil's Hole, Nevada, Bill Brown was the first exploratory diver to enter the 93 degree waters with hard hat. There is now a room in Devil's Hole named for him, where divers come into an air-filled, 112 degree room. Many subsequent expeditions used this room as a base. Brown was able to dive to a depth of 150 feet and, through the clear water, is said to have seen another 200 feet without seeing bottom.

Murray Anderson was the first American to die in a free-swimming cave diving accident on May 14, 1953. A naval reservist from Macon, Georgia, he and his companion had just begun to cave dive and fashioned a diving regulator from an aviator's oxygen regulator. For tanks, they adapted 38 cubic foot aircraft oxygen cylinders. After six previous trips and full of excitement, they drove to Radium Springs, Georgia, to explore even further in their cave. Usually they dived solo because they did not have enough equipment for both of them, but on this last particular dive they did. Anderson entered the water before his companion had exited. Passing each other they exchanged signals. Low on air, his companion surfaced but became concerned and returned to the water to look for Anderson. Circling until his air ran out, he gave up hope. Navy divers located Anderson the next morning just six feet from where the two divers had exchanged signals.

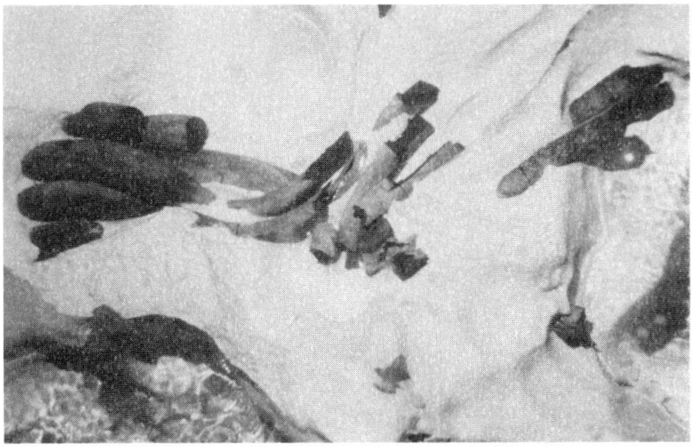

Figure 2-1 Fossilized bones embedded in the limestone ceiling of Arch Sink in Pasco County, Florida.

A major recovery operation of prehistoric animal bones began in November of 1955. Garry Salsman had grown up near Wakulla Springs, Florida, and had often manned the life guard stand overlooking the springs and wondered what was below. Practicing often in the caves nearby to refine his techniques, he longed to dive in Wakulla, but the owners would not allow it. His big break came when a movie production company was allowed to film in Wakulla. Badgering the film crew, he and his companions managed to get a job hauling equipment and being safety divers. During their time off, they explored inside the cave. On one of their excursions into the cave they found the floor of the cave littered with bones: an almost complete mastodon and hundreds of spear points from the ancient Vero Man. By now the owners were excited enough about the discoveries that they allowed Garry Salsman, Wally Jenkins, Henry Doll, Andy Harold, Gordon Whitney and Lamarr Trott to work in this cave with paleontologist Stanley Olsen from Florida State University. The crew explored the caves of Wakulla to a penetration of 1,150 feet and a depth of 240 feet without incident.

In 1957, Dr. George Benjamin began his exploration of the Blue Holes of the Bahamas. Benjamin, a research chemist from Toronto, Canada, first learned of the Blue Holes during a vacation and was intrigued. He spent all of his spare time exploring these caves, from 1957 to 1970. Noticing that the currents in the holes changed as the tide changed, he scheduled a dive during ebb tide so that, as the current began to come out of the cave, he would come out of the cave also. At first, he dived with his two sons (Pete and George, Jr.), but later was joined by a list of diving dignitaries such as Cousteau, Mount, Dill, and many others.

In 1970, Benjamin made a major effort to improve his technique and equipment so that he could dive beyond the 300 foot distance to which he was limited in the cave. It was then that he contacted NACD members, including Tom Mount, and thereafter was able to penetrate to distances of 1,000 feet at depths up to 260 feet. In fact, it was on one of these orientation dives in September of 1970 with Tom Mount that the long sought stalactites were found. On a long and deep dive, Benjamin gave the return to surface signal as he took one last flash picture. Seeing what looked like stalactites illuminated by the flash, Tom entered the Grotto Room to the full splendor of an underwater sight never before witnessed by man. There in the beautifully clear water were all the stalactites one could imagine. This proved once and for all that the formation of the area proceeded the most recent glaciation period 10-15,000 years and that the area had been above ground for thousands of years before that. Dr. Benjamin also explored the many Island sink holes, which had obvious connection to the ocean because there was a distinct fresh/salt water interface and the water depth fluctuated with the tide. In these caves, they even found some soda straw stalactites.

In January of 1959, the first recorded SCUBA dive in Little Salt Springs near Venice, Florida, by Colonel Bill Royal was made. There was difficulty getting the site recognized as a scientific discovery until human bones were discovered at a depth of 150 feet. Then, joined by Dr. Eugenie Clark, Director of Cape Haze Marine Laboratory, plus Roy Finney and Burton McNeely (nationally known underwater photographer), he found prehistoric human bones on a ledge 30 feet deep. Dr. Illius Konstantinu recovered brain material from inside one skull. Dr. John Goggin from the University of Florida, an authority on Indians, was called in to dive. He found dozens of human bones on a ledge at 40 feet. Dives were also made at nearby Warm Mineral Springs, where similar artifacts were found at depths of 260 feet. At this depth, the divers also encountered a stream of scalding water.

Dr. Brooks from the University of Florida dived to verify the existence of stalactites in Warm Mineral Springs. During one of his dives, Royal found a burned log, which was an exciting discovery because burned material makes carbon dating possible. The log was dated at 10,000 years. Even though it was found near a human jaw bone, scientists are reluctant to make assumptions about the bone. A good reason for that reluctance is seen just a short distance away at Ichetucknee Springs where mastodon bones are found routinely among beer cans on the bottom of the spring.

MODERN CAVE DIVING BEGINS: THE 1960'S

On March 20, 1960, America's best known cave diving scientist died in a cave in France. Conrad Limbaugh and his guide entered a cave without safety line and no orientation: planning to simply make a short introductory excursion together, the guide dropped a light. They surfaced inside an air pocket and Limbaugh was told to stay there while the guide retrieved the flashlight. When the guide returned, Limbaugh was gone. Because of severe storms, the search was impeded for several days. After a seven day search by Cousteau's group, the French Navy, the U.S. Navy, and a commercial diving company, Limbaugh was found in a previously unexplored part of the cave 350 feet from the spot the guide had left him.

On December 1, 1961, Grace Zinn became the first woman to make a cave diving traverse, travelling from Manatee Spring to Manatee Sink some 600 feet away at a depth of 90 feet. She and her diving partners followed the route established by Ed Bishop and Les Groves when they made the first traverse of that system earlier that year.

With all the technical advances made with equipment, especially scuba equipment, cave diving began to flourish. Not only the creative and imaginative were able to dive in the caves, but anyone who had enough money to buy equipment could dive in a cave. And because it was easy and accessible to do so, many did — without training, without being accompanied by a trained person, without the proper cave diving equipment, and without knowing whether they were psychologically suited for cave diving. Not surprisingly, many died. However, there was no established criteria by which to judge if a person was suited to be a cave diver. After two double drownings occurred within two months, an onslaught of editorials began in the Gainesville, Florida, newspaper calling for the outlawing of cave diving. It was during this period in the evolution of cave diving that legislative pressures began appearing from all sides, even within cave diving organizations (Table 2-2).

In 1962, Mike Boon began the "British " style of cave diving with his Nyhhargus apparatus (named after a crustacean often found in British caves). This consisted of a 26 cubic foot cylinder, regulator, face mask, weight belt, and no fins. The technique was to walk on the bottom carrying 20 pounds of added weight and wade from one chamber to the next. In England, cave diving was (and is) a major undertaking because the equipment had to be pushed, dragged, or hauled to extremely inaccessible locations.

American divers enjoyed easier access, so it was no surprise that when *Skin Diver Magazine* published reports of the first major traverse in the U.S., from Hornsby Sink to Hornsby Spring (a distance of 2,800 feet at a depth of 160 feet), many divers showed up to dive the traverse solo with single tanks. What to them seemed easy was, in fact, a major undertaking. It was completed by John Harper and Joe Fuller after much careful planning and aborted attempts to link up with other divers at mid tunnel so they could then continue through to the spring. In December, 1962, John and Joe met Jim Bollinger, Bill Lee, and Joyce Anthony at midpoint of the cave traverse after they had successfully connected permanent safety lines. Their penetration from the sink side had been 1,300 feet while their maximal penetration from the spring side had been 1,700 feet.

Year	Month	Legislative Effort
1964	Feb. 26	Sen. Ribicoff introduces HR 10458 S2550 into senate to regulate diving.
1964	April 1	New Jersey passes air regulation bill for diving.
1964	April 20	Judge Miller Lang of Gilchrist County calls for legislation after two single drownings occur at Ginnie Springs within three months.
1965	May 5	House Bill 1405 introduced by Sen. J.E. Cross requiring special equipment to dive and air purity.
1967	Dec. 23	*Fla. Times Union* and *Miami Herald* call for control of cave divers after quadruple death in Ginnie Springs.
1969	Jan. 8	Nebraska attempts to regular Skin Divers — Fails.
1969		Kansas makes diving illegal except where designated.
1969	Jan. 24	Suwannee River Authority attempts to stop cave diving by making it illegal to dive any spring or sink in their eleven county area.
1969		New Jersey attempts to control air in scuba — Fails.
1970		Georgia attempts to pass law regulating diving — Fails.
1971	Jan. 21	Gainesville *Sun* writes its first editorial calling for legislation after 16 year old female drowns in open sink hole.
1971	Sept. 1	House Bill 5168 introduced requiring certification for cave divers.
1972		New York tries to pass law regulating divers — Fails.
1973	March 29	Rep. Earl Dixon introduces House Bill 520-sf into state regulations.
1973	April 7	Fla. Diving Advisory Committee (FloDac) meets in Miami to discuss pending legislation proposed by Hon. Earl Dixon, Rep. Jacksonville.
1973	April 29	Second meeting of FloDac at *Aqua Shack* in Branford, Florida — Earl Dixon there to present his propose legislation.
1973	May	*Skin Diver Magazine* editorial focuses attention on North Central Florida's dilemma with cave diving deaths.
1974	July 6	Gainesville *Sun* runs its ninth editorial against cave divers.
1974	Nov. 19	Los Angeles County regulates divers.

Table 2-2

Florida and Georgia were not the only southeastern states where people were cave diving. In January of 1964, Hugh Vandegrift and Tom Grubbs dived an underground cave near Falkville, Alabama, which is plumbed to 250 feet. They explored to a depth of 45 feet, measured the width of the surface pool (350 feet), and found three horizontal passageways at a depth of 45 feet, which they marked for later exploration.

THE *AD HOC* CAVE DIVING COMMITTEE

On May 21, 1964, a seminar concerning the growing number of cave diving related deaths was held in Gainesville, Florida. The seminar was organized by David Desautels (Chairman of the *Ad Hoc* Committee on Cave Diving), the National Association of Underwater Instructors (NAUI), Frances Colvin, Mel Fried, and Jim Olsen. It gathered together speakers from the State Bureau of Vital Statistics, diving safety organizations, and diving instructor programs.

In only a four year period, 48 divers had drowned in Florida caves. In the previous year, drowning ranked third in Florida after traffic and household deaths as the cause of accidental deaths, although only 3.8 percent of the drownings were related to scuba. After some discussion, it was proposed that cardinal rules for cave diving be established, as well as a national organization designed to

Figure 2-2 Early safety efforts in Florida.

educate cave divers, hold seminars, and recommend ways to improve cave diving techniques. Many other suggestions made at this seminar were later implemented, such as posting warning signs at diving locations, making films to educate the public, requiring certification for divers to obtain air, and publishing national newsletters.

Cave diving "Down Under" was beginning also. Ron Taylor reported diving in Australia to a depth of 225 feet in the middle of the Australian plains at the Shaft, which begins as a three foot-diameter hole. The hole goes down 15 feet before there is water. Under water is a mound created by the farmer who owned the property. He had unsuccessfully tried to fill the hole with debris. The top of the mound is at a depth of 130 feet and the bottom of the mound on one side is 180 feet down. The other side descends to unknown depths.

One of the most tragic accidents to date was recorded on December 20, 1967, at Ginnie Springs near High Springs, Florida, when four students from the University of Georgia drowned. Subsequently, a small group of cave divers called the *Aquamarine Cave Dwellers* met in the spring of 1968 to discuss cave diving and its image. Invited to Camp Kulaqua in High Springs, Florida, by Elder Middag, these divers (David Desautels, Tom Mount, Leon Morrison, Gil Milner, Larry Briel, and Jim Sweeney) thought that reform could develop a new image for cave diving. The initial effort was aimed at a cave diving seminar, which was to serve as a medium for qualified cave divers to collectively establish cave diving standards, to educate those interested in cave diving, to serve as a forum for the discussion of cave diving techniques, and to serve notice to the public that the serious cave diver was concerned about the problem of excessive deaths and would try to do something about preventing them. On August 25, 1968, the first cave diving seminar sponsored by the Aquamarine Cave Dwellers began and continued for four days. This was the seed which later became the National Association for Cave Diving.

Shortly after this, the Suwannee River Authority met on January 24, 1969, to discuss legislation to restrict cave diving in the eleven-county Suwannee Valley area. Guests at that meeting included David Desautels of the Aquamarine Cave Dwellers, Lt. Shellie Downs of Alachua County Sheriffs Dept., and Chase Merritt, dive shop owner. It was suggested that the matter of legislative action be given to a select committee for further study. After three meetings, which gained national attention, the matter died in committee and the cave divers gained advocates instead of adversaries.

Back in the water, cave divers began exploring the Peacock area in earnest. In early 1969, Rick Wright and his dive partner connected Peacock Spring to Olsen, a distance of 1,600 feet, while in March of 1970 Tom Mount and Frank Martz connected Olsen to a spring they named Challenge, a distance of 2,000 feet. In 1970, Frank Martz, Randy Hylton, and John Harper were first to connect Orange Grove Sink to Challenge, a distance of 2,400 feet. This made it possible for Tom Mount and Ike Ikehara to traverse 4,000 feet from Olsen to Orange Grove, and for Harper and Hylton to traverse 6,000 feet from Orange Grove to Peacock Sink. Sheck Exley and Chuck Stevens were to top this by traversing 6,800 feet from Cisteen Sink to Orange Grove.

Figure 2-3 Typical Florida cave diver circa 1970.

Tom Mount and Ike Ikehara made the longest unassisted penetration without making a traverse when they

PRESIDENTS OF THE NACD

Tom Mount 1971-72
Bob Friedman 1973
Rory Dickens 1974
Sheck Exley 1975
Dale Malloy 1976-77
Lewis Henkel 1978-81
Terry Leithauser 1982-85
Steve Gerrard 1986-89
Dayton Saltsman 1990-91
Rick Van Eldik 1992-93
Milledge Murphey 1994

Table 2-3[1]

traveled 2,250 feet into Madison Blue Springs in July of 1970. This penetration was at a depth of 60 to 70 feet. This was topped by John Harper and Jim Lockwood, who penetrated 2,700 feet at a depth of 110 feet in Little River Springs. Again this was topped by Sheck Exley and Chuck Stevens when they made a penetration of 3,100 feet at a depth of 60 feet in Orange Grove and the exploration fever began.

THE BEGINNINGS OF THE NACD

Finally, on May 15, 1969, the incorporation papers for the National Association for Cave Diving (NACD) were submitted, just before the Second Annual Seminar on Cave Diving was held on May 29, 1969. The second seminar was an attempt to involve lawmakers and law enforcement officers in open discussions with cave divers in an effort to find a solution to the still increasing demand for anti-cave diving legislation. Following on the heels of our greatest battle for survival in the Suwannee River Valley, this seminar included the Secretary of State, all the sheriffs along the Suwannee River, and several anti-cave diving judges. Although the seminar was poorly attended by cave divers (only 41), the divers who did attend gained the respect of the law makers attending and in that regard the seminar was a great success. In the meantime, on July 2, 1969, the National Association for Cave Diving was officially incorporated by David Desautels and Larry Briel with officers Tom Mount, Dale Malloy, Gil Milner, M.D., Jim Sweeney, Ron Wahl, and Hal Watts, signing the papers.

International attention was centered on cave diving when Jacques Cousteau brought his ship, *Calypso*, to Andros and the Blue Holes of the Bahamas to film *Secrets of the Sunken Caves*, which aired on television around the world in 1970.

Pursuing its goals, the NACD officially began its instruction program on May 29, 1970, when Larry Briel, David Desautels, Dale Malloy, Gilbert Milner, Tom Mount, and Hall Watts subjected each other to an intense weekend of training and instruction. These were the first six cave diving instructors of the NACD. It was also at this time that other efforts were intensified to curb cave-related accidents. Signs and permanent lines were placed underwater in the more popular spring locations, educational publications were distributed, a speakers' bureau was formed, and our very own cave diving manual was developed and published. However, seminars continued to be the major thrust of the organization's attempts to educate both the cave diver and non-cave diver alike.

Then tragically, one of the members of the NACD died. In September 1971, Frank Martz drowned at 325 feet in Blue Hole No. 4, South Bite, Andros. He and his buddy had entered a constricted area at 280 feet that was too narrow for turning around. They continued on to a larger opening but kicked up too much silt. Martz's buddy managed to escape but Frank Martz was never seen again (his body was never recovered).

In December of 1971, a scientific project was started by Carl Clausen (State Archaeologist), Drs. Kelly Brooks (Geologist),Deevey (Limnologist), and Sublett (Human Physical Anthropologist) along with NACD divers led by Bob Friedman. They explored the far reaches of Warm Mineral Springs and Little Salt Springs for human evidence. This was the first of many scientific projects NACD divers were to participate in over the coming years. The next was a cooperative effort with the National Underwater Accident Data Center (NUADC) begun at the University of Rhode Island through support by NOAA and the U.S. Coast Guard. Because cave diving represented such a large percentage of the total number of scuba-related deaths, it was important that cave divers be involved. Collecting scuba-related fatal accident data since 1960, David Desautels had much information that would be useful to the new center.

Cave diving developed quickly in its early years. Much like the conquest of space, intelligent exploration of an underwater frontier is vital. Steps taken by responsible divers to establish Standards of Conduct published for cave diving which describe a safe, sane philosophy for the advancement of cave diving, have allowed the sport to survive without being legislated out of existence. A safe, conservative progression is how cave diving will survive in the future. Too many ill equipped, inexperienced divers have already lost their lives.

[1] Although the author states that the NACD was incorporated on May 15, 1969, the organization was re-incorporated May 21, 1973. During 1990, the NACD obtained copies of all pertinent state documents. There are no records of the organization prior to May 21, 1973, on file with the state of Florida. — Ed

BIBLIOGRAPHY

Anthony, J. (July 1963). "A Light in Hornsby Sink," *Skin Diver Magazine*. pp 24-25

Balcombe, F.G. (1953). "Cave Diving," In C.H.D. Cullingford *British Caving*. pp 350-374. London: Routledge and Kegan Paul.

Balcombe, F.G. (1944). *Members Report to the British Speleological Association*. No. 7/45.

Barada, B. (1969, August). "Let's Pass a Law," *Skin Diver Magazine*. pp. 54-55.

Barada, B. (1969, September). "Cave Diving — Education or Legislation," *Skin Diver Magazine*. pp. 32-35.

Banbury, J. (Ed.) (1972). *Proceedings of the Fifth Annual Seminar on Cave Diving*. Gainesville, FL: National Association for Cave Diving.

Beaver, E. (1964, May). "Tomb of the Mastodons," *Skin Diver Magazine*. pp. 33-35.

Bridges, L., Barada, B. (1960). *Mask and Flippers*. pp. 80-85. New York: Cornerstone Library.

Briel, L.I., Desautels, D.A. (Ed.) (1968). *Proceedings of The First Annual Seminar on Cave Diving*. Gainesville, FL: National Association for Cave Diving.

Burgess, R. (1976). *The Cave Divers*. New York: Dodd, Mead & Co.

Butcher, L. (1972, October 15). "The Deadly Thrill of Caving," *The Floridian*. pp. 9-11.

Conger, G.R., Wheeler, C.W. (1977). *Legal Issues for Florida Diving*. Gainesville, FL: WIC Publications.

Cousteau, J.Y., Dumas, F. (1950). *The Silent World*. New York: Harper and Row.

Cousteau, J.Y., Diole, P. (1973). *Three Adventures*. pp. 153-233. Garden City, NY: Doubleday & Co. Inc.

Deloach, N., Arteaga, T. (1972). *A Guide to Florida's Springs*. Jacksonville, FL: New World Productions.

Desautels, D.A. (1964). *Proceedings of Panel Discussion About Cave Diving*. Gainesville, FL.

Desautels, D.A. (1966, October). "On Cave Diving," *FSDA Bulletin*. p. 9.

Desautels, D.A. (1969, July). "Diving in Florida's Caves," *Florida Health Notes*. pp. 191-194.

Desautels, D., Hall, J. (1973). "Florida Cave Diving," In J. Erving (Ed.). *World Wide Skindivers Guide* 1973. Winter Park, FL: Erving Publications.

Drew, D. (1966, December). "A Review of Cave Diving Techniques and Apparatus in Britain," *Studies in Speleology*. pp. 163-167.

Dugan, J. (1956). *Man Under the Sea*. pp. 237-255. New York: Harper & Row.

Exley, I.S., Friedman, R. (1973). *Mapping Underwater Caves*. Gainesville, FL: National Association for Cave Diving.

Exley, I.S. (1979). *Basic Cave Diving*. Jacksonville, FL: National Speleogical Society.

Ferguson, G.E., Lingham, C.W., Love, S.K., Vernon, R.O. (1947). *Springs of Florida*. Tallahassee, FL: Florida Geological Survey.

Fisk, D., Exley, I.S. (1976). "Exploration and Environmental Investigation of the Peacock Springs System," In R. Dilamater, S. Csallny (Ed.). *Hydrogeologic Problems in Karst Regions*. Western Kentucky University.

Ford, T.D., Cullingford, C.H.D. (1976). *The Science of Speleology*. New York: Academic Press.

Frey, H., Frey, S. (1961). *130 Feet Down*. pp. 251-257. New York: Harcourt, Brace and World, Inc.

Gambe, R. (1972). "Underwater Speleology Fresh Water Diving," *International Diving Manual*.

Hulet, W.H. (1969, August). "Nameless Rivers and Sunless Corridors, " *J. Fla. Med. Assn*. pp.609-614.

Jacobs, L. (1964, October). "284 Feet Down the Devils Hole, " *Saga*. pp. 40-43.

Lavaur, G., (1958). *Caves and Cave Diving*. Crown Publishers.

Lloyd, O. (1967, April). "Cave Diving Hazards, " *Bristol Medico-Surgical Journal*. pp. 23-34.

Martz, F. (1968, December). "Exploring Florida's Lost Sink," *Atlantic Underwater News*. pp. 3-4.

Marx, R. (1978). *Into the Deep*. pp. 140-141. New York: Van Nostrand Reinhold Co.

May, J.G., (1973). *SCUBA Divers Guide to Underwater Ventures*. pp. 186-205. Harrisburg, PA: Stackpole Books.

Mohr, C.E. (1964, July). "Exploring America Underground," *National Geographic*. pp. 803-837.

Mount, T. (1968, June). "Cave Dwelling," *Dive Magazine*. pp. 24-27.

Mount, T. (1973). "Safe Cave Diving," In J. Erving (Ed.). *World Wide Skindivers Guide 1973*. Winter Park, FL: Erving Publication.

Mount, Z. (1973). "A History of Cave Diving," In Tom Mount (Ed.) *Safe Cave Diving*. pp. 20-34. Gainesville, FL: National Association for Cave Diving.

Mount, T., and A. Ikehara (1974) *Practical Diving*. Miami: University of Miami Press.

Mount, T. (1975). *Cave Diving Manual*. Gainesville, FL: National Association for Cave Diving.

North, W.J. (1960, July). "The Last Dive," *Skin Diver Magazine*. pp. 26-27.

Olsen, S.J. (1959). "The Wakulla Cave," In J.Y. Cousteau and J. Dugan (Ed.). *Captain Cousteau's Underwater Treasury*. pp. 369-373. New York: Harper & Row.

Porter, J. (1960, November). "Ohio Cave Divers," *Skin Diver Magazine*. p. 35.

Rosenau, J.C., G.L. Faulkner, C.W. Hendry, and R.W. Hull, (1977). *Springs of Florida*. Tallahassee, FL: Florida Department of Natural Resources.

Royal, W., and E. Clark, (1960, October). "Natural Preservation of Human Brain," *American Antiquity*.

Royal, W.R. "Trapped in an Underwater Cave," *Underwater*. pp. 40-42.

Schenck, B. (Ed.) (1975). *Proceedings of the Sixth and Seventh Annual N.A.C.D. Seminars*. Gainesville, FL: National Association for Cave Diving.

Sloane, B., (Ed.) (1g77). *Cavers, Caves and Caving*. pp. 177-192. Rutgers University Press.

Stephens, W.M. (1962). *Our World Underwater*. pp. 105-134. New York: Lantern Press.

Storey, J.W. (1968). "Cave Diving," In J.W. Storey (Ed.). *American Caving Illustrated*. Atlanta: American Caving Illustrated.

Tailliez, P. (1959). "The Fountain of Vaucluse, " In J.Y. Cousteau and J. Dugan (Eds.). *Captain Cousteau's Underwater Treasury*. pp. 39-47. New York: Harper & Row.

Taylor, R. (1966, August). "The Shaft," *Skin Diver Magazine*. pp. 30-33.

Vandergrift, H. (1964, August). "Underwater Spelunkers," *Skin Diver Magazine*. pp. 50-51.

Wetterhall, W.S. (1965). *Reconnaissance of Springs and Sinks in Western-Central Florida*. Tallahassee, FL: Florida Geological Survey.

Chapter 3

THE CAVE DIVING ENVIRONMENT

by Robert Tyson

Environmental awareness is essential to properly exercise the techniques and equipment that blend a formula for safety in underwater spelunking. One must constantly analyze the approaching tunnel fork, restriction, silt zone, or currents ahead. The dive team concentrates upon particular line, light, and swim techniques that are necessary to smoothly negotiate the upcoming passageway. Combining the planning, methodology, equipment, and teamwork that comprise a safe and enjoyable cave dive takes much practice; but for those who are compelled to explore this environment, the effort is rewarded by sights and challenges that few individuals have experienced.

INTRODUCTION

A true understanding of the cave environment enhances the enjoyment of a dive in addition to increasing safety. One may observe formations, cave life, water variations, and other phenomena that have been overlooked during many previous dives. One might recognize potential archeological finds that are of tremendous historical value. During descent, a dive team is exploring a pathway through geologic time that could span millions of years. For example, a cave dive in South Florida could mean an encounter with rocks that are nearly 40 million years old. This same cave may have been void of water thousands of years ago and may have been a shelter for both animal and human inhabitants. An open and curious mind must scrutinize the visual sightings to discover what is hidden from initial observations.

A masterful cave diver has learned to safely and smoothly become a *frequent visitor* to the cave environment. The simple fact that humans cannot currently breathe underwater without artificial aid assures that the diver is only a *visitor*. The word *frequent* emphasizes that the diver is in touch with personal equipment and techniques that must be updated and well utilized. Finally, the expert cave diver fulfills the above and briefly becomes one with the submerged cave environment.

GENERAL TYPES OF UNDERWATER CAVES

There are five general types of underwater caves. They are sea caves, coral caves, lava tube caves, glacial caves and, finally, solution caves. These are all formed in different geologic environments, while some share similarities in composition, shape, general location, and genesis mechanisms.

Sea caves are found in marine environments and consist of virtually any rock composition that can be physically eroded by wave and current action over a period of many thousands of years. Sediments carried by such water action act as an abrasive medium to grind away rock bodies. Sea caves are found along high energy coastlines and are laterally non-extensive. Depths are generally shallow unless the cave was "carved" during a low sea level stand in geologic history. Another reason for the lack of occurrences of deep sea cave passages is that such openings have been filled or covered with recent sedimentation and are thus hidden from the explorer.

Coral caves are found in tropical marine environments. Corals are usually composed of calcium carbonate casts, or skeletons, that have been compacted and cemented together into a formidable rock. This rock is eroded by chemical, biological, and mechanical means to create cave passages. Sea water is generally saturated with respect to calcium carbonate, therefore the cements that bond limestone are insignificantly attacked by chemical means. Biological erosion is affected by boring organisms, certain fungal accumulations, parrot fish, and inconsiderate humans. A dismal combination of biological *and* chemical degradation of coral is occurring along developed tropical coastlines by waste effluent pollution. The chemical aspects of effluent may accelerate dissolution of limestone cements and also may retard or prohibit the growth of coralline algae that help build the coral reefs. Finally, mechanical erosion by wave and current action is typically the dominant method of creating coral caves. The extent of the cavern system depends upon wave dynamics. Coral caves are usually short in passage length and are formed relatively shallow where current and wave action is strongest.

Lava tube caves are found throughout the world where geologic occurrences of extrusive igneous rock are observed. These caves are the major type explored in both Hawaii and the Northwestern United States. Kazumura Cave in Hawaii has been mapped to an extent of more than seven and a half miles. In the mountains of Washington State, more than one hundred thousand feet of lava tube caves have been mapped; some sections there have revealed widths of one hundred feet and heights of thirty or forty feet. These caves exhibit mazes, pits, multiple levels, cave adapted animals, and wet zones very analogous to features exhibited by the limestone cave. Various theories exist to explain their origin, but these caves are formed during the cooling and degassing phase of lava flows associated with volcanic activity. The study of such cave systems has been termed vulcanospeleology.

Glacier caves are those that have formed by the seasonal melting of ice near the leading edge and bottom of nearly one quarter of these rocks' volumes a glacier. A glacier is defined as a mass of ice with definite lateral limits, with motion in a definite direction, and originating from the compacting of snow by pressure. The dynamic nature and somewhat unpredictable motions of such an ice mass make glacier caves extremely dangerous to explore. The Paradise Glacier of Mount Ranier, Washington, has a location known as Paradise Ice Caves, where spelunkers have mapped over two miles of passage before 1967. Room dimensions beneath this glacier reach 250 feet long, 90 feet wide, and 25 feet high of beautiful blue-white ice. Studies show that although the cave follows stream courses, most of the passages are caused by ice melting after exposure to warm summer air that snakes its way beneath the glacier. This is just one example, but apparently far larger glacier caves are present in Alaska and western Canada where several major rivers burrow beneath glaciers for distances exceeding 10 miles. Subglacial rivers with glacial caves generally have much higher flow velocities in the summer than in winter. Extreme exposure protection is often warranted before entering an ice cave. The study of glacial caves is called *glaciospeleology.*

Solution caves are those which have formed by the dissolution of cement bonding the original rock together. This dissolution is facilitated by the circulation of freshwater within pores that make up part of the rock volume. *Porosity* is defined as the ratio of the void space within a rock to its total volume. It is usually stated as a percentage. For example, some limestones exhibit porosities of 23-25%: that is, nearly one quarter of these rock" volumes are made of airspace. Freshwater can fill these airspaces and chemically react with cements that hold individual grains of the rock together. Thus, the rock eventually crumbles and is carried away by underwater currents that develop in growing underwater conduits.

SOLUTION CAVES

Solution caves are predominantly composed of limestones that form some of the greatest caverns in the world. They are great by measure of length, depth, size, and beauty. Mammoth Cave, Kentucky, has more than 225 mapped miles of passage. The Li Nita-San Agustin system in Mexico is over 4,005 feet deep before ending in a seemingly bottomless lake. The Big Room of Carlsbad Cavern is more than one-half mile long. With delicate speleothems, which are mineral deposits formed in a cave during its "dry" lifetime, limestone caverns such as those of Virginia (Endless, Grand, and Luray) are among the most beautiful in the world to observe topside.

The word *limestone* is used loosely to include other similar minerals within a large grouping. The walls of Luray Caverns are composed of dolomite, which is recrystallized limestone with a considerable amount of magnesium. Some caves in California and Massachusetts are composed of marble, which is limestone that has been metamorphosed by time, pressure, and temperature into a rock with different properties. Gypsum is composed of hydrous calcium sulfate and can be found in the form of beautiful fibrous speleothems in Cumberland Caverns, Tennessee and Mammoth Cave,

Figure 3-1 Florida solution cave development area.

Kentucky. The caves of Overton, Nevada, were dissolved from rock salt.

Physical Features and Entrances to Solution Caves — A cave diver who plans to explore a new cave system approaches a dive plan by carefully noting the physical features and water motion at the entrance. Cave openings provide important clues to the current strength, current direction, visibility, and general nature of the rock to be encountered within.

The first and most often sought entrance is that of a *spring*. The cave opening shows evidence that water is flowing out from the system. This entrance is called an *outlet*. There may be a *headpool* around the outlet that flows into a stream called a *run*, which finally empties into a river or large surface water body. Springs may vary in current velocity and water chemistry; some along coastlines may reverse flow directions due to tidal influences. A good dive plan accounts for any unusual hydrologic changes that regularly occur in a system.

A second type of cave entrance is the *siphon*. The siphon entrance is one to enter with extreme caution and careful air planning because it is generally a reverse spring whereby water flows *into* the cave. Siphons may occur with their own headpools, runs and river connections. Occasionally, one may find a headpool containing both spring and siphon entrances. Here, the siphon entrance is relatively lower than the spring entrance regarding local hydraulic gradients.

Reversing springs periodically reverse their flow through the same outlet. An example of one might occur in a coastal area where sea water at high tide approaches and exceeds the hydrostatic head of the spring, causing it to reduce its flow and finally become a siphon until some time closer to low tide.

A cave entrance that shows no relative flow characteristics and has a general depression of ground relief leading to the water is called a *sink*. Some sinks are simply cylindrical or pot-shaped basins that are solution or collapse features. Others are linked to extensive underground cave systems that may connect with numerous other sinks. Peacock Slough near Mayo, Florida, is one such system whereby miles of passage connect a handful of sinks that are scattered amid an oak forest.

Formation of Solution Caves — The formation of solution caves requires several prerequisites. The following are some important items that must coexist to affect solution cave genesis:

1. Host rock
2. Groundwater (fresh)
3. Structural setting
4. Time

The *host rock* of a solution cave has special characteristics that distinguish it from others. It is usually a sedimentary rock whose individual grains are held together

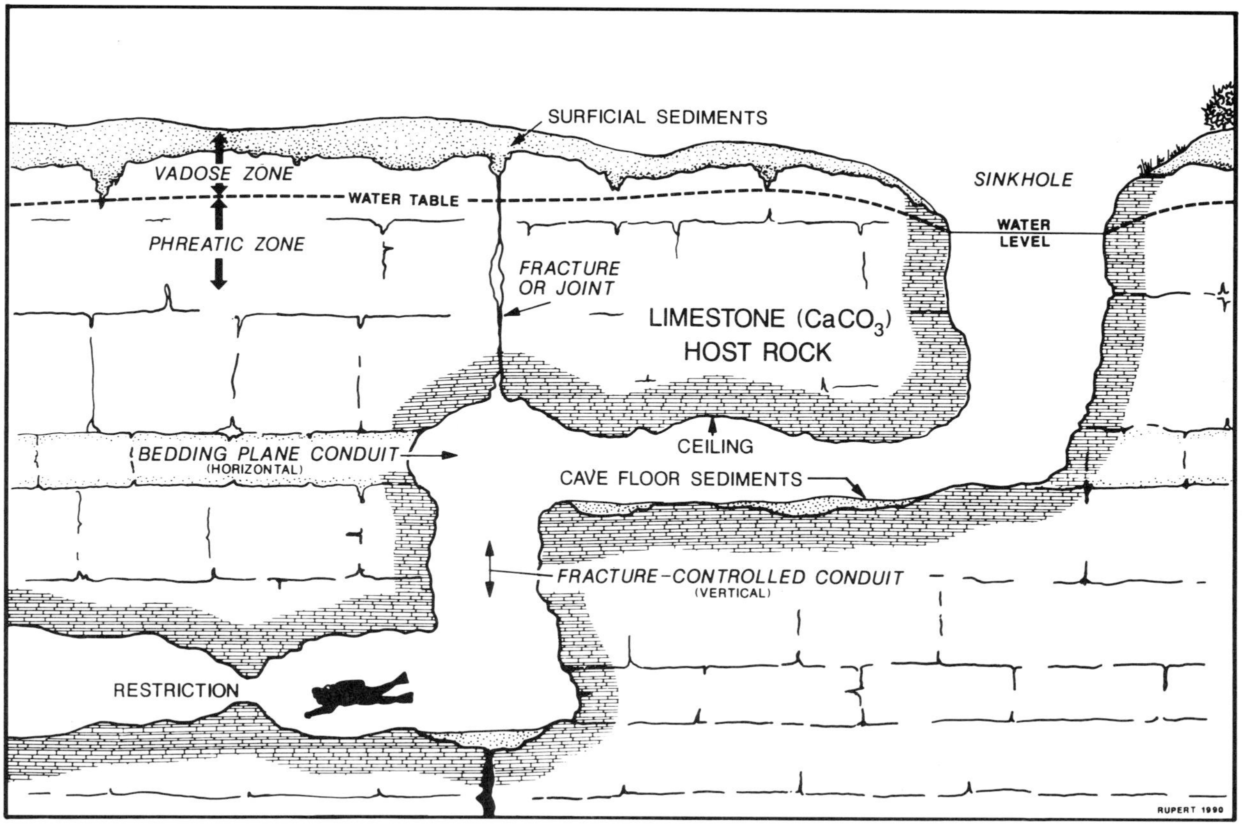

Figure 3-2 Cross-section of typical solution cave.

by calcium carbonate cement. There is adequate void space, known as *porosity*, existing between cement and grains. There is also good *permeability*, which is a rock's capacity for transmitting a fluid. Adequate permeability is essential to offer a means of mobilizing dissolved cement and to channel chemically reactive water through the host rock. Permeability is enhanced along bedding planes and fractures that often exist in the host rock.

Fresh groundwater is necessary to flow through host rock and provide a chemically reactive medium that dissolves calcium carbonate ($CaCO_3$) and then flushes the dissolved mineral away. Compared to seawater, fresh water is generally more acidic because of increased levels of dissolved carbon dioxide (CO_2) and humic acids, while having less buffering agents. The typical pH of fresh groundwater is about 5.6 while that of seawater is 8.1. The acidity allows aggressive dissolution of calcium carbonate that slowly breaks down the cement that bonds original grains together.

The groundwater must also be part of a dynamic system that continually flows to allow fresh, chemically unsaturated water to pass through rock pores and transport newly dissolved cement away from grains. A static, non-flowing system may eventually reach a point where the water is saturated with respect to calcium carbonate and can no longer dissolve the mineral. If taken to extreme time limits, the water may even become supersaturated with calcium carbonate and precipitate fresh cement. Thus, it is very important that the groundwater continues flowing to aid in cave genesis.

There are two basic equilibria involved in the dissolution of limestone. The first one is that of carbon dioxide plus water to yield carbonic acid:

$$CO_2 + H_2O \leftrightarrow H_2CO_3$$

The second one is the reaction of calcium carbonate with carbonic acid to yield calcium hydrocarbonate, which can then be transported away by a dynamic groundwater system:

$$CaCO_3 + H_2CO_3 \leftrightarrow Ca(HCO_3)_2$$

The key accelerator to both equations is the partial pressure of carbon dioxide (pCO_2) dissolved in the groundwater system. As carbon dioxide increases, more carbonic acid is created; more carbonic acid then reacts with the cement to yield calcium hydrocarbonate. The final product is quite mobile provided that flowing conditions exist in the groundwater system.

Structural setting is important to cave genesis. Most aggressive cave formation occurs where the juvenile passage is submerged in fresh groundwater flow. This allows maximum exposure of cements to a reactive, dissolving medium. The portions of caves that are underwater are part of the *phreatic zone*. At various periods of development, a cave environment may exist above the present water table. The dry portion of a cave is known as the *vadose zone*. Unusual *speleothems* form during cave genesis in vadose zones. Super-saturated calcium carbonate in groundwater that seeps through the cave ceiling precipitates dripstone features to leave geologic evidence of the cave's dry existence. Dripstones from the ceiling are referred to as *stalactites*, while those along cave floors are named *stalagmites*. A *column* is a vertically connected stalactite and stalagmite. Such cave appendages may be observed in underwater blue holes of the Bahamas and along the coast of Belize. They are a revelation to find because it stimulates one's imagination of what or who might have stalked the caves in periods past.

Time is always a consideration in the genesis of caves. The chemical reactions and physical water movement necessary for cave development proceed along the order of thousands of years before significant passage is opened. Today's newsworthy occurrences of sinkholes in Florida are generally collapses of older, buried caves that have lost support because groundwater levels have dropped enough to reduce strength of ceilings and allow overburden to "cave-in".

The geologic section of South Florida yields an interesting perspective of time and cave occurrences. Besides the occurrences of *surfacial caves*, there are zones buried at 3,000 and 9,800 feet beneath sea level that are notable cave intervals. They range from 47 million to 120 million years old, respectively. In comparison, most of the diveable caves in South Florida are present in rock that is less than 25 million years old.

HAZARDS OF THE UNDERWATER CAVE ENVIRONMENT

The underwater cave environment presents various hazards that make diving within it particularly dangerous. These unique dangers must be understood and accounted for prior to any underwater cave adventure, in addition to the hazards of open water diving. These hazards have stimulated creative thoughts leading to the invention of specific equipment and techniques that greatly increase safety and comfort for the trained cave diver. Without such specialized equipment and techniques, cave diving is extemely unsafe. To the well-prepared cave diver, the environmental hazards present a technical challenge that is also a source of extreme satisfaction.

This discussion divides cave environmental hazards into the following categories:

A. Water hazards
B. Visibility hazards
C. Structural hazards
D. Exposure hazards
E. Cave-life hazards

Water Hazards — Underwater caves present hazards by virtue of the properties, contaminants, etc. of the medium that fills them. Some caves with restricted water flow may develop numerous thermoclines due to temperature stratification of the water. Some coastal caves equilibrate water temperatures with those of the surrounding ocean or gulf. For example, a relatively warm sink near Hudson, Florida leads to a deep cave that has a water temperature of 59 degrees F. This temperature is roughly that of the Gulf of Mexico during the winter. Unusual exposure protection must be planned for this cave because most diveable sinks maintain 72 degrees F in the immediate area. The thermoclines and colder waters become more hazardous as depth and time of exposure are increased.

Water density may vary within some caves, particularly those along a marine coastline. The shallow passages of freshwater may lead to deep zones that are saltwater filled. This occurs in ground water along coastlines because freshwater is less dense than saltwater; it essentially "floats" as a lens above the saltwater. Although it is not a direct hazard, this increase in water density, as one dives deeper, alters buoyancy such that a freshwater cave diver may need to slightly increase ballast to complete a dive.

Water velocity in flowing caves presents a hazard. Current affects a diver's stamina, air supply and underwater speed. Upon entering a flowing cave at spring entrance, a diver should swim along the upper one-third of the tunnel and use proper techniques to take advantage of the lee side of the channel. Only experience can teach a diver about the peculiarities of water velocity within a particular cave system. Conversely, as a diver exerts much energy entering a flowing cave, she should take advantage of current while exiting the cave. A diver should exit where maximum current flow can aid her swimming, thus greatly reducing air consumption and relieving some physical stress toward the end of a dive.

Visibility Hazards — Hazards to visibility are usually due to particles suspended in the water column. Figure 3-3 shows the classification of sediment particles by size. *Boulders, cobbles* and *pebbles* are the larger sized particles, and though frequently seen in subaquatic caves pose no visibility hazard to the cave diver, because they are difficult to suspend in the water column.

Granules are small enough in size to become suspended in the water column by swift currents or similarly vigorous movement of water due to DPV wash, panicked movements by the diver, etc. Because of the relatively heavy weight of granules, they settle out of the water column almost immediately after any disturbance has subsided. Any current rapid enough to suspend granules in the water column will quickly move them past the diver. In such a situation, the swift moving current would present a greater hazard than granules suspended in the water column.

Next in size to granules, *sand* consists of particles varying between 2 mm and 1/16 mm in diameter. Like granules, sand settles out of the water column fairly quickly following its suspension by a local disturbance. Any currents strong enough to suspend and carry sand or granules will easily remove the smaller particles of silt and clay from the passage. If the current increases enough to suspend sand, the weight of the sand particles will cause them to fall to the cave floor as soon as current speed decreases.

Following sand, *silt* is the next smallest sediment size consisting of particles in the range of 1/16 mm to 1/256 mm in diameter. Although certainly this test is not recommended for underwater use, silt particles can be distinguished from smaller sizes by their gritty feel when rubbed between one's teeth. The smaller particles, less than 1/256 mm diameter, are clay. The combination of these two grain size groups present the single most dangerous hazard to a cave diver. In heavy current, silt particles may move out and dissipate, but they often effect poor visibility between the dive team and the exit. Silt particles are dispersed more easily than clay particles because a higher threshold velocity is required to make clay move within water. Clay-sized particles may take several days to settle in stable laboratory conditions. Thus, visibility loss due to clay turbidity may not be easily "waited out" in a low velocity cave system. A cave diver must have complete confidence in properly practiced techniques to safely exit such a hazard. Moreover, proper techniques are necessary to minimize the risk of silt/clay turbidity.

Size in mm	Particle Name
<1/256	Clay
1/256 - 1/16	Silt
1/16 - 2	Sand
2 - 4	Granule
4 - 64	Pebble
64 - 256	Cobble
>256	Boulder

Figure 3-3 Sediment particle size classification.

Structural Hazards — The structural hazards of cave diving are best experienced in a dry cave situation where one may observe these hazards while being somewhat assured of air supply and eventual exit reference. The foremost of structural hazards is the *ceiling*. A diver entering a cave situation must be aware of his finite air supply and no direct access to the surface because of the ceiling. While diving within daylight visibility of the surface near a cave entrance, one is technically performing a cavern dive. A similar dive at night or within the confines of a cave ceiling beyond visual reference to surface becomes a cave dive and warrants special air consideration, equipment, and techniques. The uneven nature of most ceilings makes them seem to have flailing fists that slap the head of an unprepared diver and grab all manner of equipment. A ceiling may also provide a stabilizing fin hold or a place to rest for the trained diver who recognizes and respects the natural opportunity. In cave systems where the ceiling is composed of soft, easily eroded limestone, one must cautiously enter and observe exhaust bubbles as they reach the ceiling. If the ceiling begins to crumble and the resulting sediment turbidity reduces visibility, one must carefully assess whether diving that particular cave is a safe venture. One always maintains a visual or physical reference to the exit in such a volatile situation.

The *sidewalls* of a cave present certain hazards that are generally associated with permanent or temporary guideline locations. One must be careful not to embed a guideline within soft walls, because in a total no-visibility emergency, a returning dive team may follow this line until it feels as though it is running directly into a wall. Walls with various horizontal cracks can also invite a poorly-run guideline into dangerous areas that may mislead a stressed dive team into unnecessary restrictions.[1] When exiting a cave with high velocity current, one must always be cognizant of the passage ahead to avoid being slammed into a wall at a sharp turn. Such an encounter readily reminds one of the massive gear being worn.

Open water divers are respectful of *bottom* characteristics, and this respect is demanded in full within a cave environment. In some cave systems, a strong flutterkick from 10 feet off the bottom can result in a puff of "smokey" silt that may or may not amuse one's dive partners. If amusement has been achieved, one might be affectionately nicknamed *Choo-Choo,* otherwise a silty return may be in store for the exiting dive team.

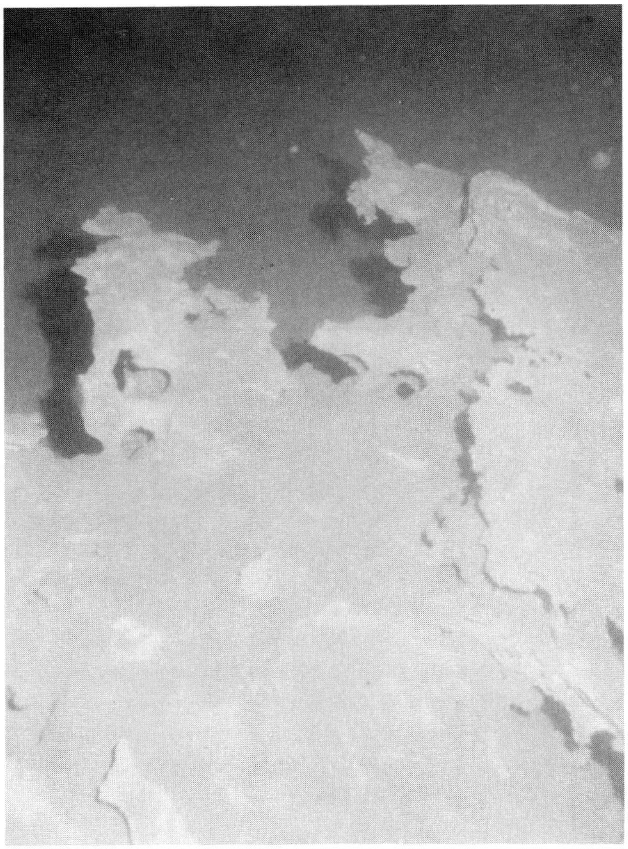

Figure 3-4 "SILT"

The *horizontal component* of many cave systems is similar to a children's pinball/marble game fashioned in a maze. A careful use of guideline techniques and an acute development of cave referencing will increase one's enjoyment and safety while exploring such systems.

The *vertical component* of some cave systems creates many depth variations during a single dive. A dive team must carefully monitor maximum depths because of the up-and-down nature of some passages. One must also take extreme caution while diving these systems after recovering from a sinus or ear infection. Several divers have been caught in a situation where they experience an ear or sinus squeeze while exiting a low ceiling cave where maximum depth is located near the entrance. They were able to enjoy a shallower dive to a maximum horizontal penetration, only to return to a stressful, painful situation while trying to negotiate the maximum depth point near the exit. An acute situation may occur if a diver ventures upward into a vertical chimney that can often be observed along cave ceilings in North Florida. The immediate ten to twenty feet relief in some chimneys may lure the susceptible diver into a dangerous trap whereby his/her body's sinuses may suffer extreme damage and pain to execute an exit. If one is caught in such a predicament, good buddy communication and a calm, patient attitude may allow time, spare air, and relaxation to clear the blockage.

Restrictions are structural hazards where at least two opposite walls are situated so that a diver faces narrow passageway. At one time, the term *minor restriction* referred to a narrow passageway which the diver could safely squeeze through without altering any personal equipment. The term *major restriction* was used for a narrow passageway which required the removal of one's air supply to negotiate the passage. Removing one's air supply in a cave environment is an unsafe practice from a systems analysis standpoint. It clearly presents a breach in the buddy system equal to the maximum amount of time necessary for one to doff tanks, negotiate the passage, don tanks, and wait for the remaining team members to follow and don their tanks. A myriad of other considerations exist such as low visibility, poor guideline management, buoyancy variations, potential separation of one from the air supply, and a duplication of all these factors during exit. A safe cave diving philosophy cannot advocate this practice at the expense of exploration or potential disaster.[2]

---

[1]The general term for guideline hazards of this type is *line trap.* — Ed.

[2]Because of these considerations, removal of one's diving gear is not recommended. Today, cave divers use alternate gear configurations such as side-mounted cylinders to negotiate tunnels which would require removal of back-mounted cylinders. The terminology has simi-

Exposure Hazards — Exposure hazards in cave environments deserve special emphasis over open water situations, because the diver simply cannot execute a buoyant assent to the surface and await assistance topside. When a cave diver enters the water, she is in control of time and depth exposures during the dive.

Time is very important while exploring underwater caves. It is a measure of the diver's stamina and can relate to cumulative physiological stress. The absorption of nitrogen by one's body while underwater is relative to time. It is a source of stress if any delay happens during exit. It is a measure of the finite air supply strapped to each explorer's back.

Depth exposures in underwater caves bring special considerations. As depth increases, the partial pressure of nitrogen dissolved in body tissues increases, hence more extensive decompression is necessary before surfacing. Compressed air is denser at depth, thus causing greater air consumption even if respiratory rates are constant. These factors combine to make air planning for deep cave dives extremely critical. Depth creates unusual and quite variable psychological effects upon individuals. These effects may lead to impaired judgment and inability to properly respond to emergency situations. Depth alters buoyancy characteristics and may demand that a diver alter her suit or buoyancy compensation device(s) to displace more water during deep cave dives.

The combination of *time and depth* exposures greatly adds to the air supply demands of a cave diver team. Adequate decompression air must be planned for prior to any deep penetration. Special consideration during planning must be given to bottom time and maximum depth calculations, for they seldom correspond to any single penetration point within the cave. Safe decompression air must be accounted for in the event of a lost air supply among the team.

Decompression practices during cave dives may be quite different than open water situations. Each diver should provide an emergency decompression supply to be tied off at the deepest anticipated decompression depth. Decompression stops are sometimes located in cramped restrictions where the entire team must seek a stable depth in a small area. Some divers bring liquids in squeeze bottles to keep body fluid levels high during long stops. Thick neoprene gloves are often clipped to decompression bottles to comfort cold hands after long exposures. Some divers bring paperbacks, while others devise unusual amusements to pass the time while awaiting the surface interval. Because of the heavy and strenuous climbs that are associated with exiting some systems topside, one must carefully consider that the body is still eliminating excess nitrogen in the blood during surface intervals. A surface decompression rest should be included after any deep cave dive where exertion is necessary to return to one's vehicle or camp.[3]

larly changed. A *major restriction* is one which cannot be negotiated using back-mounted double cylinders. Safe passage of a major restriction requires alternate gear configuration. A *minor restriction* is a narrowing of the cave passageway which can only be negotiated by divers passing single-file. Safe passage of a minor restriction requires use of an alternate air source with a long hose (5 feet is the minimum acceptable length, with 7 feet recommended). A restriction which requires careful, deliberate maneuvering is called a *squeeze.* A low area which forces the diver down into contact with the floor for just a short distance is called a *belly-rub.* — Ed.

Cave-Life Hazards — Cave-life hazards are generally no different than those encountered by an open water diver in fresh or saltwater environments. Aquatic life hazards in freshwater are generally encountered near the water's edge or in shallow areas. Such reptiles as water moccasins and alligators are quite common in Southeastern United States environments. Similarly, in marine environments, dangerous aquatic life are usually encountered at the open water entrance to a cave. They include various sharks and moray eels.

This brief mention of dangerous living cave animals must include a comment about human impacts upon cave life. Delicately balanced ecosystems exist within cave environments, and cave divers must enter a system with extreme respect for the creatures who inhabit and survive there by the simple rules of nature. Living populations are generally sparse and no unnecessary collection of cave creatures should ever be practiced or advocated by team members. One is a visitor to a closed and segregated habitat where any detrimental action may have far-reaching consequences.

INDIRECT EXPLORATION FOR NEW CAVE LOCATIONS

The avid cave diver eventually yearns to explore new caves which have never been dived. Exploration for virgin cave territory must be methodical and thorough to yield worthwhile results, because serendipity only works for the largest and most accessible locations. A preferred approach is to search from general to specific localities. Consequently, a search of literature, maps, and finally field resources should serve the curious mind quite well.

A literature search should concentrate upon finding regional carbonate geology that is near the surface and has notable freshwater resources. One should begin by searching the United States Geological Survey's or other national surveys' books that outline geologic provinces. After prospective geology has been regionally found, the State Bureau of Geology is an excellent source of valuable details. For example, the Florida Bureau of Geology has a printed bulletin entitled *Springs of Florida.* These sources put one in the ball park and help limit detailed study to areas of most promise. Master's and

[3]Because of the weight of typical cave diving gear, the practice of making a surface decompression stop of 5 to 15 minutes is recommended following *all* cave dives. — Ed.

Doctoral theses from scientific disciplines are occasionally relevant to cave environment subjects. A letter to the geology department of a nearby university may yield a detailed topic list of theses and abstracts. If a particular thesis is of interest, it can be read at the library of the same college, or a copy may be loaned to a local public library. Federal and state caving organizations such as the National Speleological Society are excellent sources for locating wet and dry cave regions. Because of the economic implications of recent sinkhole developments, some states have sinkhole research institutes that publish their findings. The association of karst with freshwater resources brings state water management districts and environmental regulatory agencies into consideration because of their responsibilities to the public as protectors of sufficient quantities of high quality groundwater.

Many of the above information resources will offer their findings in the form of maps. Map research is extremely important because it may lead to a precise location of virgin karst section. *Surface geology maps* limit regional areas if one assumes that the entrance is from the same geologic unit as that of the surrounding land. *Topographic maps* show relief relative to a datum such as sea level. Sink holes on topographic maps are noticeable if a marked depression exists above the water level of a small pond. The appearance is that of a watery bullseye outlined by concentric contour lines at varying distances away from the water. Each conutour line marks the location of equal elevations above the given datum. The contour interval determines how many lines are drawn. For instance, a planar surface with 100 feet of relief is mapped with 5 parallel lines if the contour interval is 20 feet and 10 such lines for a corresponding 10 feet interval. *Infrared photographic maps* may show several clues for springs or sinks. Intense red coloration may be indicative of increased plant activity around karst features in dry climates. If an isolated sink is surrounded by forest, it will appear as a deep blue dot within redder hues of plant material. Infrared maps of coastal areas may reveal freshwater cave outlets under marine waters if a notable temperature difference exists between the two waters.

Field research combines the literature and map resources whereby one travels to areas of particular interest. Prior to leaving public domain, one must establish local contacts to obtain landowner permission to explore their property. A truthful, tactful approach is generally appreciated by landowners and extreme courtesy should be extended toward properties once permission is granted. Local contacts may clue one into adjacent properties where springs, sinks, or other features are present. A flowing stream in karst environments should be followed to its headwaters. Clear runs that branch away from a river path should be explored. A large depression rimmed with oak trees in a general pasture area might be a discovery site. The presence of certain plant life, such as weeping willows, signal the existence of a water table very near the surface. Generally, one must be observant of the topography and surroundings that occur at different known cave sites and then one might apply research and comparison to relate this knowledge to new areas.

When karst environments occur along coastlines, one must not forget the possibility of caves existing offshore. For example, South Florida's coastline extended to present day depths of 450 feet as recently as 12,000 years ago. Subaerial exposure of these lands may have yielded cave formation in the order of hundreds of years. Depth recorders and Loran C navigation methods may be quite helpful in locating ancient depressions and offshore sinks. Offshore fishing holes can actually be large sinks with cave section below. In shallow water, some offshore springs have characteristic surface boils where water appears to churn and swirl.

Finally, inaccessible property may be explored from the air by light plane or helicopter. This is most useful in heavily overgrown areas. Stream runs may be quickly followed to head springs. The overhead viewing vantage may help in finding deep springs that might otherwise be overlooked beneath river runs.

SUMMARY

The underwater cave environment is one of constant, slow evolution. The origin of underwater caves is variable and several important processes are involved in the formation of solution caves. The hazards of such an environment require special equipment, training, and experience to safely explore unknown corridors. An understanding of such hazards should compel the enlightened diver to: (1) seek open water adventures, or (2) delve deeply into the safe methods of cave diving. It is a personal decision based upon one's self-honesty. This enclosed environment is unique and must be respected by all visitors. It offers a supreme challenge, but gives no quarter to those unprepared.

BIBLIOGRAPHY

Brentz, J.H., 1942. "Vadose and Phreatic Features of Limestone Caverns," *J. Geology*, Vol. 50, No. 6, pp. 675-811.

Davies, W.E., and I.M. Morgan, 1977. *Geology of Caves.* U.S. Government Printing Office, p. 19.

Davies, W.M., 1980. "Origin of Limestone: Caverns," *Bull. Geol. Soc.* S.M. Vol. 41, No. 3, pp. 475-628.

Dilamarter, R.R. and S.C. Csallany, 1977. *Hydrologic Problems in Karst Regions,* Western Kentucky University, Kentucky, p. 481.

Exley, I.S., 1973. "The Environment of Cave Diving." In Mount, T. *Safe Cave Diving.* National Association for Cave Diving.

Gardner, J.H. 1935. "Origin and Development of Limestone Caverns," *Bull. Geol. Soc.* AM 46 pp. 1255-1274.

Gilboy, A.E., 1985. *Hydrogeology of The Southwest Florida Management District,* Technical Report 85-01, p. 18.

Holiday, W.R. 1982,. *American Caves and Caving.* Barnes and Noble Books, New York, p. 348.

Jakues, L. 1977. *Morphogenetics of Karst Regions.* Halsted Press, New York, p. 248.

Jennings, J.N. 1971. *Karst.* M.I.T. Press, Cambridge, p. 252

Poulson, T.L. and W.B. White, 1969. "The Cave Environment," *Science* 165 pp. 971-981.

Sweeting, Marjorie M. 1973. *Karst Landforms.* Columbia University Press, New York, p. 362.

Swinnerton, A.C., 1932. "Origin of Limestone Caverns," *1 Bull. Geol. Soc. AM,* m. 43. pp. 663-694.

Warwick, G.T., 1962. "The Origin of Limestone Caves," in Cullingford, C.H.D. *British Caving.* Routledge and Kegan Paul Ltd., London. pp. 83-119.

Chapter 4

CAVE DIVING EQUIPMENT: A Guide to the Tools of the Trade

by Mike McCaskill

In its highest reaches, the sport of cave diving is a way of coming to grips with the natural environment of the underwater cave. To become integrated into these surroundings, the diver requires specialized equipment and training. The right equipment can make cave diving a safer and more enjoyable activity — the wrong equipment can make it an uncomfortable and even hazardous sport. Yet equipment remains a tool. "Tackle psyche" (faith in equipment) should not become more important than the art of technique. The "art of safe cave diving" requires the use of both specialized equipment and technique.

Equipment procurement is the first step necessary in beginning the sport of cave diving. For most divers, it represents a substantial investment. Unfortunately, many divers are quickly dissatisfied with their initial purchases in terms of comfort or performance. Often, attempts to cut costs end up in even a greater outlay of money.

Observing a group of experienced cave divers is one of the most useful methods of avoiding mistakes in equipment purchases. The brands may vary; however, there are definite reasons for the popularity of certain styles of buoyancy compensators, backup lights, etc. Although each diver has his own prejudices toward equipment, experienced divers are uniform in their demand for functional gear that has a high degree of reliability.

Equipment is of historical importance to the sport, as it often has defined the limits of cave diving. Many cave divers are technical innovators and advances made in cave equipment have led to advances in open water diving. Pride in workmanship often is evident in home-built reels and lights, and it provides motivation for technologically inspired divers. There are numerous reasons for the cave diver to take more than a passing interest in the tools of the trade. This chapter is designed to help the diver select the proper equipment and analyze gear so that all dives are made under safe conditions.

LIFE SUPPORT EQUIPMENT

Life support equipment includes cylinders, valves, tank configurations, back plates, harnesses, regulators, pressure gauges, hoses and buoyancy compensators.

Cylinders

The cylinders currently available to cave divers are those available to general sport divers. Choices are limited by construction material and size (air volume). The two materials are aluminum and steel. The differences are minimal, with steel probably best for cave divers because of the advantages of buoyancy, size, and air availability. The main advantage of aluminum is its resistance to corrosion.

Probably the most popular tank for cave diving is the 104 cubic foot steel, set in a double tank block (Figure 4-1). The main advantage is the available volume of air. Even though the two tank arrangement is the most popular, it is not the only configuration that allows safe cave diving.

A single cylinder can be used for safe cave diving if the diver's plan is based on the limits of the tank. It is just as feasible to dive a single tank fitted with a *Y* valve as it is to dive a set of doubles fitted with a dual valve manifold.

Most experienced cave divers select the double tank block. The advantages are: greater negative buoyancy with which to offset the effects of exposure suits, and a larger air capacity which allows longer penetrations. Other configurations have an even greater air capacity than doubles; however, their use may be limited to divers who are physically capable of handling the weight.

A triple tank design (Figure 4-2) requires a custom-made manifold (Figure 4-3). Typically, the existing triple tank system in this design uses aluminum 80's. However, any cylinder could be used in this system. The main disadvantage is extreme weight.

Another concept developed in the 1960's is the Delta Tank configuration (Figure 4-4). Initially, the third tank in this configuration was used as a safety tank and its air supply was excluded from pre-dive planning, serving only as an emergency supply. Today it can be used in stage diving to increase the air supply. The third tank is attached between a set of doubles with a custom-made quick release mechanism (Figure 4-5). Normally this cylinder would be a steel 71.2 because of its negative buoyancy and smaller size.

Cylinder Valves

Single Tanks — Three types of tank valves are available for single tanks, the *K, J,* and *Y* valve. The once popular J valve was made obsolete by the development of the submersible pressure gauge. It is not acceptable for use in the cave environment, where its reserve can be activated by accident and its lever can become a source of entanglement.

There are severe limits on the use of a K valve in cave diving. Although two second stages can be available by adding an octopus regulator, only one first stage can be attached to a K valve.

Figure 4-1 Double 104's.

The best system to use when diving with a single tank is the dual outlet *Y* valve. The *Y* valve affords the use of two complete regulator systems. In the event of a malfunctioning regulator, the diver can shut it off and switch to the operational system (Figure 4-6).

Double Tanks — Double tanks offer obvious advantages to the cave diver. However, they require a method of manifolding (connecting) the cylinders. There are many ways to manifold tanks but for cave diving, safety and dependability are the foremost considerations.

Permanent Dual Valve Manifold — By far the safest, most reliable, and trouble-free method of connecting tanks at this time is the permanent dual valve manifold. (Figure 4-9) Currently few manufacturers offer this manifold on a commercial basis. The assembly has two separate on/off valves, which can be turned on or off independently of each other and still maintain a common air supply for each regulator.

This system incorporates the use of two separate single hose regulators and gives the diver the option of using either regulator should an uncontrollable free-flow or malfunction occur. The diver or his partner can shut off the malfunctioning regulator in case of a problem. However, all auxiliary equipment attached to this regulator (i.e. low pressure BC inflator, submersible pressure gauge) will be lost. Divers can minimize this effect by dividing equipment between both first stages.

The following is a list of possible air supply problems that could be controlled by the utilization of a dual

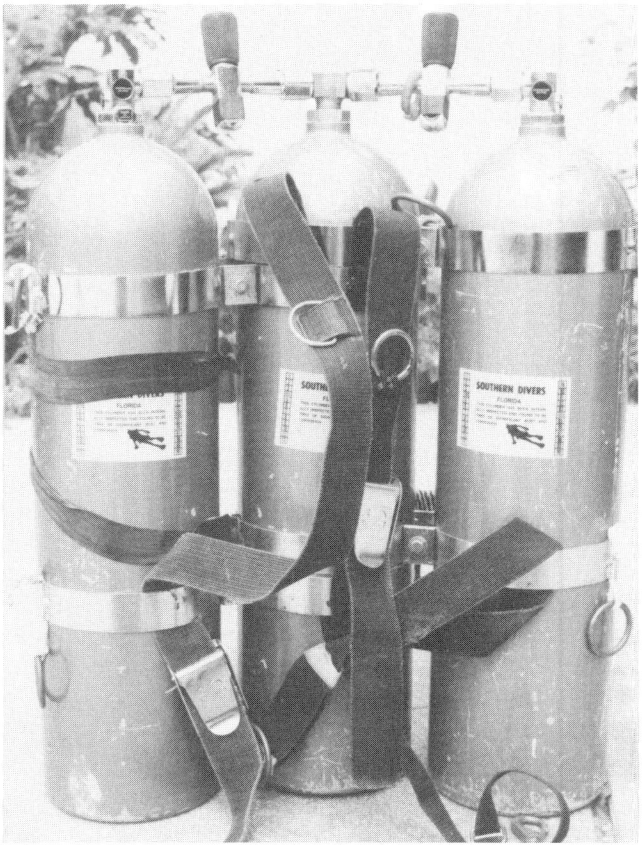

Figure 4-2 Triple tank block design.

valve manifold, as reported by Lewis Holtzendorff in a 1975 *NACD Newsletter* article "The Dual Valve Manifold vs The Conventional Manifold."

1. Free flow from second stage.
2. Free flow from BC inflator.
3. Blown valve-to-first stage O-ring.
4. Burst intermediate pressure hose.
5. Blown hose O-ring.
6. Burst SPG hose or bourdon tube in SPG.
7. Leak from first stage.
8. Obstructed air flow due to first stage malfunction.
9. Obstructed air flow due to second stage malfunction.
10. Leaking valve.
11. Obstructed air flow due to valve.

Figure 4-3 Custom manifold for triples.

Air supply "accidents" which cannot be controlled by either conventional or dual valve manifold are as follows:

1. Ruptured manifold over-pressure disk (blowout disk).
2. Leaking manifold connection.
3. Ruptured tank.
4. Blown tank-to-valve O-ring.
5. Obstruction(s) in manifold blocking air flow from one or both tanks.

Tank valve malfunctions are extremely rare but they can occur. Both tank valve malfunction and manifold failure could result in a rapid and uncontrollable depletion of a diver's available air. This possibility is a primary reason dive partners should remain close together during the entire dive.

Permanent Single Outlet Manifold — The single outlet manifold is structurally strong, reliable, and trouble-free. However, it is limited to only one outlet for regulator attachment. Should a diver have a regulator malfunction, he is dependent on another team member for air. Their air supply is lost to the team, reducing the total air supply of a two-person team by half. Considering the possible air supply problems, the permanent single outlet manifold is inferior to the dual outlet manifold.

Figure 4-4 Delta tank configuration.

Two Independent Systems — It is possible to use two single tanks, each with a regulator attached, mounted on a double backpack or harness. However, this system is practical only for special considerations or needs and requires careful air management (See Chapter 12).

This system is popular among open water divers because it offers rapid conversion from a single tank to doubles. However, this system is structurally weak and

Figure 4-5 Custom quick release mechanism.

not dependable in a cave environment. Contact with the cave's walls and ceiling can result in a disruption of the system's integrity and a blown O-ring with corresponding loss of air.

Backpacks and Harnesses — Little needs to be said of backpacks and harnesses, except that backpacks are generally preferred for single tanks and harnesses for doubles. However, each diver must evaluate the integration of each item of equipment into the system. For example, when using doubles with a horse collar or belly bag BC, a harness arrangement is preferred.

In the case of back mounted wings, a custom-made back plate is necessary. Whatever unit is used, it should be snug and secure to prevent excessive movement of the tanks during the dive. A crotch strap can keep tanks from riding too high on a diver's back.

Tanks do not have to be worn on the back. If required to dive a particular cave system, tanks can be front or side mounted. Whatever mounting system is used, it must allow a diver to keep proper trim and swim efficiently.

Figure 4-6 Dual outlet Y valves.

Regulators

The demand regulator is the heart of compressed air scuba; it is of primary importance for every diver. Furthermore, flawless performance is paramount for the survival of the cave diver. Unlike the open water diver, the cave diver cannot freely ascend to the surface if regulator difficulty occurs. Selection of a regulator for cave diving should not be taken lightly. It follows that every regulator used for cave diving must be maintained to the highest possible operational standards.

There are several criteria to consider. The regulator design must be dependable, rugged, yet simple. The regulator must deliver an adequate volume of air under all diving conditions. Resistance to inhalation and exhalation should be minimal. Air flow should remain constant regardless of tank pressure and depth.

Many different regulator types are available on today's market. The most popular design in cave diving is a balanced flow-through piston or balanced diaphragm regulator of proven dependability and quality. Attempts to save money while purchasing a regulator should not take precedence over performance and quality.

Regulator Accessories and Modifications — Modifications on regulators are based on the total system used (i.e. single tank with *K* valve, double tank with single outlet manifold, type of regulator, accessories to be used, etc.). For example, any type of single outlet valve mandates the used of an octopus regulator (Figure 4-7).

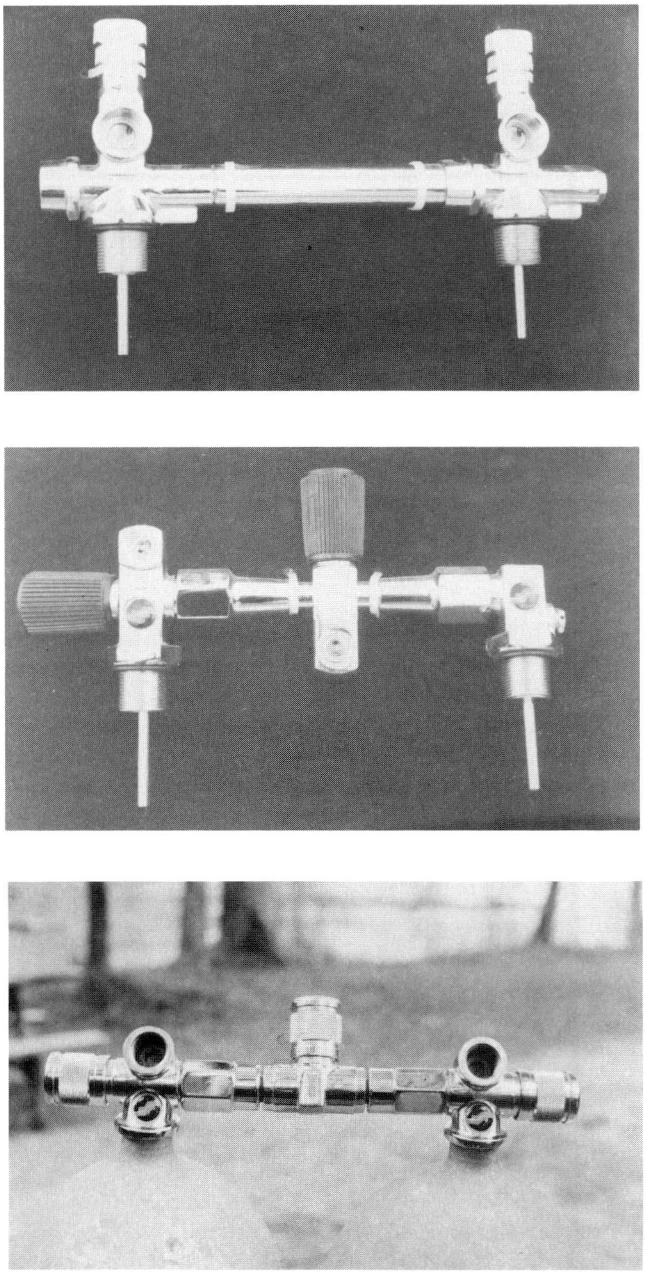

Figure 4-7 Three different dual valve manifolds.

Modifications deemed necessary for all valve configurations include the addition of a submersible pressure gauge and a power inflation mechanism for the buoyancy control device. With two second stages, this total system is referred to as a *quadrupus system.* If a dual outlet manifold is used, the submersible pressure gauge is attached to one first stage, while the BC inflator hose is attached to the other. The design of the regulator(s) usually determines the placement of these devices. Another safety modification for cave diving is the use of a five foot (or longer) low pressure hose on one of the second stages. The normal length hose is replaced with a five foot (minimum) hose on the regulator that will be given away to a team member in a shared air situation. The long hose allows single file swimming through restrictions, facilitating the team exit in emergency situations. The long hose can be dealt with by placing it around the neck, looping it in the middle with a band or surgical tubing, or by other popular ways (Figure 4-8). Any method is acceptable as long as the diver is able to make the entire length of the hose available without effort. The secondary second stage must be easily accessible, while remaining out of the way. Special care must be taken to avoid getting silt in it.

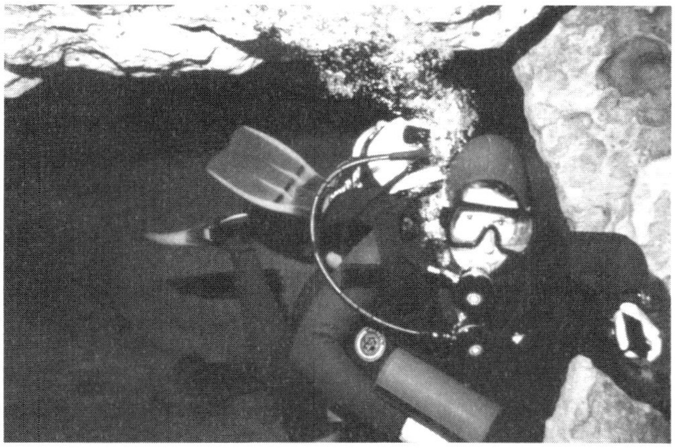

Figure 4-8 Single outlet valve with octopus regulator.

Some cave divers prefer to give the primary second stage to the distressed diver and others prefer to give the secondary second stage. In either case, the procedure must be understood by both partners in advance. Divers should breathe from both regulators before the dive to ensure they operate correctly, and at the conclusion of the dive to determine if any problems were created during the dive.

Submersible Air Pressure Gauge — The submersible air pressure gauge (SPG) is used to monitor a tank's air pressure. This gauge is mandatory for safe diving. It is the equivalent of a fuel gauge on an airplane. It would be foolish for a pilot to fly without knowing the available fuel supply. Likewise, it would be suicidal to cave dive without knowing available air at all times. The gauge should be placed in a position easily reached yet not where it will drag or catch on the guideline.

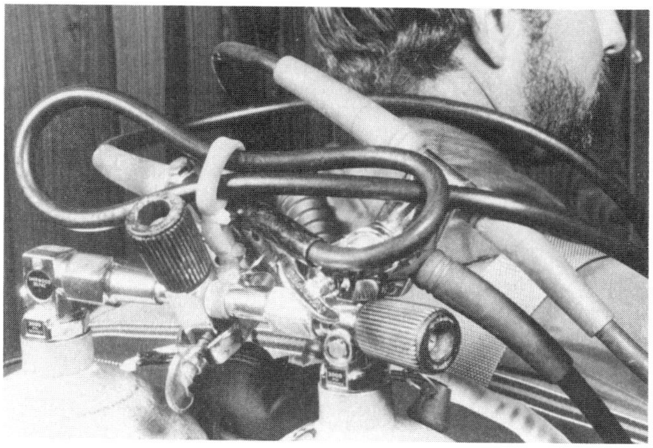

Figure 4-9 A long hose storage method.

A pressure gauge must accurately measure the amount of air in a cylinder at every level. There are other features that enhance an SPG. The dial face should be easy to read and luminous for use in restricted visibility and low light conditions. Some submersible pressure gauges have internal lighting. A swivel fitting facilitates reading the dial face.

Buoyancy Compensator Power Inflator — A buoyancy compensator (BC) enables the cave diver to efficiently control buoyancy during a dive. The BC allows the diver to compensate for wetsuit/drysuit compression resulting from increased pressure at depth. It allows the cave diver to maintain neutral buoyancy regardless of depth and equipment used.

Operation is by one of two methods: power inflation or oral inflation. A power (or automatic) inflator uses a low pressure air port off the first stage of the regulator. The power inflator allows easier control and more efficient use of air at depth than oral (manual) inflation. Oral inflation of the BC is most feasible at the surface; however, each diver should test his power inflator before entering the water.

There is a third method of inflation that should be avoided. Some buoyancy compensators are equipped with CO_2 cartridges for emergency inflation. These should be removed and the insert plugged to prevent accidental inflation that could pin a diver to the ceiling of a cave or cause an uncontrolled ascent. If a plug is not available, a spent cartridge can serve the same purpose.

SPECIALIZED EQUIPMENT

Throughout its history, trends in cave diving have often been determined by specialized equipment. One concept that has emerged over the years is the principle of redundancy. Similar to the astronaut who faces the alien environment of space, the cave diver carries redundant systems as a safety measure. The best example of redundancy in cave diving equipment is the practice

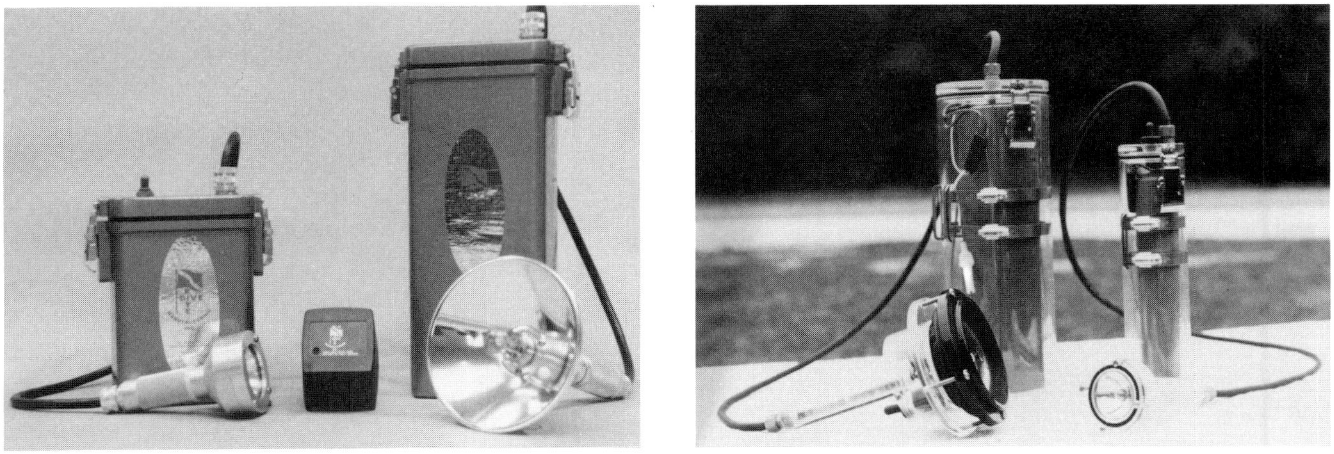

Figure 4-10 Primary lights of various types.

of carrying more than one dive light. Although only one light is needed for a dive, backup lights are carried in case of any failures. The following chart (Table 4-1) displays equipment items in terms of redundancy for a properly equipped cave diver.

Consideration of the cave environment must be made when determining equipment for a dive. In other words, equipment must match conditions. For example, when diving a system where decompression is planned, a capillary depth gauge should be carried. Systems with dark walls require high wattage lights. Consideration of the relationships between equipment is also necessary. If a permanent line is being put down, a neck or helmet-mounted light is more practical than a hand-held light.

Primary Lights — The primary light is one of the most important tools of a cave diver. When a diver's primary light fails, the dive must be turned. Thus, dependability is a basic requirement of primary lights. A diver using a primary light with insufficient power cannot safely cave dive for several reasons. Proper illumination of the system is basic to referencing; a diver with a weak primary light may be unable to signal other team members; and an underpowered primary light can be a source of stress. Thus, illumination must also be a fundamental consideration. Primary lights usually represent a large investment for each cave diver and it makes little sense not to have one that allows the diver to function safely.

Primary lights are available from dive gear manufacturers and there are also cave divers who make their own. Advancement in primary light design has been rapid in recent years, especially with new batteries available which extend burn time, make higher watt lamps feasible, and reduce the size of the power pack. Choosing a primary light is not a simple task as there are a variety of power packs, lamps, and combinations available (Figure 4-10).

The two basic performance areas of a primary light are burn time and output. Divers continually face a trade-off between long burn times or high output. 30 watts is considered the minimum output for a primary light but much higher wattages are available. As previously discussed, primary light output needs to be closely matched between team members. A light with a burn time of 90 minutes might seem adequate, but cave divers often plan repetitive dives. If a light takes twelve hours to recharge, a 90-minute burn time might be insufficient for the day's diving.

Ideally, a diver has the option of interchanging bulbs with different wattages to control output and burn time. However, a light must have sufficient power in order to use this option. For example, a diver with a light that has a short burn time while using a 30 watt bulb will not be able to move up to a higher watt bulb. On the other hand, a light with a three or four hour burn time using a 50 watt bulb would have sufficient power to move up to an even higher watt bulb. There are a variety of lamps and batteries available for primary lights and new types continually come on the market. Divers should examine the casing for the lamp and ensure that the bulb is well-protected. A lamp that is easily broken is unsafe. Additionally, no diver wants to repeatedly replace an expensive bulb. Some primary lights have adjustable beams, a very useful option. Currently, the most often used bulbs are halogen, sealed beam, and photo lamp (projector). The photo lamp type has gained in popularity with the development of reflectors that enhance its illumination properties.

Because a primary light is used throughout each cave dive, it should have rechargeable batteries. Disposable batteries are cost prohibitive in the long run except when used in backup lights. The most commonly used battery types are wet nicads (nickel-cadmium), dry nicads, gel cells, and lead-acid maintenance free batteries. However, this field has experienced rapid advancement in the past five years and cave divers need to stay abreast of new development in batteries.

There are numerous features to look for when purchasing batteries, although sufficient power remains the primary consideration. Cost, size, amp hour rating, number of charging cycles, maintenance, and charge rate are all significant factors. The time it takes to recharge batteries is often a factor in repetitive diving. Ideally, during a long surface interval, a diver can recharge the batteries to a high percentage of their capacity. Long recharge times reduce flexibility in planning dives.

Because batteries often make up a high percentage of the cost of a primary light, a diver should find out the expected life of the batteries. Divers must be aware of any special characteristics of the batteries they purchase. Some rechargeable batteries, i.e. nicads, develop a "memory" over time and need to be fully discharged with each usage. On the other hand, some rechargeable batteries can suffer damage if they are totally drained. Certain types of batteries can be ruined and cause damage to the entire system if they become wet, while others are unaffected by water.

A limiting factor on batteries is size. The batteries must fit into a canister that can be handled comfortably. Finally, a diver's primary light needs to be regularly maintained and inspected to ensure reliability. Primary light failure is a frustrating, as well as potentially hazardous, experience.

Safety Lights — In addition to the primary light, a minimum of two (maximum of three) safety (backup) lights is recommended for safe cave diving. Desirable qualities in backup lights are durability, reliability, high illumination, and compactness. Rechargeable batteries can be used in backup lights; however, at least one light should have disposable batteries. Having batteries with different properties is a safety measure; lights with rechargeable batteries tend to lose power suddenly at the end of their burn time while disposable batteries weaken at a steady rate and may burn for a longer period of time.

Not only should a diver use a variety of power sources, but different types of safety lights should be selected. Environmental conditions (pressure, temperature, water composition, etc.) can cause light failure. If all safety lights are the same type, they may all fail from the same cause.

Many different kinds of safety lights are available (Figure 4-11) and some can be upgraded with powerful rechargeable batteries and brighter bulbs. Upgraded safety lights can put out a surprising amount of light for their size. Carrying at least one high wattage backup light provides an additional safety margin.

All lights must be tested before each dive to ensure they are functioning and fully charged. Of all the equipment used in cave diving, lights have the highest failure rates. If a backup light is needed during a dive, it must function properly to ensure the safety of the diver.

Buoyancy Control Devices — Buoyancy compensators enable cave divers to control their buoyancy underwater. This control facilitates the art of good cave div-

Systems	Recommended Number
Air System	
Tanks	1 to 3
Manifold with Dual Outlet	1
Regulators	2
Submersible Pressure Gauge	1
Lighting System	
Primary	1
Secondary	2 to 3
Buoyancy Control System	
Less than 120 feet	1
Deeper than 120 feet	2 (auto & manual inflators)
Guideline / Reel System	
Gap and/or Safety Reel	2 or more
Lead Reel	1 per team
General Items	
Watch/Timing Device	1 to 2
Depth Gauges	1 to 2
Knives	1 to 2
Exposure Suit	1
Slate and Pen cil	1 or more
Submersible Dive Tables	1 set
Directional Markers	3 or more
Compass	1
Mask	1 to 2
Fins	1 pair

Table 4-1

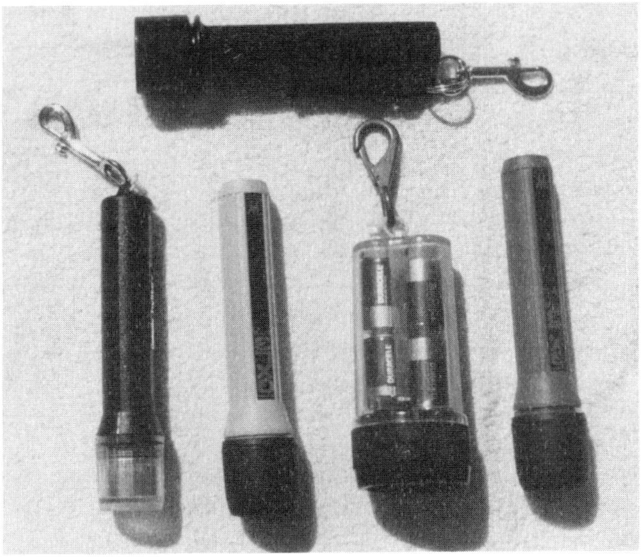

Figure 4-11 Safety lights.

ing techniques. There are several different designs for buoyancy control devices. Different types of BC's will meet the needs of different diving conditions. There are four basic designs available: backmounted (wings), belly bag, jacket type, and horse collar BC's. Additionally, drysuits can provide buoyancy control (Figure 4-12).

Most BC's have a durable outer shell (usually nylon, such as cordura) and a polyurethane plastic inner bag. A quality BC will incorporate over-pressure relief valves, oral and power inflation devices, quick-dump valves, and grommets for venting water and air from the space between the two bags. D-rings and pockets are handy for holding line markers, decompression tables, slates, and backup lights.

The most preferred BC for cave diving is the backmounted BC, commonly referred to as *wings.* It provides lift at the top of the back, where it is most comfortable, and complements the prone, feet up, head tilted back position of the cave diver. Models of backmounted BC's range in design from simple bags to integrated diving system.

An alternative unit for cave diving is the belly bag. Belly bag type BC's are useful because they offer lift nearest the diver's center of gravity. However, as with the horse collar BC, lift is under the diver pushing up, which is uncomfortable. Another disadvantage is the additional straps and buckles present in this unit.

The jacket type BC is the most recent buoyancy compensator used among cave divers. The main drawback to this BC is that it provides lift at the shoulders, which is convenient at the surface but not conductive to good cave diving technique. The horse collar BC suffers from essentially the same problem and although often used in the past, it is now the least desirable style of buoyancy compensator for the cave diver.

The drysuit's primary function is thermal regulation; however, it is also an excellent buoyancy control device. Non-neoprene, variable volume drysuits are recommended if buoyancy control is a consideration. Horse collar BC's should not be worn with a drysuit — wings

Figure 4-12 Five cave diving BC's. (Clockwise from lower left: jacket, wings, drysuit, belly bag, & horse collar.)

Figure 4-13 Right to left: 1200′ capacity reel, 500′ capacity reel, gap reel, and finger spool.

and belly bags are preferred. Whichever type BC is selected, it must not interfere with suit valve operations. Any diver who wants to use a drysuit should learn emergency procedures before diving in it. These emergencies include: blow-up, inverted swim-out, valve malfunction, and suit flooding.

Buoyancy control is essential to silt avoidance and the use of a backup BC could prevent a hazardous situation developing in case of primary BC failure. Also, a secondary BC is recommended for deep dives (below 120 feet) because of the additional lift required. A dry suit can be an excellent secondary buoyancy control device.

Safety Reels and Guidelines — The most valuable equipment a diver has for a safe return to the surface is the safety reel and guideline. Visual referencing and compass navigation are useful skills to develop; however, the guideline is the only guaranteed method of leading a diver back to the surface.

Cave diving reels are now commercially available, although some divers still make reels. Basic characteristics to consider when purchasing or building a reel are: size, line capacity, ruggedness, and neutral buoyancy. (Buoyancy is only a factor in larger reels.) A diver must also choose between an open or closed type reel. A closed type reel may be less likely to jam; however, if it becomes fouled it cannot be worked on during the dive. All reels must have a handle, winding knob, locking device, and line guide.

A variety of materials can be used to make the different parts of a reel. Reels must be made from strong and durable materials — certain plastics (such as acrylic), aluminum, and stainless steel all have characteristics that are favorable to reel construction.

Types of Reels — There are three types of reels: lead, safety, and jump (gap) reels. In most instances, the lead reel is used to provide a continuous line from the surface to the permanent line. Certain systems require several hundred feet of line to reach the permanent line, others are within 100 feet of the surface. Most lead reels hold 400 to 500 feet of line and have sideplates of about 6″ in diameter.

All cave divers should carry a safety reel, an intermediate size reel used as a navigational aid in emergencies. A safety reel should contain 200 to 300 feet of line. Jump or gap reels are even smaller, and are used to jump from one permanent line to another. They usually have 100 to 200 feet of line with 2.5″ to 3″ sideplates. Each cave diver must always carry enough reels on a dive to ensure he is never without one, even after a jump is made.

Special reels exist for installing and removing permanent lines. A reel with 8″ sideplates and a 3″ buoyancy chamber can accommodate over 1000 feet of line. This is the maximum size reel a diver can handle effectively. Sometimes a *finger spool*, which is simply a spool (usually plastic) that is held between the thumb and forefinger, is used to deploy permanent line in a new system (Figure 4-13).

Guideline — For safe and effective operation of any reel, the correct type of line must be used. Guidelines are made from nylon, as organic fibers do not work well in water. Furthermore, nylon does not float, unlike some synthetic fibers.

Braided line should be used on reels because it is

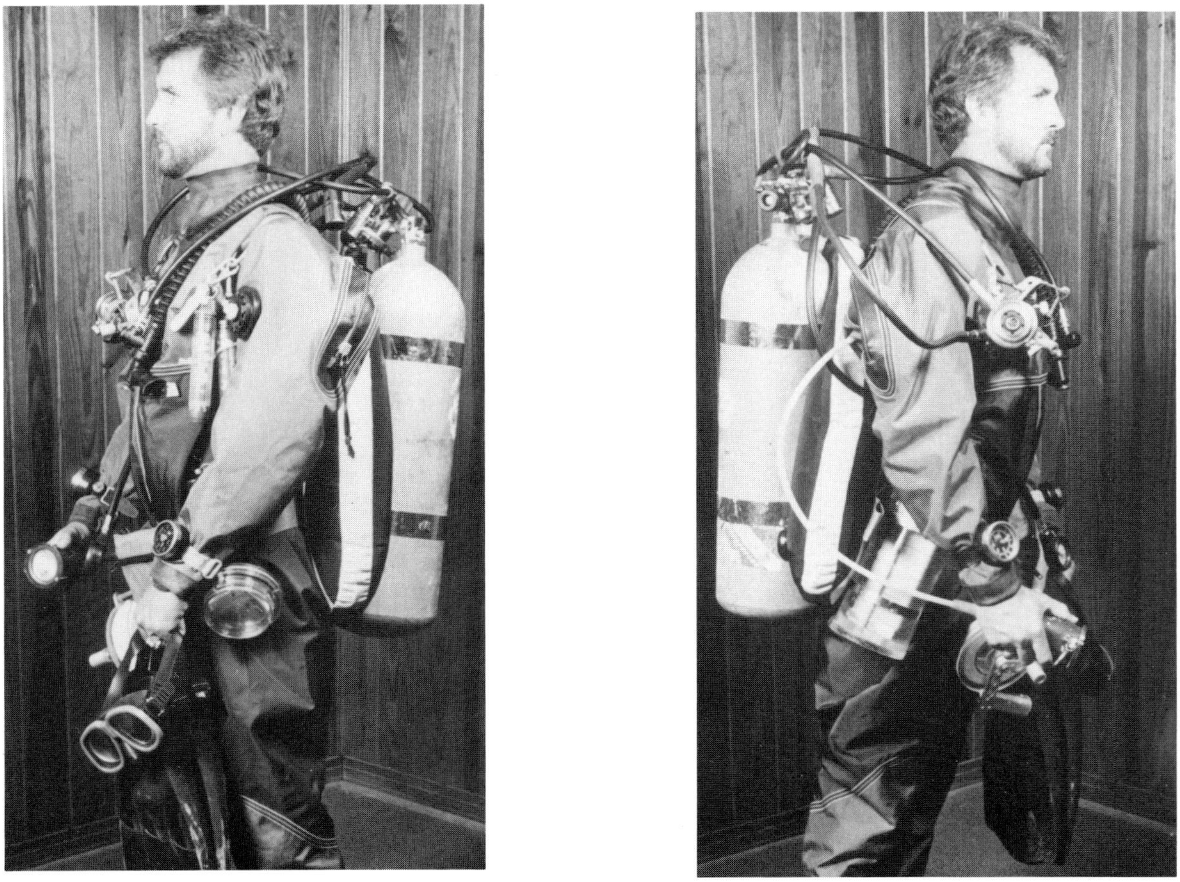

Figure 4-14 A & B: A fully outfitted cave diver.

resistant to wear. Guidelines should be between #18 and #36 in size. Anything smaller does not have sufficient strength; anything larger is too bulky to handle effectively. Through experience, divers can determine if they prefer stiffer or more flexible line. Line should be inspected periodically for any signs of wear.

Exposure Suits — Both wetsuits and drysuits are used in cave diving. Cave conditions dictate the suit which is best for each circumstance. For example, if the cave has a water temperature of 72°F and depths of 60 fsw to 100fsw, a wetsuit would suffice. A drysuit is recommended for colder water and/or greater depth. Also a drysuit is beneficial on long dives, even in 72°F water.

Each type of exposure suit has attractive features. Wetsuits are usually less expensive, more durable, and easily repaired. A wetsuit will be warmer with the addition of a hooded vest. However, drysuits are inherently warmer than wetsuits and provide redundant buoyancy control.

INSTRUMENTS AND TOOLS

In cave diving, time, depth, decompression, and direction must be accurately ascertained. Certain tools are required to gain information and communicate with other members of the dive team.

Dive Watch or Timing Device — In selecting a watch or timer, the diver should be concerned first with dependability and performance rather than price. The watch or timer should be easy to read and not prone to accidental reset. Regardless of the timing system used, beginning time of the dive should be recorded on the data slate. Divers can easily become slack in this practice when using dive computers and other automatically activated timing devices.

Depth Gauge — A depth gauge is required on all dives and it must conform to any special needs of the diver. Some gauges stop when they reach certain depths — divers must be aware of any such limits before they make exceptionally deep dives. A depth gauge must be calibrated at a variety of depths in order for the diver to have accurate information, because most gauges read shallow or deep at different depths (Figure 4-16). Capillary depth gauges are useful for making accurate decompression stops.

Compass — A compass has two functions for cave diving: mapping and orientation. Navigation is accomplished via the guideline, not by a compass. A compass

Figure 4-15 A typical compass.

should be carried on every dive and it can be mounted on a slate for convenient use (Figure 4-15).

Knife — The ideal cave diving knife is illustrated in Figure 4-17. It is small, razor sharp, and accessible. Dive knives are usually made from stainless steel and they can be attached in a variety of ways. If straps are used, the knife should be placed on the arm, rather than the leg, for easy access. In addition to a knife, many cave divers carry a line cutter for increased safety.

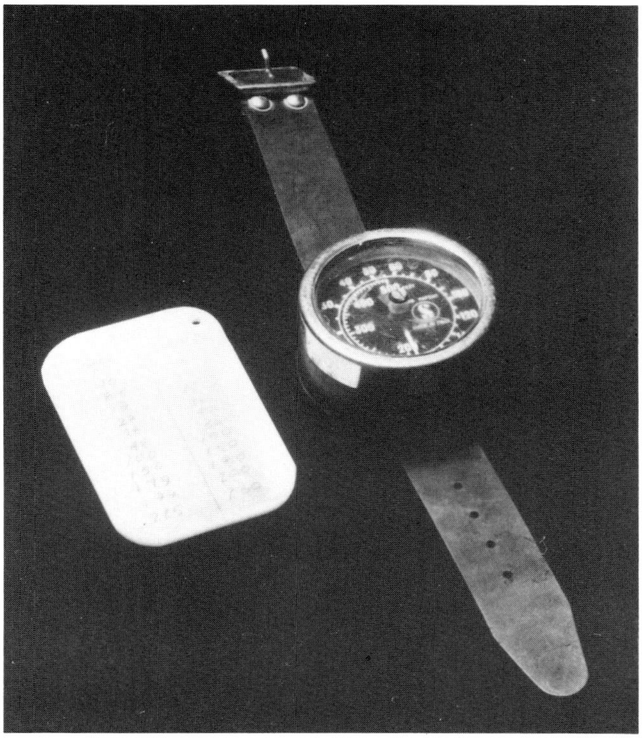

Figure 4-16 Depth gauge with calibration curve chart showing corrected vs. actual.

Directional Markers — Directional markers are used as orientation aids in cave systems with multiple permanent lines. The marker is placed on the line the divers are leaving to indicate the direction out. In the past, a variety of devices have been used as directional markers but now they are commercially available. Whatever is used as a marker, it must be easy to attach yet remain securely fastened to the line during the dive (Figure 4-18).

Decompression Tables — Decompression tables are the only acceptable method for making planned decompression stops. Even if planned stops are written on the slate, the tables should still be carried on the dive in case of deviations from the dive plan (Figure 4-19).

Dive computers are now widely available and are commonly used in open water diving. They provide much useful data to the diver and can extend no-decompression limits by computing time spent at different depths, instead of basing limits on maximum depth. Current models aim towards avoiding decompression dives. One model even shuts off if the diver enters a decompression mode. When decompression models are used, dive tables still should be carried as backup. Cave divers can employ computers as tools but should not become dependent on them.

Slate and Pencil — Slates are used to record data pertaining to the dive and as a means of communication between team members. A slate must be small enough to fit inside a pocket or pouch, but more than one can be carried. The data slate can be permanently marked, leaving blank spaces where the necessary data should be entered (Figure 4-19).

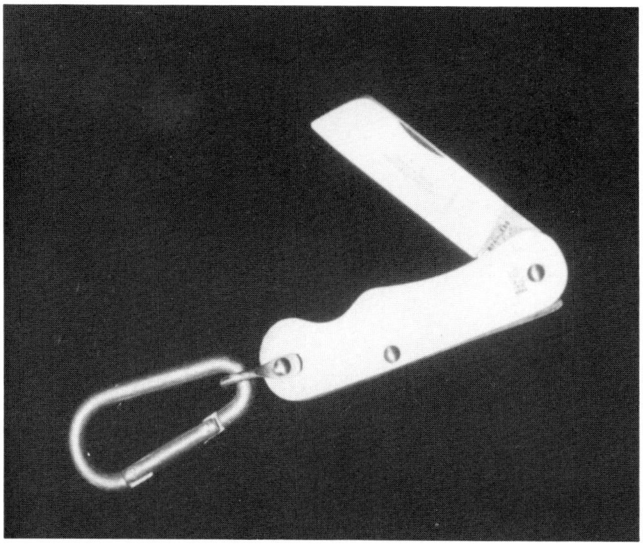

Figure 4-17 Knife useful for cave diving.

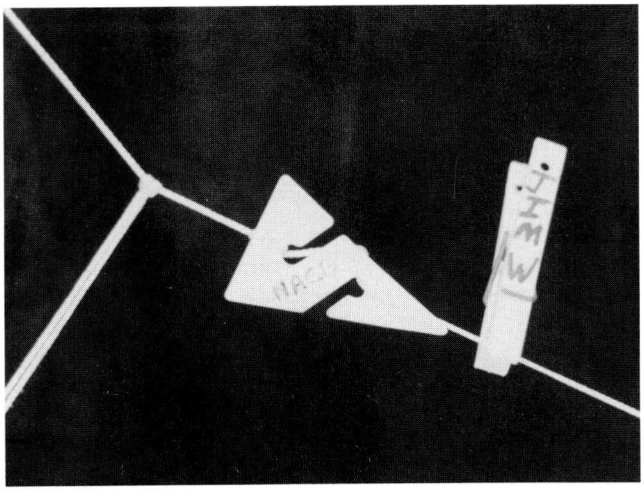

Figure 4-18 Directional Markers.

Specialty Tanks — Specialty tanks fall within the following categories: 1) decompression on air, 2) decompression on oxygen or mixed gas, 3) stage tanks for air extension, and 4) safety tanks. They are typically used with a sling instead of a backpack or harness (Figure 4-21). The sling can incorporate snap clips for attachment to the diver's harness or simply be carried by holding the sling.

The desired function of the tank determines its placement. For example, a decompression bottle of compressed air would be tied off at the deepest anticipated decompression stop. Special precautions must be taken with oxygen, which requires proper equipment and filling. Furthermore, oxygen bottles should never be placed below 20 feet.

Diver Propulsion Vehicles — Cave divers have relatively limited horizontal ranges based on swimming with fins. A diver propulsion vehicle (DPV) opens up new frontiers to the cave diver. DPV's offer the dual advantage of increased speed and decreased exertion, thus improving range and air consumption (Figure 4-20).

DPV's are commercially available in several different designs. The diver rides in some vehicles and in others is towed. Although riding offers certain advantages, it is impractical in many cave systems. Two essential features of any DPV considered for cave diving are proven reliability and sufficient power. Any diver interested in submersible propulsion vehicles should first contact a certified cave instructor who has experience with DPV's.

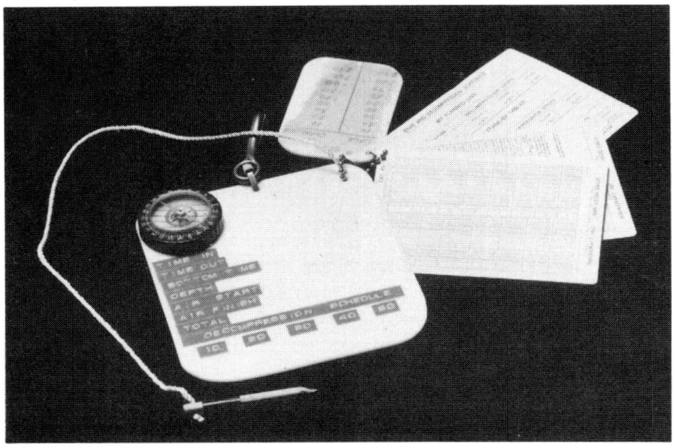

Figure 4-19 Slate & pencil with dive tables.

Figure 4-20 Cave diver using a DPV.

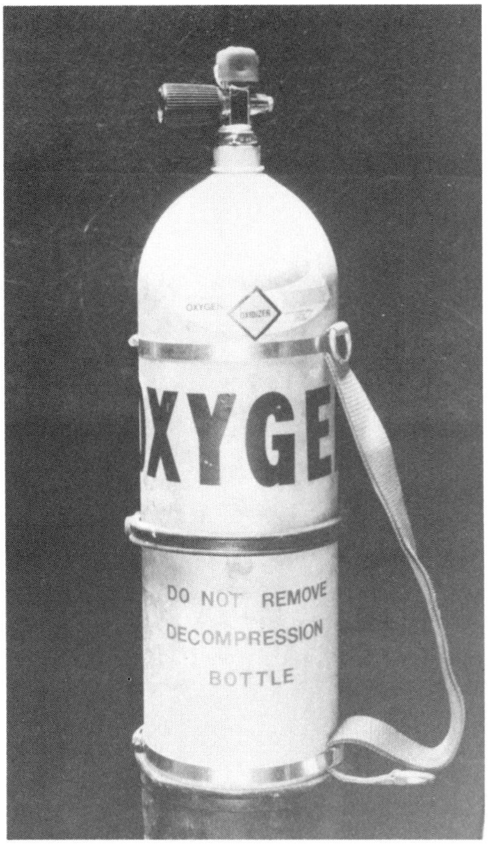

Figure 4-21 Specialty tank with sling. Note D-rings which allow for attachment to main harness.

Chapter 5

EQUIPMENT CONFIGURATION
by Bill Gavin

INTRODUCTION

There are dozens, if not hundreds, of possible cave diving equipment configurations and to examine each of them would require an encyclopedic volume of text. Not only would this be boring, it would also be unnecessary, since most of these configurations would be less than optimal. A much more efficient way of approaching the subject would be to study a successful configuration and discuss why it works. Such a configuration would almost certainly come from a group of cave divers that are devoted to serious exploration. Out of necessity, these divers will have streamlined and optimized their gear in order to allow them to go farther, deeper, and stay longer, while searching for new passages to explore. There is probably no more driven an individual than one who is lured by the desire to swim through tunnels that have never felt a diver's presence, holding a reel in her hand and laying new line as she pushes back the edge of the world.

There is a configuration that has been used for several years by a group of Florida-based cave divers while exploring some of the most demanding cave systems in the world. Much of the success that this group has enjoyed can be directly attributed to a gear configuration that does not hinder a diver during extended exploration efforts. Simply put, if everything works every time you get in the water then dives are not aborted, gear does not hinder you, you go farther more often, and **FIND MORE NEW PASSAGE**. The relationship between the number of problem-free dives and the number of successful exploration dives is direct and obvious, yet it cannot be stressed enough. A gear configuration that reduces problems will inevitably improve a diver's chances of success as well as survival. Many cave divers have adapted part or all of this configuration when the benefits were recognized. While it is by no means universal it is still worthy of study based upon the record of successes enjoyed by those who have used it.

It must be stated that since this configuration was developed by and for Florida-based cave divers, it is not appropriate for cave diving in all parts of the world or even the USA. In fact, it isn't even appropriate for ALL caves found in Florida. In very small systems, where passage size precludes the use of back-mounted doubles, then some form of side-mount configuration is obviously superior. And in certain parts of the world, where logistics make it extremely difficult to transport heavy equipment, then perhaps composite cylinders are a better choice. However, the majority of cave dives are made in systems that are both large enough and accessible enough to use more conventional tank configurations. This has proven to be the case in every part of the world where extensive underwater systems have been found. Inevitably, when the cave got large enough or long enough, double 104's[1] were called for. While the future of cave diving certainly will see an increased use of composite cylinders and rebreathers as well, it is likely that 104's will be popular for a long time to come.

What becomes apparent as we examine this configuration is that every detail, no matter how small, is important. If you change one small thing about a cave diver's gear, she may never notice the difference. Change 8 or 10 of these seemingly insignificant details and suddenly this person is going twice as far in the cave, on less air, and with less effort. She is able to achieve this improvement because her equipment is no longer hindering her. This approach has proven successful with divers that had a decade of cave diving experience, as well as with relative novices. Many of these divers experienced a drastic improvement, virtually overnight, by altering a few "minor" details.

Of course, many cave divers are not particularly interested in exploration and might assume that gear is of less importance to them. This is partially true in that "tour dives" can be made successfully even if gear is not configured optimally. Yet, by applying the same principles, recreational cave divers can conduct dives that are easier, safer, and more enjoyable.

Regardless of a diver's personal capabilities, there is no limit on how good her gear can be. Every effort should be made to configure it in the best possible manner. Setting up your gear is like studying for a test. If you don't study carefully, and study the right material, you simply won't do well. Similarly, if your gear is not carefully prepared, you increase your chances of having problems before, during, and after the dives. On the other hand, if you are willing to put in the time and effort, you can offset a lot of personal deficiencies by improving your gear. People who weren't born with Einsteinian intelligence can still do well on tests by studying carefully. Similarly, a person who wasn't blessed with a low breathing rate can still go farther in a cave by optimizing her gear. It's a matter of preparation.

Gear can and should be perfect every time you arrive at a dive site. On rare occasions it may be necessary to repair a piece of equipment that fails just prior to a

---

[1]The 104 cubic foot cylinders referred to are no longer available from the manufacturer. However, they are still in use by many cave divers. The information presented is applicable to most back-mounted double-tank configurations. — Ed.

dive. This is an exceptional event and does not justify showing up to dives with gear that always needs to be rebuilt. If a diver has gear problems and failures on a regular basis, it indicates a lack of preparedness and a poor attitude. This type of person needs to reevaluate her approach to cave diving. If a diver's buddy exhibits this type of behavior, it should be a major warning sign and cause for serious discussion.

One of the key principles of gear configuration should be *KEEP IT CLEAN.* This cannot be stressed enough. Everything should be as streamlined and low profile as possible in order to reduce drag and avoid line entanglement hazards. A corollary to this principle is, *IF YOU DON'T NEED IT, LEAVE IT AT HOME.* Carrying 5 reels on a dive that doesn't require more than one (or even none) is counterproductive. Cave divers have enough equipment that is vital without adding to the burden unnecessarily. You may be able to make tour dives while carrying every piece of gear you own, but when it comes to long exploration pushes you MUST be selective. No one ever reached the top of Mt. Everest by carrying a lot of equipment "just in case it might come in handy." Every dive should be planned to some extent and unnecessary gear shouldn't be worn.

For years, many cave divers have had the mistaken impression that the more homely it looks the better adapted for cave diving it must be. This has resulted in some divers who look as though their gear mated with a roll of duct tape and a surplus store, with maybe an old inner tube thrown in for good measure. There is nothing efficient or even all that functional about "ugly" gear. It generally takes up more space (drag), and fails more often. Part of this problem stems from the early days of cave diving when virtually everything had to be homemade. Today, very few cave divers build their own gear. Most of what they need has been developed and refined and can be purchased at any dive shop in a cave diving locale. Contrast this to the days when Frank Martz had to invent the auto-inflator by gluing a tank valve into a life vest. This does not imply that homemade gear is inferior but rather that it should be just as clean as commercially manufactured equipment if not better. Don't just throw something together with duct tape because it's quick and easy. Take the time to do it right.

HOGARTHIAN GEAR CONFIGURATION

The Hogarthian gear configuration is named after William Hogarth Main, who has the distinction of being a driven perfectionist who will not rest until every piece of gear he uses is at its absolute best. It has been the author's privilege to dive with and learn from this individual for the past decade. During this time a gear configuration gradually emerged which was the result of years of effort directed toward increased efficiency on long demanding dives. Originally it was referred to as the Hogarthian configuration in only a semi-serious manner. However, the name has persisted, and is a fitting tribute to the individual who inspired it. Many other people have made contributions to this configuration, and where it is possible (i.e. known) credit will be acknowledged. Each item or subsystem of gear will be discussed along with reasons for selecting and configuring in a particular manner. As stated earlier, it is not intended to cover all configurations that are possible. The principles involved are really what this chapter is about. Feel free to adapt this.

TANK CONFIGURATION

Not surprisingly, the tank configuration of choice is the double 104 c.f. setup as shown in Figure 5-1. These tanks have been the workhorse of cave diving for the past 15 to 20 years because of the tremendous volume of air they supply. However, all discussion of double 104 configuration applies almost universally to any double tank configuration.

A set of double tanks consists of three separate components.

1. The tanks
2. The manifold used to join the tanks
3. The bands used to stabilize the tanks

Occasionally it may be advantageous to attach something else to the tanks but this should be kept to a minimum. Remember, KEEP IT CLEAN! Anything that protrudes from your tanks, particularly from behind, is a line entanglement hazard as well as increasing your profile, with the possible result of getting you STUCK. As little as 1/8 inch can make a major difference in going through a tight spot. Any piece of gear that is attached to the back of the tanks will receive severe abuse from impact with the ceiling.

Tanks

The tanks themselves are pretty simple and should be kept that way. Don't adorn them with tank boots which

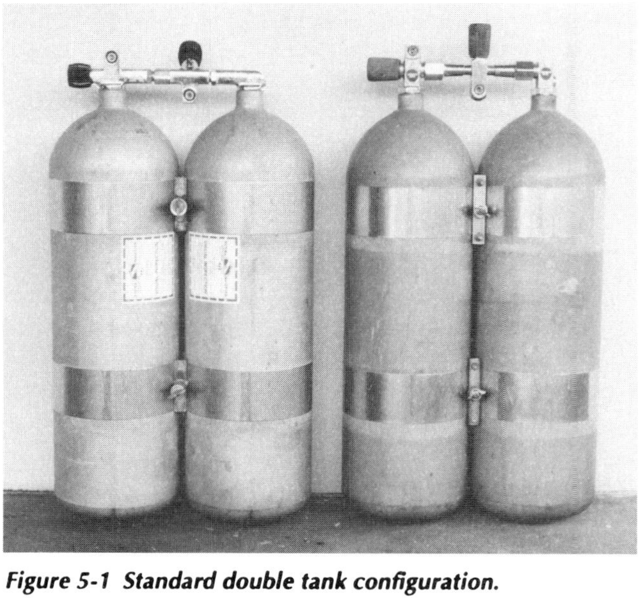

Figure 5-1 Standard double tank configuration.

raise your profile in all three dimensions. Boots also tend to hang up in tight rocky restrictions because they are relatively soft and dig into the rock. Hard steel slides through much easier provided it is free of projections created by misplaced gear.

Tanks require very little maintenance, but they benefit greatly from special attention at filling time. If the individual attaching the fill whip to your tanks doesn't carefully blow it dry, call it to her attention. It may be the 114th tank she's filled that day, but it's the first one of yours and you've got an investment to protect.

Manifold

The manifold that joins your tanks is one of the most important pieces of gear you will ever own. Years ago, cave divers dreamed of something called the *ideal manifold*, or more commonly the dual outlet manifold. The dual outlet manifold was envisioned as a manifold that would allow two tanks to be joined together with two regulators attached. The desire was for each regulator to be capable of being isolated in the event of a failure while still allowing the diver use of the ENTIRE air supply from both tanks. Dr. George Benjamin was the first to actually fabricate such a manifold and some of these "homemade valves" are probably still in use. The idea proved so successful that eventually diving equipment manufacturers began to produce the new type of manifold. This was a triumph for cave divers and the excellent safety record that cave diving has enjoyed must in large part be attributed to this breakthrough. Today it is hard to imagine what cave diving would be like if we couldn't go to the local dive store (at least in cave diving areas) and buy a dual valve manifold.

Recently, however, there has been a great deal of discussion about alternative valve configurations for double tanks. Many cave divers have done "paper analyses" of the pros and cons of manifolds vs. independent K valves, etc. Though some of these studies have been very thorough and somewhat interesting, they would be more useful if backed up by experience IN THE WATER.

While it is healthy to reexamine the way we do things from time to time, we must also be careful not to be seduced by *change for the sake of change*. If cave divers twenty years ago went to the trouble of inventing and fabricating the dual valve manifold, even though single K valves were certainly an available option, then maybe they had some good reasons. Obviously they had some excellent reasons, like being able to access their entire air supply while retaining redundancy in case of a regulator failure. The dual-valve manifold solved a lot of problems without creating a lot of new ones, which is not the case with independent setups.

The most serious problem associated with diving independent valves involves handling an out-of-air diver. Advocates of independent systems often state that if all divers used separate valves there would never be a catastrophic failure resulting in an out-of-air diver. There is obviously a serious flaw in this logic, in that it assumes that out-of-air situations are always the result of gear failures. In reality, THE OVERWHELMING MAJORITY OF OUT-OF-AIR SITUATIONS ARE CAUSED BY HUMAN ERROR. Cave diving is a very busy activity, both mentally and physically. Psychologists use the term *task loading* to describe a situation where a person is given many things to do at once. It is a known phenomenon that the more things a person attempts to do at one time the more often she makes mistakes. Whether a diver is too stressed because of task loading, or just pushes her critical air supply from carelessness or peer pressure, the result is the same. She is out of air because she had a mental failure and no gear configuration will change that fact. However, a gear configuration that places additional task loading on the diver does make it more likely that she will make a mistake. Once the error occurs, there is no amount of paper logic that will solve the problem. It is up to the diver with air to sort things out and she stands a much better chance of doing this if the valve arrangement she is using allows her to make simple decisions.

Imagine that your dive buddy has informed you of the depressing fact that she is out of air: how do you get her out of the cave using your independent valve arrangements? This is the time when the task loading caused by independent tank set-ups is at its worst and it couldn't happen at a more critical point in the dive. Which regulator do you give her? Do they both have long hoses? Which one is in your mouth? A diver who is shifting regulators back and forth during the dives is also changing her procedure for assisting an out-of-air diver unless she has at least three regulators. One way to avoid this is to dive at least one Y valve, attach your long hose to it, and clip it off. However, this prevents you from handing off the regulator that is in your mouth since it has a shorter hose (see discussion under *Regulators*). Since handing off the regulator from the mouth is considered by many to be the safest methodology, this is not a good alternative. Another option would be to dive two long hoses, but now you must find a way to cleanly store them where they won't become entangled with each other or anything else.

So where is the regulator you need to hand off? If you are diving independent valves with one long hose then you can only provide your buddy with air from one tank. What if she breathes faster than you during the exit? Chances are, even if your breathing rates are normally equal, the diver who ran out of air will be breathing much heavier during the exit. Should you give her the regulator that is attached to the tank with the most remaining air? If you have only one long hose, that is not an option. What happens if one tank is exhausted with a few hundred feet left to go? Buddy breathe the rest of the way? What about restrictions?

These problems have led some divers to actually dive twin Y valves with FOUR regulators and TWO long hoses. The sad part is that they don't realize that by cluttering and complicating their gear they have greatly increased their chances of problems occurring which are just as dangerous as manifold failure and much more likely to occur. Suppose this person actually has to hand off one of her long hoses. Visualize yourself as the out-of-air diver, watching your buddy fumble through four regulators trying to locate, unfasten, and hand one to you, amidst the snarl and tangle created by four L.P. hoses, two H.P. hoses, one or more inflator hoses, primary light cord, and other cave diving equipment. If you really want to terrorize yourself, add two primary reels and three gap reels to the picture. To say that this diver could literally drown with air on her back points out the high probability that you will drown before she manages to provide some FOR YOU.

Let's look at just one problem that might occur if the "swimming dive shop" actually manages to execute the regulator hand-off to the out-of-air diver. During the exit, her partner, excited a little by the situation, breathes heavily and exhausts one of the two available tanks. She must now convey the need to switch to the second long hose, execute this maneuver, and someone must store the now useless long hose #1, or drag it behind them as they continue their exit. The second or third time it hangs up will either convince them to store it or send the whole situation over the edge. When you consider the increased chances of blown O-rings and the interesting search through four regulators to figure out which one to isolate, line entanglements, difficulty accessing and removing gear (regulators, back-up lights, reels, etc.), and the stress caused by these problems, it should become clear that twin Y-valves are one of the worst configurations imaginable. It is impossible to configure such a system in an uncluttered manner, thus violating principle #1—KEEP IT CLEAN!

Contrast any of these approaches with the diver using a dual outlet manifold who simply hands off her long hose and concentrates on getting out alive. It is easy to see that this diver has fewer decisions to contend with, which is fortunate since she probably couldn't tell you her name at that moment in time. That is the key point, that out-of-air situations are not calm and ordered events. They are unexpected and chaotic and reactions must be instinctive and immediate or they probably won't do any good.

The diver who thinks these are just hypothetical problems has probably never been in an out-of-air situation. These are very real problems that are difficult to handle even for the best divers. As many people will attest, an out-of-air diver will often grab the regulator from her buddy's mouth, despite training, discussion, and promises to the contrary. If out of air for long enough, anyone will react this way. At this point the diver with air (on her back if not in her mouth) had better have some quick solutions. In any conceivable out-of-air scenario, independent valves make the situation more complicated at a time when responding correctly and quickly can easily mean the difference between life and death.

If cave divers were perfect automatons that never made mental errors then the independent arrangement might be safer than the dual valve manifold, but cave divers do make mistakes and that is what many of these valve analyses fail to take into consideration. Given that we are human beings and prone to error, then it makes sense to select the simplest alternative when life support equipment is involved. The dual-valve manifold has none of the task loading problems that plague the independent valve configuration. While it is reasonable to consider all the possibilities, we must remember that after hundreds of thousands of cave dives, NO ONE HAS EVER DROWNED AS A RESULT OF A BROKEN MANIFOLD. This is a fact that advocates of independent systems seem to have completely overlooked. It makes no sense to switch to a more complex system because of a failure that rarely occurs and has never cost a life.

Given this discussion, it is curious that there is so much interest in independent valve systems. After two decades of cave diving, representing hundreds of thousands of dive, we are trying to solve a problem that doesn't seem to exist except as a potential in someone's statistical paper diving scenario. Whether this is misplaced enthusiasm or simply someone trying to make their mark on cave diving is unclear. The fact remains that the dual valve manifold has been and will continue to be the best choice for the vast majority of cave diving situations.

Valve Knobs

A potential failure with any valve involves the knobs used to turn the valve on and off. If these knobs are made from a brittle plastic they can break apart when struck against a ceiling. This leaves a diver with no way to isolate the associated regulator. If this impact also results in an unseated valve O-ring, then the diver has just had a catastrophic air failure. Her valve is on, leaking madly, and she has no way to turn it off. The solution to this is simple. Replace all such knobs with a softer rubber variety that is not prone to this failure mode.[2]

Tank Bands

Tank bands are much less controversial items than manifolds, but should not be taken for granted. Pay particular attention to the quality of manufacture and be sure to use bolts of adequate strength (minimum 5/16 diameter). Bands should be fabricated from thin gauge stainless steel. Avoid thick, plastic coated bands, as they add to the profile of the tanks. In a tight, rocky restriction, anything that adds even 1/8 inch, as these bands do, is enough to ruin your day. Take the trouble to find or manufacture broad spacers for assembling the bands

[2]Metal replacement knobs are preferred by some cave divers. However, they don't absorb contact with the cave as well as the rubber ones. This means they are more likely to bend the valve stem, and perhaps cause a dive-ending air leak. Their advantage is that they slide off rock easily and are thus hard to turn off unintentionally in tight passage. — Ed.

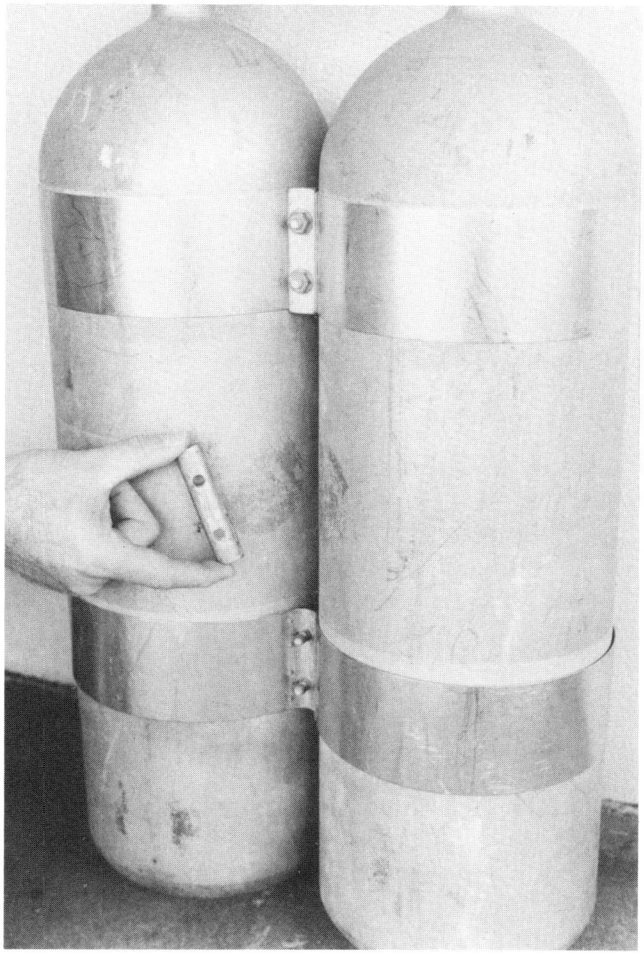

Figure 5-2 ***Band Spacers.***

like those shown in Figure 5-2. These can be made by sawing a piece of 1 inch diameter aluminum rod in half, and cutting to the appropriate length (usually 1.5 to 2 inches). Washers do not provide enough strength or bearing area: the bands will deform and possibly fail.

REGULATORS

No subject in cave diving is more hotly debated than what type of regulators to use and how to configure them. Let's cover the obvious stuff first.

Regardless of what regulators you select, certain things apply. Remember—KEEP IT CLEAN!

On the subject of keeping it clean, EXTREME attention should be given to routing all hoses so that they do not protrude outside the profile of the tanks. This prevents damage to hoses from impact with walls, ceiling, etc. Surprisingly, many divers who should know better seem to ignore this. Hoses are attached to regulators with little thought and the result is both ugly and hazardous. Yet other divers consider this so important that it may be grounds for not using a particular first-stage regulator. Contrast the appearance of the two arrangements shown in Figure 5-3. Certainly the orientation of hoses should be considered when a regulator is selected.

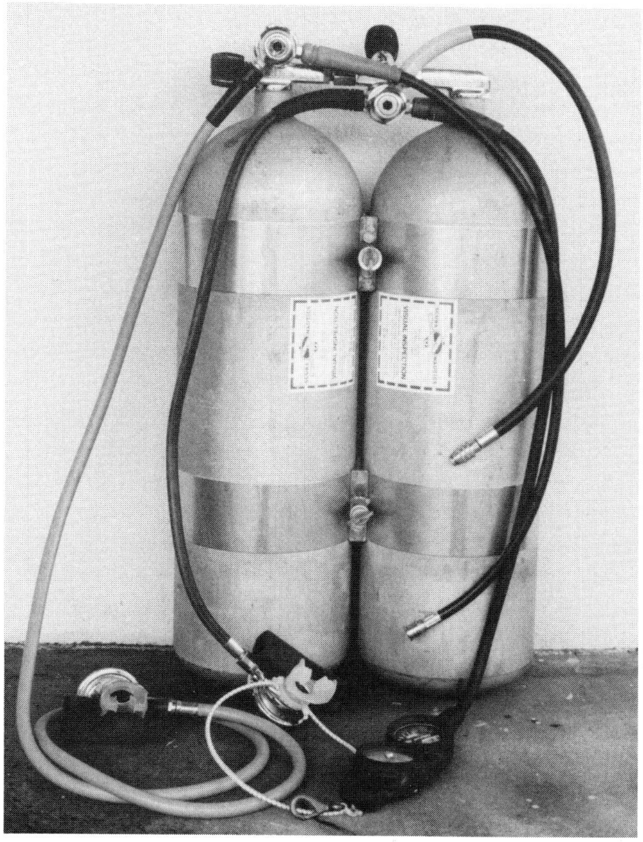

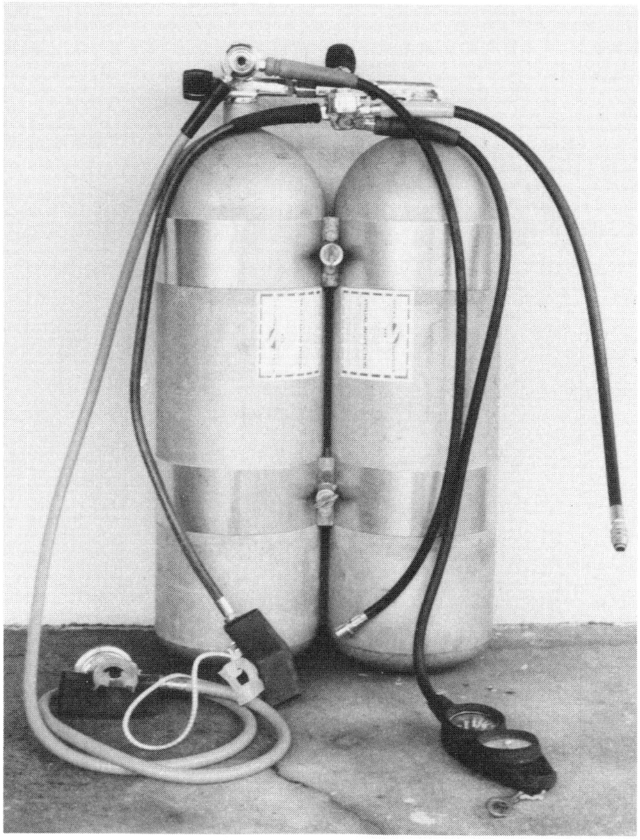

Figure 5-3 A streamlined vs. an unstreamlined configuration. This was achieved by replacing the center post regulator's first stage with a better configurated model.

What kind of regulators should you use? Almost all modern regulators are safe and reliable, but obviously some are better than others. You can't rely on the manufacturers to tell you, so you'll need unbiased sources. Of course other cave divers are a good source of information. Find out what they're diving and how it works. Ask around a lot, though, because people have a habit of getting enamored of a particular regulator for some strange reasons. Pay attention to the way a person's gear is maintained when evaluating their advice on regulators. An individual who is meticulous in all aspects of gear selection will usually be more discriminating about the regulators she uses.

Remember that the most expensive regulators are NOT necessarily the best, i.e. they may not provide the ideal combination of performance AND reliability. In general, you want to avoid the bottom-of-the-line in regulators because they won't perform (breathe easily) at the depths and demanding work rates that cave divers encounter. You also want to be very careful of so called high performance regulators. Many times they simply aren't that good or they are very finicky. A regulator that breathes like a dream but fails often is of dubious value.

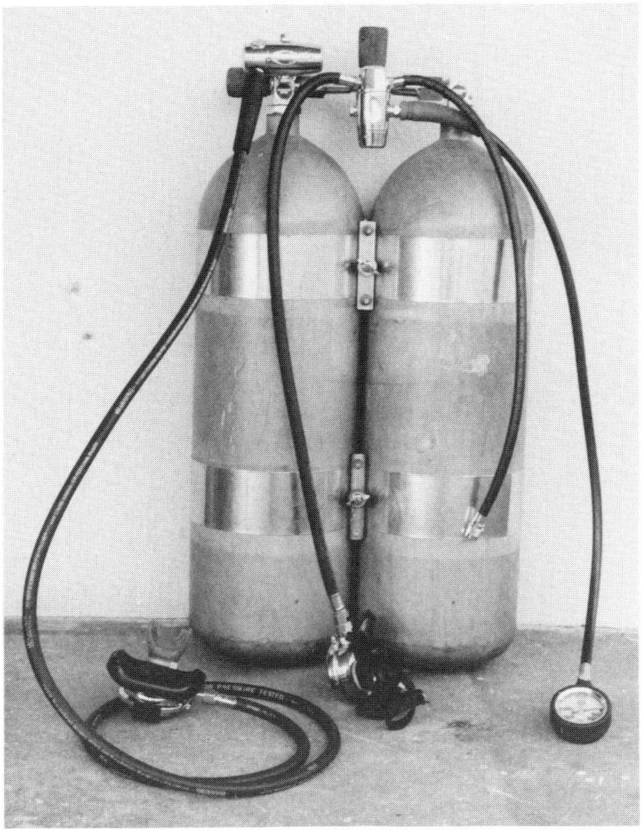

Figure 5-4A Proper hose arrangement using another brand of regulators and manifold.

It is almost impossible to predict how a regulator will perform at depth by breathing it on the surface (in the dive shop). Breathing a regulator on the surface will

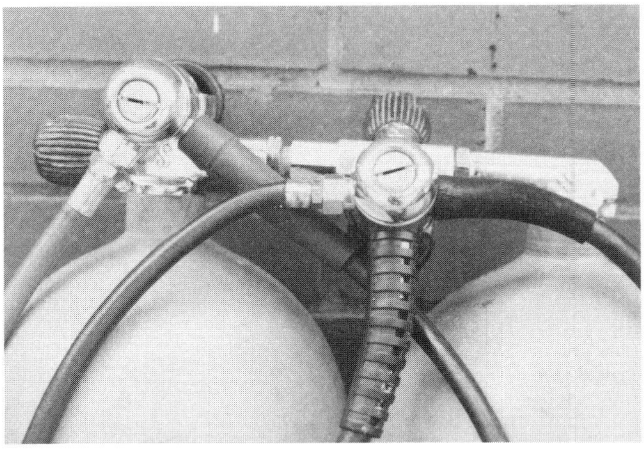

Figure 5-4B Streamlining first stage hoses with another brand of regulators.

give you a subjective evaluation of its cracking pressure. Cracking pressure is simply how much negative pressure you must exert in order to cause the demand valve to open and flow gas. However, the ability of a regulator to deliver high flow at depth is seldom a function of cracking pressure. For example, a regulator that requires two inches of water negative pressure to begin flowing gas, may deliver much more gas at depth than a high performance regulator that begins flowing gas at only 0.5 inches of water. This has to do with the orifice size in the regulator and the amount of travel that the demand valve can move through (how far it opens). The fact is that at deeper depths and/or higher breathing rates the cracking pressure has little impact on the work of breathing associated with a regulator. So how do you know whether a regulator will perform well at depth? Ask cave divers that make frequent deep dives what regulators they use.

Another good rule to follow is not to test a brand new regulator in cave diving situations. Wait until a unit has been on the market for a year or two and someone else has discovered all the problems it may be plagued with. Cave divers tend to use dive gear at extremes that

Figure 5-4C Streamlining using the same brand of regulators as Figure 5-4B, but with DVM with DIN fittings instead of yokes.

sport divers don't encounter, so wait until a regulator has a proven track record before you spend a lot of money on it.

Hose Configuration

The greatest debate in cave diving may well center around the configuration of regulators. The main point of contention is whether you hand off the regulator in your mouth to an out-of-air diver, or give her your secondary that is attached somewhere else. In the Hogarthian configuration, the primary regulator is equipped with the long hose. This is the regulator that is normally breathed during the dive, and it is also the regulator that is handed off to an out-of-air diver. Advocates of this methodology are often reluctant to make serious dives with someone who hands off the secondary. For numerous reasons, some even refuse.

Figure 5-5A Handing off regulator with long hose stored under arm & around neck: diver removes second stage & inverts it.

It is obvious that the regulator you want to hand off is the one with the long hose, but why should this be the one that is normally in your mouth? There are several reasons. First, this is the easiest regulator to find in a stressful situation. Your buddy informs you she's out of air. You realize you've got to do something FAST, and the vacuous feeling in your stomach doesn't help matters at all. At this instant all the paper theories dissolve in the water that surrounds you and the simplest of facts requires the mental effort of differential calculus. Taking the regulator from your mouth and handing it off is much simpler than locating and unfastening one. Obviously you know where it's at: you're breathing from it. There is no snap to hang up, so you can release it instantly. This provides the out-of-air diver with a regulator in the fastest and most reliable way possible. Contrast this with the diver who must first locate her secondary (how many times have you groped repeatedly for a piece of gear that you knew was right there?) and then unfasten it from whatever clip, pouch, velcro, rubber band, or other device she is using to hold it. There have been several in-

Figure 5-5B Diver bends head forward as the long hose is extended toward the partner.

Figure 5-5C As it is offered, long hose clears diver's head & extends out from under arm.

stances where a diver attempting to hand off a secondary regulator (i.e. not from her mouth) had difficulty in locating and unfastening the second stage. Meanwhile, her out-of-air buddy was getting more, well,...out of air. Remember, nothing is as easy to do underwater as you think it will be, and nothing is EVER easy in a stressful situation. Any regulator methodology which makes the out-of-air diver wait longer than she already has is asking for trouble.

Now suppose that you don't get the chance to hand off the regulator at all. A very real possibility (probability?) is that an out-of-air diver may be so stressed either from being out of air for too long or just from panic that she is going to rip the regulator out of your mouth. If it's the one with the long hose then she's got what she needs. All you have to do is pick up your secondary and put it in your mouth. This is much easier for you since you have not been out-of-air for nearly as long as she has. If you wear your secondary *around your neck on a neckstrap* then it is absolutely simple — it's right there in front of you where you need it and doesn't even need to be detached. Some divers will even wear the neckstrap so short that they can reach their secondary with their mouth without using their hand.

Another realistic scenario is an out of air situation in bad visibility. If your buddy (or you) runs out of air in zero visibility, then the basics apply. Like, everybody has a head, and everybody's head is in about the same place. Similarly, the mouth is usually located at the front and bottom of the head and there IS AIR THERE! In this situation, an out-of-air diver WILL take the regulator from your mouth: count on it. She has no way to signal you that she needs air and would like for you to locate and deliver a regulator for her. It is also unlikely that she will be able to remember exactly where and how you attach your secondary, since there is no universal method. She may not even know who she is trying to get air from if the dive team is larger than two. But, if they are all human then she'll know where to reach for what she needs. If you're lucky she'll give your second stage a gentle tug before she takes it from your mouth. This will give you maybe 0.5 seconds to realize that you need to find your secondary — FOR YOURSELF. By now she already has your primary. It's much better if the regulator she just took from you has a long hose.

Another problem associated with handing off the secondary regulator is that its operating condition at the instant needed is unknown. Specifically, secondary regulators tend to fill up with silt and debris during many dives. Although it is generally not difficult to clear them, it is not a task that should be imposed on an out-of-air diver. A diver who has been breathing normally can afford to choke on a little mud for a few seconds, but this is enough to send an already stressed diver into a full state of panic. Some people might argue that they do not want to hand off the primary regulator and then be forced to deal with a malfunctioning secondary. The point here is that you are going to have to deal with this anyway. The out-of-air diver is not going to be satisfied with a regulator that doesn't work — she is going to take the one out of your mouth, which is the one you SHOULD have given her in the first place. So keep your secondary in good condition and remember that it's better to swallow some mud than to have a panic stricken diver cause you to swallow lots of water.

Divers who advocate handing off the secondary have made vague comments about two divers being out-of-air if you hand off the regulator from your mouth. This is ridiculous since it takes only a matter of seconds to hand off the regulator and switch to your secondary. Are these people saying that it is okay for an out-of-air diver to wait during this time, but not them? The fact is that in an out-of-air situation one diver already needs air BADLY. You do not have time for reasoning like, "I'll give you some air when I can find my other regulator but I'm not going to risk my safety by giving you the one I'm breathing."

What is the diver going to do if for some reason she cannot deliver air to her buddy via her secondary because it is hard to find, detach, or filled with sediments? Write her a note that says she's sorry? Does she think this person is going to calmly die while she fumbles for her extra regulator? If she does not give this person air in a reasonable length of time HER BUDDY IS GOING TO GET THE AIR EVEN IF THIS ENDANGERS BOTH OF THEIR LIVES — period. There are plenty of statistics to back this up. Any reasoning that ignores this is unrealistic. One final point: how do you feel about diving with a person who has blatantly expressed by the way she wears her gear that she is unwilling to give you the regulator she is breathing from if you need it?

Remember the earlier discussion about diving independent valves with a K valve, Y valve, and the long hose regulator clipped off? Having read the section on regulators it should now be obvious why this configuration was considered unacceptable. Many times an out-of-air diver cannot wait and WILL take the regulator from your mouth. Indeed, some situations FORCE this action. The diver who is wearing her regulators in the Hogarthian configuration is prepared to deal with this. In fact it is common practice for many such divers to advise their partners to simply take the regulator and not pretend that they are going to have time for elaborate signals and discussion of the topic. If they do have time to signal, fine. If not, at least you know what to expect.

Excuses For Not Breathing The Long Hose

So why is there a debate about handing off the regulator from your mouth? Apparently there is a natural reluctance to give up the regulator you are using, particularly in a stressful situation. All divers probably feel this to some extent, but when this anxiety becomes great enough to affect the way a person responds to a critical situation then the safety of the dive team is compromised.

One reason that is cited for not handing off the regulator from your mouth is that the long hose causes a loss of regulator performance. These people want the ultimate in ease of breathing and feel that breathing through the long hose during the dive is not acceptable. Divers who claim this seem to be saying that the regulator performance is inadequate for normal diving situations, but is okay to hand to an out-of-air diver in an emergency. This is dubious reasoning at best. While the long hose does cause some loss of performance it is minor at the depths encountered in normal cave diving. At deeper depths the introduction of helium into the gas mixture causes reduced density and improves regulator performance. The work of breathing for a typical regulator supplying air at 200 fsw, is roughly the same as that regulator supplying a Heliox mixture at 1000 fsw.

The worst case for regulator performance is in the intermediate depth range from 150 fsw to 200 fsw, where air is still commonly used on many dives. Recently, a large bore, 7 foot-long hose became available which reduces the pressure drop through the hose, thus restoring much of the performance loss caused by the length.

Another reason cited for not breathing the long hose is that long hoses with proper fittings are not available for some high performance regulators of foreign manufacture. Divers using these regulators are forced to breathe from the short hose regulator and hand off the secondary with long hose. This is in fact an issue of money more than availability and a very poor excuse. A diver that can afford such a regulator can afford the expensive hose or custom adaptor required.

Some divers rationalize that the high performance regulator they wish to use is too sensitive to be used as a secondary. These divers do not wish to be forced to switch to a regulator of lower performance in an out-of-air situation. This implies that what is good enough for their out-of-air buddy is not good enough for them. What is wrong with the regulator they intend to give you if you need it? For their sakes it had better work or they will soon be separated from their high performance toy anyway.

Many years ago, cave divers began diving octopus regulators to make a buddy-assisted exit from a cave more feasible. Then a diver named Ray Elman had the bright idea that a longer hose on this regulator would make this much easier. However, this raised a question. Which regulator should you breathe? Most active cave divers at that time chose to breathe the second stage on the long hose and still do today. The decision to breathe the long hose was based upon sound judgment. Divers who have used this configuration for almost two decades have found no reason to change and many reasons not to.

An issue that has arisen lately is the question of how much long hose is long enough. For years, the five foot long hose was the standard and few people deviated from it. However, since 1985, more and more divers have been purchasing diver propulsion vehicles, or scooters, and using them in caves. This has led to a re-evaluation of the buddy-assisted exit scenario. The seven foot long hose is quickly replacing the five-foot hose as the standard for cave divers. It provides the extra length needed for buddy-assisted exits on scooters. Hoses longer than seven feet are more difficult to store and are generally not considered necessary, though this depends upon both the gear configuration and the type of scooter used. The best advice is to practice with a seven foot long hose and only go to a longer one if you absolutely must.

Long Hose Storage

Which brings up another topic of heated debate. Having covered whether to breathe the long hose or not, we are now faced with the problem of how to store it. Before we discuss the most commonly used methods lets talk about some desirable features of hose storage. First of all, it has to be CLEAN. We can't have this hose dangling all over the place nor can we have it protruding beyond a reasonable profile. Second, but of equal importance, we have to be able to get it deployed FAST, first time, every time, with no chance of snags or screw-ups. Third, it has to be stored in such a way as not to damage or weaken the hose. Fourth, we MUST be able to deploy this hose and restore it in its normal position while in the water. This last one may seem odd but as we shall see, it is important. Having laid down the ground rules for hose storage, let's look at the two most common methods.

Method number one is the "coiled behind the neck" method shown in Figure 5-6. In this method the hose is doubled over several times, wrapped with a rubber band or similar device, and stuffed between the manifold and the diver's head. The profile of the hose is within that of the tanks, but it is located in an unfortunate position. The manifold area is a very busy spot to begin with. It is important that a diver be able to reach both her on/off valves, and it is desirable that she be able to feel individual hoses to check for leaks that she cannot see. Such leaks may be caused by a bad O-ring or hose and can develop during the dive. In the event of a totally blown O-ring, the diver must quickly determine which regulator to isolate (it isn't always obvious), and she must reach the correct valve. Having the long hose in the way while

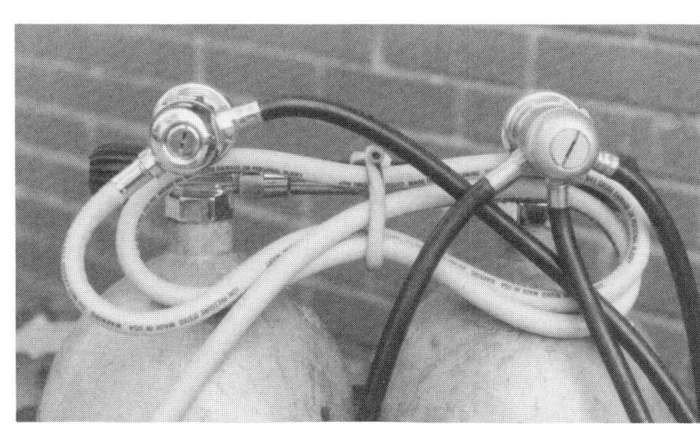

Figure 5-6 Coiled behind the neck storage.

trying to feel for escaping air is an unnecessary hindrance to say nothing of actually isolating the regulator. Perhaps the worst aspect of this hose storage location is that it is in an area that is often involved in line entanglements. Trying to sort out a line tangle that you can't see is bad enough without having seven feet of hose coiled up in the same area. Based on these problems, this doesn't seem to be a clean method of hose storage.

What about deployment? Provided the hose does not snag on a regulator yoke knob or valve handle, or get tangled in another hose, it comes out okay. Depending upon your point of view, that may or may not seem like a satisfactory situation. If you are the person waiting for air it probably won't.

One modification to this method is to attach a piece of plastic pipe to the manifold and shove the hose in this pipe. Alternatively, this pipe may be oriented vertically along the side of the tank. It reduces the chance of a snag during deployment and offers some protection for the hose. This technique goes a long way toward solving many of the typical coiled-behind-the-neck problems. However, the size of the pipe must be kept small in order to reduce bulk and this causes strain on the hose at bends. This is a problem with the rubber band method as well, but it is probably worse with the small diameter pipe.

Last but not least, what about replacing the hose in this configuration underwater. Very few people have the flexibility necessary to replace the long hose in this configuration without assistance from their buddy. For many reasons the hose may be pulled out during the dive. Whether it is for an S-drill, gets snagged, or is actually handed off to an out-of-air diver, it is difficult to replace. What if you're doing a stage dive and have a failure after dropping your stage bottles? Once you have managed to get the out-of-air diver back to those bottles, the most efficient (i.e. fastest) way to exit the cave is to get her off your air and on to her stage bottle, which should take her all the way home. At this point it is necessary that you replace your long hose in its normal position. It is probably not reasonable to expect an already stressed partner to delay the exit while she assists you with your hose. It is obvious that there is a problem with replacing the hose in this position because many of the divers who use this method are extremely reluctant to pull it out for a normal S-drill (safety drill) at the start of a dive. Perhaps a variation of this method can be developed which addresses these problems, but the typical rubber band behind the neck has many drawbacks.

The second method is the one that is employed by the Hogarthian style diver. The origin of this method is obscure but it is known that veteran divers such as Exley, Goodman, Sullivan, Eckhoff, Main, and many others were using this method at least as early as the late 70's. In those days, the most common length for long hoses was five feet. The hose was run under the diver's arm, around her neck, and IN HER MOUTH. To hand off, the diver simply took the regulator from her mouth, passed the hose over her head by raising the second stage slightly, and handed it to the out-of-air diver. This was easily accomplished in one swift motion. The diver with air then put the secondary regulator, located on a strap around her neck, in her mouth and the dive team exited the cave. In the event of having the regulator ripped from her mouth by an out-of-air diver, the diver with air simply lifts the coil of hose over her head. Fairy tales about being choked by the hose were simply not true. Once the out-of-air diver gets your regulator she isn't going anywhere without you. This method kept the hose close to the body, eliminating any chance of snags. It could be deployed very rapidly, with virtually no chance of a severe hang-up that would prevent access, and it placed no sharp bends on the hose, therefore not weakening or damaging it. Finally, it could be restored by the diver, quickly and without assistance, to its normal position.

This method worked perfectly with five-foot hose, but the extra length of a seven foot hose created a problem. Wrapping the regulator under the arm and around the neck simply didn't take up enough length. A solution to this has been to route the hose under the light case, around the neck, and in the mouth, as shown in Figure 5-7. The extra distance to go under the light case takes care of the extra two feet of hose. This method works

Figure 5-7 Long hose tucked under light case.

well if you wear your primary light case on your right side. Practice with this method has indicated that the regulator can be handed off quickly and the 7 foot hose is long enough that it can be cleared from under the light case AFTER the out-of-air diver HAS AIR. An alternative to routing the hose under the light case is to place a loop under the waist belt to take up the extra length. Then the hose is looped around the neck and IN THE MOUTH.

Perhaps the best method would be some type of flat pouch oriented along the divers right side or beside the tanks. Problems with fabricating and attaching such a pouch will have to be solved, but this might be superior to any current method. A variation of this has been used in Mexico, but it involved shrouding the double tanks with a fabric cover. While this looks great on video, it creates drag and would probably suffer from abrasion.

Accessory Hoses

It has been argued that dividing up accessory hoses is advantageous so that when a failure occurs that requires isolation of a regulator you will still have something that works (pressure gauge or inflator). This is somewhat dubious since there is no way of predicting which regulator will fail, and you are going to exit the cave at this point anyway. The accessory you need most at this point is your inflator. This will speed your exit and save air. While it would be reassuring to have a working pressure gauge, it doesn't buy you much at this time. So the overriding consideration when arranging these hoses is — KEEP IT CLEAN! One thing that does bear consideration: if you are using a dry suit with an auto-inflator, then every effort should be made to place this inflator hose on a different regulator from your BC inflator hose. This way you will always have one source of automatic buoyancy control. You can even switch this hose back and forth between your suit and your BC if the fittings are compatible.

In keeping with a clean configuration, it may be necessary to shop around for hose lengths that are shorter or longer than normal. For example, LP inflator hose and corrugated inflator hose as well, are often much longer than one would desire. It will take a little more effort, but finding a shorter hose may pay off significantly in how clean your configuration is. Both inflator hoses and submersible pressure gauges must be securely fastened in an out-of-the-way spot to prevent entanglements. Quite often, divers will attach the pressure gauge but neglect the inflator hose, leaving it to float above their heads. This not only makes the hose difficult to access quickly it also increases chances of entanglement and may cause

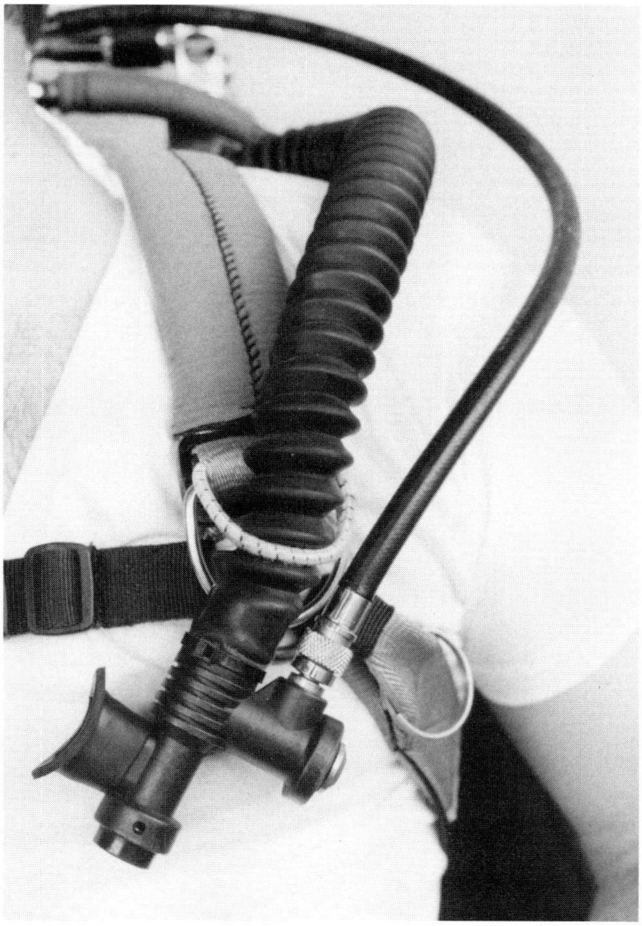

Figure 5-8A Inflator hose secured.

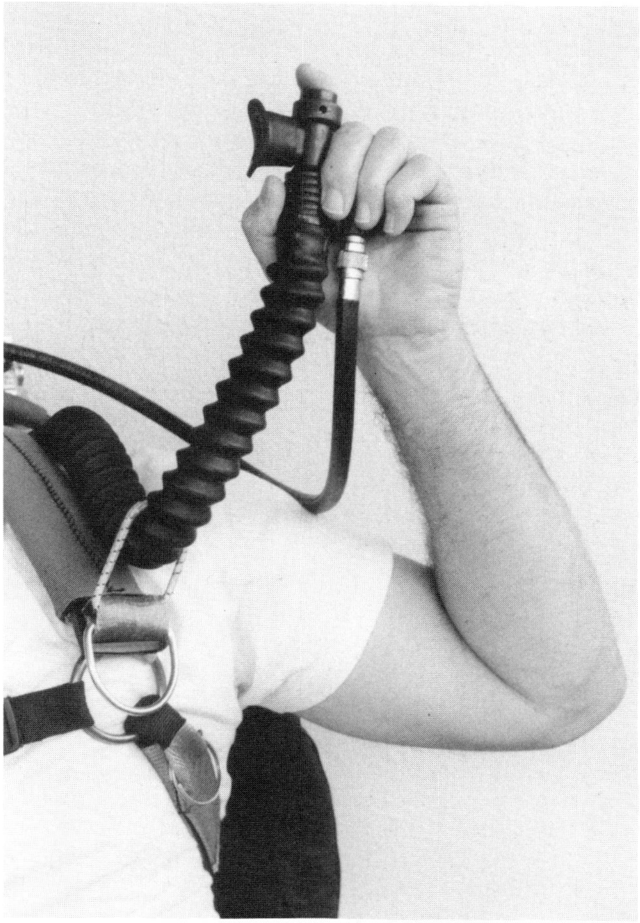

Figure 5-8B Accessibility for venting inflator hose.

damage to the cave, especially in delicate systems with extensive vadose formations. Two methods of attaching the inflator hose are available. One uses a piece of bungee cord while the other runs the LP hose under the arm. The bungee cord method allows the hose to ratchet up and down on the corrugations of the oral inflator hose. It is pulled out to dump air and then pulled back up to keep the inflator out of the silt (Figures 5-8A & 5-8B).

A quick word about consoles before we leave regulators entirely. Small consoles that house the pressure gauge and one other gauge, such as a depth gauge, CAN be used for cave diving if desired. They are somewhat inconvenient since you must detach your console from wherever you have it stored each time you want to check any of the gauges located on it. For this reason, they are not suited for survey work as you will have to unhook the console at each station to read the depth. The same applies if the compass is housed on the console. Most divers doing extensive survey work either mount the compass on the survey slate as shown in Figure 5-9, or hold it in their hand. The depth gauge is worn on the arm so it can be read quickly at each survey station.

There are many variations on where to place the pressure gauge. The main features are that it must be easily accessible and not increase the chances of entanglements or hang-ups in small restrictions. Some divers like to attach the gauge in a position in front of them so that they can see it without using their hands. Others prefer to attach the gauge off to one side so that it does not increase their profile and cause snags in tight restrictions. A few mount the gauge on their arm in the same manner as a depth gauge. There are advantages to each of these methods and each diver must experiment to determine what is best suited for her. Wearing the gauge on the front however, does seem to place it in a position more likely to be damaged or to snag on outcroppings.

Figure 5-9 Slate-mounted compass.

BACKPLATES AND BCD'S

It is safe to say that the vast majority of cave divers have chosen the back-mount buoyancy compensator backplate over all other configurations. This is because of the stability that is provided by placing the BC near the tanks as well as the comfort and simplicity of the design. What few divers know is that Greg Flanagan originated the backplate design in 1979. The first backplate was fabricated from sheet aluminum that had started out life as a road sign. Flanagan used this material to fabricate a prototype that was as clean and functional as any backplate produced today. His idea has affected cave diving almost as much as the dual-valve manifold.

There is little to be said about this configuration that isn't obvious. It is the most stable buoyancy system available because it places the center of buoyancy (which is the BC) near the center of gravity, the tanks. Having CG and CB at about the same point is a natural characteristic of the submerged human body. That is why a swimmer can remain in almost any attitude in the water with little effort. However, when we introduce a large mass external to the body, in the form of tanks, we upset this relationship. To offset this mass, we use a buoyancy compensator to keep us from falling to the bottom. This BC has relatively little mass but a large net buoyant force acting on it. The farther apart these two devices are, the more unstable the diver is in any attitude where CB is below CG, as with front worn compensators. Of course, if the diver is upside down, with tanks toward bottom and BC toward ceiling, then she is VERY stable but not very happy. After years of fighting the force couple that was created from "belly bags" and heavy tanks, the backplate and backmount compensator system was a welcome development. Though jacket-style BC's saw brief popularity, they have essentially been abandoned because of their inherent drag and problems associated with shifting air. The backplate and backmount buoyancy compensator system has become the accepted state

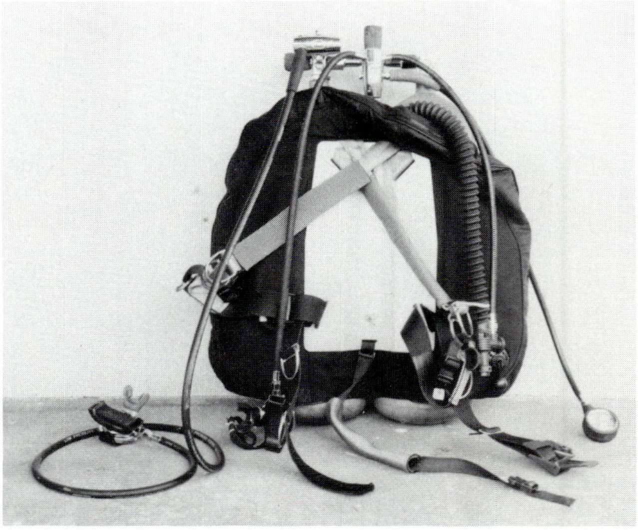

Figure 5-10 A set of double 104's with regulators, wings and backplate attached.

of the art for all double tanks configurations.

PRIMARY LIGHTS

Primary lights come in a great variety of sizes and shapes with differences in both the type of batteries used and the type of light heads or bulbs. This is because different caves as well as different cave divers are served better by some light styles than others. For the purpose of discussing the pros and cons of lights we will divide the issue into two topics, namely batteries and bulb style.

Batteries

The next several years will be an exciting time for cave divers that are interested in light technology. The promise of rechargeable lithium batteries of sufficient capacity for diving lights is just around the corner. What this will mean is smaller lights of greater capacity. For now, though, we must be content with available technology in rechargeable cells. Primary, or non-rechargeable cells, do not present an economically attractive alternative. (The word *primary* as used to describe batteries has nothing to do with the way cave divers use the word to describe their main lights.) There are three types of rechargeable cells that are commonly used to provide power for cave diving primary lights. They are:

1. Wet cell NiCads (nickel cadmium)
2. Dry cell NiCads
3. Gel cells (typically lead calcium)

Wet cell NiCads are swiftly becoming a thing of the past for primary lighting systems. Though they were extremely rugged and served for many years as the battery system of choice, they also were very messy and maintenance intensive. Constant attention was needed to keep the packs clean, filled with electrolyte, and cycled to provide full capacity. Their main advantages were their ability to tolerate abusive discharge rates and then be recharged at rates which would destroy most other cells. As batteries became available which did not require as much time and effort to maintain, fewer and fewer cave divers elected to use wet cell NiCads.

Dry cell NiCads overcame many of the maintenance problems associated with wet cells, but there were some sacrifices. Divers could no longer fast charge their battery packs off their car batteries. However, most divers found they were willing to purchase multiple packs in order to avoid the maintenance hassles of wet cells. Unfortunately, these cells have one other problem. Typical of NiCads, they would develop a "memory" if not cycled regularly, and then fail to deliver full capacity. This was especially noticeable in small rechargeable back-up lights which often failed within a few minutes of being turned on. Main was among the first to suggest that ordinary alkalines were better suited for back-up lights than rechargeable NiCads. Since these lights are rarely used they do not get cycled often enough to keep rechargeable batteries at full capacity. But this fact also makes the use of non-rechargeable alkalines a perfect candidate for back-up lights. Some divers developed the habit of burning their back-up lights during decompression to cycle the cells, not realizing that the high intensity lamps used in these lights had a short life span — about 20 hours). As cave divers discovered that their rechargeable back-ups were highly unreliable the switch was quickly made to alkalines. But, there was still a desire for lower maintenance rechargeable batteries for primary lights.

Lead acid batteries, utilizing a gelled electrolyte, solved the maintenance problems associated with wet cells and did not exhibit the memory problem that NiCads were prone to. Their main drawback is that they have a lower specific energy density than NiCads (power to weight ratio). In spite of this, they have become by far the most commonly used cells for primary lighting systems today. The combination of low maintenance and reliable burn time have outweighed other considerations for most cave divers. They are inexpensive and are available in a variety of sizes and capacities, which gives the light designer tremendous flexibility. Though there are still a few hold outs who cling affectionately to their NiCads, there is little doubt that Gel cells will continue to dominate the primary light arena until further advances in battery technology occur.

SPECIFIC ENERGY DENSITY OF COMMON BATTERIES USED TO POWER CAVE DIVING PRIMARY LIGHTS

CELL TYPE	WATT-HRS/LB (5HR RATE)
Lead-acid	6-10
Nickel cadmiium	12-15
Lithium chlorides*	50-100

**There are many different chemistries being investigated for Lithium cells and energy densities vary. All values given here are approximate and for comparison only. Energy density is also affected by packaging design.*

Bulb Styles For Primary Light Heads

Light heads come in various bulb configurations as well as various designs for each of these. For the purpose of this discussion we will categorize them according to the type of bulb used (Figure 5-11). These categories are:

1. Sealed beam heads
2. Test tube heads
3. Projector bulb heads

Sealed Beam Light Heads

Say what you will, there is little doubt that the sealed beam light head has been, and still is, the most successful style light head in cave diving. There are, of course, many reasons for this. Sealed beam bulbs (almost always in size PAR 36) come in a variety of wattages that happen to fall in the useful range for cave divers. *Useful* is defined as bright enough for a primary light without requiring a battery pack the size of a stage bottle (although underwater cinematographers may take exception to this definition). Indeed the most common definition of *acceptable brightness* for a primary light is based on the light output of a 30 watt sealed beam bulb, although these have largely been displaced by the 37.5 watt quartz halogen sealed beam bulb. Most lists of cave diving equipment requirements will include a statement like: "Primary light of intensity equal to or greater than a 30 watt sealed beam."

The early innovations of Frank Martz no doubt paved the way for much of the sealed beam bulb's popularity. And it didn't hurt when Bob Goodman began building and selling primary lights of legendary quality using sealed beam heads and wet cell NiCads. These lights provided extraordinary reliability, adequate burn times, and ample brightness. For all these reasons they are still popular today, though most divers have replaced NiCads with Gel cells. The highly polished reflector and precisely manufactured bulb provide an efficient and consistent light source. No matter what the origin of a sealed beam head it should provide the exact light output as someone else's for a given wattage and voltage. Still, sealed beams aren't perfect. They have a nasty habit of imploding on extremely deep dives (usually in the 300 fsw range, plus or minus 50 fsw).

Test Tube Light Heads

Many divers who wanted a light head that would survive extremely deep dives have selected the test tube style configuration. This style light head uses a small halogen bulb, enclosed in an O-ring sealed glass tube, and mounted in a polished parabolic reflector. The main advantages of this configuration are its depth capability and the fact that bulbs of extremely high wattages (100 watts and higher) are readily available. This can be very useful in lighting up rooms or tunnels that exceed 100 feet in width. The negative side of this is that large battery packs must be carried or burn times will be very short.

One advantage that is often cited for test tube style heads is the ability to focus the light output from tight spot to broad flood by moving the parabola back and forth. However, this feature is mostly defeated by the fact that specific parabolic reflectors are generally designed to do one or the other (i.e., broad illumination or tightly focused beam) and lose efficiency when applied otherwise. Thus, a reflector that was designed for a tight spot beam will result in concentric bands of shadows when "focused" for broad illumination. A reflector that was designed for a flood type beam can rarely be positioned to provide a tight spot pattern at all.

There are some disadvantages associated with the test tube style light head which deserve mention. Test tube heads are generally more fragile that sealed beams because of the fragile, exposed test tube. However if thick walled glass test tubes are used then this disadvantage is mostly negated. Test tube style heads are also GENERALLY less efficient because the light from the bulb must travel through the water before being reflected off the parabola. This means that a 50 watt sealed beam will probably put out more light than a 55 watt test tube style head, especially in murky or turbid water. Test tube heads are also highly variable in light output from a given bulb, depending upon the reflector used. There are dozens in use, salvaged from all manner of sources, some very good, and some not much good at all. If you elect to purchase this type head be sure you see what the light looks like IN THE WATER. The refraction caused by water improves some and hurts other reflectors, but it will definitely change. Trying to make a comparison in air is almost useless. Try to make a dive using the test tube light you are interested in with another diver who is using a sealed beam of comparable wattage. Then make your decision after factoring in the type and depth of diving you typically do.

Figure 5-11 Test tube, projector bulb, and sealed beam light heads.

Projector Bulb Light Heads

Projector bulbs come in a variety of voltages and wattages, making it possible to have one light do many things. Projector bulb light heads are very small and compact which reduces drag and makes it easier to construct rugged light heads that will handle great depth. However, this small size has a disadvantage. The small reflector makes this type bulb somewhat less efficient than sealed beam or test tube style heads with larger parabolas. This means that greater wattage bulbs must be employed which requires larger battery packs. While many of these bulbs are ideally suited for underwater cinematography they may be less than ideal for typical cave diving.

Goodman Handle

One thing that is certain about light heads is the advantage afforded by the Goodman style handle shown in Figure 5-12. The diver slips her hand through the handle, with the head resting on top of her hand and her fingers free to pull through the cave, operate an inflator, read a pressure gauge, or hold on to a scooter. The flashlight style handle does not leave the fingers free to perform other tasks, thus rendering one hand useless except to hold the light. With the tremendous surge in popularity of diver propulsion vehicles in cave diving, many divers are finding the Goodman style handle more suited to their needs. The odd thing is that prior to scooters the Goodman style handle was probably even more valuable since it made pulling your way into a high flow cave much easier. Divers who are unfamiliar with this style of handle consider its appearance strange, but its contribution to speed and efficiency on long dives is impressive.

Having covered primary lights in some detail it is now appropriate to make a couple of general comments. First, a primary light should have a burn time long enough for the dives you plan to do with some margin of safety. A minor delay can turn into a major problem if you run out of light before the dive is over. This has in fact resulted in fatalities where air planning was adequate but light planning wasn't. How much reserve you need depends on the specifics of the dive, but at least 30 minutes is advisable. As a general guide, a primary light should provide two to three hours of burn time. Second, the useful range of wattage for typical primary lights is from about 30 to 100 watts. From 37.5 to 50 watts is ideal for most situations. Remember that a 100 watt bulb is going to require at least twice the weight and size battery pack that a 50 watt needs to achieve equivalent burn time.

Back-Up Lights

It may seem unnecessary, but for the sake of thoroughness, lets define what a back-up light is. A back-up light is any light that is used in the event of a primary light failure, regardless of its size or shape. According to this definition we could dive with three large canister lights, using two of them for back-ups in the event of a primary light failure. In the past this might not have been such a bad idea since the high voltages associated with over-volted NiCad packs caused frequent bulb failures. Today though, the switch to Gel Cells has pretty much eliminated this problem. It is not unusual to make 200 to 400 dives without a primary light failure. In view of this, we would be hindering ourselves unnecessarily by carrying more than one primary, unless we had some special purpose like underwater photography. If a primary light does fail, we are going to exit the cave at this point. From then on, we are no longer sight seeing: in fact, we are just trying to follow the line out without getting lost or wasting too much time. Because of this, back-ups do not have to be nearly as bright as primary lights. We want these lights to be bright enough to exit the cave with, but small enough not to hinder us during a normal dive. They must also be extremely rugged and reliable since when we need them we really NEED them. They had better be able to provide this reliability with minimum maintenance and their configuration must be one that is easily stored. Quite a bit to consider. Let's make a list of the choices we have to make:

1. Number require (and desired)
2. Style (size, shape, etc.)
3. Brightness required
4. Burn time required
5. Type of batteries (rechargeable or not)
6. Where to carry them

For many years the standard requirement for cave diving had been a minimum of three lights per diver.

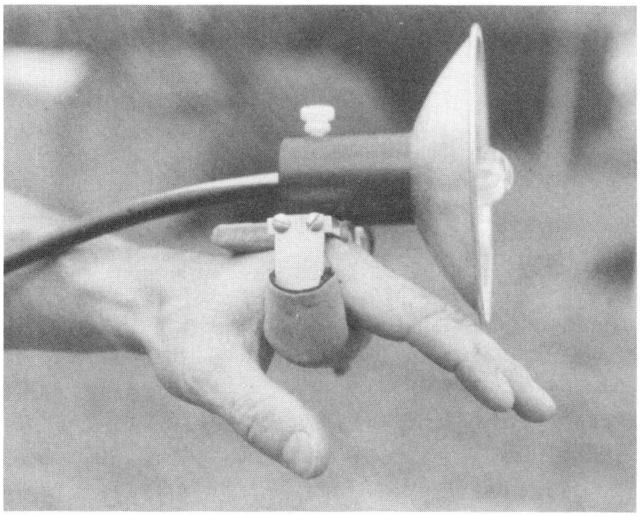

Figure 5-12 Goodman style handle.

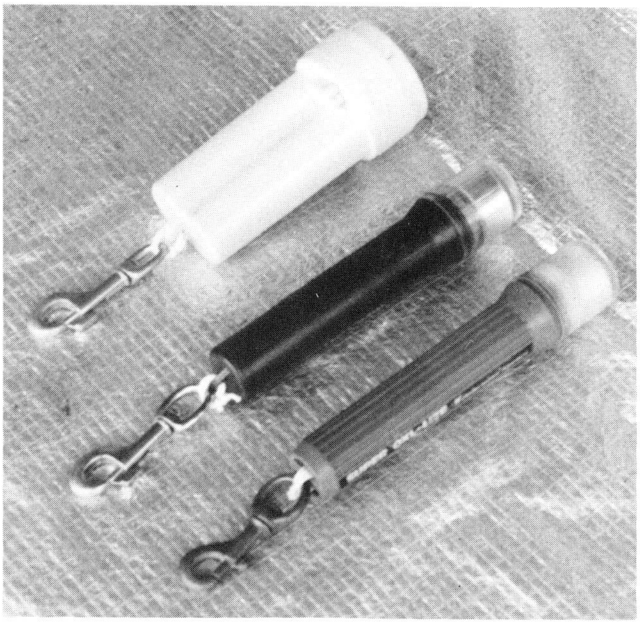

Figure 5-13 Assorted back-up lights. The more streamlined the better.

This dates back to an early estimate that the probabilities of a light failure occurring during a dive was about one in fifty. Therefore the probability of two lights failing on the same dive was one in 2500, and for three lights this shrunk to one in 125,000. Pretty good odds even without considering that your buddy has three more. This makes the odds of a total light failure (all yours and all of your buddy's) one in 15,625,000,000. In spite of this there have been instances where divers claim to have witnessed a half dozen or more light failures in a single dive. What's wrong with this picture? The most likely explanation was that the lights didn't "fail" but rather they burned down right on schedule. If your light has a burn time of 90 minutes and you're doing a 90 minute dive, don't be surprised if your failure rate is high. The next explanation is one that few will admit to but is probably widespread: poor equipment maintenance.

The fact is that today's cave diving lights are much more reliable than those in past years. Their MTBF (mean time between failures) may be as high as 200 dives or more. If your lights fail frequently there are two possibilities. Either you've got the wrong light — or the lights are on and you're not home. Actually this may literally be the case. The most popular back-up light used in cave diving employs a screw down lens to turn the light on. If not backed off several turns past where the light goes out the batteries can discharge even though the light doesn't appear to be on. These lights can also be pressure activated if not backed off far enough. In this case the light didn't fail at all — the diver did because she burned the light before she needed it.What all this is leading up to is that three lights per diver is still an adequate number. In fact it is more so today than ever before. If a diver is solo diving (or just nervous) then carrying a fourth back-up light is fine. But carrying five or six or even more lights is both a hindrance on long dives and probably a safety hazard. Reducing your chances of a total light failure to one in 10 trillion while increasing your chances of a line entanglement to one in ten is a poor trade off. Actually it goes beyond just a line entanglement hazard. Every extra piece of gear that you carry makes it harder to access every other piece that you're already wearing, for two reasons. First, they get in the way of each other and second, you've got to remember where more things are.

The most popular style of back-up light for cave diving is probably the three C-cell cylindrical light using a screw down lens as the on/off switch. These lights are inherently simple and rugged. They provide enough brightness for following line while still being small enough to store cleanly and not hamper a diver. Remember to back the lens off until the O-ring is just covered and they will rarely fail. These lights provide a baseline for both brightness and bulk. A light that is significantly less powerful is going to make following a line more difficult. A much larger light will be difficult to store cleanly and will hinder you unnecessarily.

Primary alkaline cells are the most suitable batteries for back up lights because of their long shelf life, extended burn time, and low cost. Maintenance consists of rotating new batteries into the light every few months (if not used) and cleaning the O-ring. Since back-up lights are generally not maintained as well or as often as primary lights they must be simpler in nature. This makes the use of rechargeable cells for back-ups undesirable.

Figure 5-14A Hogarthian back-up light configuration: secured.

One of the neatest (and simplest) innovations in cave diving gear configuration was Bill Main's solution to the problem of where to carry backup lights. In the late 1970's he began attaching his back up lights to his shoulder straps using D-rings and pieces of bicycle inner tube cut into 3/4 inch wide bands. The result was completely streamlined and easily accessible lights as shown in Figure 5-14. This became the standard Hogarthian configuration and remains unchanged today.

One final word about back-up lights. Because we rarely use them during a normal dive we tend to take them for granted. We use them during decompression, or after the dive, or just to take the trash out at night. The problem is that bulbs (as well as batteries) have a limited life. If the bulb in your back-up light has an average life span of 20 hours and you've spent 19.5 hours using it to read during decompression then you're going to have a problem some day. Remember that the next time you reach for a cave diving back-up light for some nonessential purpose.

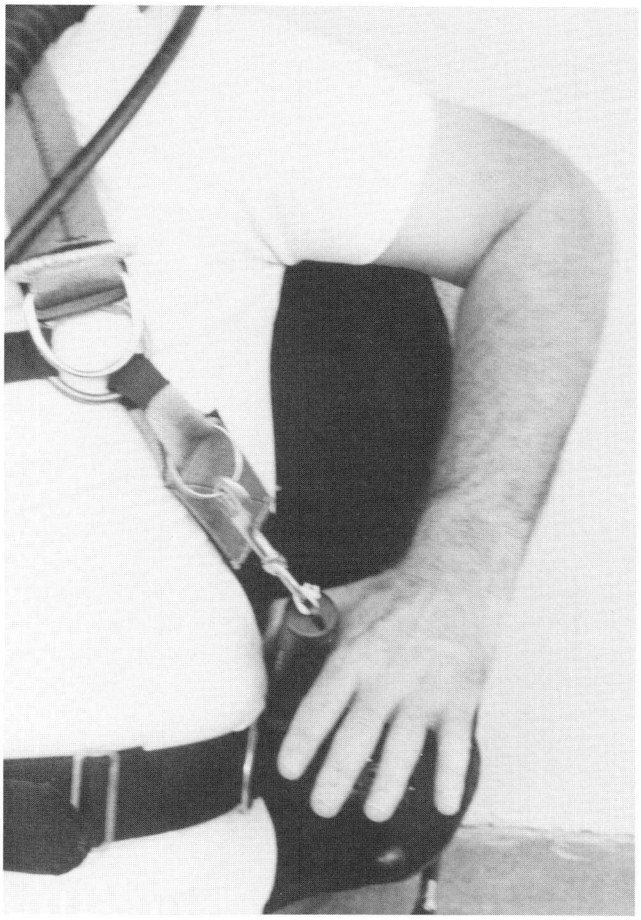

Figure 5-14B To use, grasp light as shown, then ...

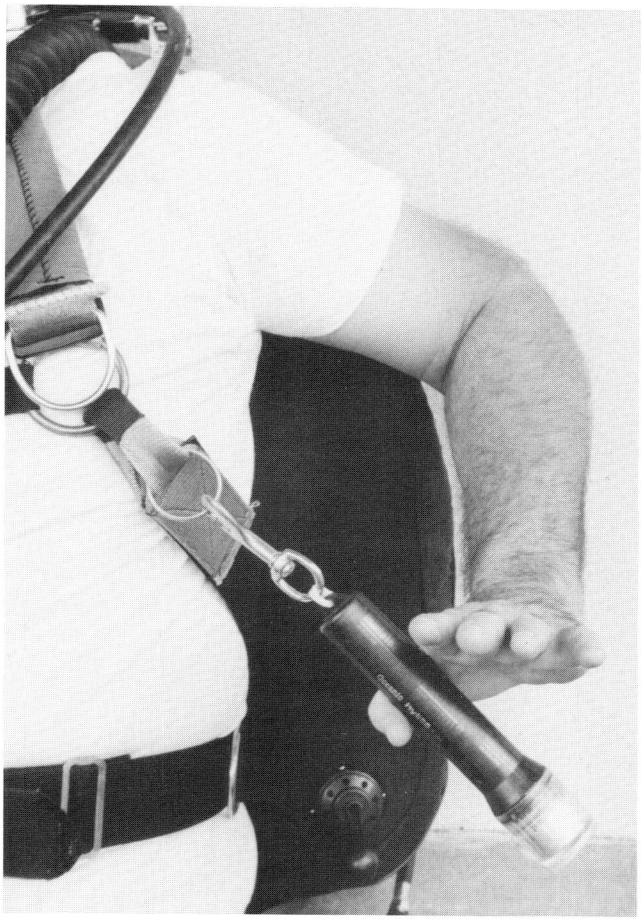

Figure 5-14C Pull light free of retaining band & release clip.

DIVE EXPOSURE SUITS

Cave diving is an activity that takes place all over the world in almost every climate. Thus the degree of thermal protection needed will vary considerably. If you are diving in very warm water (as found in Mexico's Yucatan peninsula) then the requirements for keeping warm are not very severe. For shorter dives a thin (1/8 inch) neoprene wet suit may be all that is needed. However, because of the extremely long nature of most cave dives, more protection than this is usually required in most parts of the world. The decision that most cave divers must make is whether to buy a good 1/4 inch farmer-john wet suit or to go for broke (sometimes literally) and buy a dry suit.

Wet Suits

Wet suits have the advantage of simplicity, which makes them cheaper and in some ways more reliable than a dry suit. Since they have no seals or waterproof zippers to deteriorate, wet suits will generally last longer with less maintenance than dry suits. They are also easier to learn to dive since they do not represent an air volume which must be adjusted in order to achieve buoyancy control. Wet suits also produce less drag in the water giving them a slight advantage over dry suits in swimming (or scootering) speed. And finally, with the newest and stretchiest neoprene suits, there is a greater flexibility and range of motion with wet suits.

Unfortunately, wet suits do not keep a diver as warm as a dry suit even in shallower water. On deep dives (approaching 200 fsw and beyond) they are almost completely ineffective because of suit compression. This would seem to indicate that wet suits are suitable for shallower dives or for short deep dives. While this is for the most part true, there is one caveat. Very deep dives, with the associated extreme suit compression, can permanently reduce a wet suit's thermal insulating qualities.

The general trend among divers using wet suits for very long dives is multiple layering. By wearing thin tunics or even full 1/8 inch suits in addition to their 1/4 inch farmer-johns they seek to eliminate water movement in and out of the suit. There is of course a trade-off in that the more neoprene you put on, the less flexibility you have. This negates at least one of the advantages of diving a wet suit.

Dry Suits

Dry suits have been the object of a love-hate relationship with cave divers for many years. We love them when they work and when they don't we contemplate alternative hobbies. Dry suits are more complex and require much more maintenance than wet suits. The fact that they are more complex results in an availability of suits from various manufacturers that range widely in quality and cost. As a general rule, a dry suit is not a thing to be economical about. That is, if you've decided you have to have one, spend every penny you can. The cheaper dry suits won't last as long or work as well as the more expensive ones, leaving you disappointed and wet. Expect to spend $1000 or more on a high quality dry suit.

Dry suits can be loosely described by two categories. There are neoprene dry suits which are made of the same material as wet suits. Neoprene dry suits are perhaps a compromise between wet suits and fabric dry suits. They are generally close fitting, like a wet suit, and are almost as flexible. They allow the diver to wear a thin sweater or undergarment, but achieve most of their insulation from the thick neoprene. These suits keep a diver much warmer than a wet suit because she is kept relatively dry, but they are still affected by depth. As the diver descends and the neoprene is compressed there will be a loss of buoyancy as well as insulation.

Fabric dry suits offer the ultimate in warmth because they allow the diver to wear a heavy undergarment. Since air is added to the suit to equalize pressure (and since the undergarment has open interstitial air spaces) the undergarment is not compressed and thus retains its insulating quality. By far the best material for an undergarment is Thinsulate, a 3M product which was developed into dry suit undergarments during the U.S. Navy's Passive Diver Thermal Protection System programs. Thinsulate retains more of its insulating value when wet or damp than any comparable material. For very long or very deep dives, or any combination of the two, a high quality dry suit with Thinsulate underwear offers the highest degree of warmth.

Dry suits present the opportunity for yet another advantage in warmth. Since many long or deep dives involve helium mixtures, it is necessary to carry a separate small tank to inflate the dry suit. This is because the thermal conductivity of helium is so high. (For comparison, an 80/20 HeO_2 mixture has a thermal conductivity 84 times greater than air.) While this at first seems like an added nuisance it can be a major plus. Rather than using air in this bottle the diver can substitute argon, an inert gas. Argon has a thermal conductivity of about 0.68 times that of air. This means that you will stay considerably warmer in a dry suit that is filled with argon versus one filled with air. Of course you will still lose heat through respiration and any unprotected extremities, but it does amount to a significant difference. Carbon dioxide would theoretically be an excellent choice also, but has problems associated with the formation of carbonic acid if the diver sweats (causing a burning sensation like sunburn) and CO_2 inside a dry suit might increase the chances of skin bends. Argon seems to have none of these problems and is readily available.

Dry suits offer a tremendous advantage in thermal insulation over wet suits, especially on deep dives. There are of course some disadvantages. Cost of a high quality dry suit is about three times that of a good wet suit. This is somewhat offset with time as the valves and underwear will last indefinitely. The only thing that wears out is the shell itself. But dry suits are also harder to dive. They require the same attention to buoyancy control that a buoyancy compensator does. In fact it is like diving with two BC's. This may increase safety since there is a redundant source of buoyancy available, but it does task load the diver. The decision to buy a wet or dry suit must be based on the type of dives you are doing (and want to do). If you contemplate the very long or the very deep in cave diving then you have little choice.

One final piece of advice. If you elect to buy a dry suit, get one with a front style zipper entry even if the cost is significantly higher. The durability and reliability of a dry suit zipper is greatly increased when it is not being stressed by arm movement at the shoulders, by tanks pressing on it, or air pressure trying to pull it apart when the diver is in normal swimming position. Front zippers have been observed to last three to four times longer than the same type zipper mounted on the back.

STAGE DIVING EQUIPMENT

Stage diving is obviously an advanced form of cave diving. It is also a vital part of serious exploration. Many people will cave dive for years without ever stage diving. Others will use this technique almost every time they get in the water. Stage diving should only be attempted once all other gear problems have been sorted out and the diver has gained experience. If there are still problems with gear or technique then stage diving will only aggravate them. Once a diver has mastered the normal equipment of cave diving she can greatly expand her capabilities by moving on to stage diving if she has the desire.

Stage diving is not just a way to go further in a cave. It is a way to increase safety. The presence of additional sources of air in the cave should make any dive safer if it is planned correctly.

Stage Bottles

Almost any single tank can be used as a stage bottle but some are more suitable than others. In general the tank should not be extremely negatively or positively buoyant. This rules out many tanks such as 104's. A negative tank will slow a diver and cause her to work harder since she must over-inflate her BCD. Many divers have tried using larger capacity stage bottles to increase their range only to find no advantage. Some realize immediately that the heavier bottle is hindering them to the point that the extra air is barely able to cover the extra work. Others remain confused as to why they can't go much, if any, farther on a larger cylinder. They overlook the most important aspect of a stage bottle, that it be close to neutrally buoyant.

By far the most popular and perhaps best suited tank for stage diving is the Luxfer aluminum 80 cubic foot cylinder. The physical size, air volume capacity, and buoyancy of this tank are as near an ideal compromise as any cylinder that is presently available. Next on the list are such tanks as the Kidde 80, the Catalina 80, and the standard steel 71.2 cubic foot tank. All of these tanks have reasonable buoyancy characteristics and are large enough to be useful as stage bottles.

Some tanks that are definitely not recommended for stage bottles are: steel 104's (Sherwood/Pressed Steel), steel 95's (Scubapro's Faber), and aluminum 90's (US Navy).

Steel 104's and 95's are simply too negatively buoyant to be used efficiently as stage bottles. Adding buoyancy tubes will increase drag and make doffing and donning these bottles more difficult. Aluminum 90's (Navy 90's) are too positive. They will float when still partially full making them awkward to handle and upsetting the diver's buoyancy.

One thing should be noted about stage bottles. If you waste a lot of time taking them off and putting them on, they will do you little good. Stage bottles (like all gear) should be configured as cleanly as possible to speed up the process of getting them on and off. You should practice with your stage bottles to the point that you can remove or replace one in less than one minute. Otherwise you are wasting valuable time and gas. Few things are as frustrating as watching your buddy struggle for five minutes with her stage bottle while you waste your own gas and get colder by the minute. It is interesting to note that many people who take inordinate amounts of time to don stage bottles are the same ones who are searching for larger capacity bottles to use.

Figure 5-15 Stage bottle rig.

Regardless of which tank you choose to fashion into a stage bottle, the method and hardware will be about the same. There are many variations on this theme, but only one will be addressed. The differences are minor and only experience will determine which particular modifications are best suited for each individual.

The basic stage bottle rig consists of a metal band (hose clamp, etc.) mounted about 1/3 of the way from the bottom of the tank. A strap or rope is placed under this band and a clip or snap is attached at this end. The opposite end is attached to the tank valve and a second snap is secured here. The two snaps serve to attach the bottle to the diver. This author began using the method shown in Figure 5-15 in 1988. It is faster and simpler to rig a bottle using rope like this than the traditional flat nylon strap. The rope is first doubled and pulled through a piece of tubing (rubber, nylon, etc.) about 1 foot long. This makes for a more comfortable handle for transporting the bottle. The looped end of the line is then passed through a brass snap and the handles passed back through the loop. This end is then placed under the metal band which is tightened in place. The brass snap is held in place below (not under) the band and prevents the rope handle from pulling free. The opposite end of the rope consists of two free ends which are led around the valve after being looped through a second brass snap. Trim the leftover rope, burn the ends, and you're finished. If desired, a rubber strap may be placed on the tank before the rope is secured to the valve. This is handy for securing the pressure gauge hose, etc. Simple enough? If you are using a Luxfer 80, the nylon hose should be about 15 inches long. You will need about 5 feet of 1/4 inch braided nylon rope. The rubber strap can be cut from an old tire inner tube.

Stage Bottle Regulators

The stage bottle regulator is often chosen without much thought and is frequently a "leftover" regulator of questionable condition and quality. Since the stage bottle is not the diver's primary source of gas there is a tendency to put less effort into its preparation. The consequences of this are predictable: frequent failures and aborted dives. Choose the regulator for your stage bottle as though your life depended on it, since obviously it DOES. Many divers will pay top dollar for the highest performance regulator available to use as their primary and use anything they can get a good deal on for their stage bottle regulator (not to mention their secondary). Maybe this is why some people don't want to hand off their primary regulator. The point is that EVERY regulator you breathe from is just as important as ANY other. (The only exception to this is a regulator that is strictly for decompression. This regulator will generally be used at shallow depths and low work rates and can be switched underwater if necessary in an emergency.) Your stage bottle regulator is used at the point during the dive when you are probably working the hardest because you are carrying the most gear. Don't cut any corners in its purchase and maintenance.

There are two choices in routing the second stage supply hose from your stage bottle. The traditional method is to fold the hose in front of you so that the second stage can be placed in the mouth right side up. Though this is not an issue with some regulators, it is still necessary to place a bend in the hose. Many people find this uncomfortable since it places a twisting or tugging force on the mouth piece. This can be especially aggravating when riding a scooter (DPV).

An alternative method is to use an octopus length hose and route this around your neck and in your mouth, much the way the hose would normally come over your shoulder if you were using a single tank with backpack. This is much more comfortable and has the advantage that the second stage is easily located if dropped from your mouth. There is a disadvantage to this method if you are wrapping your primary (long) hose around your neck. Care must be taken not to cross the two hoses and not to confuse them. Different color mouth pieces help avoid this confusion. While this hose is around your neck it will be difficult to hand off your long hose, but this should not be necessary anyway if your buddy is also staging. If you must assist an out-of-air diver while you are staging, the simplest procedure is to hand off the stage bottle regulator and then immediately hand off the entire stage bottle to the out-of-air diver. This is another good reason for practicing stage bottle removal. If you are fortunate enough to have a stage bottle available when your buddy needs gas, count your blessings.

SUMMARY

A diver's cave diving ability is a function of three things. The first is her natural physical and mental ability. Some of this is innate, but all of us can improve in this area by hard work. The second is gear. No one has any predisposed advantage in this area. You may not be making record setting dives, but your gear can be as good as anyone who is. The last is desire. It determines how much effort you will put into the first two areas, and how far you will decide to go with the ability you develop. Physical ability, skill in the water, experience, and judgment can only be developed over many years, but gear can be perfect just as soon as you make the effort.

This chapter can be looked at on two levels, and hopefully it is valuable on each. First, it can be viewed as a presentation of a specific gear configuration that has proven very successful. While this is worth something to the reader it is perhaps less important than the second level. The second level can be thought of as "Zen and the Art of Cave Diving Equipment Maintenance." It is more subtle and requires that the reader look for underlying values. To put it as simply as possible, a cave diver must care about the work she is doing on gear and the quality of the final result. She must put aside ego, impatience, and excuses, and settle for nothing less than perfection. Those who do so will discover on their own the value of such effort. Those who don't will never quite understand what the others are talking about.

Chapter 6

TEAM MANAGEMENT

by J. Billy Young

Close observation of any group of cave divers will reveal that cave diving is an individualistic sport. Cave divers have different reasons why they enter the underwater cave environment and they each set different goals for cave diving. While conforming to the rules of cave diving, divers certainly exhibit nonconformity with regard to the equipment they favor and ingenuity and creativity in solving problems with equipment and the environment. Yet the buddy system is an integral, essential part of cave diving.

Under favorable conditions, the buddy system functions to provide companionship for a shared adventure. Under adverse conditions, the buddy system can turn a life threatening situation into a minor emergency and allow the team to return safely to the surface. The key to success in maintaining a safe buddy system lies in preparation, understanding, and unification of the members into an efficient, functional team.

The "ideal" dive team would consist of divers equally matched in knowledge, training, ability, and equipment. However, this ideal is not always reached. Concessions are necessary when establishing the criteria of the dive plan to compensate for any limitation of team members. The team management concept includes: preparation and planning, execution, buddy assistance and rescue, and team member responsibilities. Each of these topics plays an important role in the overall success of the team, just as each diver plays a part in ensuring its success.

This chapter will examine how a good foundation for a team is created, how the team should prepare and execute a dive, and how each team member can contribute to overall team safety.

TEAM SELECTION

Finding a suitable diving partner can be a frustrating experience, particularly in cave diving. A diver should strive to closely match training and experience with prospective dive partners. Fortunately, national training programs have developed standards which ensure that every certified cave diver has the knowledge and ability to safely dive in caves.

Team members need to be compatible as individuals and compatibility begins before divers ever don a single piece of equipment. Divers who share personal friendships and have mutual respect for each other generally maintain good communication underwater. This type of camaraderie increases unity as a team, uniform purpose, and better buddy awareness.

Team members should have similar goals and share the same philosophy toward self-imposed limits. Divers with widely differing views in regard to safe depths, decompression, etc., will not want to make the same type of dives.

The selection of qualified team members must also address the issue of equipment. Beyond assuring that each team member has all the equipment necessary for cave diving, divers should have comparable primary lights and air supply systems in order to dive together. Other chapters cover the safety considerations of having equally matched equipment. Moreover, maximum benefit from equipment is derived when divers have comparable systems.

TEAM SIZE

Dive teams can consist of any number of members. However, dive teams ***should*** consist of only two or three members. The idea behind team diving is to reduce risk, but teams of more than three can actually increase risk. First and foremost is the consideration of buddy awareness. If more than three divers dive as a team, it is very difficult for team members to maintain buddy awareness. A simple solution is to divide a large group into smaller teams. In choosing whether to have two or three person teams, each size has advantages to consider.

1. Two Person Team Advantages
   - A. Communication
   - B. Buddy awareness
   - C. Silt control
   - D. Speed and efficiency
2. Three Person Team Advantages
   - A. Additional backup equipment and air supply
   - B. Additional primary light for better referencing
   - C. Additional physical support and assistance

From a safety standpoint, the three person team offers the greatest advantage, provided the cave size will accommodate the larger team. Two person teams on the other hand, tend to be more efficient, particularly in smaller cave systems where a lead diver may have difficulty maintaining visual contact with a third diver (and vice versa). Most dives can be performed with either size team.

Preferably, different teams do not dive the same system at the same time; however, more than one team can safely dive in a single cave system if certain procedures are understood and followed. Separate teams may choose to use a common temporary line to avoid running two lines. Each team should avoid crowding the other and maintain a separate dive plan.

If a common temporary line is used, the team that is chosen to reel up the line must be absolutely sure that the other team has exited the system before they remove it. By attaching a message to the reel, any question about a team's status is eliminated. If there is no communication between the teams during the dive, the line should be left. It should also be left in place if a group of unfamiliar divers is encountered who have apparently taken advantage of the line.

When more than one team of divers are in a system, there is greater likelihood that silt and percolation will affect visibility. While exiting, divers should be prepared for reduced visibility and should show consideration for teams still in the system.

DIVE PREPARATION

After the dive team is formulated and dive planning procedures are started, a team leader should be appointed to coordinate the plan and direct the dive. The leader is generally the most experienced diver or the diver most knowledgeable of the cave system. The team leader lays out the dive plan but receives input from all team members when setting goals, establishing limitations, and discussing general criteria.

The most important consideration is developing the dive plan around the least experienced member of the team. The plan should not exceed this person's ability. Similarly, diving with a new partner requires special attention to detail in preparation for the first dive. The first few dives should be technically easy, in the safest environment possible. Once the communication barriers are broken and both divers are confident in each other's ability, more difficult dives may be attempted.

The team leader will usually handle the reel if a temporary guideline is necessary, although another team member can be allowed to handle it in order to gain experience. In determining positions for the dive, the least experienced diver is placed in the middle of a three person team. Positions are to be maintained until the turnaround point, at which time the order is reversed.

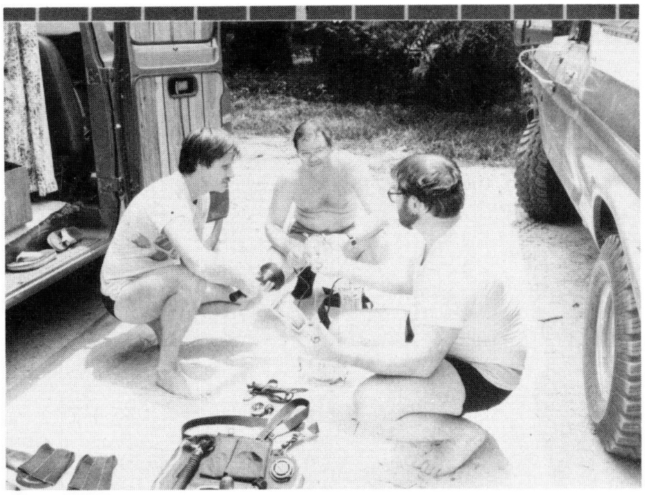

Figure 6-1 Communication lines before guidelines.

After the plan is devised, team members should review each other's equipment before beginning the dive. Once in the water, equipment checks are performed by each individual and cross checked by team members.

After this part of the pre-dive procedure is completed, a short octopus breathing drill (an *S-drill*) should be undertaken in open water or at the mouth of the cave. This exercise conditions teams members to react quickly and confidently in the event of a real emergency.

TEAM EFFECTIVENESS

Effective team management creates an atmosphere of comfort and safety for team members. To achieve it, each member of the team must follow certain procedures.

Buddy awareness is critical to successful team management. Awareness is a term used in cave diving to describe the diver's ability to know what is occurring on a moment to moment basis. It is a "feel" for the environment, diver activity, and line placement. Awareness seems to improve with experience and is a key to successful diver performance.

Good communication goes hand in hand with buddy awareness. Maintaining good communication depends on each team member's alertness and response. Because cave dive teams normally use an in-line swimming configuration, periodic spot checks of trailing divers are required. Natural bends in the cave are good locations to visually check team activity. Hand signals are not necessary at all visual checkpoints; however, the *OK* sign may be used whenever a response is desired. Hand signals need to be illuminated by placing the hand in the primary light's beam, but care must be taken to avoid shining a light directly in another team member's face.

Another aspect of awareness concerns *referencing. Cave referencing* refers to the close visual inspection of cave landmarks made by each diver during the course of a dive. Although every diver must always know the location of the guideline and remain in close proximity to it, the presence of the line makes some divers pay little attention to the cave itself. By identifying landmarks, cave referencing reinforces navigation and reduces stress. Divers can recognize where they are in a cave at any given moment if they are committed to cave referencing. Cave referencing is an individual act that adds to team effectiveness.

Another component of team effectiveness is buddy assistance. On any cave dive, a team member can make the dive more comfortable by rendering assistance during routine procedures. For example, the diver in front of the reel person on exit should undo all wraps and tieoffs and keep the line taut. This simple procedure helps to ensure that the team makes a smooth exit from the system. If a dive is made in order to accomplish specific tasks, such as surveying, research, photography, or other

Figure 6-2 "S" Drill.

projects, physical assistance and lighting can add greatly to team efficiency. The key to efficiency is assigning each diver a role and having the dive plan specify these responsibilities. If divers are aware of their responsibilities, they can be in a position to provide assistance when required.

Buddy assistance should be differentiated from buddy rescue. A definition of each follows.

Buddy Assistance — providing aid or support to another team member, thereby improving the efficiency, safety, and overall well-being of the entire dive team.

Buddy Rescue — rendering aid to a team member in imminent danger or a life-threatening situation and successfully assisting the distressed diver to the surface.

Buddy assistance includes providing aid in fairly commonplace occurrences such as making equipment adjustments for a team member or freeing a team member from simple line entanglements. The concept of buddy rescue in regard to cave diving is discussed in the following section.

Buddy Rescue

The cave environment creates a special set of circumstances to consider when dealing with buddy rescue. Compared to open water diving, the chances of successful rescue of an unconscious, non-breathing victim are diminished considerably because of the potentially circuitous route to the surface. However, the example of an unconscious, non-breathing victim represents the worst case.

With proper preparation, buddy assistance, air use management, and all of the other prerequisites for safe cave diving, buddy rescue remains an improbability rather than a distinct possibility. The chapters on emergency procedures cover what to do in case of an emergency. The focus of this section is on prevention, and on avoiding situations where rescue may be unsuccessful.

A dive team should never exceed a point in the cave where team members do not have the equipment, "consumables" (air and battery power), or abilities to successfully assist or rescue another team member if a problem or emergency arises. A rescue attempt is in jeopardy on any dive where a team has exceeded its limits.

Environmental hazards that could affect the ability to provide assistance or rescue include restrictions, silt, current, and depth. Avoidance is one solution to these hazards and it should be practiced in extreme cases. One example of an extreme case would be a major restriction — a passageway requiring the reconfiguring of equipment other than the standard back-mounted doubles. In the past, before alternate gear configurations were widely known, cave divers sometimes removed their air bottles to pass through major restrictions.[1] However, these conditions are present to some extent in every cave system. Obviously, avoidance is not always the answer.[2]

Properly preparing for known hazards minimizes risk and allows for the successful implementation and completion of emergency procedures. An essential part of successfully dealing with environmental hazards includes knowledge of the cave system, preferably obtained through one team member's first-hand experience and research. Establishing safe limits, particularly in regard to depth, also helps minimize the impact of the environment in case of an emergency.

Perhaps the hazards that represent the greatest threat to the diving team are self-imposed. In most cases, environmental hazards are pre-determined, but poor judgment and poor technique represent safety violations that may threaten the entire team.

To cope with the stressful complications that may occur on a cave dive, the cave diver makes mental and physical preparations. Adequate preparation comes from training, conditioning, and experience. The higher the experience level, the less likelihood of high stress levels.

The worst possible result of high stress levels is panic. If a team member reaches a state of panic, that individual may lose control of his performance because the threat of death has overcome all reasoning. Of all rescue or assistance possibilities, this situation is one of the most complicated and potentially dangerous a diver can face.

Dealing with a panicked (or near-panicked) diver requires caution. Assurance should be given to the stricken diver, who should be approached cautiously. Divers should begin the exit as soon as conditions have stabilized and proceed in a calm and unhurried manner. During the exit, concentration on basic principles of cave diving is essential. The diver should be carefully monitored for additional signs of stress along the way.

---

[1]The safest choice in this situation is turn the dive (avoidance) rather than remove your air supply. — Ed.

[2]The diver can the utilize an alternative gear configuration, such as side-mounted cylinders, to deal with this significant environmental hazard on subsequent dives. — Ed.

The key to dealing with panic and fear is recognizing the symptoms in early stages and providing assistance to curb its progression. Signs include difficulty with basic skills, constant equipment problems, lack of response to communication efforts, lack of eye contact, unusual physical movements, and wide eyes or dilated pupils. Any indication of an unusually high stress level is sufficient reason to terminate the dive.

SELF-RELIANCE AND TEAM MANAGEMENT

Almost every diver can provide accounts of buddy assistance, and perhaps many of these would have been major emergencies if a buddy had not been available. The buddy system provides a backup if it is needed, but it is each diver's responsibility to be prepared for emergencies and be as self-reliant as possible.

If a diver is dependent on his buddy, the buddy system cannot function. Even if one diver has more experience, every team member should be prepared to render assistance. Although it may sound ironic, a key ingredient to the buddy system is self-reliance.

Team Responsibilities

Cave divers must not only accept responsibility for themselves, but for the team as well. The first responsibility a diver has to the team is honestly presenting self-ability. If a person cannot present information without fearing a threat to his ego or peer pressure, he is shirking his responsibility to the team.

The second responsibility concerns overall team safety. The decision to abort or terminate a dive, for whatever reason, should not be questioned. Furthermore, a diver should not suffer recrimination for his decision to call the dive. An atmosphere of trust and acceptance helps foster mature and responsible judgment in each team member, as well as reduce stress.

The unification of divers into an effective team requires common goals and a positive atmosphere. A person sensitive to ego threat may go along with goals that do not reflect his own, and thereby participate in a dive plan that is beyond his limits. A performance-oriented diver may push other team members beyond limits once the dive has begun, or make another diver feel guilty about calling the dive once back on the surface, and thus endanger the team on future dives. There is nothing wrong with setting ambitious goals for a dive, but each diver must remember he is a member of a team and has responsibilities to that team.

SUMMARY

This chapter has been devoted to establishing the merits of team diving and providing guidelines for successful team management. Effective dive teams are a cornerstone of safe cave diving but they do not come about by accident. In order to fully enjoy cave diving, divers need to form teams with others who share their goals and who they trust in stressful situations.

Teamwork is a coordinated effort and provides not only a greater margin of safety, but increases task effectiveness. The sharing of experiences makes the sport more enjoyable and rewarding. However, effective team management requires total commitment from each individual, mutual objectives and purpose, and complete understanding of each individual's motivations. Close communication and awareness is critical to the team's success and the measure of how the team performs as a unit.

Chapter 7

DIVE PLANNING & POST DIVE REVIEW

by Milledge Murphey, Ph.D.

SECURING INFORMATION

The gathering of information relative to dive site, conditions at the site, subaquatic cave map(s) (if such exist for the site selected), equipment needed, meeting places and times, buddy selection and acquisition, travel arrangements, emergency information and equipment, and many other informational elements must be considered in order to ensure safe, enjoyable cave diving. Dive planning is a subject which is infrequently treated in cave diving literature, and it is frequently overlooked or minimally covered in openwater scuba diving courses and in some cavern and cave diving courses. Most persons recognize that a sound dive plan is an integral part of safe, enjoyable cave diving. Many believe that such planning is almost as necessary as redundancy in air cylinders or reel and line use.

Clearly, the success (and enjoyment) of each cave dive depends upon a single consideration (covered in exemplary fashion by Jeffrey Bozanic elsewhere in this book): *air supply* and planning for its use. Dry cavers can successfully cope with many of the emergencies which they encounter over a response time of hours or even days. Cave divers typically have only minutes within which to deal with emergency situations, and frequently, the problems encountered by the cave diver significantly reduce the margin of available time for problem solving. There is generally little or no time to use waiting for help, and unlike their openwater counterparts, there is no direct access to the surface where response time may greatly increase. In cave diving, when the air supply expires, so may the diver.

Exactly what is meant by dive planning? The dive plan is usually considered to be a summary of what dive team members want to accomplish, how they want to accomplish it, and when and/or where the team interfaces directly with its limitations in the overhead environment. Further, it is properly a "thought rehearsal" for the actual dive (much like a flight plan is for an aerial flight), wherein as many problems or alternative situations as possible are anticipated so that the team can plan suitable responses to each potential contingency.

USE OF CONSUMABLES

Adequate cave dive planning is critically important in several areas which include, but are not limited to: use of consumables, establishment of limitations, management of tasks and task loading, limitations imposed by the site, resource management (including human resources), and communication problems and the need for standardization of signals. Planning for the use of consumables must include a discussion of *air, light* and *stamina* (all of these areas have been thoroughly detailed elsewhere in this book).

As air consumption is fully covered in Chapter 12 of this book, it will be mentioned only briefly here as a basis for other planning considerations. Among the considerations which must be utilized in planning for judicious air use are: the experience of the cave divers in question; consideration of environmental specifics including water clarity, temperature, flow direction (spring or syphon); site access; and other factors. Another contingency involving air consumption is planning for drastic air loss, including the potential for complete air loss. Cave divers must plan and practice air sharing in two person and three person teams (or more if applicable). Finally, the plan must establish turnaround limits for air, distance, and time milieu[1].

Planning regarding light should include not only ambient surface and sub-surface light, but more importantly primary and back-up lighting for use subaquatically. Fully charged batteries in all lights, fresh bulbs, O-rings, wiring, and adequate burn times are musts in the lighting plan. Finally, wattage and brightness of *all lights* to be used on the dive may play major roles in planning decisions relating to diver order for the dive, reel person determination, etc.

The third area is perhaps one of the most elusive and least often adequately considered by cave divers during their planning. Stamina is directly related to age, physical condition, duration of the dive, thermal exposure, equipment drag, physical loads imposed by the dive and site, and finally psychological and other factors. As cave diving is an activity which contains a high degree of risk in its pursuit, diver conditioning is of critical importance. Diver stamina is directly related to the level of physical condition of the diver; being *in shape* is perhaps one of the best "insurance policies" which a diver can maintain to insure her safety. Being in good to excellent physical condition may enable a cave diver to successfully withstand the rigors of thermal exposure, physical load, and psychological stress.

---

[1] *Time milieu* refers to such factors as: inert gas exposure, thermal exposure, stamina, burn time of primary lights, ambient surface light during entry and exit, park operation hours (when applicable), etc. — Ed.

Factors which all cave divers must monitor include:

1. Reduction of dive depth and time when over forty years of age.
2. Maintenance of an "ideal" body weight as stipulated by the U.S. insurance industry.
3. Cessation of alcohol, tobacco, and recreational drug use.
4. Not cave diving when fatigued or emotionally upset.
5. Hydration before, during, and after diving.
6. Engaging in a program of regular exercise such as aerobic swimming, jogging, or cycling.
7. Recognition of personal physical, psychological, and experience limitations, and diving well within them at all times.

SETTING LIMITATIONS

As this book contains the previously referenced chapters by Bozanic and others which cover many of the critical limiting factors (and planning for them) in great detail, I will outline herein those factors which limit all cave divers. It must be recognized that cave diving is an absolute experience in that the subaquatic cave environment is singularly unforgiving should one enter it without proper training, planning, and equipment.

Cave divers must be formally trained and as a group, pair, etc., determine the critical air supply prior to diving. Additionally, the reserve air available for decompression must be determined for each diver in the presence of others participating in the dive.

A second and equally critical factor is time. Air supply obviously limits time under water and, therefore, these two elements are inexorably linked when planning a dive. At any given depth, an individual diver has a finite air supply and therefore a limited amount of time within which to penetrate a subaquatic cave. One time related factor is the establishment of *exit time* so that enough air will remain with each diver to allow complete decompression (if planned). Failure to consider and establish turnaround times, exit times, and decompression times ***before the dive***, can result in confusion and the occurrence of incident or accident scenarios for the diving team.

Depth is another of the absolute factors which is linked to air supply and time. The diving team must plan for, agree upon, and establish a maximum depth limit which no member of the team will exceed. Depth determines decompression planning, as does time, and therefore preplanning regarding its limit is essential. In considering depth limitations during planning, the group and each diver within it must honestly face her experience with nitrogen narcosis, and not give in to the ever present temptation to exceed known personal depth parameters. Similarly, personal air consumption rates at depth must not be pushed for the purpose of staying with the group. Depth must be planned with exact limits set so that it is absolutely controlled by all group members, resulting in conservative air use during the dive and availability of air for the potential emergency and decompression components of the dive.

Planning for decompression is detailed elsewhere in this volume, therefore my purpose is to outline planning considerations as they relate to allowable decompression. As with all other elements planned for in cave diving the decompression schedule must be decided upon prior to submerging. Thus, if the dive plan is executed precisely, there will be no necessity (beyond routine double checking) for subaquatic calculation of stop depths and times. During planning related to decompression, cave divers must consider the predisposing factors related to decompression sickness (age, obesity, sex, etc.), and take all available precautions to mitigate against its onset including pre-dive and post-dive hydration, oxygen use during decompression at the 30,[2] 20 and 10 foot stops, additional "safety" time at the 10 foot stop, extended post-dive rest taken at the surface, and other practices for safety.

Penetration into subaquatic caves is of interest to all cave divers and must be carefully planned prior to diving. Obviously, the experience of the individual member of the dive team must be considered during such planning. It is a prudent practice to limit penetration distances to the comfort limit of the most inexperienced diver on the team. Inexperienced divers may, with gradual increases in penetration limits, become experienced in a safe manner, enabling them to penetrate farther and/or explore new passage in time. To attempt long, deep penetrations with minimal experience may be courting disaster, as panic can quickly overtake the inexperienced diver under adverse conditions at great penetration distances.

The psychological factors involved in cave diving as well as other hazardous activities are well known and are discussed elsewhere in this book. It is well established that repeated practice of the emergency procedures and techniques involved in safe cave diving can produce a safe reaction level in cave divers. This level of safe practice, developed to the degree of stimulus response, can result in minimal tendency to react in an irrational manner when under stress. Those divers who are unable to maintain this level of reaction-based behavior due to seasonal cave diving only should always gradually reenter the cave diving realm (upon resumption of cave diving after a substantial absence from the activity).

---

[2]Use of 100% oxygen deeper than 25 fsw is potentially hazardous and remains controversial, though some divers routinely use it during D/C as deep as 30 fsw. Nitrox is acceptable for use at 30 fsw, and for most deeper D/C stops encountered following dives made on air. — Ed.

THE DIVE SITE

Sites for cave diving are as physically varied as are the divers who seek to visit them, thus careful planning regarding the specific site to be visited must be undertaken. The entry and exit points and techniques vary, and available equipment, stamina, experience, and technique acquisition must be evaluated and planned. Other factors to be considered in site planning include selection of a suitable number of team members, planning for maintenance of contact with the full team complement, and planning the exact location of decompression stops. Configuration of the subaquatic cave and its flow and silt features are also matters which require planning to insure safety and enjoyment.

TASK MANAGEMENT

All of the foregoing having been considered, the prudent team should clarify the expectations of each member regarding the dive, so that no single feature or potential feature of the dive remains undiscussed. Responsibilities of each team member must be agreed upon with assignment(s) made for reel person, line person, and checker. All members should be familiar with the protocol involved within the team, as well as with other teams which may be encountered in the cave during the dive. Finally, complete equipment matching, S-drill rehearsal, and discussion of contingency plan(s) must be thoroughly completed. Each diver must be familiar with her personal resources and those of all other members of the team. Elements including knowledge of one's buddies' equipment type and configuration is mandatory. Contingencies such as location and deployment of auxiliary air supplies and other factors must be clearly explained by all team members during the pre-dive planning session. The careful development of complete contingency plans for all possible occurrences during and after the dive is perhaps the most critical phase of the planning feature in cave diving. Such plans will never be needed or used if all dives go according to plan. However, in the unlikely event of a mid-dive equipment failure, physical difficulty of a diver, or other (innumerable) potential problem(s), these detailed contingency plans and rehearsal of them will become the critical factor between a successful dive and one with an ominous termination.

SITE CONSIDERATIONS

Among the plans which must be made include those which relate to the unique characteristics of the location at which the dive takes place, time of day of dive, and numerous other factors. Several topics included herein appear obvious, however more than one group of experienced cave divers has journeyed to a remote site to discover that they had, through failure to plan thoroughly, inadvertently left at home the critical piece of equipment for use in reaching the water, thus aborting the dive.

Absolute lines of pre-dive communication must be established and maintained among all team and team support members in order to ensure trouble-free dive planning and execution. Additionally, preplanning regarding location of decompression stops (if needed) is a requirement which must be addressed and understood by all members of the team. Finally, best use of all available equipment for a specific dive by a specific team is of paramount importance to the planning effort. Should the plan call for DPV, stage, or mixed gas techniques, all team members should agree on how best to use the combined material support (collectively used but individually owned by team members). Equipment quality and maintenance is usually an individual concern; however, in dive planning, all available equipment should be distributed according to the task(s) planned for the team and its individual members.

COMMUNICATION

Obviously, the subaquatic cave environment poses unique environmental conditions which mandate careful planning. Among the considerations requiring planning are potential use of Rimbach or touch contact communication, light communication, sound, hand signals, the slate and pencil, and others. *All team members must be thoroughly familiar with all potential communications methods, and all potential signals within each method must be agreed upon.* Lack of light, turbid water, buddy separation, depth-related nitrogen narcosis, confusion, improperly utilized signal(s) and an infinite variety of other potential problems necessitate absolute agreement during the planning phase of the dive by all team members. The consequences of failure to consider *all possibilities* when discussing communication prior to the dive may prove fatal.

An additional factor to consider is the order for use of handsignals during a cave dive. The dive team should discuss and agree upon use of light, hand, slate and pencil, sound, touch-contact and other signals prior to diving. Such agreement can be the key to avoiding confusion during the dive, and to the level of potential confusion which may exist during an emergency. As an example, if a diver begins using touch contact communication while in clear water, at 200 feet penetration, and at a depth of 60 feet, team members might be well advised to abort the dive due to the presence of an inexperienced, ill-trained, and fearful team member.

Finally, cave diving communication is difficult; it is a skill which must be practiced frequently, modified often during planning sessions with new dive partners who do things in a slightly different manner, and agreed upon prior to every dive. Clearly, as verbal communication is impossible while underwater, use of the aforementioned methods is mandatory. Difficulties encountered during normal cave diving conditions are numerous, and use of any communication under water, especially during subaquatic speleology, should be minimized to prevent confusion. For example, darkness renders hand signals difficult to discern and use of slate and pencil may be difficult due to limited space, visibility, or other environmentally imposed conditions. All potential problems can be successfully mitigated if all team members will insure that they are "speaking the same dialect" within each potential communication system they may utilize during the dive. It is recommended that all cave divers adhere to the published standard cave diving hand signals contained in the NACD book, *Handsignals for Diving*, thus ensuring the use of standardized signals and eliminating confusion. Further, it should be mentioned that this system is compatible with most openwater hand signal systems, and is thus convenient to use in training new cave divers. An understanding and use of these signals is basic to personal safety during cave diving.

SUMMARY

To summarize this chapter, the author refers the reader to all of the more specific topical chapters contained herein, prior to initial cave dive planning and post-dive review sessions. Rereading this chapter on an "as needed reminder" basis is advised. Further, the following quick reference outlines may be of assistance for use during a preplanning review:

Steps in Dive Planning

1. Pre-departure
2. Site briefing
3. Objectives
4. Emergency procedures
5. Contingency planning

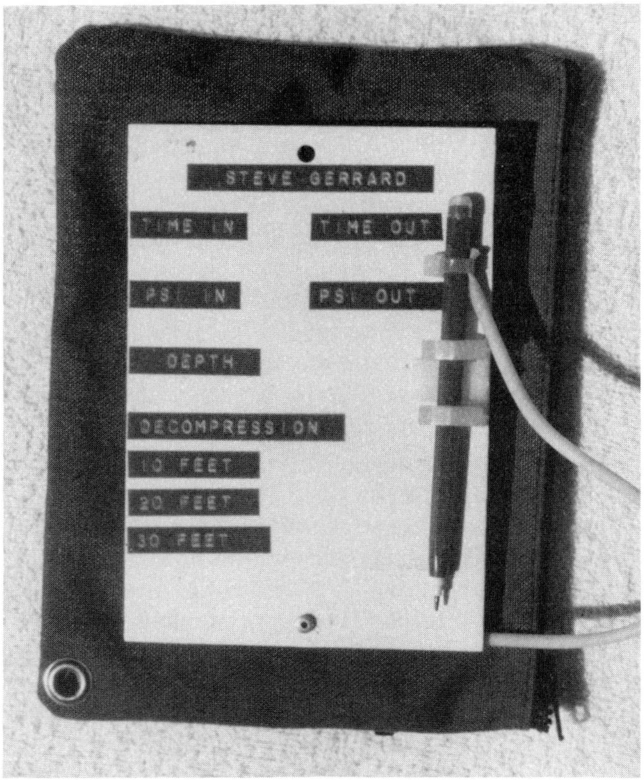

Figure 7-1 Typical cave diving slate.

Dive Planning Tools

1. Checklists
2. Dive logbook
3. Slate(s)
4. Pressure gauge
   A. Record air use/consumption
   B. Record planned turnaround (CAS)
5. Depth gauge
   A. Maximum depth planned may differ from your depth gauge reading during the dive. It is a good idea to read the depth at a known shallow land mark and also at maximum depth. A change in the shallow water depth reading may reflect a similar change at maximum depth. Gauge read ings may change during deep, extended dives.
6. Watch/Dive Timer
7. Compass
8. Computer

Post-Dive Review

The post dive review serves many purposes and may be the most enjoyable portion of a successful dive. Divers share the experiences which occurred during the dive and this catharsis is often extremely pleasant. Other positive aspects of the post-dive review include:

1. Conducted at the surface prior to exiting the water, it allows time to rest following the dive, thus enhancing nitrogen purge from the body, and delaying the exercise which results from dive site exit.
2. All post dive slate recording may be completed during this time.
3. It is the "social" portion of the dive.
4. Discussion of problems may be accomplished in the light of immediate past experience of the dive.

Figure 7-2 Post dive review.

5. Equipment problems/successes may be discussed with immediate clarity.
6. Future dives/explorations may be planned.
7. Discussion of unique or interesting cave features may be clearly pursued.
8. The plans for exit from the site and the walk back to the vehicles can be finalized.
9. The gear storage scenario, post dive meal, trip home or repetitive dive can be discussed.

With the completion of the post dive review, log entries can be transferred from slate to logbook, and all team members can savor another safe cave dive, *unless* there has been an incident or accident. The post dive review, under these more negative conditions, may become a rescue planning session; or the more macabre recovery dive.

The retrospective analysis of cave diving accidents has provided the following basic safety procedures for cave diving.

1. Obtain appropriate training for cave diving prior to diving in caves.
2. Use a continuous guideline-to-openwater at all times.
3. Reserve at least 2/3 of total air for exit from the cave.
4. Never exceed 130 feet in depth during cave diving.
5. Always use a minimum of three battery powered lights during cave diving.

If these principles are always observed, and the planning principles outlined in this book are followed, cave diving can be safe. If a sound postdive review is carried out, this dive, and those in the future will be safe, comfortable and rewarding.

Chapter 8

SWIMMING TECHNIQUES

by H. V. Grey

A basic tenet of this book is that safe cave diving is an art, as well as a science. Nowhere is this more evident than in propulsion techniques. A reef diver, for example, who drags his feet or carelessly kicks up the bottom, can do irreparable damage to the reef ecosystem, but probably won't be personally inconvenienced by this. But the same diver, in a cave with a silt floor and a low ceiling, can reduce 100-foot visibility to a couple of inches, or even destroy it completely, in a matter of only a few seconds. Tragically, diver-induced silting is a major contributing factor in many diving accidents in submerged caves .

If underwater caves were large, stagnant, siltless, and virtually indestructible, then open-water swimming techniques would be more than adequate for safe cave diving. However, most underwater caves have attributes which, singly or in combination, greatly complicate the problem of propulsion. These environmental features include: high flow; silt on floors, walls and ceilings; small passageways with low vertical clearance; restrictions; soft clay walls and ceilings; fragile formations; unstable rocks and projections; dark, light-absorbing walls and silt; and pre-existing low visibility (from causes such as particulate matter suspended in the water). Just as standard open-water equipment configurations and air management rules are inappropriate for cave diving, so are standard open-water swimming techniques.

The goal of the cave diver should be to achieve a balance between ***cave conservation, safety, efficiency, and silt control.*** It may be necessary, for example, to sacrifice efficiency in the interest of not damaging the cave or minimizing silt. On the other hand, in an emergency it might be advisable to tolerate a certain amount of silt in order to beat a hasty retreat. These are judgments which have to be made according to the specific situation. But all four factors should be kept constantly in mind.

FLUID DYNAMICS

Fluid dynamics is the study of how things move through fluids — both liquids and gases. The following sections outline principles that pertain to a diver's movement through the water.

Vertical Movement — Scuba diving is one of the few physical activities which permits one to experience a simulated sensation of weightlessness. When a diver is neutrally buoyant, the gravitational attractive force of the earth is effectively counterbalanced by the buoyant force of the water and the use of additional buoyancy-compensating devices.

Ascents and descents are achieved by applying force in the desired direction of travel. This is accomplished by swimming, pulling on or pushing against a fixed object, or inflating or deflating the BC. Occasionally, if the vertical correction is minimal, as for negotiating a rise in the floor or dip in the ceiling, merely inhaling or exhaling may be sufficient. (Ideally, the diver should be looking and thinking ahead 20 to 50 feet when possible, anticipating required changes in depth.)

Horizontal Movement — While the neutrally buoyant diver is effectively *weightless*, he is by no means *massless*. (*Weight* is a force equal in magnitude to mass multiplied by acceleration due to gravity.) The diver experiences mass in terms of the energy required to initiate and maintain forward horizontal motion from a position of rest relative to the water.

A neutrally buoyant diver "swimming" through a vacuum would encounter no frictional resistance. In accordance with Newton's First Law of Motion, once an object is set in motion it will continue until it collides with something. Water, however, offers a large physical resistance to a solid body traveling through it. Therefore, it is important to minimize the surface area which contacts the water, presenting as streamlined a shape as possible (see Figs. 8-1A and 8-1B).

Because of the apparent sensation of weightlessness, divers are often unconcerned about carrying additional, nonessential pieces of gear. (*If three lights are good, aren't five better?*) Some divers will even carry extra lead weight. Not only must this additional mass be pushed around the cave, requiring the expenditure of extra energy, but excess weight requires that the BC be more inflated. This both enlarges the diver's frontal profile and increases friction-induced drag.

The diver should also take care to make sure that "danglies" such as submersible pressure gauges, backup lights, line reels, inflator hoses, etc. are attached as close to the body as possible. This not only contributes to streamlining, but prevents those items from damaging the floor of the cave or becoming entangled in line.

Buoyancy and trim are treated extensively in another chapter. But a few main points about buoyancy are salient to this chapter on swimming techniques. If the diver is negatively buoyant, some of his swimming energy will have to be directed upward in order to keep him from sinking deeper. Likewise, if he is trimmed so that he is

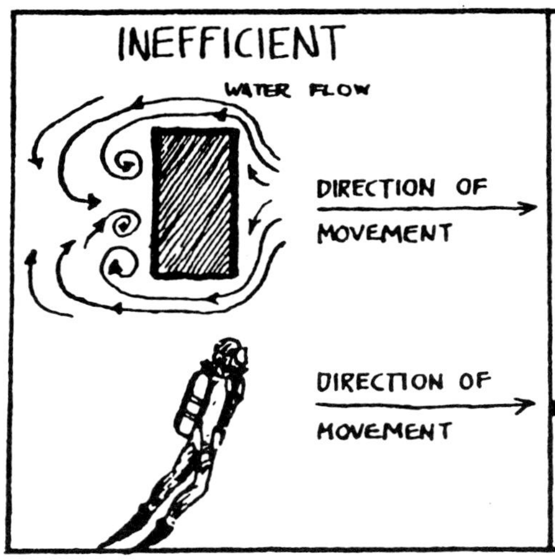

Figure 8-1A

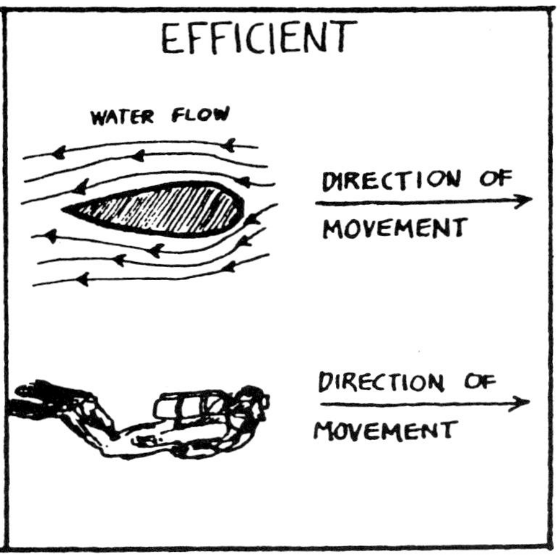

Figure 8-1B

feet-heavy, he will have to make himself negative in order to counteract the upward tendency of his swimming angle (see Fig. 8-2). Not only does this waste energy and cut down on efficiency by using physical motion to do what should be done with the BC, it also directs the fin turbulence down to the floor of the cave, which can stir up silt.

If the diver is under-weighted and positively buoyant, he will have to kick in a downward direction to keep from rising. If he is top-heavy, he will have to be positively buoyant in order to compensate for his downward swimming angle. Again, this is inefficient because swimming energy is being used to counteract buoyant force. Upward-directed fin turbulence may also knock loose silt particles off the ceiling, which can cause unnecessary damage to the cave (see Fig. 8-3).

The most efficient angle of attack is a level, horizontal attitude. Thrust efficiency is maximized since it is in the direction of travel, and the presenting frontal area is as small as possible, minimizing drag. Fin turbulence is directed straight back, which fortunately minimizes silt disturbance in most horizontal passages (see Fig. 8-1B). The horizontal trim position also allows the cave diver to perform several modified kicks for silt avoidance which require a rigid, bent-knee posture.

Generating Thrust — Initiating forward movement from a position of relative rest (or accelerating from a constant velocity) requires *pushing* in some fashion or other against another object, such as water or rock. An astronaut floating free in the vacuum of space has nothing against which to push, and so cannot effect acceleration with any conventional "swimming" movements.

If a diver were to try to move through the water by pushing against another diver of equal mass floating free in the water, they would both be forced away from each other at approximately the same speed. So half the diver's propulsive energy would be wasted pushing the other diver away. In the same way, pushing against water is inefficient, too, since only part of the energy is translated into forward movement. The rest is spent displacing the water backward.

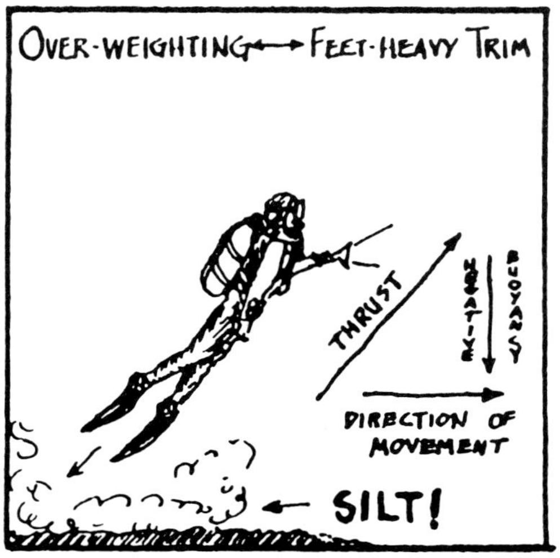

Figure 8-2

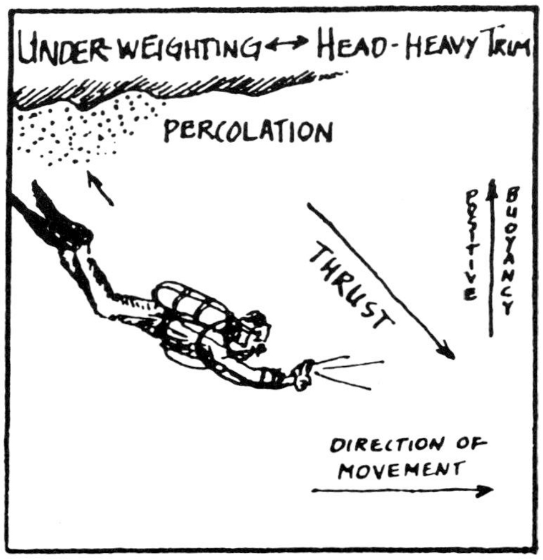

Figure 8-3

It is much more efficient to push against a fixed, immovable object, such as a solid outcropping of rock. The rock doesn't give way and all the energy is applied to propulsion. Unfortunately, however, this almost invariably results in damage to the cave. Although pulling techniques have been long used by cave divers, we are now beginning to recognize that most of the submerged caves we dive in cannot tolerate this type of impact from the large number of divers now visiting them. Extreme discretion should always be used in deciding to employ pulling techniques, as they ***always*** leave scars wherever they are used. If we are to preserve our beloved caves in a condition anything like their pristine state, we must be willing to sacrifice speed and efficiency for conservation.

ASSESSING THE CAVE

Flow — According to the Bernoulli Principle, the velocity of water moving through a conduit increases as the diameter of the conduit decreases. This is because the only way for the same volume of water to move through a smaller space in the same amount of time it takes to move through a larger diameter space, is for the water to move faster. Thus, when a cave passage narrows, the current will be stronger (see Fig. 8-4).

Flow will usually be strongest in the center of a tunnel, since the water there is farthest away from friction-producing rock surfaces. Unless there is significant breakdown on the floor, the combination of gravity acting on the water and the smoothness of the layer of silt on the floor will usually make flow fairly strong there as well. The diver will usually find that flow is weakest near the ceiling or walls, especially when there are irregular rock projections which disrupt the smooth flow of water.

Flow has advantages as well as disadvantages. Current is similar to wind. It can produce the effects of a "tailwind" or a "headwind." Whenever the flow pushes the diver toward the point of exit from the cave system, it increases the safety of the dive (all other things being equal). Likewise, whenever the flow pushes the diver away from the point of exit from the cave system, it decreases the safety of the dive.

Syphons should be approached with caution. Even a moderate syphon can greatly increase air consumption during the exit. Special air-supply planning is required to dive syphons with safety. The Thirds Rule is seriously inadequate for such situations.

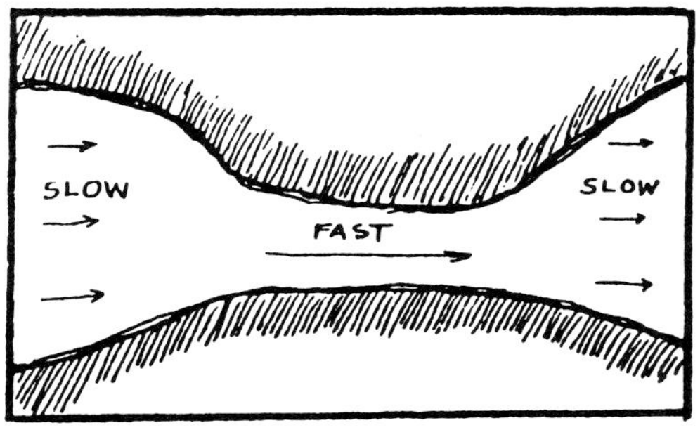

Figure 8-4

In some systems, the flow can reverse. These systems can have seasonal or daily reversals. Ocean blue holes have fierce reversing tidal flows where the diver must time a lengthy penetration around the slack period at the end of low tide. The divers enter with the last remnants of the tidal influx and exit with the outflow. To safely execute such a dive, the divers must know exactly when the flow reverses; otherwise, they risk having to exit against what can be a formidable syphon. Local tide charts are not specific enough for cave diving purposes; reversal can be as much as four hours off local surface tides. There can even be a significant difference between the cave system's tides and the surface water directly above it!

In large passages or in small tunnels with only very slight current it is sometimes difficult to detect the direction of flow. One way to determine flow is to observe the movement of suspended particulate matter.

While it is always important to avoid stirring up silt for both conservation and safety reasons, it is critical in systems or areas where there is very little or no flow at all. In stagnant areas it can take weeks for some kinds of fine clay or organic silt to settle. Very fine particles, which would ordinarily be carried along by even slight flow, can accumulate on all the cave surfaces. The silt on the floor can be several feet thick and so light and fine that the diver may not even be aware of touching it. If a cave diver accidentally silts-out a passage, the situation can sometimes be handled more easily if the divers are mentally prepared, and have an adequate air supply, to wait for the suspended particles to settle. But this is not effective in locations where there is no flow and where the "silt" is composed of clay or fine organic particles.

Size and Configuration — Large cave passages offer several advantages for swimming techniques. The flow is usually less than in smaller portions of the tunnel. Divers can stay well above the floor, use more efficient swimming strokes, swim side by side, turn around and communicate more readily, and more easily render buddy assistance or share air.

There are also negative aspects to large passages. The diver should usually try to avoid the full force of the current by staying near one side of the tunnel or the ceiling or the floor, and to maintain line orientation. This may be impractical in large chambers. In extremely large chambers disorientation can occur if walls are dark or primary lights cannot otherwise penetrate to a cave surface.

Small passages generally require much more skill and experience. The diver is forced to swim closer to the floor and his choice of propulsion techniques is more limited. Silt avoidance is often a primary concern in small passageways. Turning around, communicating, and assisting a buddy are, of course, more difficult under such conditions. However, the diver is usually close to a wall or ceiling. If these are hard surfaces, they can be used for pulling or pushing, and for directional orientation.

When a passageway narrows, flow becomes stronger. Cave divers sometimes carry drop-weights to combat the force of flow welling up out of a restricted vertical chimney. The weights are left at the bottom of the chimney so that the diver has normal buoyancy for the rest of the dive, then retrieved on the way out. As flow increases towards the point of becoming unmanageable, the mere force of the current decreases safety dramatically, independent of the current's direction. Drop weights used in such situations should be attached to the diver, and carried well past the point where they are needed. This prevents the diver from becoming accidentally swept into the current and pinned against a wall or ceiling. Use of helmets may also be appropriate in such circumstances.

Drop weights are also carried to assist in maintaining depth during decompression. They may be used to offset the increasing positive buoyancy which occurs near the end of a dive as the air bottles are emptied. Some drysuit divers use them to permit greater inflation of the drysuit during decompression, allowing for greater warmth.

In horizontal passages with significant flow (or where negative buoyancy is insufficient to combat flow in a vertical chimney), swimming, pulling, or kicking techniques have to be used. If the passage is narrow enough, divers can straddle or brace against the sides or floor and ceiling, and work their way forward. Fortunately, because of the high flow, silt is usually no more than a temporary problem. However, both conservation and safety must be given high priority.

Silt — In some high flow systems, there are sections of the cave where the passages are completely free of all silt except for large, heavy sand particles which settle out almost immediately. This gives the diver the option of pulling and kicking, or even becoming negative and crawling along the bottom on his elbows and knees if necessary, without fear of causing a silt-out or damaging ancient silt formations. If the silt is light and fine, but the flow is still heavy, any silt that is inadvertently stirred up will be swept out of the cave fairly quickly. However, this is hardly a license for careless silt technique. Not only does it impact the cave, but other divers may be in the system, too. The original team might even find itself having to swim back out through the silt cloud.

When silt is thick and fine, and flow very moderate or nonexistent, the silt that is stirred up usually will not have time to settle out or be swept out of the cave before the divers exit the cave. The conservation- and safety-conscious cave diver should glance back occasionally (even when swimming in moderately large tunnels) to check on silt and percolation. This is especially important in small tunnels where even a single careless fin stroke can drastically reduce visibility. Small, silty tunnels should be avoided by novices until they have perfected their silt technique and are comfortable in zero-visibility conditions. If the diver feels that the cave conditions exceed his level of competence, he is wise to turn the dive.

In low tunnels with silt floors, even experienced cave divers must move slowly. Should the diver miscalculate his buoyancy and find himself plunging down into the silt, it is probably best to make no swimming movements at all. It is usually best to inflate the BC and wait for positive buoyancy. Most likely, less silt will be stirred up by landing in it than if the diver attempted to swim upward. When possible, though, the diver should try to arrest his descent. If contact with the cave floor is unavoidable, the diver should try to minimize damage and silting by landing on only a single hand.

When a diver finds himself in this situation, he should immediately begin inflating his BC. He should continue holding the power inflator/deflator mechanism and continue inflating the BC until he either begins to rise in the water column or contacts the cave floor. The object is to ***quickly over-compensate*** for the negative buoyancy with somewhat ***excessive positive buoyancy***. Thus the diver needs to be ready to gradually deflate the BC to a neutral state as he rises away from the floor. When contact with the floor is likely, the diver should place his arm and hand so that he can land on one or two fingers. (This will not be possible if he is oriented vertically with feet down, or if he has "turtled" into a face-up, tanks-down position. In either of these cases, he should remain as still as possible, allowing himself to land as gracefully as possible under the circumstances.) When landing on the fingers, the diver should allow them to sink into the silt until downward motion stops, then simply keep balanced on them while ***gradually*** inflating the BC as described above.

Delicate Formations — Many of the most beautiful formations found in submerged caves took thousands of years to develop. Stalagmites and stalactites which are broken cannot regenerate themselves. Once broken, they are broken forever. Nothing is as heart-rending in an underwater cave as seeing rubble piles of speleothems caused by divers who are thoughtless or who have exceeded their skill level. But decorated caves are by no means the only ones susceptible to diver damage. Rock and silt are also an important part of a cave's legacy. Occasionally, porous limestone projections will break off if kicked or pulled on too roughly (an important consideration when tying off line). Even the ceilings, walls, and floors can be permanently scarred if they are composed of packed clay. The diver should try to avoid swimming techniques which damage the cave whenever possible, even if it means moving more slowly and carefully and not being able to penetrate as far into the cave.

Depth — Fortunately, swimming near the top of a tunnel not only keeps the diver as faraway from silt on the floor as possible and usually out of the strongest part of the current, it also minimizes depth, and thus minimizes air consumption and decompression requirements. This is particularly important in deep caves. Excessive exertion should also be avoided, especially at excessive depth, because of the accelerating effect on inert gas absorption. The diver should try to move with as little exertion as possible, stabilizing himself against the cave in order to rest when necessary. It is commonly said that cave divers are only "one breath away from death." It might be advisable to give some consideration to the length of that breath. Trying to swim against a heavy current at extreme depths should probably be avoided altogether.

PROPULSION TECHNIQUES

Swimming Techniques — for movement through large passages or where silt is not otherwise a factor.

Frog Kick — The diver is trimmed horizontally, in a face-down position. He begins the stroke with both legs straight, then draws each leg outward with knee bent in a plane horizontal to his body, then snaps his legs back together straight. The fin blast is directly behind the diver. However, because of the power of the stroke, silting can occur if it is performed too close to the floor (See Fig. 8-5).

Flutter Kick — Swimming horizontally, face-down, the diver moves one leg up and the other down, then alternates. The wake turbulence angles upward and downward as well as straight behind the diver, and can disturb silt as much as 8-12 feet away. For this reason the horizontal flutter kick should be used only in large or siltless tunnels (See Fig. 8-6).

For a change of pace, the flutter kick can also be performed with the diver swimming with level trim, but with the body rotated 90° on the longitudinal axis. Fin turbulence is directed in a horizontal plane behind the

Figure 8-6

diver, as with the frog kick. The flutter kick can even be performed with the diver swimming upside down. For example, when it's necessary to swim underneath a line which is up on the ceiling (See Fig. 8-7).

Dolphin Kick — The diver is trimmed horizontally and swims face down. The legs are held together, and bend and flagellate like a big tail. The entire body tends to oscillate up and down. This is a powerful stroke and is good as a change of pace, but because of the enormous downstroke blast, should only be used in very large passages where there is no chance of disturbing the bottom.

Swimming Techniques — for movement through moderate-sized passages with silt floors.

Modified Flutter Kick — This technique is probably one of the most commonly used in cave diving. The diver swims with horizontal trim, with knees bent and held rigidly in place. Only the ankles move. Fin move-

Figure 8-5

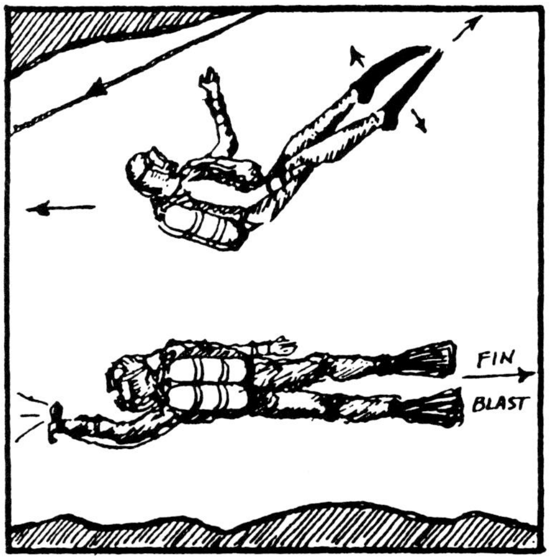

Figure 8-7

Figure 8-8

ment is so restricted that the turbulence is directed behind the diver or slightly upward (See Fig. 8-8).

Modified Frog Kick — Same as the modified flutter kick except the fin movement is side to side. This is also very effective in controlling silt. However, the stroke is wider than the modified flutter kick, so extreme care should be exercised when swimming through heavily decorated areas.

Shuffle Kick — A flutter or modified flutter kick is done with the bottom leg stationary below the kicking leg so as to deflect the fin wash. This is a slow stroke, but fairly effective for controlling silt (See Fig. 8-9).

Shoveling or Scooping — In a heavy current where there are no good rock handholds on the floor, walls or ceilings, it is possible to make forward progress by pulling along the silt or (preferably) sand on the floor. One reaches out, digs one or both hands into the silt, and pulls himself forward. This obviously will stir up a lot of silt, but may be about the only practical way to move if the current is too strong to swim against. And of course, strong flow will tend to dissipate the disturbed silt, and heavy sand will quickly settle. This technique should only be used where it is clear that disturbing the silt or sand will not permanently alter this feature of the cave.

Pushoff Techniques — for passages with strong flow, or low ceilings and heavy silt.

Ceiling Pushoff — The diver makes himself slightly positive and moves forward by pushing against the ceiling with his heels, alternating feet. This can be combined with arm pulling techniques when handholds are available. Again, extreme discretion should be exercised when contemplating this technique if there is any risk of damaging the ceiling (See Fig. 8-10).

Braking — When swimming against a current, slowing down is not usually a problem. However, when swimming with a strong flow, it is possible to lose control, especially in large tunnels. This could result in the diver exceeding safe ascent speed or even missing his decompression stops. The cave diver can brake himself by grabbing onto rock projections and avoiding the strongest portion of flow by staying close to walls and ceilings. If there is no silt, or if there is only heavy sand, the diver can get very negative and brake himself along the floor. If all else fails, the diver can actually turn around and swim against the current as he is being swept out.

Turning — In large passages the diver can turn easily while using normal swimming strokes by kicking harder with the leg opposite the desired direction of turn, making a few pulling swimming strokes with the arm opposite the direction of turn, or rolling and arching into the turn. This can usually be done without having to slow down.

In small tunnels, however, it is necessary to slow

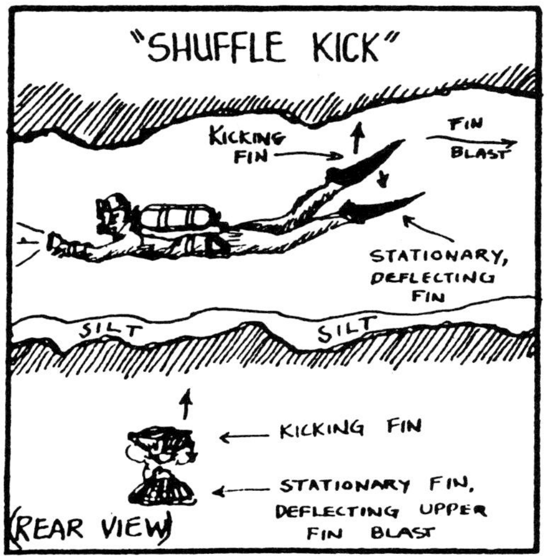

Figure 8-9

Figure 8-10

down in anticipation of a turn. If there are low ceilings and thick silt on the floor, the diver will probably already be going slowly. Additional turning movements must be made with extreme care in order to avoid silting. If the diver is close to his turn-around psi, it's generally better to turn the dive a few hundred psi early in a wider portion of tunnel, than to push ahead into a smaller tunnel where turning around is difficult.

In tight sections of the cave, tucking the legs up to form a tight ball and then pivoting with the hands is recommended. Some passages do not permit turning around, however, and the diver is essentially committed to proceeding forward until he reaches a wider spot, or trying to back out. In addition to not being able to see in the direction of travel (and probably being silted out as well), the diver's tanks may function like a spear barb or ratchet cam so that he cannot force the tanks backwards because of an irregularity in the ceiling. The diver will most likely have both arms out in front for crawling and pulling purposes, and may not be able to reach behind to maneuver the tanks down.

It is for this reason that some exploratory cave divers prefer ***worming*** in new, tight tunnels — that is, going feet first. This is especially wise in a restricted vertical passage, where the diver could find himself having to struggle back through a restriction upside down. Needless to say, small tunnels and restrictions require excellent technique, experience, and good judgment.

Stopping and Hovering — The ability to stop and hover motionless in the water is largely dependent upon good trim and buoyancy. If at all negatively bouyant or feet-heavy, the diver will usually have to engage in continuous little sculling or finning motions in order to maintain his equilibrium. These are frequently done unconsciously once the diver has stopped in order to perform some engaging task. It is particularly dangerous if the diver tends to be trimmed feet-heavy so that he naturally gravitates to a vertical position when at rest. In this position, even the slightest bit of fin movement can stir up devastating clouds of silt.

There are several different techniques for stopping, to be used depending on cave configuration and task requirements. Inducing positive buoyancy and resting against the ceiling is very effective, if the ceiling is fairly close at hand and is composed of fairly hard rock. Holding onto a wall projection with neutral or slightly positive buoyancy is also good, although it only leaves one hand free. Sometimes becoming negative and settling on the floor of the cave is effective, if the silt is fairly firm and coarse-grained and unlikely to be damaged. Another technique is to position one's body with head-down trim with either neutral or slightly negative buoyancy, and then stabilize with one hand on the floor, preferably on an outcropping of rock if any are available.

If there are no cave surfaces suitable for bracing or balancing, the diver should assume a neutrally buoyant, level attitude, with knees bent and fins well above the floor. This may be very difficult to maintain because of rolling or pitching tendencies inherent in the diver's trim. Slight adjustments can be made by moving the arms front or back to shift the center of gravity, or spreading the legs apart.

Figure 8-11

CONCLUSION

The above techniques require good trim and buoyancy control, body positioning, and above all, practice. Remember that every open-water dive is an opportunity to practice cave-diving techniques. Large cave tunnels with good flow and visibility conditions provide excellent opportunities to practice more advanced skills and experiment with new techniques. As with most other cave-diving skills, over-learning is one of the best ways to insure proficiency, especially in an emergency.

The cave diver must have constant ***conscious*** awareness of body positioning and propulsion techniques in order to keep cave damage and silting to a minimum, and to maximize safety and efficiency. Proper attention to swimming techniques can make all the difference between an enjoyable, productive dive and a disaster.

Chapter 9

BUOYANCY CONTROL, BODY POSITIONING AND PROPULSION

by Rory Dickens

This chapter investigates the techniques for controlling the buoyancy and body positioning (trim) while cave or cavern diving. Diving safely in caves requires that the cave diver control buoyancy and trim in a skilled manner. By understanding the basic theoretical concepts of buoyancy and trim, the cave diver can apply these concepts to her own diving. This understanding can lead to an increase in the cave diver's skill in controlling her diving system.

THEORETICAL CONCEPTS OF BUOYANCY

Any discussion of buoyancy must start with Archimedes' Principle: *a fluid exerts on an immersed body a buoyant force which is equal to the weight of the fluid originally occupying the boundary surface, and whose line of action passes through the original center of gravity of the displaced fluid.* In essence, when an object is totally submerged it displaces a "piece" of water that has the same shape as that of the

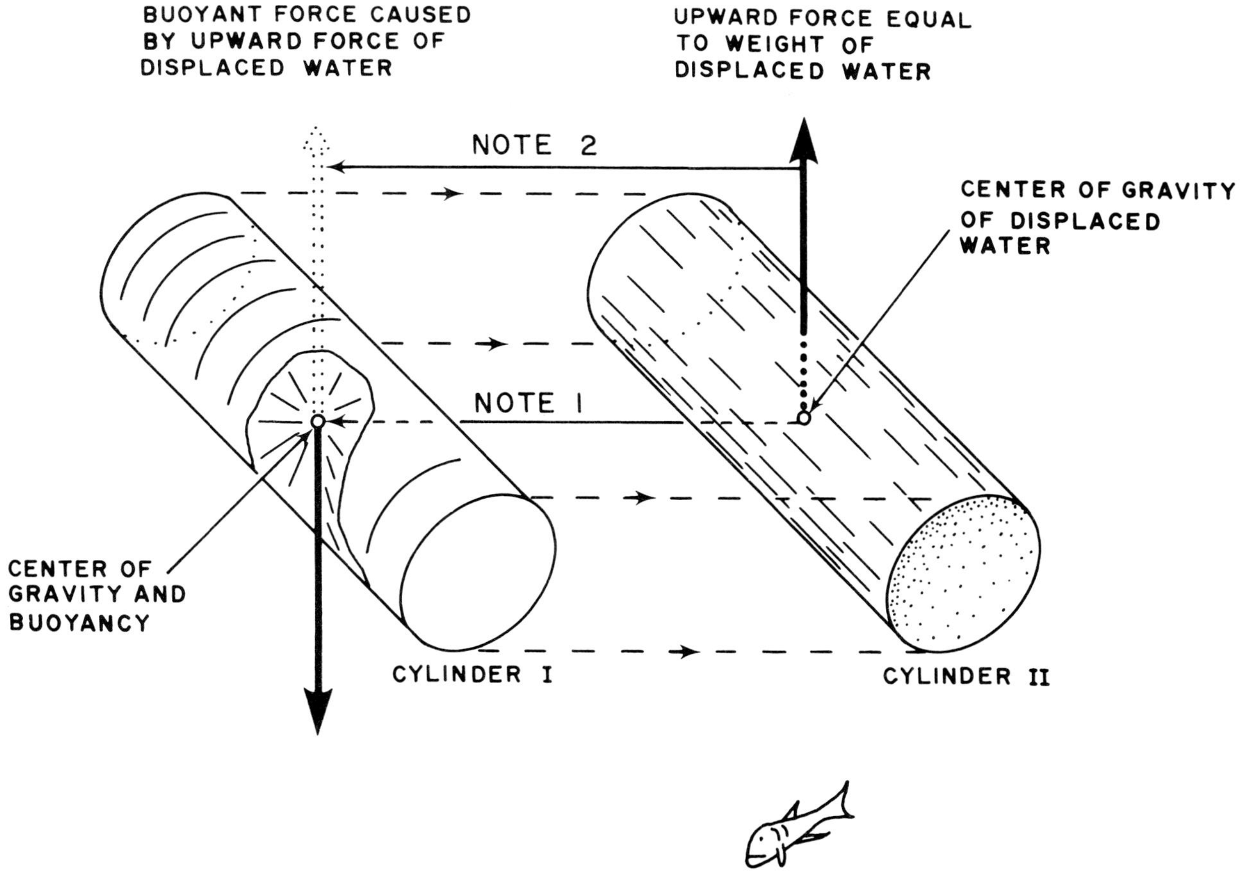

Figure 9-1

outer surface of the object being submerged. The buoyant force of Archimedes' Principle is equal to the weight of the "piece" of water and acts vertically upon the submerged object. Figure 9-1 illustrates this concept.

Two centers of gravity are involved; one related to the displaced fluid (piece of water) and the other related to the object. The *center of gravity* of the "piece of water" becomes the *center of buoyancy* of the object. Visualizing the displaced fluid as having the same shape as the submerged object, the point where the weight force acts on it is the same as the point where the buoyant force acts on the submerged object. Thus, the center of gravity of the displaced water represents the center of buoyancy of the submerged object.

Figure 9-2A represents the end view (cross section) of a solid cylinder of uniform density, while Figure 9-2B represents a similar cylinder differing only in that it contains a cavity. When both cylinders are totally immersed in water they will displace the same volume of water and will, as a result, experience the same buoyant force.

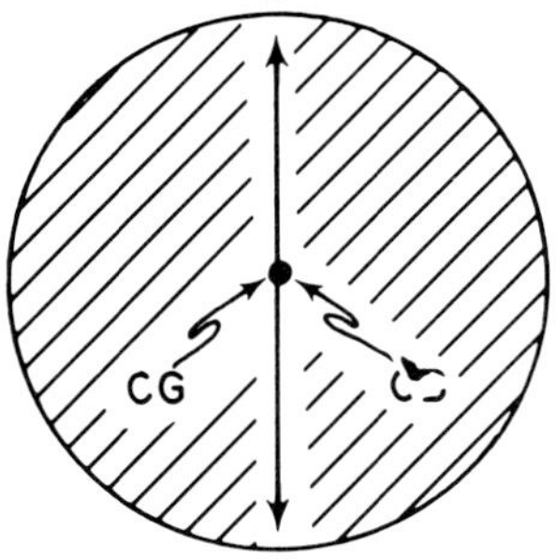

Figure 9-2A

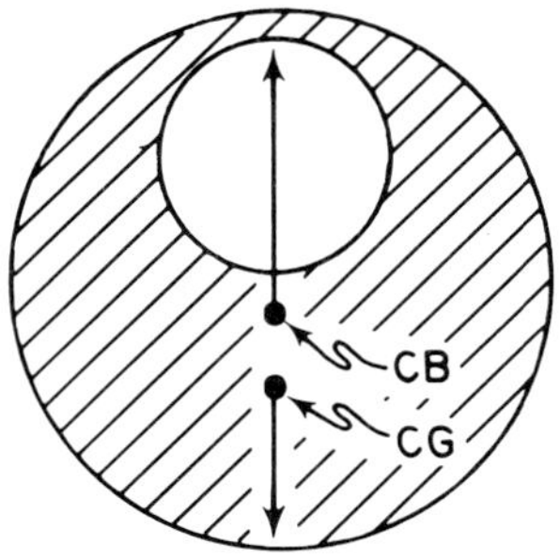

Figure 9-2B

Figure 9-2A shows that the solid cylinder has its center of gravity (CG) and center of buoyancy (CB) at the same point: the center of the cylinder. The cylinder containing the cavity (Figure 9-2B) is in a different condition. The center of buoyancy is still at the center of the cylinder, but the center of gravity is now below the center of the buoyancy.

In effect, only a body of uniform density will have a center of gravity and a center of buoyancy at the same point. A cave diver, equipped with heavy tanks and a buoyancy compensator, is not of uniform density and will be in a buoyancy situation more closely depicted by Figure 9-2B than that of Figure 9-2A. By inverting the hollow cylinder depicted in Figure 9-2B, a situation is generated as illustrated in Figure 9-3A. This is a more realistic model for the cave diver's state when totally submerged. The object described in Figure 9-3A is in a state of unstable equilibrium. If this object is rotated either slightly clockwise or counterclockwise, a force couple is created and the object will rotate to a state shown in Figure 9-2B, which is a condition of stable equilibrium.

Figure 9-3B shows a view of a diver along the diver's longitudinal axis. The human body has a relatively uniform density when viewed along the longitudinal axis, with the weight equally distributed on either side of the axis. In this condition the diver is best described by Figure 9-2A, where the center of gravity and center of buoyancy are at the same point. Here the diver's body will be in a state of neutral equilibrium.

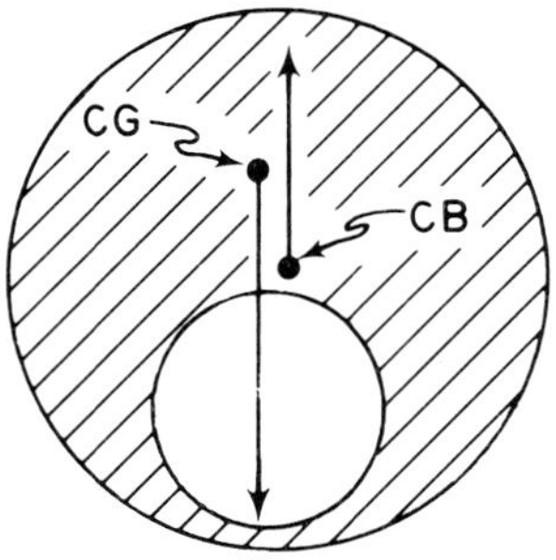

Figure 9-3A

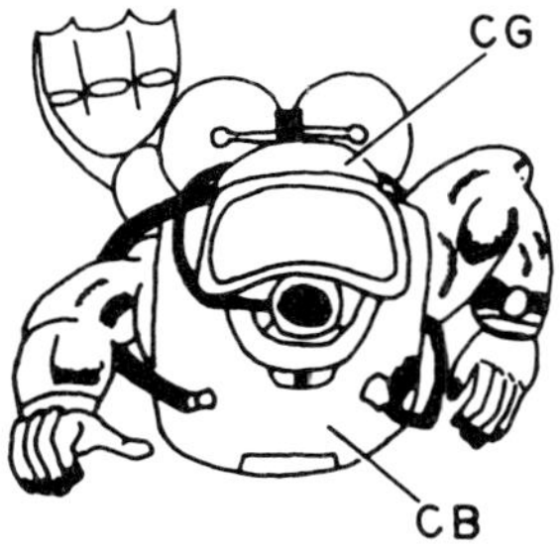

Figure 9-3B

The diver's body, the massive tanks on top of the diver and the air compartment of the buoyancy compensator beneath the diver constitutes the diving system. The addition of tanks and compensator causes a loss in the longitudinal symmetry that was enjoyed by the diver's body alone.

If the buoyancy compensator is worn on the chest, the center of buoyancy of the newly created diving system will remain in about the same place relative to the diver's longitudinal axis. However, the center of gravity will experience an upward shift, resulting in a state of unstable equilibrium similar to the object shown in Figure 3A. If the diver starts to roll to either side, the resulting force couple will tend to continue to roll her to an inverted position as depicted in Figure 9-2B. The cave diver will wind up in a state of stable equilibrium, but unfortunately she will be upside down.

If the buoyancy compensator is worn on top of the tanks, it will create a state of stable equilibrium around the longitudinal axis, and if the diver rolls, the force couple will tend to bring her back to an upright position.

Ideally, a cave diver wants a state of neutral equilibrium around her longitudinal axis, as she might desire to swim on her side or in an inverted position. In such a situation the center of gravity and the center of buoyancy would both lie on the longitudinal axis and no force couples would be generated when the diver rotates around this axis.

If a diver is not in a state of neutral equilibrium

around her longitudinal axis, she must exert some effort to overcome the force couples in order to swim in any position other than upright. This effort would detract from the propulsion effort. A cave diver has a certain amount of total effort available based on her breathing rate. The more of this available effort that is used to maintain body position, the less there is available for propulsion.

One method to achieve neutral equilibrium is to add lead weights at the waist below the compensator vest until the center of gravity lowers to the center of buoyancy. One disadvantage of this technique is that the compensator vest must be further inflated to account for the additional weight. This will cause an increase in drag which in turn requires the cave diver to increase the propulsion effort to cover the same distance.

The cave diver could also achieve neutral equilibrium by bringing the tanks as close to her back as possible, and at the same time, using a buoyancy chamber on top of the tanks. Such a chamber would be separate from the diver's compensator, thus causing complications in buoyancy control. Neutral equilibrium usually has to be compromised with the requirements for buoyancy and trim control.

Every cave diver must consider the consequences of adding equipment. If weight is added to the right or left of the cave diver, the diver will have lateral separation (side to side) between her center of gravity and her center of buoyancy. This results in lateral instability, which will cause the cave diver to roll right or left. This instability can be eliminated by keeping the weight on both sides of the body equally distributed. For example, if a cave diver has two heavy backup lights, they should be placed on separate sides.

STATIC CONTROL OF BODY TRIM AND BUOYANCY

Figure 9-4 shows a cave diver from the perspective of the diver's lateral axis (across the shoulders). It is around this axis that the cave diver controls trim. Assuming that a cave diver is motionless in the water, if her center of gravity is either forward or aft of the center of buoyancy, a force couple is introduced and the cave diver will either trim head down or head up. The degree of this attitude will depend on the distance the center of gravity and the center of buoyancy are separated. A distance of only a few inches can cause a diver to trim out in a vertical position (which is especially embarrassing when this position is head down). Equilibrium cannot be established until the force couple disappears. Thus, a cave diver must achieve stability control around both the longitudinal and lateral axes (right and left roll and head pitch up and pitch down).

In Figure 9-4 the center of gravity (CG) is shown aft of the center of buoyancy (CB). In this situation the force couple will cause the cave diver to rotate into a head up position. Such a position is usually desirable for an open-water diver but not for a cave diver. In Figure 9-5 the cave diver's center of gravity is shown as forward of the center of buoyancy. The cave diver, as depicted in this diagram, will rotate in a clockwise direction into a head down trim position. For a cave diver this is usually a more desirable position, because it allows her to keep her fins away from the silt on the floor of a cave. Because this position is more desirable for cave diving, a weight belt should be avoided. A weight belt will cause the cave diver's center of gravity to move aft of her center of buoyancy and into a head up trim position. Because most cave divers wear exposure suits, they have to add some weight to their diving systems. The specific methods of adding such weight is discussed later in this chapter.

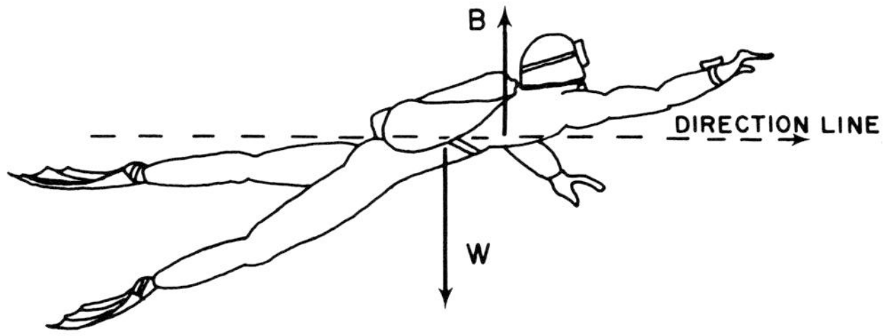

Figure 9-4

The diver's buoyancy and, to some extent, the location of her center of buoyancy, is controlled by an air container referred to as a *buoyancy control device* or a *buoyancy control system.* These devices can be broadly categorized as fixed volume and variable volume. Most scuba compensator devices will be of the variable volume type. A submarine is an example of a fixed volume compensator. To change the buoyancy of a submarine, air (at ambient pressure) is blown into and released from rigid chambers, causing the submarine's buoyancy to increase and decrease respectively. The variable volume compensator also contains air at ambient pressure. The compensator's container must be flexible in order to change its volume as air is added and removed.

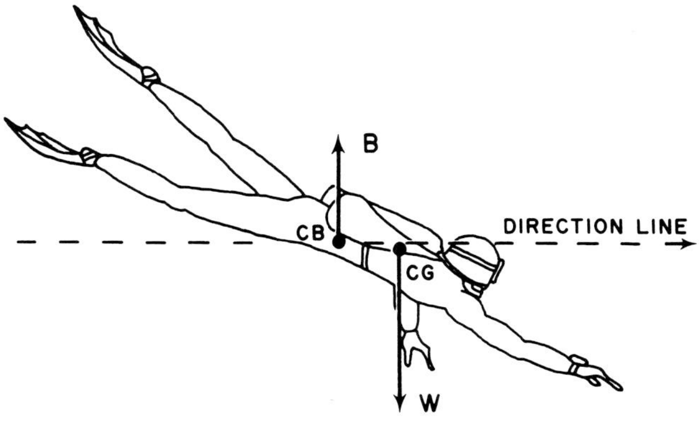

Figure 9-5

There are some characteristics that are common to all buoyancy compensator devices (BCD's). A compensator has an oral inflation/deflation tube, but in cave diving BCD's are filled by the injection of air from the first stage of the regulator. A compensator has an over pressure valve which prevents the bladder from bursting. A dump valve should be positioned on the BCD so that the diver can dump air when in a level or head down trim.

The greatest volume of the compensator is usually toward the bottom. This location of volume causes the center of buoyancy of a diver to be closer to her center of gravity. As a result, a diver has more control over her trim. Some BCD's have both the injector and dump valves on the end of the oral inflation tube. One problem with this arrangement is the possibility of pushing the wrong button because of their proximity. The inflation of the compensator at a time when deflation is expected (or vice versa) can place a cave diver in an embarrassing position. A safer arrangement is the separation of the two controls, which many BCD's have.

In most diving situations the compensator is not kept completely full. When not completely inflated, air can move along the length of the BCD as a diver changes position; this movement of air will cause the cave diver's center of buoyancy to change. If a diver's weight is properly distributed, she can take advantage of this feature to alter her static trim state. By assuming a head down attitude, the air will move to the bottom of the compensator. In turn, the center of buoyancy will move behind the center of gravity, causing a head down trim. Conversely, when the diver assumes a head up state of trim, the air will move to the top of the BCD, and a head up trim state will be maintained.

There is one situation where this property can cause a diver considerable difficulty. On a dive along an uphill, silty tunnel, a diver is forced into a head up trim position. The movement of air to the top of the compensator may force the diver's fins into the silt. This is one example of the considerations that go into a cave diver's choice of compensator and the necessity of coping with any negative aspects of the buoyancy control system.

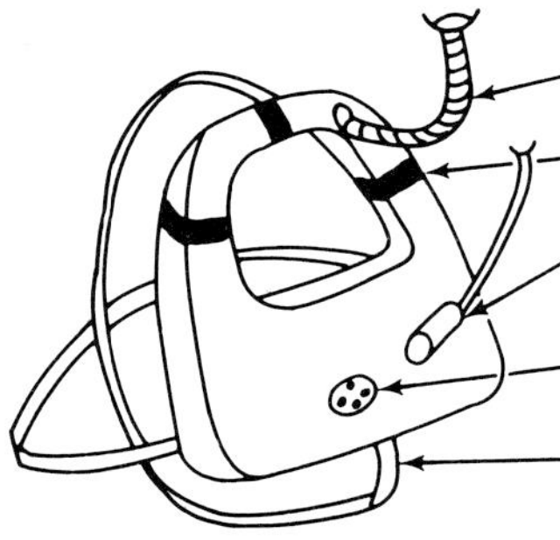

Figure 9-6A

TYPES OF COMPENSATION DEVICES

The Compensator Vest, also known as the horse-collar or front-mounted BCD, was one of the original compensator devices manufactured in the United States. Before the advent of this compensator, cave divers in Northern Florida were using, with some degree of success, plastic jugs as compensators. Figure 9-6A illustrates a compensator vest, and it shows items that are common to most compensator devices. Some cave divers restrict the neck of the compensator vest with tape, as this causes the center of buoyancy of the compensator to move down.

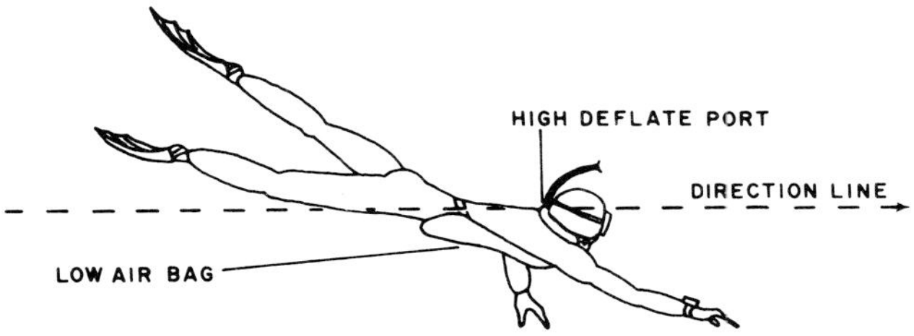

Figure 9-6B

In the early years of cave diving this BCD was considered by many cave divers as the only acceptable type to use for cave diving, and it probably was the most suitable compensator available for cave diving at the time. However, there are presently many different types of compensators on the market that are suitable for cave diving, and the compensator vest is used infrequently by today's cave diver.

Figure 9-6B illustrates a side view of the compensator vest on a cave diver who is trimmed head down. From this diagram one of the principal advantages of the compensator vest can be identified. The collar of the compensator turns up over the neck of the cave diver. One rule that applies to all BCD's is that "any air that is above the dump valve cannot be dumped through that valve." If the dump valve is placed at the top of the collar, the upturn of the collar places it above the main air volume, even when the diver has a head down trim state (Figure 9-6B). Because of this configuration, the diver is able to dump air from this BCD even in a state of head down trim. This feature seems to be unique to the vest-type compensator.

In addition to the advantage of dumping air in a head down trim, this BCD offers the cave diver excellent control of trim and buoyancy and is usually the least expensive type of compensator. There are, however, disadvantages to using it, which are listed below.

1) A cave diver is lying on a bag of air when using the compensator vest, causing her to be in a state of unstable equilibrium as shown in Figures 9-3A and 9-3B.

2) A cave diver is compressed between the compensator and her tanks, which can restrict breathing.

3) A compensator vest requires a complicated arrangement of straps for attachment to the cave diver's body. The combination of the BCD straps and tank straps create an array of straps encircling the user that can be uncomfortable and restrictive.

4) The air chamber of a compensator vest creates bulk directly in front of the cave diver's chest, thereby restricting chest expansion during inhalation and movement.

The back-mounted compensator (or wings) is a U-shaped container that wraps around the tank; it is placed between the tanks and the diver's back. Figure 9-7A illustrates a back-mounted compensator. The neck volume of the bag is usually small in order to keep the center of buoyancy as far aft as possible. At present, the back-mounted BCD is the buoyancy control device preferred by many cave divers. Its advantages and disadvantages are spelled out as follows.

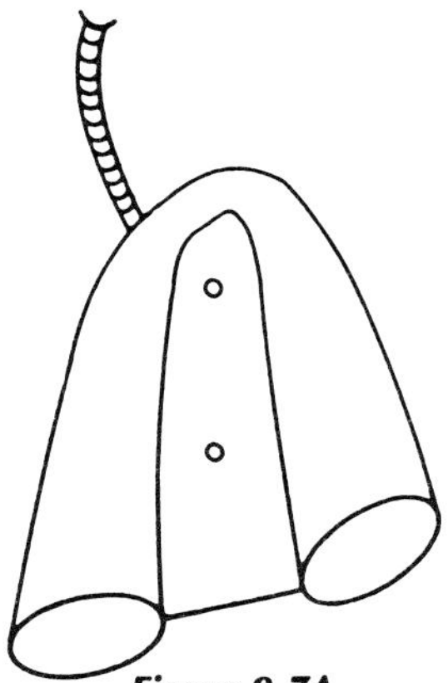

Figure 9-7A

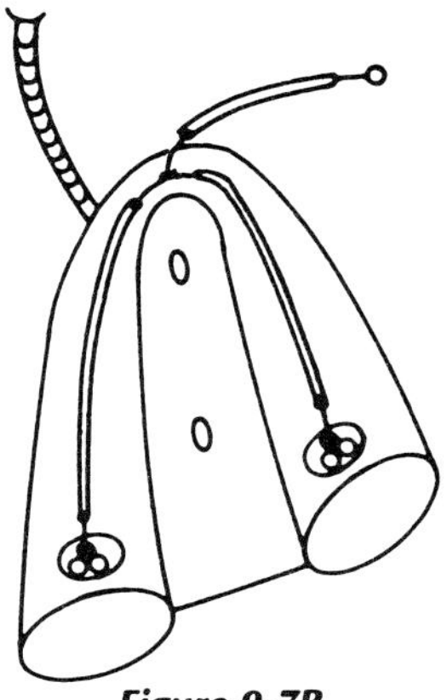

Figure 9-7B

Advantages

1) The compensator can be integrated into the backpack, thus reducing the number of straps needed for the diving system.

2) A cave diver's movements are less restricted with an air bag over the back.

3) A diver hangs "suspended" from the compensator and is not compressed between the tanks and air bag.

4) A diver is in a state of stable equilibrium around her longitudinal axis. When relaxed, the diver tends to rotate into a vertical position. (In some cave diving situations this could be a disadvantage.)

Disadvantages

1) When trimmed head down, a cave diver must roll to the side to dump air from the BCD. This could be avoided if dump valves were mounted on each side of the top/rear of the bag. (See Figure 9-7B).

2) When in a state of head down trim the bag does not always fill equally on both sides.

3) The oral inflation tube can be difficult to locate, as its point of connection to the BCD is above and behind the diver's shoulders. (See pages 47-48 for the description of a technique to overcome this problem.)

4) The BCD is out of the diver's reach. If a cave diver experienced runaway auto inflation, she could be pinned to the ceiling of a cave. It might be difficult for the diver to deflate it without assistance.

The compensator Jacket is illustrated in Figure 9-8. It is constructed similarly to a sleeveless coat, and it is donned and worn very much like a coat. The jacket has a small volume neck, and the greatest air volume is carried in the sides of the device. Some of these BCD's have air chambers on the back as well as the sides. This BCD places the air under and behind the diver's arms. The compensator jacket has some of the desirable features of both the compensator vest and the back-mounted compensator. Correspondingly, it has some of the disadvantages of both.

The compensator jacket is probably the easiest of the three BCD's to don. It can be made into an integrated tank-compensator-backpack system. By attaching accessory items such as lights, reels, etc. to *D-rings* on the tanks and jacket, a cave diver can don her entire cave diving system like a coat. Any diver who has worn a drysuit on a hot day can appreciate the advantages of this system. This system allows for a very short interval between donning the drysuit and entering the water; as a result, the cave diver is less likely to become overheated. When using a dry suit, the BCD and its accessory hoses need to be configured in such a way that the diver has easy access to all dry suit valves. Generally speaking, horse collar and standard jacket-style BCD's do not permit this. Back-mounted wings and ADV-style jackets seem to be preferred by dry suit divers for this important safety reason. Remember to consider this whenever outfitting yourself for drysuit diving.

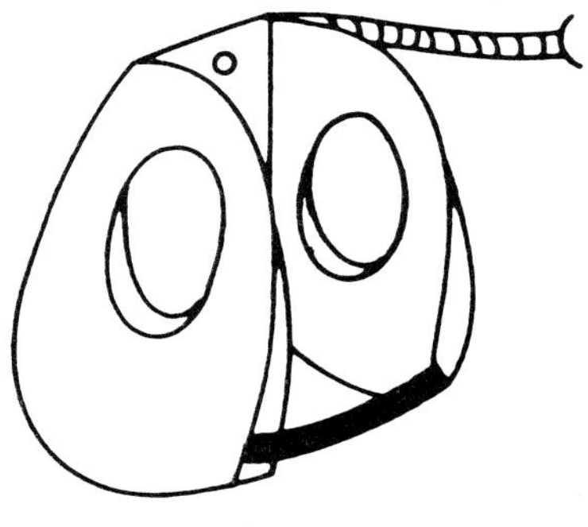

Figure 9-8

The compensator jacket inflator hose can be very accessible, depending on the manufacturer. When in a head down position, a diver may have to roll, but not to the extent required by a back-mounted BCD. A compensator jacket that has a dump valve at the top with a lanyard attached reduces the need for roll.

With the compensator jacket, the cave diver's chest is not as constricted as it is with the compensator vest. However, the diver does not have the degree of freedom of movement that a back-mounted BCD allows. The compensator jacket provides the greatest volume of air at its bottom, which creates favorable trim characteristics.

The compensator vest, the back-mounted compensator, and the compensator jacket are the three most common types of BCD's. Each type has its own set of

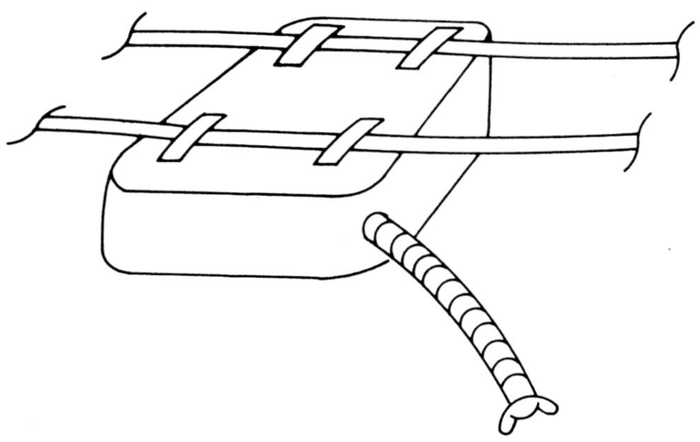

Figure 9-9

advantages and disadvantages. It is a matter of individual preference as to which BCD best suits a cave diver's needs. Often divers simply stay with the compensator they used when they learned to dive. Familiarity is an important factor in cave diving efficiency, although a diver should remain open to trying another buoyancy control system. This text does not suggest that one compensator type is superior to any other.

A *Belly Bag* is shown in Figure 9-9. Mounted on straps, it is located near a diver's center of gravity and provides precise control over trim, but leaves a diver in a state of unstable equilibrium. The additional straps and discomfort from air pushing up against the diver are the major drawbacks to the belly bag. This design is not particularly suited for open-water diving and they are produced on a limited basis by specialty cave diving manufacturers.

A drysuit, which can be used as a buoyancy compensator, is an accepted environmental protection system for cave diving. Even in warmer regions, many cave divers have converted to drysuits from wetsuits because of added comfort. The drysuit offers more than just additional comfort: it can also serve as a backup BCD. For cave diving purposes, if an inflation/deflation hose is being used, it should be mounted high on the shoulder of the suit.

The drysuit should not be used as a diver's primary compensator. It acts as an extremely long air compartment, and when a diver changes trim, air may move the full length of the suit. This movement of air can result in radical trim changes. In a head up trim attitude, air may pool in the neck region of the suit, causing discomfort for the diver. In a head down attitude, air movement to the legs may cause too much head down trim. Most cave divers insert only enough air in their drysuit to make it comfortable, and use their primary compensator for buoyancy control. However, for a diver using double 104's or other considerably negative gas supply system, compensator failure can be a serious incident and the backup provided by a drysuit could be a life saver.

STATIC CONTROL OF BUOYANCY AND BODY POSITIONING

A diver's state of buoyancy is determined by the density of her body and equipment in relation to the water in which she is immersed. A diver's goal is to have a buoyancy control system that can accomplish needed changes with ease, and gives the diver control of buoyancy throughout the entire dive. In order to have control of buoyancy from start to finish, several different factors must be understood.

In most cave diving situations, a cave diver wears an environmental suit to avoid prolonged exposure to the relatively cold underground water. Furthermore, divers usually experience depth changes of sufficient severity to cause the exposure suit to undergo different states of compression. During a prolonged cave dive with doubles, a diver can easily consume ten pounds of air. Continuous air consumption and changing depth while wearing an exposure suit will cause the diving system to experience many changes in buoyancy.

Changes in buoyancy also occur when a diver encounters water at different temperatures. Colder water is denser than warm water and causes a slightly greater buoyant force for the same volume of displacement.

A cave diver normally desires a state of neutral buoyancy, with a state of neutral equilibrium around the longitudinal axis and head down trim around the lateral axis. The equilibrium states of a diving system can be determined by the results of a diver shifting weight and the shape of the BCD. Static buoyancy is simply tested by a diver remaining motionless in the water. An important factor for cave diving is the capability of a diver to "get negative" under all conditions of the dive. In order to control buoyancy, a diver must be capable of negative buoyancy.

Most cave divers wearing double steel 104 cubic foot capacity tanks have little trouble remaining negatively buoyed, even when the tanks are near empty.

However, at the end of a dive the cave diver is least negative because of the depletion of air. *Drop weights* placed at a decompression stop ensure negative buoyancy during decompression. For divers using double aluminum tanks, a lead bar placed between the tanks and the backpack helps counterbalance their positive buoyancy, and helps to achieve a state of stable equilibrium around the longitudinal axis. Having the weight between the tanks is also much more desirable than on a belt around the waist.

Another useful test for a cave diver is the static trim check. After donning her complete cave diving system, the diver should go to depth and achieve neutral buoyancy. The diver then assumes a horizontal position and tries to remain motionless. Ideally, this position can be maintained without effort. However, in most cases the diver will find that she starts to assume a head up or head down trim. Preferably, the cave diver settles into a head down trim.

To adjust the trim state for a head down trim, weight should be moved forward and buoyancy volume moved aft. A three to five pound weight can be mounted to the top inside of a set of doubles; this will cause a large force couple that shifts the diver into a head down trim. Taping the neck of the BCD, as previously discussed, helps move buoyancy volume aft. A cave diver should consider the placement of air volume when purchasing a BCD.

After adjustments, a diver should be able to take up any body attitude without effort. Although this is an ideal state, through careful testing a cave diver can come reasonably close to this goal. Once equilibrium and trim are established, the diver need only be concerned with buoyancy during the dive. This can be easily controlled by injecting and exhausting air from the compensator. A properly functioning auto (power) inflator for the BCD is mandatory for safe cave diving.

DYNAMIC BUOYANCY CONTROL AND BODY POSITIONING

A diver must be able to control her buoyancy and body position while motionless and through changes in depth. A further consideration is control while swimming horizontally through the water.

In Figure 9-10, the cave diver is shown trimmed head down: in Figure 9-11, the diver is shown trimmed head up. In both situations the buoyant force ***B***, the weight force ***W***, and the drag force ***D*** act in the same direction regardless of the body attitude. This is not the case with the lift force ***L*** and the thrust force ***T***. The lift force, which is relatively small, will be upward if the angle of attack is positive (Figure 9-11), and downward if the angle of attack is negative (Figure 9-10). The magnitude of the lift force increases as the angle of attack increases, and when the angle of attack is zero (level trim), the lift force will be zero. The thrust force is a result of the action-reaction forces between the fins and the water. This force will normally be directed forward along the diver's longitudinal axis.

The thrust force can be broken into two components, one along the direction line and one along the vertical. Figure 9-12 illustrates the thrust force broken into its components when the angle of attack is negative (head down trim), and Figure 9-13 indicates the thrust force components for a positive angle of attack (head up trim).

In both situations, part of the thrust force acts along the direction line, and it is this component of thrust that propels the diver. When the angle of attack is negative, as shown in Figure 9-10, the vertical component of the thrust force will act down in the direction of the weight force. If the angle of attack is positive, as shown in Figure 9-11, the vertical component of the thrust force will act up in the direction of the buoyant force. Thrust force is totally directed into forward propulsion only when a diver's angle of attack is zero. The direction line should not be confused with the horizontal. The direction line is the direction the diver is moving through the water. If the buoyant force and the weight force are equal, the forces of the diver will be balanced and the diver will move in a direction opposite to the thrust force. As long as a diver is neutrally buoyant, her direction line will be in a direction opposite the thrust force and all thrust will be used for propulsion. Consequently, the most efficient way to move underwater is in a state of neutral buoyancy. Not only does the neutral state allow a diver to get the most use out of

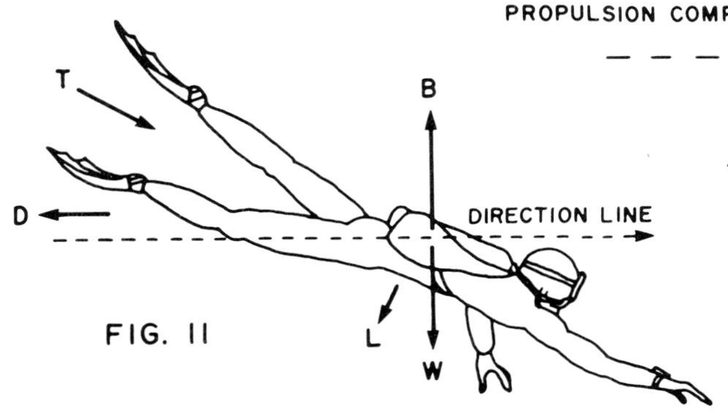

Figure 9-10

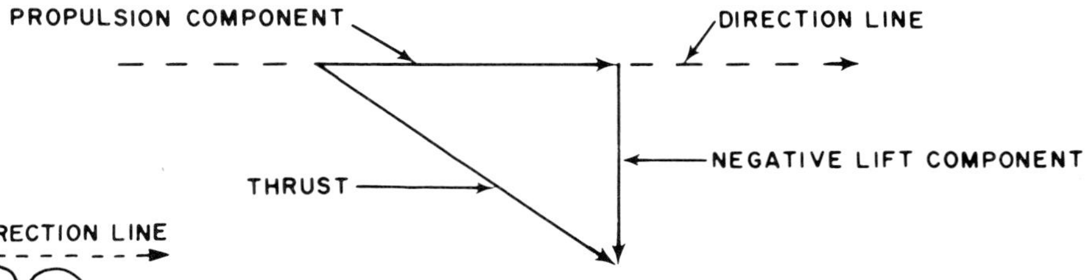

Figure 9-11

her propulsion effort, it also keeps the frontal area of the diving system at a minimum and reduces the drag force to a minimum.

The trim state of a motionless diver is a result of the relative positions of her center of gravity and center of buoyancy. When a diver is swimming, the situation is entirely different. As previously stated, a diver's buoyant force must equal her weight force in order to swim in a neutral trim state at a constant depth.

When a diver's buoyancy is less than her weight in the water, she must swim in a head-up position (trim) if she wants to maintain a constant depth. This happens because the smaller buoyant force will be overcome by the larger weight force, causing the diver to sink gradually, unless the thrust force contains an upward component to counter-balance the sinking force of weight. This upward component occurs only if the diver is in a head-up position, in which part of the thrust of her kick is directed upward. The diver drops her feet below the direction line while rotating her upper body above the direction line. The more negative the diver is weighted, the more vertical the diver must be positioned for counter-balancing her weight while in motion. This position diverts part of the diver's expended energy of propulsion to maintain constant depth. The over-weighted diver will use more air to cover a given distance. Normally, this is an undesirable condition for the cave diver.

Conversely, when a diver's buoyancy is greater than her weight in the water, she must swim in a head-down position if she wants to maintain a constant depth. In this case, the diver's positive buoyancy requires that the feet be above the direction line and the upper body below it in order to prevent her from gradually floating upward. This occurs because the larger buoyant force has to be countered by a downward component of the thrust force, a condition that exists only if the diver is moving horizontally in a state of head-down trim. This causes the same air consumption problems noted above. It is also an undesirable condition for the cave diver, as it tends to pin her to the ceiling. If the diver loses control of trim near the bottom of a vertical shaft, it can result in explosive "blow-up." This type of accidental loss of buoyancy control has been implicated as a causative factor in at least one cave diving fatality: Bill McFaden's death at Little Dismal Sink. (Inert gas narcosis has also been implicated in that accident.)

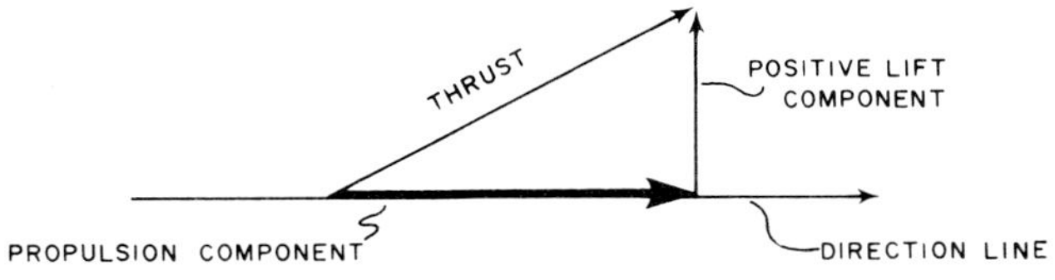

Figure 9-12

While underway, the relative positions of a diver's center of gravity and center ot mass have little effect on the trim state. Different sets of rules govern trim when a diver is motionless and when she is underway. A cave diver must take into account both of these conditions when making a cave dive.

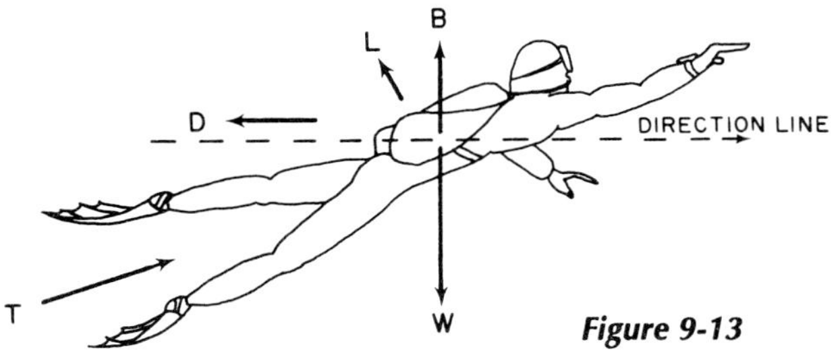

Figure 9-13

DIVER SPEED AND PENETRATION DISTANCE

The drag force is proportional to the frontal area of the diver, therefore air-distance ratio will increase as a diver decreases her frontal area. A second factor controlling drag force is a diver's speed through the water. The effect of speed on drag is often misunderstood by divers, but it is crucial to efficient use of energy. Two rules govern this effect:

1) At very low speeds, the drag force on a diver is proportional to the speed of the diver through the water.

2) As speed increases, the drag force becomes proportional to the square of the speed through the water.

At very low speeds, a doubling of the speed will only result in a doubling of the drag force. However, as the range of speed increases, a doubling of the speed will cause the drag force to increase by a factor of four. Divers are frequently in a transitional range between these two effects and need to understand the consequences of changing their speed.

The greatest portion of a diver's thrust force is used to overcome drag. Therefore, an increase in swimming speed by a factor of three will mean an increase in effort somewhere between three and nine times, depending on the speed at the start of the increase. Because air consumption is closely tied to effort, maximum speed will not result in maximum distance. There will be some swim speed between minimum and maximum effort at which the air-distance ratio is the greatest.

To illustrate, consider the two extremes of effort. If a cave diver remained motionless until all air was consumed, her air/distance ratio would be an unacceptable zero. On the other hand, if a diver swam at maximum effort, air would be rapidly consumed. Assuming the diver could sustain maximum effort for the entire swim, her air/distance ratio would be very low, because much of her effort would be wasted on overcoming the large drag force created by the high swim speed. Any anticipated gain in penetration distance from a higher swim speed would be negated by an unacceptably high air consumption rate. Figure 9-14 illustrates the relationship between air distance ratio and swim speed.

In addition, there are also physiologic limitations on efficiency as swimming speed increases. Skeletal muscles will continue to function when not fully supplied with oxygen. But as the length of time during which they are being inadequately oxygenated increases, an *oxygen debt* is being accumulated. The diver experiences this as gradually becoming "out of breath." Eventually, to repay this oxygen debt, the diver will have to slow the frequency of skeletal muscle contractions considerably, perhaps even stopping completely, to "catch her breath." This condition is familiar to most people through activities on the surface such as running or swimming. Underwater, the efficiency of respiration is decreased by at least two factors: immersion in water requires more energy simply to expand the chest to inhale; and the use of scuba gear further decreases respiratory efficiency. Both of these effects are increased significantly as the diver descends in the water column. This means that the oxygen debt is incurred more quickly and "paid off" more slowly when immersed. And the deeper you go, the higher the "interest rate" on your "oxygen debt" gets.

All cave divers can benefit from knowing what speed range is the most efficient for them on long distance horizontal swims. The actual speed will vary from one individual to another depending on swimming ability, physical conditioning, metabolic rate, etc. Divers can experiment to discover their optimum speed. One method would be to swim in full cave diving gear in a swimming pool at constant depth. Each run is timed over a measured distance equivalent to the distance normally covered by the diver. By using different speeds, the diver can obtain corresponding pairs of values for air/distance ratio and swim speed. The diver can then make a plot of air/distance ratio versus swimming speed (as in Figure 9-14) and determine her most efficient swim speed range.

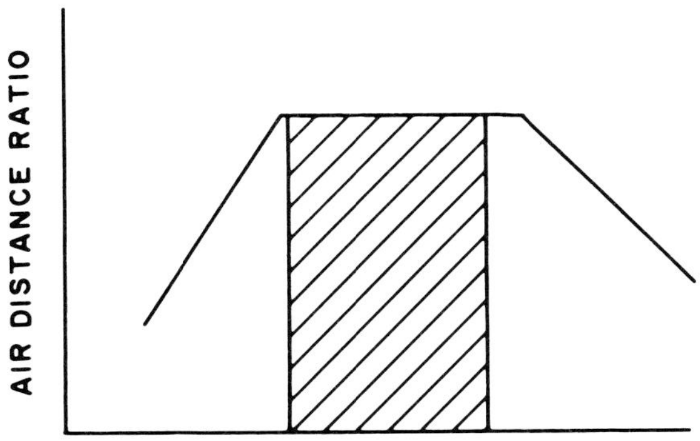

Figure 9-14

DIVER PROPULSION VEHICLES

The Diver Propulsion Vehicle (DPV) is now employed extensively in cave diving. The DPV should be trimmed slightly nose down and be from one to two pounds negative. The nose down trim allows a cave diver to use her own positive buoyancy and head down trim to keep the propeller thrust upward when in low areas. In very low areas, a diver can carefully heel kick (that is, walk on the ceiling using her heels but not part of her fin to contact the ceiling of the cave) if the DPV takes a nose down trim. This technique damages the cave, and should not be used routinely.

Proper trim for the DPV can be accomplished by the combination of adding weight and a buoyancy chamber to create a force couple that causes nose down trim and a slight negative buoyancy. A buoyancy chamber can also be used to offset torque, which is prevalent in some DPV's. The single-motor DPV tends to torque to the port side (left when facing forward). This can be countered by placing a buoyancy chamber on the left side of the DPV as shown in Figure 9-15 (which is a head-on view of a DPV).

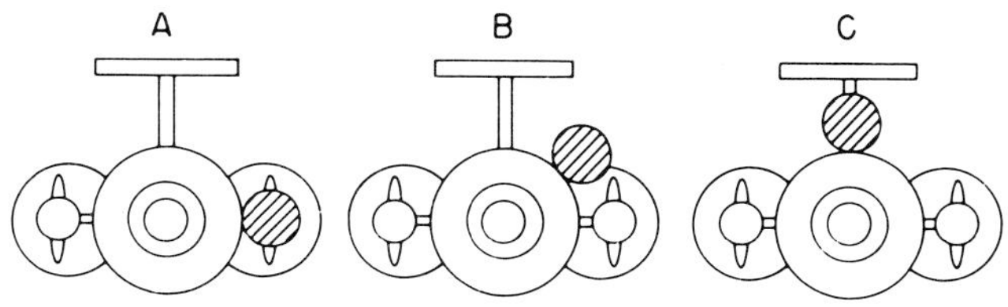

Figure 9-15

INDEX OF TERMS

Air/Distance Ratio: the distance traveled over a horizontal distance (usually measured in feet or meters) divided by the air consumed in psig. The value is normally determined from log book entries and corrected to the surface equivalent. This may be done using the following equation:

SA = (DA x atma)

Where:

SA represents the Surface Air consumption;

DA represents the Depth Air consumption; and

atma represents the pressure in *atmo*spheres aboslute for the depth at which DA was calulated.

For example, if you used 800 psig to cover 400 feet at a depth of 66 fsw, the value for DA would be 400/800 or 1/2 (0.5) foot per psig. Since the pressure at 66 fsw is 3.0 atma, SA would be (0.5 times 3), or 1.5 feet per psig. For dive planning of air consupmtion, the SA value can be converted to anticipated air consumption for another depth under similar diving conditions. This is done by dividing SA by atma for the new depth. The equation is:

DA = (SA / atma)

For example, if the same person as in the previous

example wishes to make a similar dive to 99 fsw, the value for DA will be 1.5 divided by 4, or 0.375 feet per psig using the same air supply system. If she begins her dive with 3000 psig and plans to limit penetration to 1000 psig, the diver can anticipate a maximum penetration of 1000 times 0.375, or 375 feet when CAS is reached.

Attitude: The position of the diver's longitudinal axis with respect to the direction line. It is a measure of the degree of head down or head up trim.

Buoyant Force: The upward force of displaced water on a submerged object.

Center of Gravity (CG): the point where the weight force appears to act on an object (related to the balance point of that object).

Direction Line: the direction of the path a diver is making through the water at any given time.

Drag: the force of resistance to the movement of a diver through the water.

Dynamic: refers to the diver when swimming or otherwise underway.

Force Couple: two forces acting along parallel lines but in opposite directions such that a twisting effect is caused on an object subjected to the force couple.

Lateral Axis: an imaginary line running through the center of buoyancy of a diver such that it is parallel to the diver's shoulders. It is around this axis that trim occurs. (See Figure 9-16)

Longitudinal Axis: an imaginary line that runs parallel to the spine of the diver and passes through the center of buoyancy (see Figure 9-16). This axis is parallel to the tank axis if the tanks are properly worn.

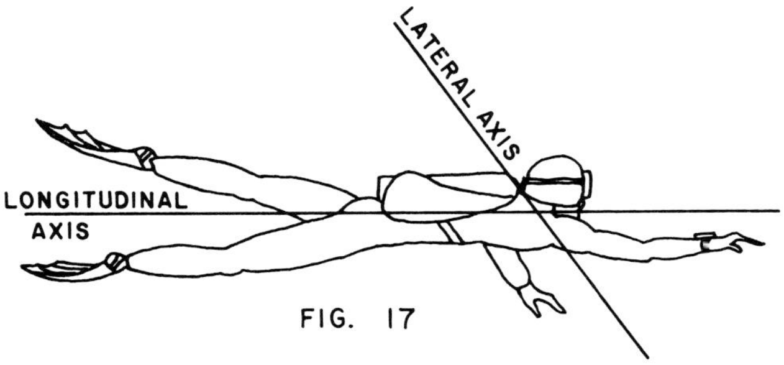

Figure 9-16

Neutral Equilibrium: the state of a body in water such that when it is moved by a disturbing force from an original position, the body will remain in its new position after the disturbing force is removed.

Stable Equilibrium: the state of a body in water such that when it is moved by a disturbing force from an original position, the body will return to its original position after the disturbing force is removed.

Static: refers to a diver who is not swimming or not otherwise underway.

Torque: a twist that tends to cause rotation that results from the application of a force couple.

Trim: the control of the angle of attack around the direction line (head up, level, and head down).

Unstable Equilibrium: the state of a body in water such that when it is moved by a disturbing force from its original position, the body will continue moving into a position of stable equilibrium after the disturbing force is removed.

Chapter 10

GUIDELINES

by Steve Gerrard

Always be sure of your exit! An understatement to be sure. Cave diving can appear ***deceptively easy***. Without proper training and experience, venturing into underwater caves is very hazardous and potentially fatal. For a cave diver without a guideline, or one who uses it improperly, the risk increases dramatically. One of the cardinal safety rules of safe cave diving is to have a continuous guideline.

The guideline is the cave diver's primary navigational tool. Cave passageways often form complex labyrinthine mazes that even the most experienced cave divers cannot keep track of using only mental referencing. Tunnel often looks different from the opposite direction of travel, and small side-tunnels which join the main passage at an acute angle can be overlooked easily.

Guidelines are used for a variety of purposes: permanent and temporary placement, gaps and jumps, survey, exploration, communication and safety. They vary in size, type and color. Careful procedures and proper application promotes a safe cave dive. No two caves are alike and each dictates its own specific needs and considerations. The use of the continuous guideline from the surface throughout the cave system ranks as one of the most important rules for the diver to successfully follow.

Figure 10-1 Typical nylon twine used for cave diving guidelines.

MATERIALS

The best guideline material to use underwater is nylon. It is synthetic, will resist deterioration and is, therefore, far superior to natural fibers such as cotton. Polypropylene is discouraged as it floats and can be difficult to manage underwater. Another type of guideline sometimes used is kernmantle, which is monofilament nylon that is sheathed in braided nylon. Usually much thicker and heavier, it is popular in high traffic underwater caves, sumps or systems with extreme conditions. Although durable, it is more difficult to handle, requires larger reels, and once nicked or cut, it can break.

TYPES

The two basic types of nylon guideline commonly used are *braided* (or *woven*) and *twisted* (or *laid*). Braided line is preferred because it maintains a higher degree of command and resilience, and it resists wear from rough surfaces and continuous use. Twisted lines are stronger, less expensive and easier to find at the local hardware store. Many explorers prefer to use twisted line, while tour guidelines are usually braided.

White is the most suitable color for guidelines. It stands out against the background in the wide diversity of caves. Yellow, orange, and red may be used if the cave is white or light colored. The development of a fluorescent guideline could well be the way for the future.

The size or diameter of the guideline is an important element. Too large or too small of a diameter affects the amount of line which can be wound on the reel, its placement, tautness, and controlability. Measurement is gauged either by fractions of an inch, or by a standardized cordage numbering system with examples ranging from 1/16" through 1/4" (#18—#36). Currently, the most popular size guideline is #18 or 1/16".

USE

In popular underwater cave systems, the permanent guideline is usually found far from the entrance making it difficult for the unqualified diver to find. It is essential for the cave diver to maintain a continuous guideline from outside the cave as this follows our No. 2 rule from Accident Analysis.[1]

Line placement begins with the initial tie-off starting outside the cave entrance in open water to enable a direct, unobstructed ascent to the surface. In conditions such as poor visibility, night or dusk, the cave diver may choose to place the initial tie-off at or near the surface. Exceptions to this may be dictated by current, other divers, or the cave itself.

The initial tie-off can be made on objects such as rock projections or the end of a branch or log. Most cave divers prefer to make a fixed loop, tied with a non-slip knot (such as a bowline or double granny) and large enough for the reel to be placed through, at the end of the guideline. A sturdy rock projection serves as the best tie-off point. The tie-off can be accomplished with efficiency and speed by taking the guideline through the fixed loop, forming another loop that is adjustable. Place this adjustable loop around the projection, snug the guideline around the projection, wrap at least twice and, pulling forward on the reel, snug the guideline into place. (It should not spin around the projection when pulled on if it has been properly secured.) Sometimes, a closed-end object such as a large log must be used. The tie-off in this case is done by pulling the single fixed loop around the log and then threading the reel through the fixed loop. Then proceed with two additional wraps of the reel if there is enough room to pass it around the log.

Line Placement — When installing a temporary guideline, a secondary tie-off serves as a back-up in case of unintentional or misguided tampering by other divers, poor initial tie-off, or the breakage of guideline due to normal wear. Exact placement of the secondary tie-off is decided by personal judgment, but it is usually a short distance inside the cave.

A basic rule for laying the guideline is always place it low so that you don't force the divers to pass underneath it. Swimming under a guideline is a sure recipe for entaglement of regulators or manifolds in the guideline. Place the guideline in the easiest, safest area of the cave passage and use the least number of tie-offs necessary so that you can have a more expedient exit. In the event of low visibility, each tie-off that must be negotiated by feel will slow the team's exit. If the low visibility is due to poor technique during an air-loss emergency with the team now sharing air, extra delays in the exit may result in injury or death. A taut line is also a must in case your exit depends on following the guideline by feel due to loss of visibility. Loose guideline is a nightmare and might get you or your team hurt.

Wherever the cave passageway turns, it is usually necessary to place a tie-off. Even in a long section of straight tunnel, periodic tie-offs must be placed to keep the line taut. Nylon which is soaked with water will stretch up to 50% before reaching its breaking point. This is one of the reasons it is prefered for guidelines. But this also means that currents will stretch out and create slack in long unsecured sec-

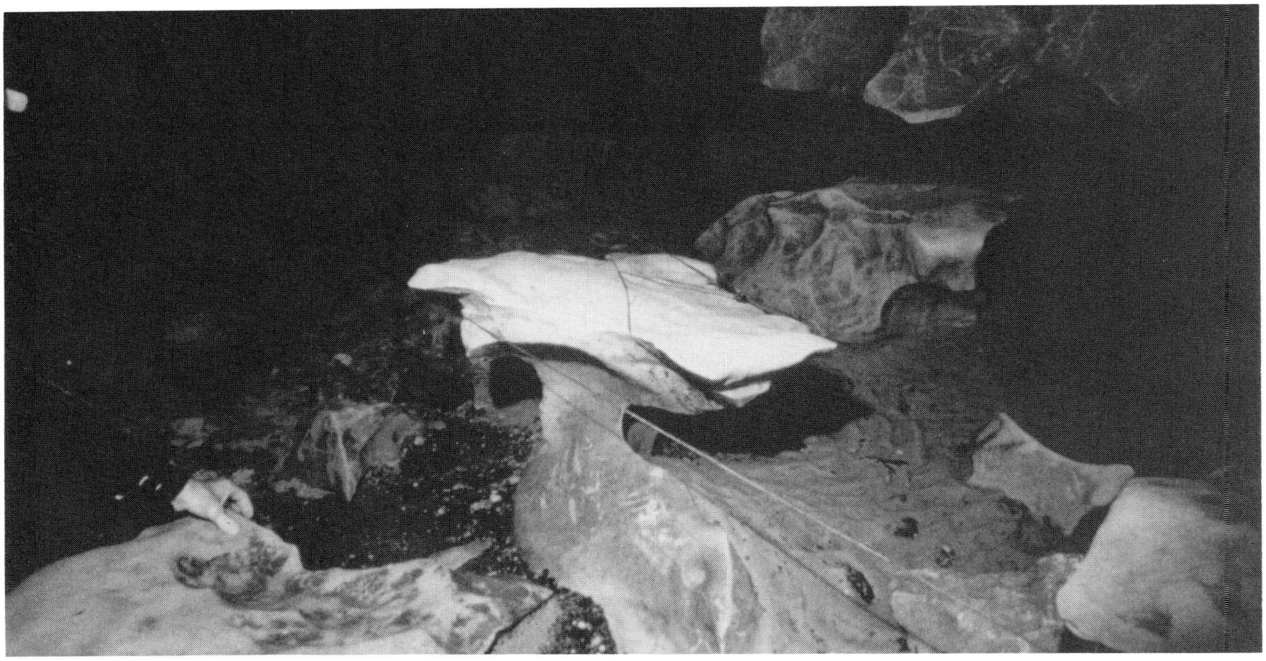

Figure 10-2 A properly placed & suitably taut guideline.

[1]The basic safety rules are derived by an analysis of cave diving accidents to determine how they might have been prevented. The process is called Accident Analysis. Traditionally, there are five rules based on accident analysis. (1) Be properly trained for the type and the location of the dive. (2) Maintain a continuous guideline to be sure of the way out. (3) Reserve *at least* two-thirds of your air for exiting the cave. (4) Limit your depth to 130 fsw. (5) Carry at least three lights per diver. — Ed.

tions of nylon guideline.

It is a good conservation practice to place guideline where it will have the least contact with the cave wall between tie-offs. But the primary purpose of the guidline is safety, and the best general rule to use in placing the line is to place it so that it will be in the optimal configuration for exiting by feel in absolute zero visibility by divers using the touch-contact method of communicating. (This technique is covered thoroughly in Chapter 19, pages 156-157.)

Team Procedures — The person running the reel should be the first diver into the cave and the last one out. This rule must be followed to prevent one of the dive team members from being separated from the guideline. During entry, the second diver on the team should assist in laying the line by checking for proper placement and for slack in the line, for line traps (see below), and for loose wraps or otherwise poor tie-offs. If the second diver sees a preferable location for a tie-off, he can loosen and re-locate the particular one in

Figure 10-3 Second diver illuminating tie-off.

question. Whenever the reel person is using both hands to make a tie-off, etc., the second diver should illuminate the working area for the reel person.

During exit, the team members simply turn and exit, without passing any other team members. This causes the team to exit in the reverse order of entering. The diver directly in front of the person running the reel (the second diver) should maintain communication with the reel person, loosen and remove all tie-offs, wraps and placements, take up any slack in the guideline, and make it as easy and safe for the reel person to wind the guideline onto the reel as he can. To take-up slack in a line while swimming past it, place the index or middle finger of each hand on opposite sides of the guideline, about eighteen to twenty four inches apart. Move the hands in opposite directions so that the arms are out in front of the shoulders, catching the guideline on the extended fingers. This will take up slack equal to the distance between your fingers, and you can let the guideline slide over your fingers as you swim past. To take up more slack, just move one arm forward and the other arm back toward your hips, creating an *N* shape in the guideline as it passes your extended fingers.

If there is a third person on the dive team, he should assist the second diver in similar ways whenever the second diver is working with the guideline.

Wraps — The most popular type of wrap is the *lock-wrap*. It involves placing the guideline around a small open-ended object or projection with one wrap, then make a second wrap by taking the reel under or over the guideline so that the line crosses over and wraps around itself. This places one loop around the projection, and a second loop around the guideline right where it loops around the projection. This insures that the line feels continuous as you follow the line by feel past the wrap. (Without the "lock," you will have to feel around the object as you follow the line wraps.) As you pull the guideline, the lock allows the line to become taut without much further tightening around the object. If your dexterity is good, you can make the lock wrap by twisting the guideline twice, then placing it over the small open-ended object and pulling forward.

A slightly more secure version of the lock wrap can be made by taking two wraps around the object, then one wrap around the guideline. This produces a round turn around the obejct with a loop around the guideline's standing part.

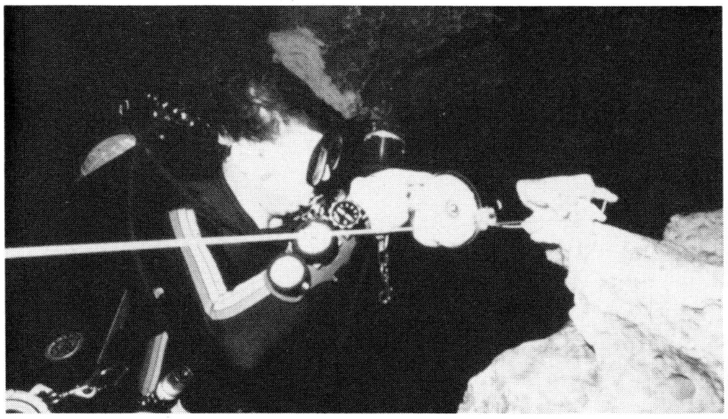

Figure 10-4 Tieing-off to permanent line.

The lock-wrap is the best choice where changes of direction occur or where medium to high flow of water exists. Many cave divers use it exclusively. The lock-wrap is expecially useful for improving speed and efficiency during low visibility exits when following the guideline by touch.

The *speed-wrap* is used for efficiency and speed during penetration. Simply wrap the guideline around the object once or twice but do not "lock" it. One wrap produces a loop around the object, two wraps produce a round turn. For it to work safely, the guideline must be taut. An artfully done speed-wrap will look snug and compact.[2] The speed-wrap is good for straight stretches of cave without much current.

Once you reach the permanent guideline, the idea is to keep the connection simple. Most cave divers place the reel over or under the permanent guideline, bring it back, reel up the slack, (repeat procedure a second time if necessary), lock the nylon screw or other spool-locking device, and clip the reel to the guideline so it will not dangle or drop to the floor. More wraps of the reel means more to undo on the way out, but it is usually a personal preference. Do not make it complicated.

Guidelines should be kept low, taut and placed in the safest area of the cave passage. Some caves may require the guideline to be placed near the ceiling. Do not place wraps on small or weak-looking objects unless doing so is unavoidable.

Line Traps — A nemesis that you should avoid when installing a guideline is the *line trap.* Line traps are created when there is a sharp bend or curve in the passageway with some type of undercut, ledge or crevice. If not anchored properly, the guideline will "swim" into the low area or crevice while being pulled taut around the curve or bend. If you fail to tighten a well-placed guideline, current may loosen the wraps and blow the slack line into these small spaces. If you have to depend on this guideline to exit by feel, you could have a major problem. The line trap is an obstacle that will drastically impede your exit. There is NO need for line traps to occur and they can be a major hazard.

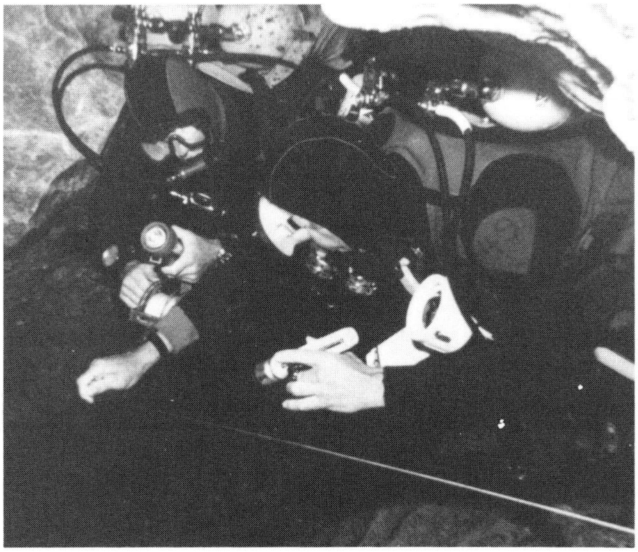

Figure 10-5 Teamwork during exit.

The Exit — When exiting the cave system as a team, the diver with the reel is the last diver out. This is a sacred law of safe cave diving. Realistically, the reel person has the most work and responsibility throughout the dive, including the exit. But the diver exiting ahead of the one with the reel should also be responsible and working hard. Two divers working in concert results in a safer and more efficient exit. Teamwork is always the best way.

GAPS and JUMPS

A gap or jump is a space between two permanent guidelines in an underwater cave. The separations may vary from 6 inches to 60 feet or more. The standard distance is usually 10-20 feet but that decision is controlled by the experience and the judgment of the cave diver producing the gap. The term *gap* is used to refer to the space from the end of one guideline to the beginning of another. The term *jump* is used to refer to the space from the middle of one guideline to the middle or to the end of another. Essentially, a *gap* is a space between two guidelines in the same passageway, while a *jump* is the space between two guidelines at the intersection of different passageways. When this space has been temporarily connected using a gap reel, the two permanent lines are said to be *gapped* or *jumped.*

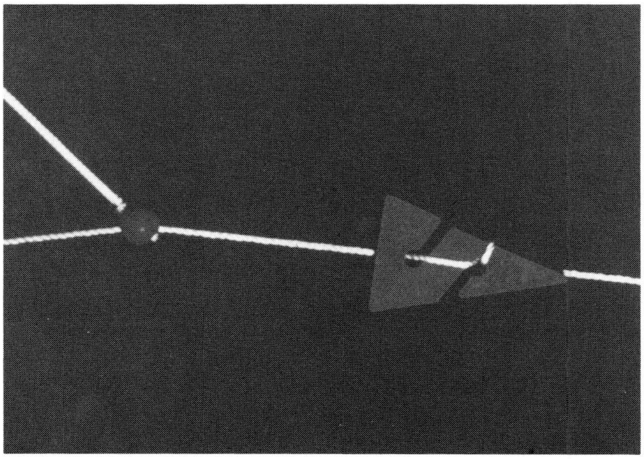

Figure 10-6 A properly marked Y-intersection.

In most cases, distinct permanent lines are separated by a gap or jump. However, in certain situations, the permanent lines are sometimes connected by a *T* or *Y* intersection.Whenever a *T* or *Y* occurs in the line, whether because that's how the permanent lines are installed or because you have created one by placing a gap or jump reel, a suitable temporary line marker should be placed on the *EXIT* side of the line. This is

[2]Whether using the lock-wrap or the speed-wrap, the wraps should be placed around the object in a "closed" rather than an "open" fashion. This means that the wraps will look as though the guideline goes around the object at one point, rather than having the line "stretched out" as it winds around the object. This helps in keeping the wrap snug, and in negotiating a speed-wrap by feel in the event you must follow the line out in low visibility. — Ed.

an important safety procedure that should never be omitted. If you have to exit by feel in a low visibility situation, imagine how you would feel if the line you are following joins another line where you must go right or left. One choice leads to the entrance, the other choice leads further into the cave. Wouldn't it be comforting to feel your line marker on the side you entered from, clearly indicating the route to the entrance and to safety?

To maintain a continuous guideline when gapping or jumping, the safest procedure is for the lead diver to place all lines. Do this in the following way. Tie-off the gap or jump line to the permanent line. Place a line marker on the exit side of the permanent line, within a few inches of the point where the gap or jump line joins the permanent line. In addition to marking the correct exit path where a *T* or *Y* occurs, it also creates a visual and tactile reference point. This is useful even when no *T* or *Y* is formed by the temporary line placement (as sometimes occurs at gaps). Communicate with all other team members to be sure they note the gap and don't simply play "follow the leader," swimming past the gap or jump unaware. Swim across the gap or jump and make the connection to the other permanent line. Each team member should visually reference the gap or jump from its end-point by turning and looking back to its point of origin on the permanent line. This gives each diver a mental image of what this line intersection will look like during exit with normal visibility. Make a mental note of any projections or outcrops that you might encounter if exiting by feel in low visibility.

When exiting, the lead diver who placed all the lines going in is now the last diver coming out. This same diver is responsible for reeling in any temporary lines and removing line markers placed by his dive team. By not passing any other team members, no divers are stranded when the temporary lines are reeled in. Lines or markers placed by other dive teams should be left undisturbed.

In low visibility and other emergency situations, it is best to leave all temporary lines in place. It is possible for team members to accidentally pass each other in low visibility without realizing it. When divers are maintaining touch-contact during a low visibility exit following the line by feel, handling a reel properly is too difficult for even the most experienced divers. Temporary lines are also left in place whenever the exit must be timely, such as after a significant accidental air loss.

Depending on the particular situation, there may be time and suitable conditions to tie-off the line directly to the permanent line or to the cave. This permits the diver to retrieve the reels from the dive while exiting by cutting the reels free from the line. However, this procedure is *potentially very hazardous*. It takes additional time, and the divers may become disoriented during the maneuver. If visibility is low, there is an increased chance of error. It is also possible that the wrong line will be cut, or that the line will be cut in the wrong place. This could be fatal. *The safest and quickest method is to simply leave all reels and line markers in place, and exit. Reels and markers left in a cave can be retrieved on another dive.*

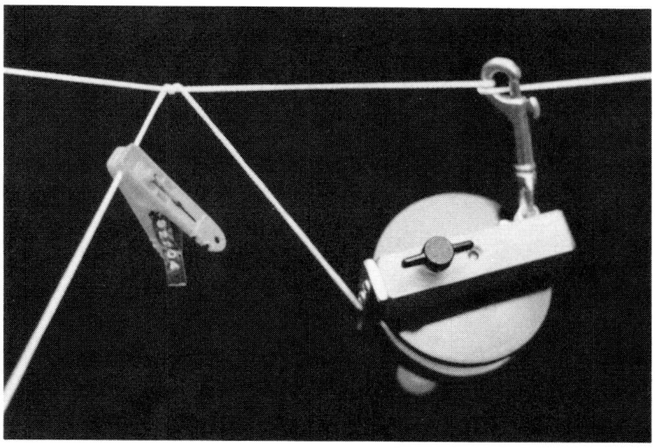

Figure 10-7 Securing the gap reel to the second permanent guideline.

There are three ways to connect the gap line and reel. The reel may be attached directly to the permanent guideline; it may be hooked to the nearest wrap or tie-off in the permanent guideline; or it may be anchored to a projection or outcropping and wrapped once around the permanent guideline, then placed across the gap or jump.

When attaching the gap line directly to the permanent guideline, place the fixed loop around the permanent guideline, then pass the reel through the loop, and snug the lines together. This is usually fast and convenient but sometimes with smaller or older permanent guidelines this could weaken or pull the permanent line from its position. Connecting the gap or jump line to the nearest wrap insures an anchor and is safe, but sometimes one may not be available. On rare occasions, the gap line can be tied off on an open-ended projection that is near the permanent guideline, then simply wrapped around the guideline once before swimming across to the second permanent guideline.

Once the intersection is produced, communication becomes the vital ingredient to insure safety and certainty as to the direction out of the cave. The use of temporary or permanent directional markers is an important tool to accomplish this.

Types of markers that have been employed during the past three decades are clothespins, outrigger clips and plastic arrow markers. Markers should always be placed close to the intersection on the EXIT side of the permanent line. But remember, NO directional marker is fail-safe. Be sure to reference the intersection as well, in order to insure a successful exit. Never assume, guess or gamble your way out of a cave.

The swim across the gap to the second permanent line is established by the reel person signaling the command *stop* or *hold* to the remaining team members. Once the other guideline is reached, the gap or jump line is attached in the same fashion as the temporary guideline from the entrance to the main permanent guideline. Styles of attachment will vary among individuals. The goal is to make sure the attachment is secure, simple, easy to remove, and maintains the "continuous guideline" to the exit. Once completed, the reel person signals that the team may cross. With short gaps this structured procedure is not difficult. With very long gaps where the reel person may go around a corner or swim out of sight, the procedure is modified. Here, as the lead diver swims around a corner to place the line, the second team member follows him just to the corner. If there is a third team member, he stays at the permanent line. This enables the second team member to have visual contact with the lead diver and with the permanent line. If the distance, cave configuration, or other conditions prevent this, then run the gap or jump reel in the same manner as was done with the primary reel when entering and locating the main permanent guideline.

Visual Gaps — Many gaps are relatively short in distance, often six feet or less, and are sometimes bridged without a line due to laziness, perceived·low risk, or personal choice. Cave divers who use DPV's, or who traverse from one opening to another swimming in one direction only, or those who fight to minimize bottom time during lengthy and arduous dives may be tempted with this choice. Safe cave diving clearly dictates "***Always*** use a continuous guideline." As a result, visual gaps remain a controversial issue in the cave diving community and a source of philosophical debate. No cave diving organization or training program condones the practice for safety, professional and liability reasons.

Snap and Gap — One way to minimize the risks of the visual gap, and increase efficiency while maintaining the continuous line, is the *snap and gap*. Permanently installed, a small bronze or brass bolt clip is attached to a length of braided nylon guideline that spans the distance of the breach. Simply pick-up the snap, stretch it across and clip it on. This clearly simplifies the entire gap procedure while still maintaining a safe, continuous guideline. This tool will grow in popularity and use in the years ahead.

Short Jumps — A few cave systems incorporate spaces of 12 inches or less between the permanent guidelines. The philosophy is to maintain the distinct guideline while avoiding the *T* intersection. In a situation where a cave diver must follow the guideline by feel, and comes to the end of the line, the diver reaches out for the perpendicular guideline, finds the directional arrow marker and continues to the exit.[3]

[3]These are locations which are ideal for a *snap and gap*. If one is not in place, the lines should be connected with a gap reel. ***"Always*** use a ***continuous*** guideline." — Ed.

SAFETY REEL

All cave divers should carry a designated safety reel and guideline of the same type used for gaps and jumps. This reel is used in the event of losing the permanent guideline during poor visibility, or when searching for a lost buddy. Never dive without your safety reel.

If a diver becomes separated from the permanent guideline during a silt-out, he should establish a secured tie-off point and relocate the permanent guideline. This is done by referencing the specific area by feel and carefully deploying the safety guideline in a systematic fashion, counting the number of kicks or knots to determine distance. Once obviously too far, turn around, reel in your safety guideline and return to the central tie-off location. Repeat the same procedure in a different direction as if following the spokes of a bicycle wheel, until finding the permanent guideline. After discovering the permanent guideline, securely wrap the safety guideline and begin your exit. If in total control, you may retrieve your safety guideline and reel. But in an emergency situation, leave it and return another day to retrieve it. ***DO NOT JEOPARDIZE YOUR SAFETY!***

If doubt exists on which way is out during these adverse conditions, follow the permanent guideline to clearer water and look for familiar reference points, flow of water, silt trails, or air bubbles on ceiling to determine the correct exit. Staying *in control* is a must.

While searching for a lost buddy, a safety line can also be fastened to the permanent guideline allowing the diver to conduct the search safely. This situation would most likely occur in large rooms or wide bedding plane areas in caves.

CIRCUITS AND TRAVERSES

A circuit dive involves entering one cave passage and exiting from the original entry point by swimming at least part of the return trip through another passageway. A traverse involves entering a cave and swimming in one direction exiting to another cave opening. In circuit and traverse diving, any guidelines, reels, stage bottles, or other items placed in the passageway during the dive must remain in place to be retrieved on another dive. Both circuits and traverses may vary in complexity and length. As with other types of cave dives, they should be dictated by safe air management, time calculations, familiarity with every part of the cave route, air consumption plans, continuous guideline, passage configuration (restrictions), personal comfort, a thorough dive plan, a contingency plan and sure knowledge of your exit.

Typical failures in these types of dives involve visual gaps, failing to maintain a continuous guideline,

Figure 10-8 Various guide reels for cave diving.

following a survey map verbatim[4], pushing the limits of air, and over-estimating the ability of one or more members of the dive team. Experience through training, keen awareness and careful thought and planning are the key ingredients to insure safe, enjoyable dives with circuits and traverses.

PERMANENT GUIDELINES

Novice Lines — Many underwater caves including springs, sinkholes and cenotes, are located at popular open-water dive sites and can present a potential hazard for open water divers who enter the overhead environment. The purpose of the novice line is to help guide the open water diver out of the cavern/cave successfully while not being an invitation into the cave system. Usually large in diameter (1/2" or #60) and durable for constant use and wear, these guidelines have proven to be very effective and have saved many lives. The cave diving community strongly frowns upon any non-qualified diver(s) entering the cavern or cave environment, therefore, installation of this type of guideline is contested by some.

Tour Guidelines — Many cave systems have become popular "tour dives" for the newly trained or intermediate level cave divers and have come to be known as "sacrificial caves" due to the heavy traffic and resulting wear and tear they receive. Typically, larger durable tour guidelines have been placed in these systems to maintain simple directional requirements.

Exploratory Guidelines — Cave explorers are typically the first individuals to penetrate a cave system and play an important role in the cave diving community. Without exploration, there would be no new caves to enjoy, and no new opportunities to learn more about this beautiful environment.

The typical exploratory guideline is usually small in diameter so that more line can be packed on the reel. Twisted nylon is commonly used as it is less expensive, but braided nylon is growing in preference. Exploratory guidelines usually include small knots or markers at regular intervals to aid in measurement. A knot every 10 feet is the standard in the U.S., while in Europe and other parts of the world, lines are marked in meters. During exploration, guidelines are often deployed with long distances between wraps. As a result, there is an increased possibility for line traps, fragile wrap locations or improper placement of the guidelines. *T's,* or permanent connections of two exploratory guidelines, occur more frequently during placement of exploratory guidelines, requiring acute awareness and careful judgment during the planning and the execution of subsequent dives. For these reasons, there is a major difference in following an exploratory guideline in comparison to permanent tour guidelines, and extreme caution is advised for those of limited experience in cave diving.

The standard practice of permanent guidelines in England, Europe and other locations around the world are similar to the United States. But *T's* are used exclusively as many caves have a labyrinthine configuration such as in the Bahamas and in the Yucatan Peninsula of Mexico. Some caves offer the extreme conditions of poor visibility combined with cold water, increased depth and distance that makes permanent guideline connections desirable or the only choice for safety. It is possible that many exits may arise in different directions from *T's,* and that will result in multi-directional markers. The closest exit should always have the most markers, usually two, while all other exits are marked by one. Again, extreme care must be used.

COMMUNICATION

Throughout cave diving history, a variety of methods have been developed and employed for communicating by the use of guidelines. Color, knots, duct tape, clothespins, chemical light sticks, flashing strobes, outrigger clips, and plastic arrows markers are a few examples.

The use of duct tape was originated by cave diving explorer and instructor Lewis Holtzendorff. Cut into triangle-shape pieces, duct tape provided an inexpensive but effective way to mark guidelines and also provide a surface to write information on.[5] However because it is difficult to remove, maintain, and subject to rapid deterioration, duct tape has become obsolete. So has the use of knots. Knots at specific points in the

[4]Not all submerged cave maps are accurate. Generally, divers should not attempt circuits and traverses in passage they have not previously dived on separate familiarization dives. — Ed.

[5]These duct tape markers are sometimes called *'Dorff markers,* which is short for *Holtzendorff Markers.* — Ed.

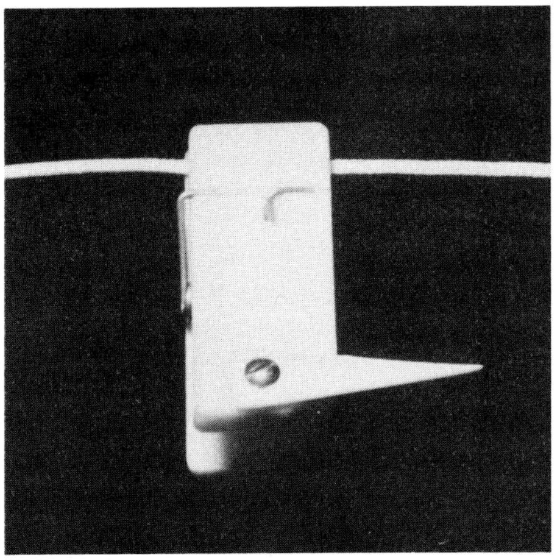

Figure 10-9 Outrigger clip with pointer.

line did provide a method of communication that was still available during zero visibility. However, the lack of standardization often caused confusion particularly during stressful situations. For that reason, this method has been abandoned.

Colored lines once intrigued the imagination but environmental conditions such as tannic acid, organic growth and normal wear have proven this method of

Figure 10-10 A properly secured Wilson marker.

communication futile. Chemical light sticks and flashing strobes have also been used but tend to be expensive, confusing and short term.

Clothespins are used for a variety of purposes and meant to be only temporary on permanent guidelines. Pins can be used to indicate maximum cave penetration, set up traverse or circuit dives, mark exits for gaps and jump lines, indicate when more than one cave diving team is using the same guideline, and for psychological reinforcement. Most clothespins are identified by personal markings such as initials or a nickname, and should never be abandoned in a cave as they become litter. Typically used to indicate exits, a clothespin may be clipped to the line with another attached perpendicularly on the first pin, pointing in the direction out. Though inexpensive and easy to use, clothespins are considered flimsy and unreliable as they may be easily knocked loose or fall apart.

The outrigger clip used for trolling in deep sea fishing became very popular during the 1970's. Though

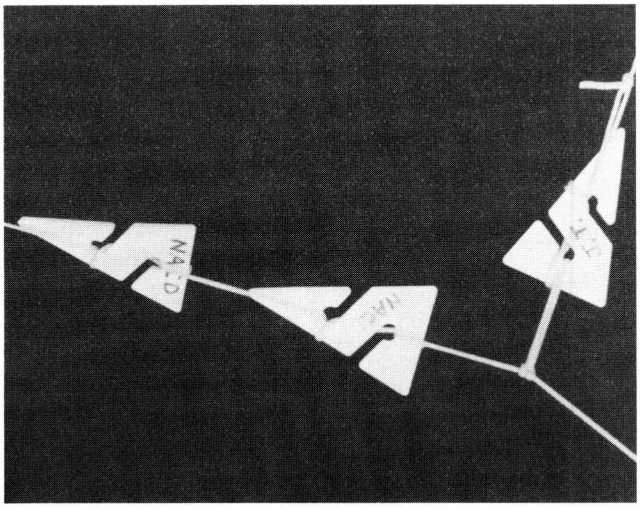

Figure 10-11 Two of the guidelines lead to exits. The closest exit is marked with double line arrows.

more expensive, they are larger, have a stronger spring and are more dependable than clothespins. These devices were subjected to the creative cave diver mind and are often enhanced with reflector tape, screw-on pointers, or are notched or cut so that the exit direction could be determined by feel during adverse conditions. Many cave divers still use this type of marker.

Around the late 1970's, cave diver Forrest Wilson of north Georgia came up with what is now the stan-

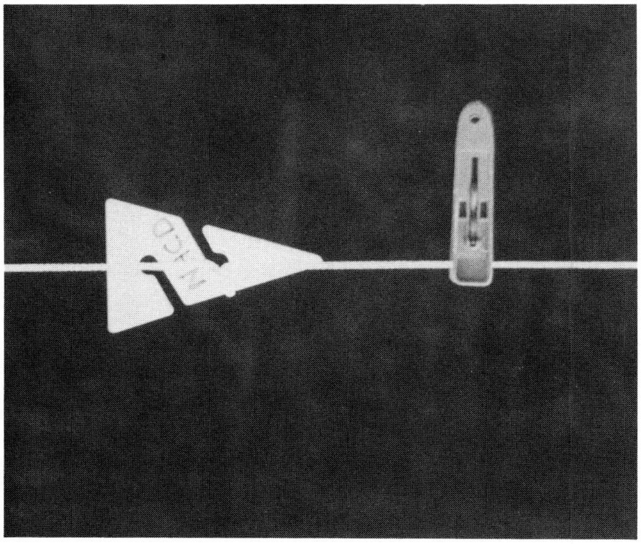

Figure 10-12 Clothespin used to re-inforce a permanently placed line arrow indicating exit.

Figure 10-13 The mid-point between two exits is indicated by line arrows placed back-to-back. Current or passage configuration may create a significant time difference in swimming to these two equi-distant exits.

dard directional marker: the plastic arrow marker. Arrow markers are isosceles triangles typically 2.75″ x 2.75″ x 1.625" and have two holes bored along the central axis with slots cut from the holes to the opposite sides. This enables the guideline to be wrapped through the slots on the arrow to lock it in place to reduce the chance of its falling off.

Plastic arrow markers dominate the procedure for guideline communications. They are produced in a variety of colors, will not deteriorate, can be written on, and are very easy to understand by visual sight or physical contact. It is a standard practice for cave divers to carry three or more along with a few personal clothespins or outrigger clips. As each cave system is different and the permanent guidelines are established in a variety of ways, the use of arrow markers will vary in frequency and purpose. Awareness and good judgment is advised.

TEAM PROTOCOL

During weekends or holidays, one or more cave diving teams may choose to dive at a popular cave location. There are several procedures for each team to consider to insure proper and safe etiquette.

One option is for the second team to go to another dive site. An alternative is to wait until the other team is finished with their dive.

A third possibility is to share the same reel and temporary guidelines, based on an agreed upon dive plan established in advance. The designated first team places the temporary guidelines. The second team follows when ready. In order to maintain communication with multiple teams in the cave, each team places specified line markers on the exit side of the temporary guideline that is tied off to the permanent guideline. If the other team's clothespin is still attached when a particular team exits and reaches the primary reel, the reel is left alone, and the exiting team pulls their clothespin. If the other team's clothespin has been removed, the exiting team removes the primary reel before exiting the cave. This procedure can work with additional teams, as long as the dive plan is established and everything is clearly understood by all. Any confusion during the dive with any team requires you to leave the primary reel in and retrieve it later. ***Be safe!***

When multiple reels/lines are used, the first team in has the right-of-way. The second team or any other teams follow in with their own temporary guidelines and use the following basic principles.

1. Always deploy the guidelines so they are clearly distinct from the first team's, and avoid crossing lines.
2. If forced to cross, the second team places their guidelines underneath the first one with the idea the first team will exit early allowing a smooth retrieval of their guidelines.
3. If sharing the same tie-off's, wraps or placements, the additional team(s) should lay their guideline(s) so that the first team is able to retrieve their line without any interference. This could cause the second team to be forced to use less favorable locations. Each previous team has priority over the next team.
4. The second team may be required to postpone their dive until additional room is available in the cave passage.
5. No temporary guideline should ever be used without the permission of the team which placed it.
6. ALL teams should use markers for communication.

Some cave divers may not want to share their guidelines with anyone and that right should be respected. Confusion will result if any team forgets to remove their marker(s) and may cause a life threatening situation. The exiting team always has the right-of-way over any other team. When teams pass each other in the cave passage be careful not to blind divers with bright primary lights.

Chapter 11

REFERENCING and ORIENTATION

by John Burge

Experienced cave divers employ a number of techniques referred to as *referencing* in order to develop and maintain a continuous orientation to their whereabouts in the cave system. These techniques are an essential element of the navigation process employed by the proficient cave diver.

INTRODUCTION

Referencing, as implied by the term, is the application of a number of different types of observations which, when combined with other cave diving techniques, enables the diver to develop and maintain an awareness of location as well as past, present, and future conditions. Much discussion is devoted in other sections of this work to the use of the guideline, line protocol, line marking, and personal identification. It is paramount that the continuous guideline *always* be the primary element of navigation, and for determining present location and "which way is out."

However, additional information in various forms can often add an increased level of confidence to the divers and can enable them to compare current conditions (flow, visibility, turbidity) with conditions which they can anticipate—both in terms of further penetration and exit.

In other words, referencing techniques augment the diver's primary navigation tool (the line) with other less well-defined, less precise means of navigation which provide both a "feel" for the cave as well as better awareness of location and conditions. It is well known that a higher level of awareness and a strong sense of orientation contribute substantially to a diver's confidence level and lower the degree of stress. It stands to reason, then, that an experienced, confident cave diver is one who develops and maintains a strong sense of orientation during a dive and a constant awareness of the surrounding environment as well as her whereabouts. Conversely, a lack of awareness and a weak sense of orientation contribute substantially to a decrease in confidence and an increase in stress. Loss of confidence and high stress lead to panic, and panic in an underwater cave is tantamount to a high probability of death. Maximum confidence with minimum stress are the two most important ingredients in the satisfactory resolution of a life threatening problem situation.

Problem development rapidly dictates priorities. Air management certainly gets priority number one, and orientation typically demands priority number two. If a high level of orientation is maintained throughout the dive, there is a much higher likelihood that problem management will go smoothly. To sum up, the experienced cave diver will not just swim into the cave. She will make her penetration laying or following line while making mental notes of where she goes, paying particular attention to the details of the cave system in order to generate a "feel" for the cave — creating confidence in her ability to sense where she is at all times.

THE BASIS FOR REFERENCING

The fundamental basis for referencing is an understanding of underwater caves in general. What is the origin of the cave? How was it formed? What is the composition of the materials surrounding the cave void (walls, floors, ceilings)? How does this material interact with water? What is the water composition and the water source for the cave?

An in-depth study of speleology is not necessary for a general familiarization of cave formation, but a little background on the subject can be both interesting and informative. (The reader is referred to Chapter 3 for more information on the geology of underwater caves.) Divers who become informed about the composition of the underwater cave environment are better equipped to develop their sense of orientation and referencing due to a broader scope of knowledge. With an elemental understanding of the formation and makeup of the cave, a diver can begin to make certain types of observations that reveal information which otherwise would be completely overlooked.

An excellent companion to the study of the geology of underwater caves is survey work. Virtually all cave divers who survey find that a keener awareness of cave features is triggered when they start taking measurements, logging readings, or sketching cave features for a survey.

Divers should keep in mind that the development of referencing skills is much more than simply remembering a few techniques. Rather, these skills come with the experience of many dives and constant attention to the cave environment. An inexperienced and less attentive diver will require numerous dives into the same cave system before she can constantly maintain knowledge of where she is located in the cave. On the other hand, the experienced cave diver will have a high level of understanding of the cave structure and composition even before entering the water. Once the dive begins, this diver maintains a constant awareness of the surroundings and environment, anticipating where the dive team is going, where it is, and where it has been.

BASIC FACTORS OF THE CAVE ENVIRONMENT

There are four important factors or cave properties which interact to generate the environment of an underwater cave. These properties always exist in one form or another and any one of them can have a strong influence on a dive. These properties are listed below, along with possible variations.

1. Flow
   - A. High/Low/None
   - B. Direction
2. Cave Composition
   - A. Hard/Soft
   - B. Karst/Lava/Coral
3. Size and Shape
   - A. Large/Small
   - B. Lateral/Vertical/Other
4. Water Composition
   - A. Mineral Content
   - B. Clear/Turbid

Each property can vary within its extremes. The composition of a cave can range from very hard to very soft. The flow can range from very high to none and can be in either direction. The combination of these factors determine the conditions for a dive. For example, a high flow, hard composition, large cave with clear water would yield very favorable conditions in terms of visibility. Likewise, a no flow, soft composition, small cave with turbid water could create very unfavorable visibility conditions. Divers can predict what type of conditions they will encounter based on the combination of these elements.

REFERENCING

Referencing is sometimes erroneously considered only the making of observations. As used here, however, the term has much broader connotations. Referencing is the making of observations ***and*** the integration of these observations into an established data base already in memory to form a higher level of awareness. Experienced cave divers make useful observations which, combined with an understanding of the cave environment, give them a high level of awareness of their surroundings. There are several categories of features and factors that cave divers can observe during a dive.

Line Position — The primary element of navigation in any underwater cave is the guideline, and it should always be in visual or touch contact. It is important also, however, to note the relative position of the line to the passage (along the wall, near the floor, near the ceiling, etc.). Furthermore, it is particularly important to note when (in terms of time, distance, or location) a line makes a marked departure from the norm. A line variation is often just as noteworthy as a significant natural feature in marking a position, just as line tie-

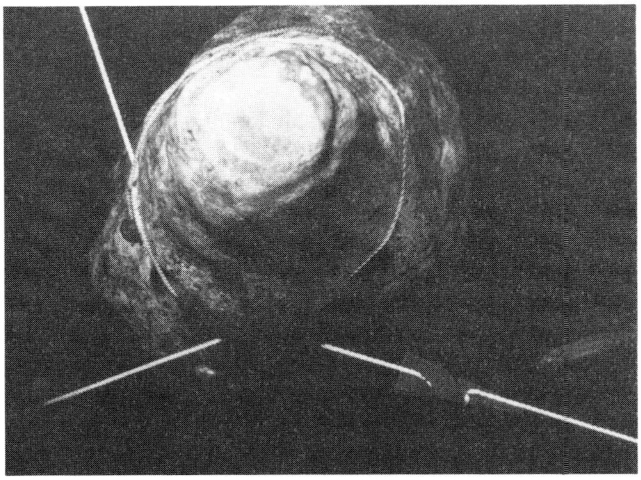

Figure 11-1 Referencing the line at this point during penetration might prove useful in case of touch-contact emergency exit.

off points, jumps, and intersections are excellent reminders of location.

Significant line points such as these are just as prominent in divers' perceptions of their position in a cave system as are notable geological formations in the cave. Divers should make a mental note and *reference* a guideline event to either the time or perceived distance, or to familiar passage geometry and features. Just as a car driver does not have to stop at a familiar intersection to read the street signs or ponder a map, cave divers who use line referencing can proceed with confidence at a familiar intersection, knowing they are on course.

Magnetic Direction — Use of a compass for navigating in an underwater cave is very imprecise. Reliance on a compass for primary navigation is absolutely out of the question and should never be considered as even a temporary substitute for a continuous guideline. Although the compass is used extensively in surveying underwater caves and is one of the essential tools for that task, it serves only a secondary and supporting role in navigation. However, it can be quite useful in that role.

Cave divers should check their compasses from time to time in order to know the general direction they are travelling, or if the passage is gradually turning. It is not necessary for a diver to take note that she is on a heading of 187 degrees. It ***is*** useful for a diver to know that a passage is tending generally south. If a diver notes subsequently that the passage is tending west, she will have a far better appreciation and mental image of where she is and where she has been. Divers who have had an opportunity to study a map of the cave can use general magnetic direction to assist them in forming a mental picture of where they are in the system.

Image Referencing (Snapshotting) — There are several terms applied to a technique called *image referencing.*

It has been called *looking back, back seat driving, snapshotting,* as well as many other descriptive terms. The technique is quick and effective, but too often neglected.

Image referencing is simply noting while traveling *into* the cave a particular reference feature a diver wishes to record onto a mental map. It could be anything from a cross section to a line tie to a breakdown. The diver swims past the reference feature and then stops to observe it *from the exit point of view* in order to recognize it on the way out.

A diver does not need years of cave diving experience to realize that caves look different on the way in from the way they look on the way out. Stopping to take a "snapshot" of a reference point serves three purposes.

First, it records the mental image that will be seen on exit. This is quite important for a diver under stress. A familiar reference is the most secure feeling a cave diver can have while managing a problem — it injects her with the confidence of knowing where she is, which way she needs to go, and how much time it will take her.

Second, the fact that the diver stops and reverses direction or position makes the event consequential and significant and therefore reinforces the memory process and locks the snapshot image into other parameters, such as time or perceived distance from the exit.

Third, snapshotting serves to reference the entire dive team to common reference locations, which serves to enhance the individual diver's own mental references.

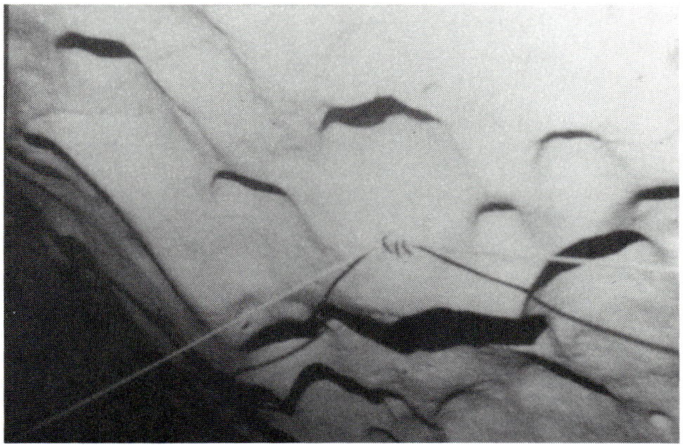

Figure 11-2 Unusual items such as this method for securing the permanent line are often worth noting.

Structural References — Perhaps the most common element of referencing is the mental recording of certain structural features in the cave. There are innumerable structural features on any cave dive, but only a few unique, noteworthy structures should be remembered for referencing. Divers must limit their referencing to only those locations and features that are the most easily noticed and mentally logged.

Topping many cave divers' lists are sections of passages with memorable shapes, cross sections, or unique bottom features. Because the dive light beam always leads the way and because cave divers tend to scan sections of passage with their lights, certain portions can be recognized readily. This is much easier and more effective than trying to reference a single cross section, even if a map with cross sectional data (which are few and far between) has been studied in advance.

Since the cave diver is nearly always in the horizontal position, bottom features are excellent references in some types of caves because they can be seen without any special effort. Typical bottom features to reference are a bottom composition which is unique to a certain location, or bottom irregularities that are obvious. These can range from bottom color, to boulders and breakdown, to concentrated groupings of eel holes. One cave in northern Florida has a particular section called *Eel City*. A diver does not need a vivid imagination or a photographic memory to recognize and reference this location. Eel City quickly becomes a familiar landmark even to first-time divers in this cave.

Side passages, protruding walls, columns, domes, and pits all lend themselves to ready identification and referencing. In fact, features such as these are usually so dominant that they nearly always are included by the cartographers who generate the maps from surveys. Their symbology is well known and widely recognized by underwater cave map users.

Depth variations also can be used as references where the depth of a particular location varies from the norm. Likewise, flow characteristics can be noted in instances where cave geometry causes flow variations that are significant enough to notice — unusually high or low flow areas or even eddy currents can pinpoint a particular locale.

Last, but very high on the list of priorities of structural features to reference, are any cave configurations which could pose a potential hazard or difficulty under abnormal conditions such as limited visibility or an air sharing situation. These typically fall into two categories:

1) Line traps

2) Restrictions

Line traps are discussed in the section devoted to line laying techniques and, of course, should be avoided as the line is laid and placed. However, even though proper attention should have been paid to the laying and placement of the line, particular attention and referencing should be made to potential line traps in the event a restricted visibility exit might have to be made. Under such conditions, a diver does not need any surprises on the way out — especially a surprise that impedes an exit from the cave under less than optimal conditions. The simple awareness of the potential of such a situation will put a diver in a much better frame of mind to solve the problem.

Any cave diver could encounter a situation where, on exit from a cave while following the guideline in limited visibility, she swims straight into a wall or very slight opening. At this point, she must be able to think logically to solve the problem. A diver who is aware the line could have moved from its original placement, and is aware of her position in the system, will not be overwhelmed with doubt about being on the wrong line, going the wrong direction, etc. Line traps are a good example of why referencing is a very necessary procedure, and why referencing skills should be developed by every cave diver.

The other frequently encountered potential hazard is the restriction. Divers should ***always*** reference with particular care and emphasis any restrictions, and all divers should snapshot them from the exit point of view ***immediately*** after negotiating the passage. A dive team may even elect to take the time to negotiate the restriction in both directions before continuing the dive. This is a very effective referencing technique and the restriction will certainly be retained in memory for instant recall should the need unexpectedly arise.

The Time-Distance Dimension — Referencing is not limited to the mental recording of locations and features of the cave. Another dimension is the time-distance dimension, an important factor in a diver knowing where she is in a cave system. There are four basic means to figure this dimension.

1) Noting elapsed time.
2) Relating known or documented landmarks with known times or distances.
3) Noting perceived distances.
4) Noting air consumption.

Preferably, more than one of these means should be employed by a diver in order to have a good sense of location in an underwater cave system, and how far the dive team is from the surface. This is one area of cave diving where many cave divers tend to have their own individually preferred methods, most of which are combinations or variations of the four previously cited methods.

For the less experienced cave diver, a rudimentary method can be simply referencing a particular feature at set time intervals.

Some divers attach clothespins or personalized line arrows on the line at certain intervals, retrieving them on exit. This is a simple but effective and reassuring technique. A diver has no doubt of her location when she picks up a personal identifier she has placed only a short while ago.

If a diver has access to a cave map, she can memorize useful reference information prior to the dive and then confirm it during the dive. These features then can be correlated to time or air consumption. With a mental picture of the map in mind, and with time and/or air checks at points of reference, a diver will have a high level of orientation to her location in the system.

Perceiving distance is a skill more easily developed by some than others. In actuality, as long as a diver perceives accurately where she is and can relate that location with time, she will be confident and positive about the dive. Generally, distances are perceived by noting: 1) sections of cave traversed, 2) air consumption, 3) time elapsed, or 4) by combining these methods of approximation.

No matter what referencing techniques are applied, the addition of the time-distance dimension to a referenced location serves to reassure divers and give them a sense of "where they are."

CONCLUSION

Referencing and cave orientation are integral to the navigation process in an underwater cave system. A diver who just pays out a reel or follows a line and swims blissfully into the unknown or who simple-mindedly follows a line without referencing the individual elements dictating the environment is being extremely naive. On the other hand, the experienced cave diver relies not only on specialized equipment, but studies charts and maps and observes natural elements to confirm her location. The guideline is the primary device in underwater navigation, but referencing and cave orientation provide navigational input which builds a body of knowledge of a diver's whereabouts, especially where she is and where she has been.

The skills that compose referencing cannot be taught in the classroom or in open water. They must be learned by application in the underwater cave environment. Highly developed referencing skills serve an extremely important role in the mind of the cave diver in developing a keen awareness and strong sense of orientation and whereabouts, which are vital to her confidence level and the ability to hold stress to a minimum in problematic situations. ***A diver's capability to maintain her orientation and a sense of where she is could make a significant difference to her and her dive team someday.*** It ***could*** mean...life or death.

Chapter 12

AIR MANAGEMENT

by Jeffrey Bozanic

Divers are severely limited in their caving experiences by the amount of air they can carry with them. Minor nuisances or slight difficulties for a dry caver can become major hazards for a cave diver because of the amount of time available to deal with problems. Any problems a diver encounters must be solved in minutes, rather than in the hours available to a dry caver. Thus, the limited quantities of air mandate the use of many other techniques and safety equipment. By themselves, however, these techniques and equipment do not preclude the occurrence of an accident. Cave divers must also understand and utilize proper air management when they dive.

Accident analysis has shown that improper air planning is one of the most important reasons why people have died during cave dives. Divers must carefully plan the use of their air, always leaving enough in reserve to successfully solve any problems which might arise with the cave.

FACTORS WHICH AFFECT AIR PLANNING AND AIR CONSUMPTION

There are many factors which affect both air planning for a dive and the rate of air consumption. Any variable which causes the exit from the cave to be slower than the penetration, or causes the divers to use significantly more air while exiting the cave, places the dive team in a potentially hazardous situation. These factors generally fall into three major categories: environmental conditions, physiological stress, and psychological stress.

Environmental Conditions — Many adverse environmental conditions can slow a dive team significantly when they turn to exit a cave. Some conditions may exist prior to the dive, while others may arise during the dive.

Reduced visibility can occur during a dive through poor swimming technique or natural phenomena (such as percolation) and may slow a diver's progress through a system. Decreased visibility may hide line traps or prevent a team from exiting through restrictions or narrow parts of a cave without slowing considerably compared to their penetration. Visibility reduction due to switching from a primary to a secondary light may have similar effects.

Siphons present a special hazard to cave divers. Divers swim into siphon systems much faster and easier than they will be able to exit. Because of greater exertion during the exit, air consumption rates increase. Furthermore, it is often difficult to appreciate the effects of current until the dive team actually turns the dive and begins exiting.

Cold causes a diver to use air more rapidly. While the effects of diving in cold temperatures may not be apparent to a diver at first, they increase with the duration of the dive. Therefore, more air will be consumed while exiting the cave. Cave divers who plan cold water dives (or long dives) can reduce this problem by wearing exposure suits designed to provide maximum warmth.

Restrictions and line traps may be easily passed while swimming in one direction, but far more difficult moving in the opposite direction. Restrictions are also far more difficult to pass while sharing air with a partner, so that in an emergency situation, progress is much slower.

Depth also affects a diver's air reserve. On shallow dives, one-third of a cylinder can last a diver a fairly long time. This gives the diver a margin in which to determine solutions to potential problems. On deeper dives, however, one-third of a cylinder will not last as long and the time available to solve problems is reduced. Coupled with this factor is the impairment of mental processes which occurs at greater depths and significantly reduces the problem solving capabilities.

Physiological Stress — Many of the aforementioned environmental factors can also contribute to physiological stresses on the diver's body. These include current, cold, and depth. Any of these conditions can lead to the expenditure of greater energy, by working harder (such as physical exertion when swimming against a current), by maintaining body temperature, or by increased breathing effort. These factors must be considered when planning air management for a dive.

Poor equipment management can also increase energy expenditure during a dive. A diver who is not streamlined and is out of trim faces more drag than a properly prepared cave diver and will have to work harder to move through the water. Likewise, poor buoyancy control can result in greater energy expenditure and air consumption.

Psychological Stress — A comfortable person breathes less than one who is anxious or frightened. Because breathing rates quicken as stress increases, air consumption is affected by the level of stress. Divers who regularly practice emergency drills will have a lower level of stress when facing a problem and therefore, they will not experience as great an increase in air consumption. Furthermore, divers who successfully manage stressful situations (see Chapter 15) will quickly bring their breathing back under control. However, an increase in air consumption in an emergency situation cannot be completely eliminated.

In a worst case scenario, wherein catastrophic air supply failure occurs at the point of furthest penetration with one-third of each diver's air consumed, both divers must exit sharing air. The psychological stress imposed on the divers by the emergency situation would increase their breathing rate, and more air would be consumed during the exit than on penetrating into the system. If there were only two divers in the team, there probably would not be enough air to safely exit.[1]

AIR CONSUMPTION

Air consumption refers to the rate at which a diver uses his air. Determining an individual's air consumption can benefit cave divers in many ways. Beginning cavern and cave divers can observe an improvement in their air consumption rate as their experience increases. More experienced cave divers may use knowledge of their air consumption rates in various ways that help them plan dives more safely and with more confidence. Some special uses of air consumption rates will be discussed later.

To understand air consumption rates, first a diver must know the total amount (the rated volume) of air that his tank will contain when full and what pressure (the working pressure) is needed to achieve a full tank. The rated volume of a tank is usually between 50 cubic feet (cf) and 120 cf. Common American values for a tank's working pressure are 3000 pounds per square inch (psig) for aluminum tanks and 2250 psig for 3AA steel tanks. Ten percent must be added to the working pressure of 3AA steel tanks to figure their volume; therefore, 2475 psig is used to determine the pressure/

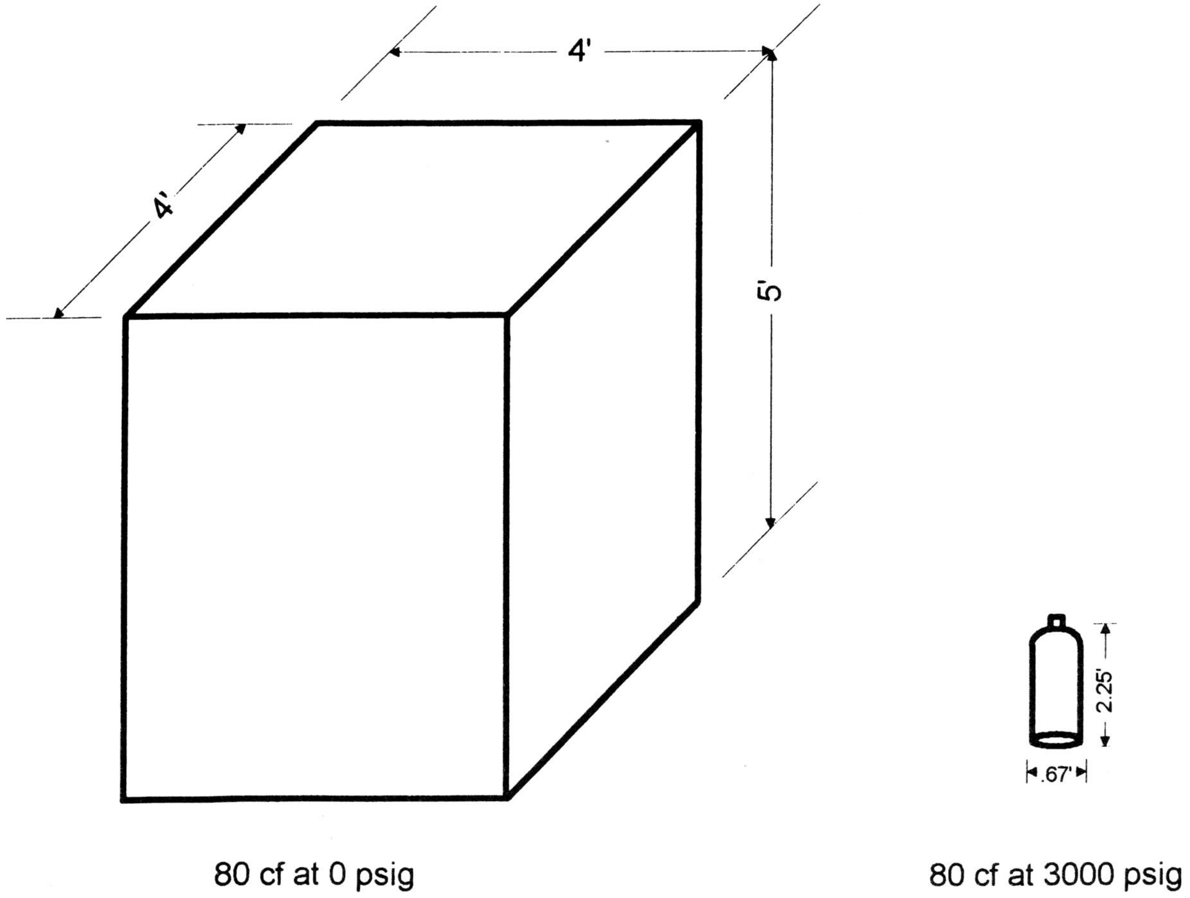

***Figure 12-1** Air compression in a scuba tank. In this drawing, the cylinder is shown about 22% larger than scale for clarity.*

[1]Assuming that they were using the Thirds Rule without providing a cushion of air for emergencies. — Ed.

volume relationship of steel 71.2 cf tanks. Rated pressure values may not be the same in different parts of the world. Moreover, new tank models may soon be available with greater working pressures while maintaining current safety margins.

Figure 12-1 illustrates a typical scuba tank. The diagram shows how much air is compressed into the tank and therefore how much can be released. Note that the volume placed in or released from the tank is measured at surface pressure.

The volume of air consumed on a dive is found by relating pressure changes to volume changes. A depletion of tank pressure is directly proportional to a depletion of the air contained in the tank. Therefore, one can determine air volume change from a measured tank pressure change. Figure 12-2 illustrates this pressure-related change in volume.

In the illustration,we assume an 80 cf cylinder with a working pressure of 3000 psig. The tank pressure changes from 1800 psig to 1500 psig, or by 300 psig. This change represents a part of the total maximum pressure (working pressure); in this case it equals one-tenth (300 psig/3000 psig), or ten percent. Because they are directly related, a ten percent drop in working pressure represents a ten percent drop in volume. At the surface, this represents a volume of 8 cf (one-tenth of 80 cf).

If a compressible volume of air is taken from the surface to depth, its volume at depth will be less because of the higher surrounding (ambient) pressure. The same relationship holds true for air released from a tank at depth. A given amount of air released at depth will not occupy as much volume as it would at the surface. During diving, this results in a more rapid drop in tank pressure at greater depths.

Although it may appear that a diver uses more air at greater depth, actually the *volume* of air per breath, if measured at depth, is no greater than the volume used at the surface. However, the *amount* of air (number of molecules) needed to create that volume is greater at depth because of the greater ambient pressure which compresses that volume. Therefore, the fixed *amount* of air originally placed in the diver's tank is depleted more rapidly at depth than at the surface, as the diver breathes the same volume per breath while experiencing greater ambient pressure.

For ease of understanding and calculation, ambient pressure should be considered in *atmospheres*

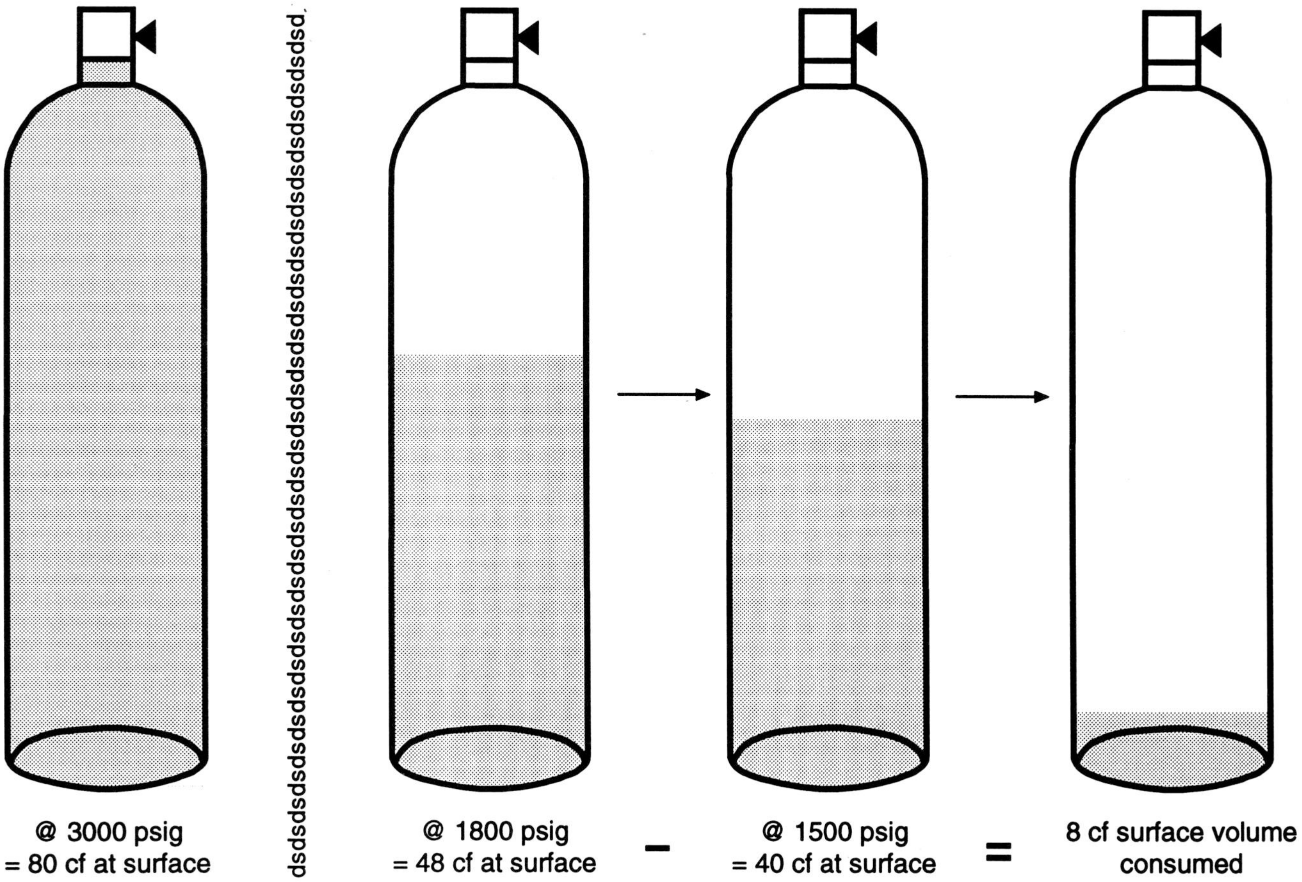

Figure 12-2 Pressure-related change in volume.

Volume Changes with Depth

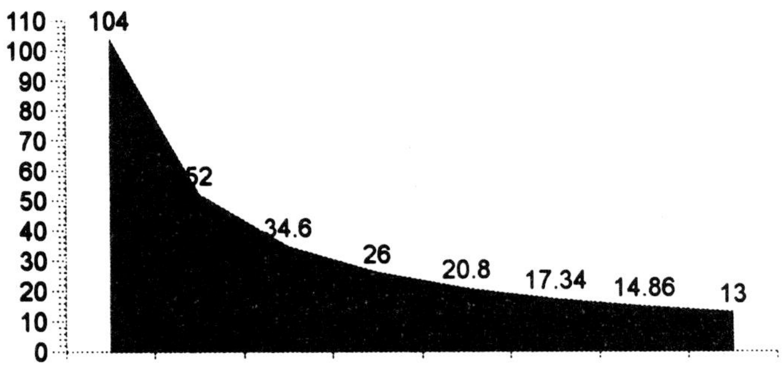

Figure 12-3

absolute. One atmosphere is the surrounding pressure at the surface. Related to the zero pressure of a vacuum, it is one atmosphere absolute. The pressure created by 33 feet of seawater is also equal to one atmosphere, but because there is one atmosphere of air above the water, the total or absolute pressure is 2 atmospheres absolute (as related to a vacuum of zero pressure).

Figure 12-3 illustrates graphically how a given volume of air is changed by depth. Table 12-1 shows the same information. To establish a reference, air consumption rates at depth are equated to surface air consumption rates. Therefore, the depth at which a diver uses air must be known in order to relate the volume of air used to a surface use-rate. A diver at 99 feet depth (four atmospheres absolute) would need 20 cubic feet of surface air to get 5 cubic feet of volume at depth. To determine a diver's *surface air consumption rate,* the amount of air used must be divided by the depth at which it was used (as expressed in atmospheres absolute).

Finally, by including the period of time in which the air was consumed, air consumption can be expressed in the common term of volume per minute. Simple division of the volume of air used by the number of minutes during which it was used yields the answer (cubic feet of volume per minute).

By following these steps, a diver can determine his rate of surface air consumption per minute. By reversing the steps, the amount of air needed for the diver at a given depth for a given time can be determined.

To illustrate, Diver A has a tank rated at 50cf with a working pressure of 3000 psig. He depleted his tank pressure from 1800 to 1500 psig during 5 minutes at 33 feet. The difference in pressure is 300 psig or ten percent of the working pressure. Ten percent of the tank's rated capacity is 5cf, which was consumed at 2 ata. Dividing the air used by the atmospheres absolute at which it was consumed, 2.5cf of surface air was consumed. Dividing this figure by the time in which it was used (5 minutes) gives a result of 0.5cf per minute for his surface air consumption rate.

Once a surface air consumption rate has been determined, a diver can determine the approximate amount of air needed for a given depth and time period. With a surface air consumption rate of 0.5 cubic feet per minute, Diver A can calculate the amount of air he will consume at 66 feet during a 20 minute period.[2] The consumption rate is multiplied by the

Cubic Feet at Surface	104	52	34.6	26	20.8	17.34	14.86	13
Atmospheres Absolute	1	2	3	4	5	6	7	8
Depth in Feet of Sea Water	0	33	66	99	132	165	198	231
Ambient Pressure in psia	14.7	29.4	44.1	58.8	73.5	88.2	102.9	117.6
Ambient Pressure in psig	0	14.7	29.4	44.1	58.8	73.5	88.2	102.9
Cylinder Pressure in psig	2640	2640	2640	2640	2640	2640	2640	2640

Table 12-1 Volume Changes with Depth. **This table shows the equivalent surface volumes in a steel 104 cf cylinder as it is taken from the surface to 231 fsw (8 ata) while the internal pressure remains constant at 2640 psig.**

[2]Assuming the same amount of energy is expended by the diver during these different dives. — Ed.

ATA	DEPTH IN FSW	Vol. @ 3000 psi	Vol. @ 1800 psi	Vol. @ 1500 psi	Δ Vol. @ 300 psi	Minutes Resting	Minutes @ Maximum Exertion
1	0	80 cf	48 cf	40 cf	8 cf	20:00	3:05
2	33	40 cf	23.99 cf	19.99 cf	4 cf	10:00	1:33
3	66	26.67 cf	15.99 cf	13.33 cf	2.66 cf	6:39	1:04
4	99	20 cf	11.99 cf	9.99 cf	2 cf	5:00	0:46
5	132	16 cf	9.59 cf	7.99 cf	1.6 cf	4:00	0:37
6	165	13.34 cf	7.99 cf	6.67 cf	1.32 cf	3:20	0:31
7	198	11.43 cf	6.86 cf	5.71 cf	1.15 ct	2:53	0:27
8	231	10 cf	5.99 cf	4.99 cf	1 cf	2:30	0:23

Table 12-2 Affect of depth on duration of air supply. **This table shows the relative amount of time a diver would get from 300 psig of air from an 80 cf tank at various depths during rest and also during maximum exertion. The figures for breathing rates are somewhat arbitrary. They are based on the assumption that at the surface, an 80 cf cylinder will last 3 hours and 20 minutes at absolute rest, and slightly more than 30 minutes (30:50) if it were possible to maintain maximum exertion at the surface until the bottle is empty. (This breathing rate works out to 11.3 liters per minute at rest and 73 liters per minute at maximum exertion. It is roughly equivalent to twelve 950 cc breaths per minute at rest and forty-eight 1500 cc breaths per minute at maximum exertion.) From the table it is easy to see that a diver wearing double 80 cf cylinders at 132 fsw theoretically could use 300 psig of air in as little as 1 minute 14 seconds of maximum exertion. (At that rate, the diver would probably pass out from hyperventilation.)**

atmospheres absolute (0.5 times 3). This result is then multiplied by the minutes at the planned depth (1.5 times 20) to arrive at 30cf. With a 50cf aluminum tank, this would be 60 percent of the rated volume; thus Diver A will use 1800 psig (60 percent of 3000 psig).

Air consumption rates are useful for determining approximate air needs for specific dives. However, they are not intended to be used during a dive to determine penetration limits. During the pre-dive planning, air rules for the dive must be determined.

AIR RULES

The air rule most often used for cave diving is called the *Thirds Rule*. Under the Thirds Rule, each individual diver reserves at least two-thirds of the starting air supply for the exit. The air supply is divided into imaginary thirds: one-third (or less) for the entrance, one-third for the exit, and a minimum of one-third held in reserve.

The reserve air exists for several reasons. First, it allows a margin of safety should the exit from the cave take longer than the penetration. Second, it provides air in case unplanned decompression stops become necessary. Finally, it represents an air supply for any other member of the dive team. Theoretically, the reserve is sufficient air for both divers in a two-man team to exit a cave, even if one has suffered complete loss of his air supply. However, in many situations the Thirds Rule does not provide an adequate safety margin. This is especially true for two-man teams.

If a team is using the Thirds Rule, each member must first determine his starting air volume. As previously stated, this can be derived from the rated volume and pressure of the diver's tanks. If all members of the team are using the same sized cylinders, then the air pressure in those tanks may be compared directly to determine relative air supply volumes for the dive team members.

Dive Team with Uniform Cylinders — In the case of a team with the same type of tanks[3], a diver's thirds are determined by dividing starting pressure by three. If a diver's starting pressure is 3000 psig, 1000 psig represents the maximum amount available for penetration. This is subtracted from the starting psig, yielding a turn-around pressure of 2000 psig. Therefore, this diver must signal for the dive to be turned when his gauge reaches 2000 psig.

If the starting pressure is not divisible by three, it is first rounded down to the nearest 100 psig value that can be divided into thirds. Dividing by three, this value is subtracted from the starting pressure to give the turn-around pressure. For example, a diver with 2900 psig would round down to 2700 psig. Dividing by three yields 900 psig, which is subtracted from the the starting pressure to give a turn-around pressure of 2000 psig. Although this might appear to be the same turn-

[3]That is, tanks with identical working pressures and rated capacities. — Ed.

PSIG	120G	100G	80G	104S	95S	95S	71.2S	52S	80A	71.2A	63A	50A
3500	120.0	100.1	80.6									
3400	116.5	97.2	78.2									
3300	113.1	94.3	75.9			95.2						
3200	109.7	91.5	73.6			92.3						
3100	106.2	88.6	71.3			89.4						
3000	102.8	85.8	69.0			86.5			80.7		63.1	50.4
2900	99.4	82.9	66.7			83.7			78.0		61.0	48.7
2800	95.9	80.0	64.4			80.8			73.5		58.9	47.0
2700	92.5	77.2	62.1	107.9	97.7	77.9			72.6		56.8	45.3
2600	89.1	74.3	59.8	103.9	94.1	75.0			69.9		54.7	43.7
2500	85.7	71.5	57.5	99.9	90.5	72.1	72.2	52.6	67.2	72.2	52.6	42.0
2400	82.2	68.6	55.2	95.9	86.9	69.2	69.3	50.5	64.5	69.3	50.5	40.3
2300	78.8	65.7	52.9	91.9	83.3	66.3	66.4	48.4	61.8	66.4	48.3	38.6
2200	75.4	62.9	50.6	87.9	79.6	63.4	63.5	46.3	59.1	63.5	46.2	36.9
2100	71.9	60.0	48.3	83.9	76.0	60.6	60.7	44.2	56.4	60.7	44.1	35.3
2000	68.5	57.2	46.0	79.9	72.4	57.7	57.8	42.1	53.7	57.8	42.0	33.6
1900	65.1	54.3	43.7	75.9	68.8	54.8	54.9	40.0	51.1	54.9	39.9	31.9
1800	61.7	51.4	41.4	71.9	65.1	51.9	52.0	37.9	48.4	52.0	37.8	30.2
1700	58.2	48.6	39.1	67.9	61.5	49.0	49.1	35.8	45.7	49.1	35.7	28.5
1600	54.8	45.7	36.8	63.9	57.9	46.1	46.2	33.7	43.0	46.2	33.6	26.8
1500	51.4	42.9	34.5	59.9	54.3	43.2	43.3	31.5	40.3	43.3	31.5	25.2
1400	47.9	40.0	32.2	55.9	50.7	40.4	40.4	29.4	37.6	40.4	29.4	23.5
1300	44.5	37.1	29.9	51.9	47.0	37.5	37.5	27.3	34.9	37.5	27.3	21.8
1200	41.4	34.3	27.6	47.9	43.4	34.6	34.6	25.2	32.2	34.6	25.2	20.1
1100	37.7	31.4	25.3	43.9	39.8	31.7	31.7	23.1	29.5	31.7	23.1	18.4
1000	34.2	28.6	23.0	39.9	36.2	28.8	28.9	21.0	26.8	28.9	21.0	16.8
900	30.8	25.7	20.7	35.9	32.5	25.9	26.0	18.9	24.2	25.9	18.9	15.1
800	27.4	22.8	18.4	31.9	28.9	23.0	23.1	16.8	21.5	23.0	16.8	13.4
700	23.9	20.0	16.1	27.9	25.3	20.2	20.2	14.7	18.8	20.2	14.7	11.7
600	20.5	17.1	13.8	23.9	21.7	17.3	17.3	12.6	16.1	17.3	12.6	10.0
500	17.1	14.3	11.5	19.9	18.1	14.4	14.4	10.5	13.4	14.4	10.5	8.4
400	13.7	11.4	9.2	15.9	14.4	11.5	11.5	8.4	10.7	11.5	8.4	6.7
300	10.2	8.5	6.9	11.9	10.8	8.6	8.6	6.3	8.0	8.6	6.3	5.0
200	6.8	5.7	4.6	7.9	7.2	5.7	5.7	4.2	5.3	5.7	4.2	3.3
100	3.4	2.8	2.3	3.9	3.9	2.8	2.8	2.1	2.6	2.8	2.1	1.6
Work psig	3500	3500	3500	2400	2400	3000	2250	2250	3000	2475	3000	3000
+10%	—	—	—	2640	2640	3300	2475	2475	—	—	—	—

For purposes of computing this table, the nominal capacities of the cylinders were used. Values given are in cubic feet rounded down to the nearest tenth. A constant temperature of 70°F is assumed for all computations. This table is representative only! You should not assume that your cylinder with a nominal capacity that is the same as one the table is the same cylinder. For example, one brand of aluminum 80 at 3000 psig has a capacity of 79.87 cf and was omitted for convenience. Also, manufacturer's tolerances may permit a variation in internal capacity of the same batch of cylinders by the same manufacturer of up to ±10 cubic inches. Therefore, no two cylinders are exactly identical, even as they come out of the manufacturing plant.

Table 12-3 Cylinder capacities at various pressures.

ing pressure as the first example, only 900 psig were available for penetration as opposed to 1000 psig.

When buddies have unequal starting pressures, air calculations are based on the diver with the least amount of air. For example, if Diver A has only 2000 psig while Diver B has 2100 psig, air calculations are based on Diver A's beginning pressure. Diver A's third works out to 600 psig (1800 divided by 3) for a turning pressure of 1400 psig. Diver B subtracts A's 600 psig from his starting pressure of 2100 to arrive at a turning pressure of 1500 psig. This allows for divers with different breathing rates to maintain their safety margin.

Dive Teams with Different Capacity Cylinders — Dive team buddies do not always use the same type of tanks. In this case, a dive team member who figures thirds based on tank pressure cannot relate this figure to other team member's thirds. Tank pressures must be converted to volumes before thirds can be determined. If this were not done, then one diver could breathe a greater volume of air entering a cave than the other team member has reserved to get him out. This could occur even though no diver used more than one-third of his air on the penetration.

When using volumes for thirds, the person with the lesser volume of air figures thirds by dividing the available air by three, to derive a third which is measured in cubic feet. The other divers use this amount of air as their calculated third. This volume is converted back to pressures in order to read it from the submersible pressure gauge. This technique can be used regardless of the cylinder sizes, or even if one diver has doubles and another has only a single tank. To illustrate, Diver A has a set of double 80 cf aluminum tanks filled to 2700 psig. The volume of air is determined by multiplying the total volume of the tanks when full (160 cf, or twice 80 cf) by the actual pressure of the tanks (2700 psig), then dividing by the pressure at which the tanks are full (3000 psig). This yields a volume of 144cf.

Diver B has a single 104 cf 3AA steel tank filled to 2400 psig. Working pressure for this tank is 2400 psig, which means the pressure at which the tank is considered full is 2640 psig (2400 psig plus ten percent). With an actual pressure of 2400 psig, volume is determined by multiplying the rated volume (104 cf) by the actual pressure (2400 psig), divided by the "full" pressure (2460 psig). This yields a figure of 94.6 cf.

Diver B has less air, therefore thirds for both divers will be based on his available air supply. Diver B's third is 31.5 cf, which is the amount that this team is limited to using for penetration.

This figure in cubic feet must be converted to a figure in psig for both divers. The volume to be used for penetration (31.5 cf) is multiplied by the pressure of the tanks when full and divided by the volume of the tank when full. For Diver A, 31.5 is multiplied by 3000 and divided by 160cf, with a result of 590 psig. 590 psig should be rounded down to 500, in order to be read off the submersible pressure gauge. For Diver B, 31.5 is multiplied by 2640 and divided by 104 cf, with a result of 800 psig.

The final step is for each diver to subtract this amount of air from the starting pressure of the tanks to arrive at a turning pressure. Diver A, with double 80's, has a turning pressure of 2200 psig (2700 minus 500) and Diver B, with a single 104, has a turning pressure of 1600 psig (2400 minus 800). Diver B obviously would have arrived at the same figure by using his pressure reading — this holds true for the diver with the least amount of air. However, using pressure readings to determine thirds, Diver A would have reserved much less air. The loss of Diver A's larger air supply at the turning point would not have left sufficient air for the team's exit.

This method of calculating thirds is not nearly as convenient or easy as the method described when all divers have the same size cylinders, but it has the advantage of working for any combination of tanks at any pressure. Table 12-2 is designed to simplify the calculations necessary by giving the volumes of various cylinders directly without mathematical calculations. The relationship between tank pressure and volume is presented for different types of tanks. For purposes of computing this table, the nominal capacities of the cylinders were used. Values given are in cubic feet rounded **down** to the nearest tenth. A constant temperature of 70°F is assumed for all computations. This table is representative only! You should not assume that your cylinder with a nominal capacity that is the same as one in the table is the same cylinder. For example, one brand of aluminum 80 has a capacity of 77.4 cf at 3000 psig but was omitted for convenience. Also, manufacturer's tolerances may permit a variation in internal capacity of the same batch of cylinders by the same manufacturer of up to ±10 cubic inches. Therefore, no two cylinders are exactly identical, even as they come out of the manufacturing plant.

The Thirds Rule is a minimum air rule. More conservative air rules can be adopted for all dives and are absolutely necessary under certain conditions. A two-person team that stretches its air supply to the limit of the Thirds Rule would probably not have sufficient air for the exit if problems are encountered and a high stress situation develops.

The air rules a team adopts for a dive must be appropriate for each individual cave system and must take into consideration any specialized equipment used (such as DPV's) and the size of the team.

The thirds rule can be modified to provide a safety cushion. One method is for the divers to subtract a certain amount of air from their beginning air supply. For example, each diver may subtract 300 psig from his pressure reading before he figures thirds. Other examples of more conservative air rules are the fourth or sixth rule, where only one-quarter or one-sixth of the air volume is used for penetration into a cave system.

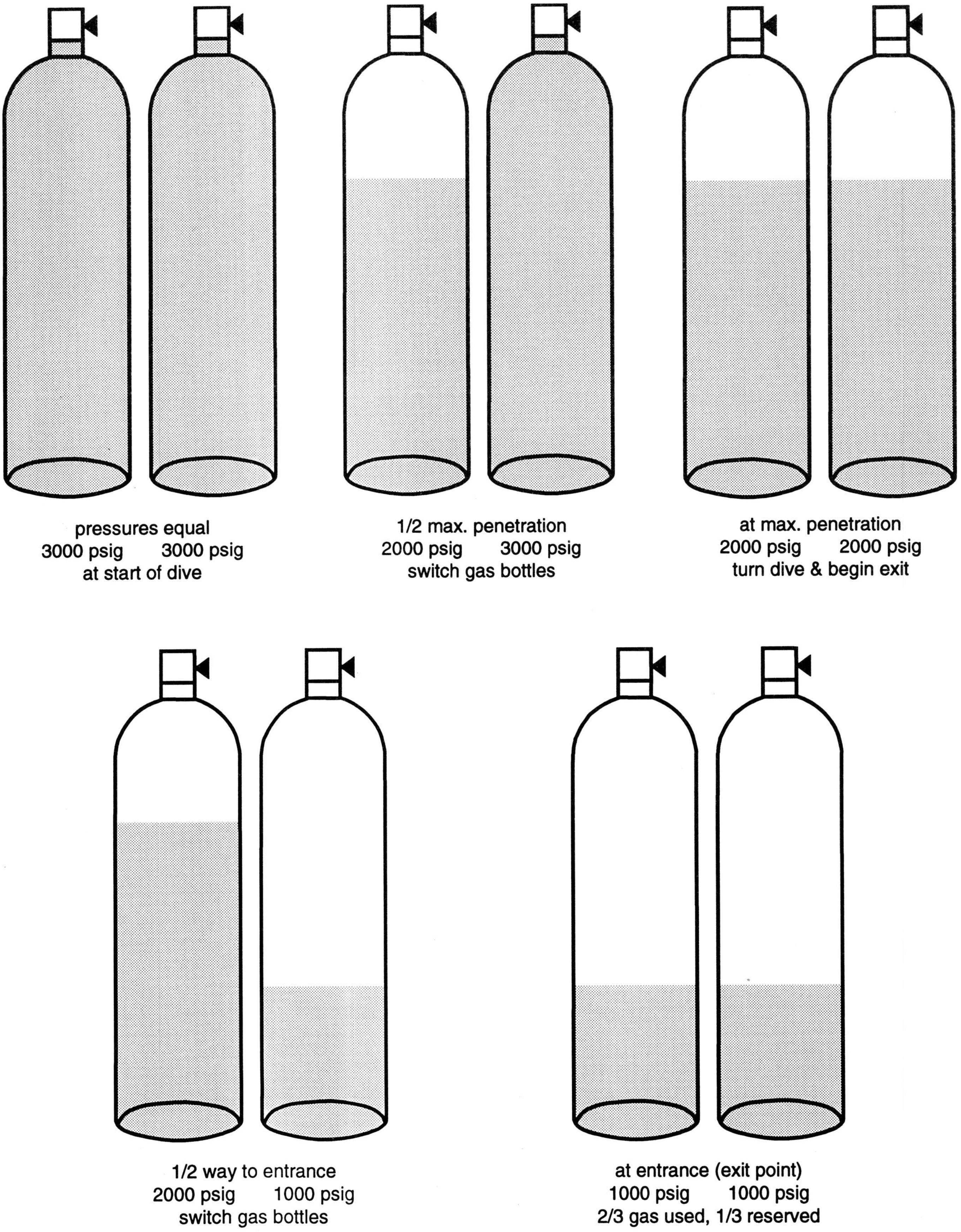

Figure 12-4 Alternating tanks using thirds.

Diving into a siphon or using a DPV mandates extremely conservative air rules. Specialized training is needed in order to undertake such diving and part of that training will cover the air rules necessary for safe diving under these circumstances.

Regardless of the air rule adopted for a dive, when the first member of a team hits his turning pressure, all team members turn the dive to exit the cave.

ALTERNATE TANK CONFIGURATIONS

Cave dives can require decompression stops, if the depth and length of the penetration dictates that decompression is required. As previously stated, one reason for reserving two-thirds of the air supply was in case of unanticipated decompression stops. However, this reserve of air should be used only for emergencies. Planning to use this air during D/C means that it is not available for emergency use. It has been committed for use during decompression. The reserve might be used for other reasons during the dive and the dive team might not have enough air to complete the necessary stops. On all dives where decompression stops are expected, decompression tanks with enough air to last all members of the dive team for the entire decompression period should be placed ten feet deeper than the first planned D/C stop. The tanks are placed deeper than the expected first stop to give the divers the opportunity to determine their standing on the tables *before* ascending to the first stop. This allows for any discrepancies between the dive plan and the actual dive.

Cave divers who wish to explore beyond the limits of double tanks can carry additional tanks. These extra tanks are known as *stage bottles*, and are usually attached below the diver. These stage bottles are utilized first, and as they reach one-third of the starting volume, are detached from the diver's body and fastened to the safety line.

Several stage bottles may be used on a single dive, creating a relay system similar to the way high altitude camps are established during major Himalayan mountaineering expeditions.

In no instance are the stage bottles ever used more than one-third during the penetration. During the exit, however, the stage bottles are commonly used down to a few hundred psig before switching to the backmounted cylinders. This allows the diver to drop the encumbering stage bottle in the event of an emergency, with as much air as possible reserved in the more secure backmounted system.[4]

Tanks do not have to be backmounted. Tanks can be worn on either or both sides of the diver's body. Each sidemounted tank is independently fitted with its own regulator and SPG. This system is normally used in America in order to negotiate passages that would not allow a diver with backmounted tanks to pass without removal of the air delivery system. Sidemounted cylinders are the standard cave diving configuration used by divers in Great Britain, and are often used by scientific researchers in locations where solo diving cannot be avoided.

1 cf = 1728 ci = 28316.736 cc = 28.32 L

1 ci = 16.387 cc

1000 cc = 1000 ml = 1 L = 61 ci

50 cf = 1415 L	95 cf = 2690 L	104 cf = 2945 L
71.2 cf = 2016 L	100 cf = 2831 L	120 cf - 3398 L
80 cf = 2265 L		

Abbreviations

cc = cubic centimeters cf = cubic feet ci = cubic inches L = liters ml = milliliters

Table 12-4 Volume Equivalents

[4]Air management principles and procedures for such advanced techniques as stage diving are covered in detail in specialty cave diving courses. Qualified cave diving instructors who have appropriate experience often teach advanced cave diving classes in stage diving, DPV diving, cave rescue and recovery, mixed gas diving, side-mount configuration diving, and others. — Ed.

Because the tanks are independently fitted, the diver has a backup and air reserved in the event of any single cylinder air failure. The use of the tanks is alternated, so that during the penetration one-third of the air in each cylinder is utilized, and during the exit an additional third of each tank is used. This leaves a third of the starting air supply in each cylinder as a reserve. This alternative is depicted in the following diagram (Figure 12-5).

Air planning is one of the most important aspects of safe cave diving. The Thirds Rule is a minimum standard for cave diving and in many cases does not provide a sufficient reserve. Divers should remember to consider tank size when determining their turning pressure and always base their calculations on the diver who starts with the least amount of air. Each diver should carefully record his turning pressure before a dive and monitor his pressure gauges during the dive to ensure he does not exceed that point.

Chapter 13

UNDERWATER COMMUNICATIONS

by Jeffrey Bozanic

Humans are communicating animals. Most of our accomplishments can be traced directly to our ability to communicate effectively. When communication is impaired, the activities one is involved in are unable to proceed in an efficient manner.

INTRODUCTION

Communicating underwater is much more difficult than it is on the surface. This stems from the phenomenon that underwater a person becomes deaf and mute. Our primary mode of communication, speech, cannot be utilized without special equipment. To overcome this problem, divers developed a variety of means to communicate while scuba diving. While these means work relatively well, a number of problems still occur which impair productive communication.

The first of these problems is a lack of standardization. Because hand signals are not the same from one diver to the next, or from one part of the country to another, some signals may be miscommunicated or misunderstood. A second problem is the lack of signals to cover situations which may arise during a dive. If the "vocabulary" is missing, divers are severely hampered in their efforts to solve problems underwater.

When communication problems occur during an open-water dive, the divers are free to ascend to the surface. Once they have reached the surface, they can discuss what was actually meant, then descend and continue their dive. When cave diving, this is not a viable option.

Because cave divers are unable to ascend directly to the surface, communications must be extremely well established before the start of a dive. Effective communication can minimize misunderstandings and lessen the impact of unforeseen situations. On the other hand, a lack of effective communication can lead directly to very serious problems in a cave. Thus, in-water communications provide the basis for problem solving and problem prevention during dives.

A breakdown in communication could lead directly to a scenario which places the dive team in jeopardy. An extreme example of this could be a diver who lightheartedly interprets a *thumbs up* signal as "I'm OK, let's go for it!" instead of its intended meaning of "Lets turn the dive." In a more subtle vein, misunderstandings or poor communication skills can increase diver anxiety, increase task loading, and generally make the members of the dive team less safe by making them less comfortable during the dive. For these and other reasons, underwater communications are a vital skill for both novice and experienced cave divers.

HAND SIGNALS

Hand signals are the most common and easily recognized form of communications used in scuba diving. The primary advantage of hand signals is that they are easily given and easily understood. Two disadvantages of hand signals are: 1) not all hand signals are standardized, and 2) divers must be in visual or touch contact to utilize hand signals.

Hand signals are a language, just as spoken English is a language. In order to be used effectively, divers must understand that signals, like words, must have identical meanings from one person to the next. To foster standardization, several texts have been written that deal exclusively with the description and utilization of hand signals. These books include *Hand Signals for Diving*, distributed by the NACD, and Norris Eastman's *Handbook on Underwater Communication*[1].

Even the aforementioned textbooks cannot include signals for every idea or thought buddies may wish to communicate. Standardized hand signals will not cover every scenario, especially for divers involved in specialty cave diving. In this event, it is certainly acceptable for divers to invent their own hand signals.

Figure 13-1 Hand signals in use during a cave dive.

[1]While Eastman's book contains many useful hand signals, over 30 of them require the use of both hands. As Mr. Bozanic explains below, such hand signals are not useable when cave, night or wreck diving. This is because the cave, night or wreck diver needs to illuminate the signals æ a skill which requires the use of one hand to hold and direct the light. — Ed.

Signals set up prior to a dive can be used by the same dive team on all subsequent dives.

New hand signals should meet the basic requirements of all hand signals. They should be able to be given with a single hand, so that they may be illuminated with a light in the other hand. They should not mimic another signal and should be distinct enough to be easily understood while diving. Cave divers involved in activities such as photography, specimen collection, mapping and survey work will probably require the development of new signals.

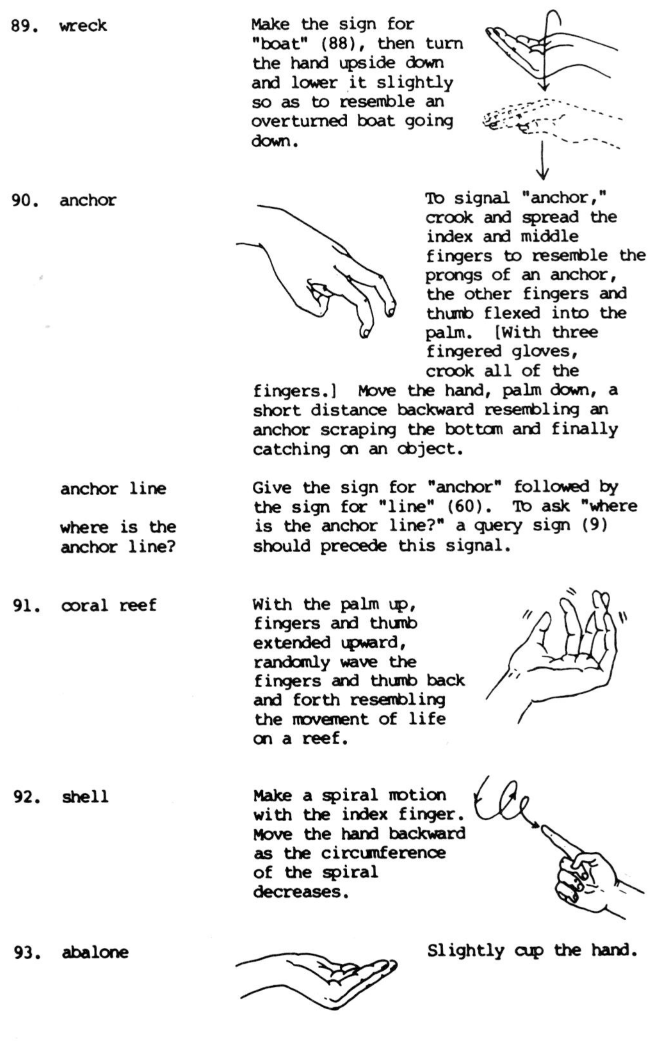

89. wreck — Make the sign for "boat" (88), then turn the hand upside down and lower it slightly so as to resemble an overturned boat going down.

90. anchor — To signal "anchor," crook and spread the index and middle fingers to resemble the prongs of an anchor, the other fingers and thumb flexed into the palm. [With three fingered gloves, crook all of the fingers.] Move the hand, palm down, a short distance backward resembling an anchor scraping the bottom and finally catching on an object.

anchor line / where is the anchor line? — Give the sign for "anchor" followed by the sign for "line" (60). To ask "where is the anchor line?" a query sign (9) should precede this signal.

91. coral reef — With the palm up, fingers and thumb extended upward, randomly wave the fingers and thumb back and forth resembling the movement of life on a reef.

92. shell — Make a spiral motion with the index finger. Move the hand backward as the circumference of the spiral decreases.

93. abalone — Slightly cup the hand.

***Figure 13-2 A page from* Hand Signals for Diving**

Hand signals must be used properly in order for communication to take place. Before a cave diver can use a hand signal, she must first get her buddy's attention. A diver accomplishes this by flashing her light back and forth several times across her partner's light beam. To assist the partner in noticing the movement of light, divers need to keep their light steady and move it slowly when they are not trying to signal.

Proper lighting of the hand signal is one of the most important considerations in a cave. While giving the signal with one hand, the diver illuminates the signal with the light held in the other hand. If the signal is made outside the beam of the diver's light, communication does not take place. The diver should also be careful not to shine a light into her partner's eyes. Generally, the light beam is directed perpendicularly to an imaginary line running from one diver to the other.

The diver must hold the signal long enough for her buddy to see and identify it. A diver may need to allow time for her partner to interpret and comprehend the signal. This will depend on the signal used, how common it is, and the skill and experience of the dive partner. All signals should be acknowledged before the team proceeds with the dive, so that the person who gave the signal knows that her partner understood the message.

There are many different types of hand signals used at various times during any given dive. Hand signals may be grouped into five categories: basic signals, environmental signals, directive signals, equipment signals, and problem solving signals.

LIGHT SIGNALS

Light signals are a means of communication using a diving light. Although many divers only use their light to get another team member's attention, it has further uses as a communication resource. Light signals are most often employed while a team is travelling through a system and it is difficult or inconvenient to turn around and use a hand signal. A light signal enables the lead diver to give a signal and receive an acknowledgment without having to stop and turn around. This increases the efficiency of the dive team, and can make the dive more enjoyable.

There are two basic types of light signals used, one for *OK*, and one for *I want your attention*. The *OK* signal is a command signal, and requires a response. The attention signal may or may not require an immediate response, depending on how it is used.

To give an *OK* signal with a light, the diver rotates the light in a circle, tracing out a circle on the cave floor or wall where the partner can see it. It is used as either a question or as an answer. The response is the same signal (if the diver is OK) and should be given at the same location where the first signal was given.[2]

Most cave divers are familiar with the practice of flashing their dive light across their partner's light beam in order to get their attention. This is a valuable method of communication, especially when a trailing diver needs to get the attention of the lead diver. This technique can be refined to achieve three separate

[2]If the partner is not OK, the proper response is the *Attention!* signal. When the lead diver turns around, the appropriate hand signals can be used to communicate the exact nature of the situation. — Ed.

meanings for the attention signal.

The first meaning of the attention signal is *Emergency, I need your help!"* To give this signal, the diver flashes her light rapidly across the beam of the buddy's light. The rapid flashing is continued until a response is obtained. If a diver receives this signal during a dive, she should be prepared to impart emergency assistance immediately, such as providing air to her buddy. This signal should only be given when there is in fact a life-threatening emergency and prompt assistance is required.

In a non-emergency situation, the signal *I want your attention* is used. This signal is the same flashing of the light across a buddy's beam, but at a slower rate. It is generally flashed two to four times, followed by a pause. Attention to a particular item or place in the cave can then be shown with the *OK* light signal given around the object. Alternatively, hand signals may be used as a follow-up to communicate desired ideas.

The third attention signal used is that for *I'm still here, and everything is OK.* This is a very slow wave of the diver's light across their buddy's beam. It notifies the partner that they may continue the dive. It is given by the trailing diver, frequently enough so that the lead diver does not have to turn around and visually verify presence. This signal requires no response by the lead diver, who may continue the dive without pause.[3]

The primary difference between the three attention light signals is the rate of speed at which they are given. This may be confusing to buddies who are diving together for the first time. If any doubt exists as to the degree of attention required, a diver should always assume it is of the most immediate type.

It is preferable that all divers use the same strength light. However, there may be times when divers are diving with lights of unequal strength. In this situation, the person with the weaker light should precede the diver(s) with the brighter light(s). Light signals given by a dim light from behind are easily missed because they are washed out by the strong light of the lead diver. With the weaker light in front, the trailing diver(s) can easily signal the lead diver. When the dive is turned, the diver with the weaker beam switches position and becomes the lead diver on the exit.

OTHER COMMUNICATION TECHNIQUES

There are times during some cave dives when it is impossible to communicate using either hand or light signals. This may be due to low visibility or the nature of the message. In low visibility, touch-contact signals may be necessary to use. They are described in Chapter 19 on *Low Visibility Cave Diving.* These signals are designed to help move the dive team to better conditions. At the cessation of need for touch-contact communications, the divers can re-establish visual communications and proceed with the dive.

All of the aforementioned techniques combined together will cover nearly all situations; however, there are times when a diver still cannot communicate a particular message. In these instances, the most likely tool for achieving a satisfactory interchange is the diver's slate. The advantage to using a slate is that any idea, even a complex one, can be communicated. The major disadvantage of a slate is the time that it requires — time to write the message in a legible manner, transfer the slate, read the message, and respond. Therefore, the slate is used when it is the only method available to communicate a message.

A diver must practice to acquire the skills necessary to efficiently use a slate. These skills include getting the slate out from wherever it is normally stowed and returning it again after use. Legible underwater writing takes practice, as well as efficient use of the limited space available on a slate. Use of key words helps conserve space and saves time.

Finally, noise may also be used as an alternate communication tool. It is difficult to employ noise (such as banging on a tank) for sophisticated communication because of its severe limitations, especially the lack of variety. Its major use is that of an attention-getting signal, in order to establish visual communication.

PHILOSOPHIES OF COMMUNICATION

A number of different techniques for communicating underwater have been mentioned in this chapter. The frequency of use and efficiency of these procedures will vary from dive team to dive team. Factors which influence the amount of use stem from the primary consideration of how well the dive buddies know each other (as dive partners). If the team members dive together frequently, the quantity of communications will often be reduced. This occurs because buddies begin to know how the other one thinks and reacts in common situations, and also because they grow more adept at reading their buddy's body language during the dive. Body language often communicates enough information to a regular buddy that supplementation with formalized hand signals is redundant.

It is important that dive teams *review signal usage before every dive.* This is true even if the team dives together on a frequent basis. Pre-dive briefings should cover not only basic hand signals, but also any special signals which might be used on the particular dive being planned. Additionally, any problems which were

---

[3]A technique which the lead diver can use to gauge the closeness of her partner is to smother her own lamp against her chest. This results in the only light visible in the cave being generated by the other dive team members. This technique is especially useful when negotiating bends or restrictions in small passageway. You can easily determine when the next dive team member has passed the curve or restriction. In 3-person dive teams, this technique can also be used by the middle diver. — Ed.

encountered in the previous dive with regard to communications should be reviewed.

Post-dive briefings on signals and communications should be conducted after the dive. Regardless of how often partners dive together, there will sometimes be poorly understood moments during a dive. These misunderstandings should be discussed in full with a view to preventing their occurrence in future dives. If a diver wanted to communicate a certain thought or concept during the dive but lacked a signal, the dive team may want to develop a new signal (if none already exists).

CONCLUSION

In the near future, new and more sophisticated methods and equipment for communicating underwater will probably become more common. Some divers already utilize communication devices which allow divers to speak to each other during a dive. This field shows a great deal of promise and will eventually enable cave divers to achieve rapid and effective communication in a much more efficient manner. However, the proper use of presently available communication methods allows for safe and enjoyable cave dives. Every dive team should place a high priority on establishing and maintaining effective underwater communications.

REFERENCES

Finley, C., J. Stone and C. Vilece, (Ed.s), *Hand Signals for Diving*, 1977, 4th edition, NACD, 38 pp.

Eastman, N., *Underwater Communication*, 1979, Beverly Publishing Co., 44 pp.

Chapter 14

EMERGENCY PROCEDURES

by Mary Fahning

INTRODUCTION

"I'm out of air!" "My primary died!" "The cave has totally silted out!" "The reel is jammed!" Some cave divers might consider these situations emergencies while others might view them as only incidents. Is each and every incident indeed an emergency, or are they only potentially dire events?

Emergencies seem to pivot around a loss. Loss of communication and teamwork stem from lack of awareness and, by themselves, do not constitute an emergency. Loss of self-sufficiency, as with a regulator malfunction, is not significant if a buddy can be signalled quickly and a backup made available. Combined together, however, these losses can constitute an emergency and further develop into a disaster/accident if action is not taken.

Obviously the best time to handle such a sequence is before it begins to happen. Prevention is the first step in emergency procedures — divers who practice prevention greatly reduce their chances of facing an emergency. Dive planning and proper procedure keep incidents from becoming emergencies.

PREVENTIVE MEASURES

Equipment

Cave divers are dependent on mechanical devices; thus planning begins with the purchase of reliable equipment with redundancy in mind. Properly adapting this equipment (as in streamlining) provides safer passage through a cave with less potential for entanglements. Care and upkeep of life support systems is essential when surface air may be hundreds of feet away.

A maintenance routine of continually checking and rechecking the performance of equipment should start before leaving for a dive site and continue into the water during the pre-dive preparations. A team check of equipment called *matching* should occur at the surface of the water wherein the dive leader lists each piece of equipment and every member of the team checks the working ability and security of each portion of his life support system.

A gear check should be conducted in the following manner:

(1) Both valves are turned on all the way to ensure that not only is the air to both regulators on, but that the diver can reach the tank valves and turn the controls without hesitation in event of regulator malfunction.

(2) Both regulators are checked to see that they function properly in the water. Even though a diver would quickly find out if the primary regulator was not functioning, a thousand feet back in a cave with an out of air situation is not the time to find out the secondary regualtor is out of order. Team members should check each other's first stages and tank valves by scanning them underwater for several seconds.

(3) The low-pressure BC inflator should be checked to see that is hooked up and functioning, and that each team member's hoses are properly arranged.

(4) All lights (backup and primary) should be held underwater and checked. All lights must be secured to prevent entanglements while remaining accessible.

(5) Divers should check to make sure they have all necessary support equipment such as safety reels, dive tables, slate and pencil.

(6) Air supplies should be checked and recorded. Turn around air supply should be computed, recorded, and announced to the team. This helps reinforce the two-third's rule and keeps the diver aware of his air limits.

If any piece of equipment is inoperable or missing and cannot be replaced, the dive should be cancelled. The pre-dive check does not take long and should be conducted in an unhurried manner. This check not only helps prevent emergencies from occurring, but it creates a positive atmosphere for the dive.

Figure 14-1 Cavern Diving Students Practicing Touch-Contact Exit.

Awareness

Planning, in the form of practice and mental rehearsal, increases divers' awareness of themselves, their equipment, their buddies, and their surroundings, and it further reduces the chances of cave divers encountering an emergency situation.

This skill has been termed *Global Awareness* by diver/author Lou Fead. It can be sharpened and nurtured in many ways. One such way is through imagination and playing with "What if's?" "What are my fears as a cave diver?" "What do I worry about?" "What could go wrong?" Emergencies evolve from something the diver has allowed to slip by him. A *globally aware* diver strives to prevent an emergency in order to avoid having to solve it. This diver closely evaluates the potential for incidents, problems, and even emergencies, and prepares via skills and mental attitude to avoid them.

Figure 14-2 Cavern Diving Students Practicing Touch-Contact Exit. In Figure 14-1 the divers are getting oriented and establishing their communications link. Here, we see a well-organized and coordinated exit.

Practice

A cave diving course allows a diver to experience cave diving safely. In a safe environment, students experience situations in an acutal cave. However, a "guardian angel" (the instructor) is there to oversee and circumvent any real problem or emergency. Upon completion of a cave diving course, students are well practiced in handling most potential emergencies and are hopefully aware of their own limitations. With time, however, divers tend to grow complacent and take these skills for granted. Practicing emergency skills can sharpen a diver's global awareness and help avoid occurrences that lead to an emergency. Divers can practice before, during, and after a dive. Even mental rehearsals away from the water enhance awareness and competence in dealing with unplanned situations. Divers who are oblivious to the possibility of using emergency skills set the stage for disaster.

GENERAL PROCEDURES

A diver's first reaction to a problem or emergency should be to *STOP*. A diver must stop and *GET CONTROL*. Cave divers must get control of their bodies and minds in these situations. A human's natural reaction when closed in is to thrash out and fight — a poor instinct in a cave. This reaction can cause loss of buoyancy control, leading to silting and a narrowing of the diver's perception. Rapid breathing is also a by-product of this instinct.

If a diver can stop and get control, he has reacted in a positive, rather than in a destructive, fashion. When awareness is maintained, a diver can proceed to do something about the situation. The diver should signal his buddy, who should already be aware that something is wrong. A properly functioning dive team maintains communication at all times.

After stopping and gaining control, a diver must *THINK*. Although the diver may be aware of recommended procedures, not all situations evolve in the same manner. Divers must assess each situation on an individual basis. By evaluating the current status of the dive, the diver can figure out a solution. Once a diver has thought through the situation, he must *ACT*. Once the decision has been made to act, divers must proceed with control and maintain global awareness.

A diver's reaction will usually include some combination of self help (self rescue) and team response (buddy rescue). A diver who stops and gets control is initiating self help. When a buddy is signalled, a team response begins. A team that works together will develop the best procedure for any given incident, problem, or emergency. A post-dive review and critical analysis of every dive sharpens global awareness and develops a diver's ability to assess unplanned occurrences.

INCIDENTS

Not all unplanned circumstances in a cave necessitate "calling the dive." Some situations fall into a generalized category called incidents. Whether the dive continues after an incident depends on air supply and stress levels. The safety of the team is always the first consideration in deciding whether or not to continue the dive.

Communication Breakdown

A breakdown in communication often is the factor which precipitates an incident, problem, or emergency. Divers should be aware of their buddy's light at all times. If a diver maintains awareness, then any unusual movement of the beam (or its absence) will be noticed. At regular intervals divers should turn and look at their buddy, who should be prepared to flash an *OK* sign. The *OK* sign is not required at every check; when the sign is given, it should be illuminated by the diver's light beam.

When a diver needs to get a team member's attention, the light should be vigorously flashed back and forth across the area where the buddy's light is pointed. An aware buddy will immediately respond to any unusual light movement; however, all divers should use slow and steady movements at other times in order to make this type of signal more noticeable. Communication is the vital ingredient of an enjoyable and successful dive but it requires teamwork and awareness.

Entanglements

Entanglements in cave diving usually occur as a result of poor line and reel usage. Generally a simple snag results from *danglies*, unsecured pieces of equipment which seem to reach out and grab the line. Swimming under or too close to a line can cause an entanglement and should be avoided. Letting the line go slack while laying or reeling it also creates a potential trap. A diver who feels any resistance while swimming should immediately stop and resist the temptation to jerk loose.

If a diver is caught but finds that the line is clear, he should check for projections in the cave as the source of entanglements. Hoses are easily caught on certain formations at the ceiling of a cave, while lights and other accessories may get wedged against rocks in narrow passages.

After discovering the source of entanglement, divers should first attempt to free themselves but should not make any complicated body movements. If unable to get free, a diver should signal a team member that there is an entanglement. The snared diver should then remain motionless while his buddy untangles him.

Reel Jams

Whenever reel jams occur, they waste time and air and take away from the enjoyment of the dive. But most reel jams can be avoided. Many reel jams are caused by improper technique, wherein a diver has allowed the line to go slack. Keep tension on the line at all times. Playing the line back and forth across the spool when reeling it in ensures that the line will not loop over the side and cause a jam. Other reel jams can be avoided by checking the line on land — laying it out and reeling it in, ensuring that the full length of line is available for the dive.

If a jam does occur, the reel should not be forced. Air supply should be evaluated, as well as team position in relation to the dive. If it happens on the way in, or if plenty of air is left, a diver can attempt to fix the jam. The diver should first get stabilized and be certain that minimal silting will occur while working on the reel. A buddy should provide lighting while only one diver works on the reel (unless assistance is requested). If the jam cannot be freed in the water, there are two options. If there is sufficient time, the line can be carefully wrapped around the reel as the team exits. If time and air are short, the line can be tied off and left, to be recovered on another dive.

Visibility Loss

Silting — Minor loss of visibility constitutes another type of incident. Improper technique, bubble percolation on the ceiling, and passage through small, silty areas can cause visibility to decrease. Proper body position and technique helps to avoid encountering this situation. However, in some caves silt may be an unavoidable occurrence in certain areas. For this reason, all visibility reductions do not necessarily dictate a hasty retreat.

When visibility does decrease, divers should remain close to the line and make an *OK* sign around the line with one hand. If visibility is minimal, direct team communication can be maintained by holding on to the arm or leg of the diver ahead. The following are some of the signals a dive team can use in this situation: a slight push for go ahead, a pull for back up, a squeeze (or loss of contact) for stop, two squeezes for *OK*, three squeezes for exit the cave, and several quick squeezes to indicate a problem.

In some cases silting may only require line contact, with buddy recognition maintained by lights. It is important that the lead diver proceed slowly and not out-distance anyone. The lead diver can assist other team members by periodically shining his light backward and downward, helping them determine their location in relation to the cave. Similar to driving a car in fog, there are occasions when dimmer lights help reduce backscatter, making cave features more visible.

In times of low visibility, divers must maintain their relationship to the cave entrance. Divers should never lose their orientation or global awareness. Going into the system, divers should use a compass to identify the direction out and record it on a slate, particularly if there is little or no flow. In a high outflow tunnel, silt will be carried towards the entrance. In these systems, remaining still for a moment or two may allow the passage to clear out. For orientation purposes, a diver should remember that clear water is generally found further into the cave or near the ceiling. However, in a syphon system a dive team may find the silt being carried along with them.

Light Failure — Primary light failure can also cause loss of visibility. Unless a diver carries a second primary light, the dive must be terminated! The safety of the team should not be jeopardized by proceeding even a little further into the cave. Lead divers must be aware of the absence of a following diver's primary light, as the backup light can rarely be expected to flash through the brighter light.

Once the problem has been communicated, the diver without a primary light should usually lead the way out. An alternative to this method of exit is for the entire team to switch to backup lights. This change not only makes all lights equally dim, enhancing dark adaptiveness, but can add an enjoyable quality to the remainder of the dive.

Inadequate Equipment Maintenance

Inadequate equipment maintenance is another source of incidents. Old, worn fin or mask straps can break, causing propulsion or vision problems. Regular inspection of these often neglected fittings can help prevent such an occurrence. If it does happen, exiting the cave is imperative. The mask can be held on by hand. With a lost fin strap a single-legged kick can be used, such as the shuffle kick. In either case buoyancy control and body positioning become more difficult and critical.

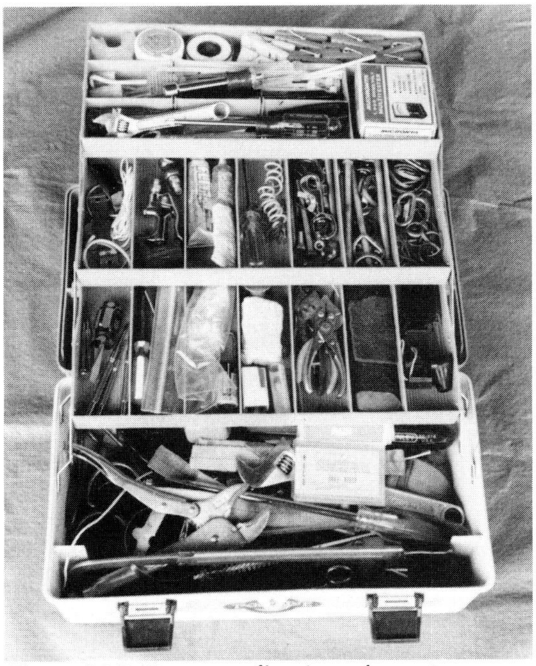

***Figure 14-3** One cave diver's equipment maintenance kit.*

Properly inspecting and maintaining equipment is a way to avoid such problems. Carrying innumerable equipment such as extra masks, straps, and lights is not the answer. Unless a diver has a special consideration, such as contact lenses, this tendency should be avoided.[1] It sometimes leads to a diver with a nightmarish array of extraneous equipment that can only cause confusion. All equipment must be neatly stowed and accessible.

PROBLEMS

Incidents, if handled properly, are an inconvenience rather than an emergency. However, any incident can develop into a problem and progress to a full blown emergency. How a diver reacts may determine the severity of the problem. Divers who stop, get control, and think before acting will avoid many problems and exercise good judgment if they do arise.

Broken Line

Lines can be broken during a dive, especially if a diver is snagged and panics, resorting to violent action in a bid to get free. Whatever the cause of a line break, divers should assess the situation in a calm manner. Since safety lines are generally laid with tension, and nylon line will stretch approximately 30-40%, a diver must be prepared for the line to recoil and shorten, possibly out of sight. Before a diver attempts anything else, a compass bearing of the direction out should be taken. Divers must also maintain good silt control.

If the line is readily visible and within reach, the diver should secure it to the cave or repair it. If a diver cannot see the end of the line leading to the entrance, a safety reel should be secured at the present position with the diver proceeding in the direction of the previous compass reading. Silt prevention techniques are key factors in this process and cannot be overemphasized. Once the line is found, the diver should secure it, mark the direction out, and tie off the line from the safety reel before cutting it.[2]

A team must assess air supply, stress, and team safety when deciding whether or not to repair the break or proceed out of the cave. The line can always be repaired on another dive as long as others are informed of its condition. In most cases line breakage can be avoided through diver awareness — awareness not only of potential entanglement but inspection of the line as it is being laid.

Zero Visibility

Although some visibility loss can present a minor inconvenience, total light failure (highly improbable if each diver carries four lights and checks them before the dive),[3] or a total silt out with complete visbility loss

[1]Divers who wear contact lenses while diving cannot open their eyes underwater without a high probability of losing their contact leanses. Accidental loss of the mask might mean loss of visibility for the remainder of the dive. Such divers sometimes carry spare masks. — Ed.

[2]The safety line will need to be tied off and left in place over the section formerly covered by the permanent line. Attempting to reel in the safety line at this point is potentially hazardous. By cutting the safety line from the safety reel, the reel can be retrieved rather than leaving it behind. — Ed.

[3]Until recently, the NACD recommended that each cave diver carry a minimum of four lights. Due to the increased reliability of underwater lights, NACD now recommends a minimum of three lights per diver. — Ed.

can be a real problem. Loss of communication within the team makes each diver a solo diver with reduced safety. For this reason it is very important that lines of communication be regained through physical contact.

In a no visibility situation, the lead diver should slowly back up until communication is reestablished. Then the team can work together (using the signaling procedure discussed earlier) to assess the situation and decide to either proceed with the dive (a silt out may have been an accepted part of a planned mud passage) or exit the cave. CONTROL is of prime importance in order to avoid entanglements; or cause further silting, which will only prolong the situation.

EMERGENCIES

Some problems leave no decisions as to continuing or exiting the cave. Buoyancy compensator leaks or regulator malfunctions immediately place a diver's life in jeopardy by removing the redundancy control necessary for self sufficiency. Such problems are only a step away from an emergency.

Buoyancy Compensator Failure

Leakage in a buoyancy compensator makes it difficult, if not impossible, to control positioning. If redundant compensating devices are worn, as is often the case when divers are using steel 100's, or if the diver is wearing a dry suit along with a conventional BC, the malfunction of one system reduces the impact of this occurrence. Taking care not to place heavy or pointed objects on the BC during storage and inspecting the bladder before each dive will help prevent failure due to leakage.

When a diver faces such a problem and only has one BC, he may be able to crimp off the hole with one hand, enabling him to exit the cave satisfactorily. If for some reason the tear is so big that it cannot be pinched off, the BC can sometimes be removed (not possible with backmounted BC's) and placed in a position to allow some degree of buoyancy control. In the case of a backmounted unit, body positioning may enable air to be trapped in a portion of the unit. In the worst situation a diver may be forced to crawl out of the cave, using breath control as an aid.

BC failure can also involve the power inflation device. Inflator hose connections can fail or the auto inflator can be made inoperable when a first stage is shut off. Oral inflation is then the only means of buoyancy control and it should be practiced periodically. Whatever the cause of failure, the dive should be terminated with the handicapped diver leading the exit.

Regulator Malfunction

Regulators are designed to operate with precision and it is important to maintain them properly. Regular maintenance of rubber parts, replacement of worn seats, adjustment of intermediate pressure, operation with the high pressure limits, and placement of hoses to prevent abrasion or banging on the ceiling will greatly increase a regulator's dependability.

All divers must be able to reach their own valves and turn them off to ensure a limited loss of air should a free flow malfunction or hose rupture occur. All dives should start with both valves turned ***all the way on*** so that the second regulator can be utilized immediately as the inoperative unit is turned off. Since the valve will only turn in one direction if already completely on, a diver will not waste air trying to figure out which way to turn it.

In a free flow situation involving a single valve manifold, it is possible to turn the air all the way off, occasionally cracking it open to breathe. If the problem involves a leaky exhaust valve, the diver should switch to the second regulator. If there is no second regulator, the diver's hands can be cupped over the exhaust ports to prevent water from entering during inhalation. Regardless of the type of malfunction, the affected diver should lead the exit from the cave.

With a dual valve manifold, regulator malfunctions present a problem but can be dealt with through self help. Without regulator redundancy, a regulator failure places the dive team in an emergency situation. This can also occur with a dual valve manifold if there is a catastrophic failure, such as a tank to valve O-ring rupture, manifold leakage, or a burst-disc rupture. Maintenance and inspection can help make such an occurrence less likely. However, if it occurs the team should be able to work as a unit to efficiently leave the cave. Regular practice of air emergency procedures helps prepare the team for such events.

Sharing Air

A diver signals for sharing air by moving the hand across the throat ("I'm out of air") and then tapping the mouthpiece ("Let's share air"). The assisting diver gives away the regulator attached to the long hose. Whether a diver gives away the regulator in his mouth or the spare, the second mouthpiece must be secured in a readily available spot, such as the neck or chest area. This location also helps protect it from collecting debris and becoming inoperable.

Which regulator a diver should give away is often debated among divers. Regardless of the technique used, divers need to find out before a dive starts which regulator their partners plan to give them in case of an out of air situation. Furthermore, divers should breathe off their partner's regulator to get accustomed to the air delivery and location of the purge button.

Once the exchange has been made, the divers should communicate their readiness to exit the cave. Time taken to assure that the long hose is not twisted, that the abandoned regulator is not a snag hazard, and that buddies are in contact with the line will facilitate a smoother and less hassled retreat. The dependent diver should lead the way to ensure that the regulator is not inadvertently tugged from his mouth, leaving him behind and airless. Divers must focus on proper technique on their exit, to avoid further stress which will further tax their limited air supply.

Lost Buddy

Solo diving should be avoided, yet buddies who do not stay together on a dive become solo divers. Loss of contact is usually a result of poor buddymanship but every team needs to have a plan in case they become separated.

Lead Diver and Alone — When a lead diver notices that his buddy's light is no longer behind him and does not see it after turning around, the reel should be tied off. Clearer water is often found near the ceiling and, by rising slightly, a diver may be able to locate his buddy's light. If there is no sign of the other diver, the lead diver then retraces his steps, taking care to look for side tunnels. If the lead diver is on a permanent line, a compass bearing should be taken and a marker placed on the line showing the direction out. If one buddy is missing from a three person team, the two divers should not separate. They should stay together and monitor air supply closely.

During exit, the diver(s) should look off the line for signs of diver passage, such as bubbles or silt disturbance. All reels should be left in place, with a note tied to the reel indicating that the diver has exited the system.

Following Diver and Alone — If a following diver becomes separated, he should reestablish contact with the line, record the compass direction of the way out on his slate, and place a directional marker on the line. The diver should evaluate his air supply and wait for his buddy's return. A solo diver should not proceed further into the cave.

After a reasonable time, taking into consideration the diver's own anxiety level and air supply, he should exit the cave, leaving a note on the line that indicates he has left the system. The diver should look for signs of his buddy on exit, in case he exited using a different passage. The diver's primary concern is his own safety and he should not jeopardize his life searching for a buddy who might be anywhere (including the surface).

Loss of Buddy and Line

Loss of buddy contact along with loss of line presents a double problem. The primary concern of a diver at this point is to reestablish line contact. This should be done in the most methodical way possible, thus enhancing the diver's problem solving ability. A safety reel should be secured at the diver's present position. After taking a compass bearing, the diver should start looking for the line at 90 degree angles to the exit heading. This should be done slowly and cautiously to avoid stirring up silt or fouling the reel. The diver should be aware of current when searching for the line, as it can easily alter the diver's intended direction.

After the line is found, the diver can follow the procedures outlined previously for lost buddies. Being a lost buddy places a diver in a hazardous situation. In a team, there is never only one lost partner. Each person in a separated team is experiencing an emergency. This is one emergency that is easily avoided if all divers maintain awareness.

Rescue / Recovery

Rescue is a controversial subject in cave diving. Various techniques have been advocated for removing an unconscious or incapacitated diver from a cave to the surface. Some cave divers have advocated keeping the victim face down, with the regulator in place, others say face up, because this is more stable as it rolls the body with the tanks acting as a keel. The best advice is for a dive team to discuss all variations, then practice them.

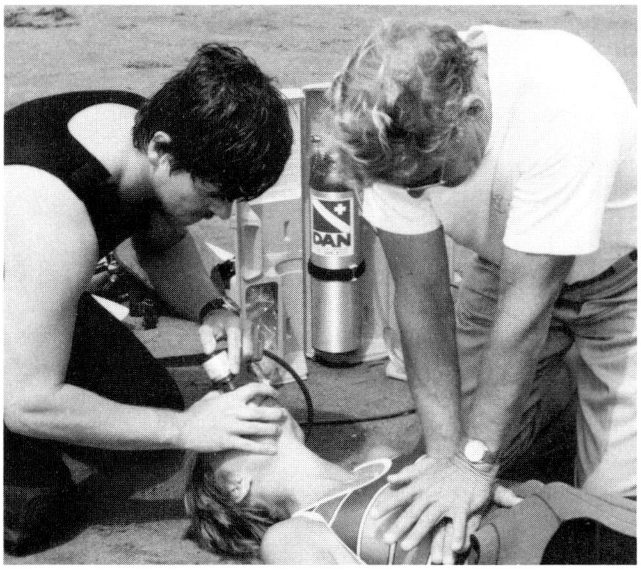

Figure 14-4 CPR Practice

When removing a victim, a diver must control both persons' buoyancy, while still maintaining silt control — visibility is even more critical in this situation. A diver must also maintain awareness of entanglements, position of his buddy's regulator, restrictions, and air supply. Divers must consider their ability to accomplish this successfully before the start of a dive when planning penetration, depth, and bottom time. Physical conditioning may be a factor in a diver's ability to successfully rescue his buddy.

Panic Outside the Team

Cave divers can exercise a high degree of control

over their own actions during a dive and successfully overcome problems that occur. However, at many cave entrances there is a popular cavern or openwater dive site where inexperienced divers may be encountered. Their actions are unpredictable and unfortunately, they sometimes wander into a cave system and panic.

More than once, a cave diver has inadvertently or through good intentions become involved in this life and death struggle. A panicked diver must be approached with **extreme** caution and if he appears totally out of control and presents a danger to others, he must be left alone. There are successful cases where a rescuer waited until unconsciousness occurred and then brought the victim to the surface for resuscitation.

Cave divers should also be aware of placement of lines at popular dive sites. Lines placed in areas of heavy traffic can be an invitation to some divers and a hazard to others. Temporary lines have been cut while in use by a cave team. Divers must consider the system and weigh the safety factors when they decide where to place a line. Divers may want to put a message tag at the start of a temporary line which explains the importance of the line to the cave diver and the danger of following it.

Entrapment

Awareness of a cave configuration can protect divers from becoming trapped. Entrapment can occur as a result of cave collapse or entering a one-way, bottleneck restriction. Although cave collapse in an underwater cave is unlikely due to the supporting effect of water, divers should evaluate the walls and ceilings of a new tunnel. Crumbling mud walls and collapsing layers of bedding plane ceilings are much more hazardous than solid limestone phreatic tubes. Entry into such areas should be made with extreme caution, if at all.

Some divers enjoy exploring small, tight leads in hopes of finding new passages. However, no restriction should be attempted that requires the removal of equipment. Any diver who finds that he is unable to back out of a tunnel should not struggle but relax. The diver's partner may be able to render assistance — a tug, push, or movement of a snagged piece of equipment may be all that is required to free the diver. If passage has been made through to an area and it is found impassable on return, some equipment removal may be necessary. As each piece of equipment is removed, self-sufficiency decreases. It is best to evaluate restrictions and not proceed if they cannot be done easily.

EXTREME PRACTICES

Development of skills to make cave passage easier is the challenge of every dive. Safety equipment and techniques have progressed steadily in recent years. "New" caves are being discovered and explored. Formerly inaccessible areas of "old" caves are being explored as new techniques and equipment are developed, expanding potential cave diving sites. The increased safety of today has expanded the limits of cave diving, paradoxically increasing the possibility of an emergency.

What might be a simple incident near the cave entrance could constitute a disaster several thousand feet back in the system. The use of scooters, stage bottles, large capacity tanks, and new tank-mountings make long or deep penetrations easier. But all distances and obstacles negotiated entering a cave system must be dealt with on exit. Distance and depth lessen the chances of survival in emergencies. Exploration potential has expanded beyond the diver's capabilities of dealing with possible disaster. Great care in planning, along with inner appraisal must be done before extreme cave diving practices are undertaken.

SUMMARY

An open mind, keyed to awareness and continued learning, is necessary for safe and enjoyable cave diving. Whether or not an unplanned situation becomes an incident, problem, or emergency is up to the diver. Personal safety can increase if divers learn from their mistakes and share their knowledge with others. Divers should analyze and evaluate every dive and develop global awareness.

Regardless of the situation, divers should STOP, GET CONTROL, THINK, and then ACT in a positive and controlled manner. Even when not in the water, divers can improve their reaction to incidents by using their imagination and running through possible scenarios. Finally, divers should never have doubts about their safety during the planning of a dive. They should heed their feelings in order to avoid pushing themselves beyond their limits. When all members of a dive team are confident in their ability to deal with any situation that might arise, they will have an enjoyable and successful dive.

Chapter 15

STRESS IN CAVE DIVING

by Robert W. Smith

INTRODUCTION

Stress has always been a subject of interest to most divers and to cave divers in particular. We are aware that we are *under stress* and concerned about *panic* while cave diving. Panic can be described as a final and critical reaction to a compounding series of stressful events. Stress affects the diver's performance in many ways which are generally more subtle but often just as dangerous as panic itself. Similarly, the phenomenon of stress occurs in many forms which may be recognized as such by the diver. The purpose of this chapter is to identify sources of stress in cave diving, describe the possible effects which stress may have upon the diver's performance, and suggest methods for combatting stress and minimizing its negative effects.

Stress is defined by Webster as a force that strains or deforms. In the context of human behavior, stress might be regarded as a force that tends to break down an individual's ability to perform. Physical stress has a tendency to weaken or injure the diver, while psychological stress leads to behavior impairment and to what we often refer to as *human error.*

The physical stresses of cave diving are presented in other sections. The present discussion will focus on psychological stress. However, factors such as exertion, cold, pain, etc., can also be a source of psychological stress to the diver. For this reason, the psychological or behavioral aspects of physical stress will be included in this discussion.

SOURCES OF STRESS

Time Pressure

A common practice of psychologists who want to induce error into an experimental situation is to put people under time pressure. The race against the clock has long been recognized as a source of both physical and mental stress with regard to human performance.

Perhaps you think that your reason for cave diving is "to relax and get away from it all." People do not ordinarily regard their means of recreation and enjoyment as a source of time pressure, but think about the profile of a typical cave dive for a moment. First, there is the dive itself. Are you going to attempt a penetration or perhaps a traverse from one entrance to another exit? One reason that traverses are avoided early in cave diving training is due to the time pressure it involves. In view of the nature of the sport, however, cave diving always involves some form of time pressure.

Take the simple exploration of a large chamber near the mouth of the cave, for example. This type of dive profile by no means eliminates the need to keep an eye on your watch and pressure gauge. The nature of the dive exploration may distract you from gauge monitoring just long enough to make things tight when you finally remember to look at your console. If you wait too long, you begin to rush and make mistakes. On the other hand, preoccupation with gauges can become a distracting and, therefore, stressful activity.

Our training usually makes us aware of this form of stress in cave diving and thus explains our reason for wearing watches. But there is another form of time pressure in cave diving which sometimes escapes attention. It occurs during pre-dive activities, and it can get us into much trouble as rushing into a cave.

Let's look at a typical, relaxing, cave diving weekend. It may start on Friday night with the rush to get our gear packed for the six hour drive to the cave. The quicker we get ready, the sooner we can leave, the sooner we can arrive at the site for the big night dive or the cookout. It is a great chance to leave some gear behind or to start out with 1800 psig of air in our tanks.

Then begins the actual dive preparation itself. On a bad day, perhaps two of your buddies have started the long walk to the cave while you are still standing around on your tarpaulin with 85 percent of the gear on your back, 10 percent still at your feet, and your spare light locked in someone else's van. This can lead to deadly impatience and two types of error: either forgetting something, or worse yet, not caring. These are, interestingly enough, the same kind of mistakes we make when concerned, anxious, frightened, terrified, or otherwise under what we commonly recognize as stress. Remember, the stress of time pressure can sneak up on you disguised as part of the general excitement of the dive and create a whole set of problems of its own.

Task Loading

Another little trick that psychologists use to get people to make mistakes in experimental situations is called *task loading*. It simply involves giving people more jobs to do than they can effectively perform in a given time period or assigning them competitive tasks which require them to do two or more things at the same time.

One thing that can be said about cave diving is that you are never bored. Perhaps one of the most sat-

Figure 15-1 Double staging and other advanced types of diving add significantly to the already high task loading of cave diving.

isfying aspects of this sport is that it is technically challenging. One must keep in mind, however, that the line which separates challenge from stress is a very thin one indeed.

Under routine conditions, the cave diver may find herself handling a reel, directing her light, controlling her buoyancy, avoiding silt, wall referencing, watching her buddy, checking her air, checking her time, and a multitude of other tasks. Under non-routine conditions or in an emergency, things can really begin to get complicated. A novice can get a little panicky just thinking about the task loading associated with a cave dive. This stress factor can affect even an expert's behavior more than she may realize.

Exertion and Cold

Scientists at UCLA (University of California at Los Angeles) have observed heart rates of 160 beats per minute (70 to 80 is normal) in divers who have just finished gearing up for an ocean dive off the beach in southern California. At this point in the diving day, the cave diver may just be ready to start a 200-yard walk through the brush to the dive site, fully equipped including dry suit and double 100's. This kind of activity tends to make even the most well-conditioned diver a little out of breath, which is exactly what you don't want at the beginning of a dive. Once you are in the water and ready to begin the dive, the possibility of overexertion still exists. Working against the current, particularly in a tight squeeze, is an obvious source of physical challenge. Perhaps more subtle is the milder, but continuous exertion associated with a long penetration dive.

The physical stress found in this type of activity is obvious. Psychologically it can also affect you, primarily through distraction relating to your physical condition, when you should be paying attention to other aspects of the dive.

The chill factor associated with diving can affect people in the same way. The staged decompression frequently associated with cave diving makes cold stress a significant factor. The chills usually affect a diver during her decompression stops when the dive is "practically over." If you think a minor distraction cannot lead to trouble at that point in your dive, consider the consequences of misreading your watch by ten minutes.

Lack of Visibility / Directional Reference

Let us consider some of the more obvious stresses associated with cave diving. One of the factors you consider is the darkness, which of course will not exist if you carry the proper lighting systems into the cave. Naturally, the possibility exists that your light may go out. This should not be a problem since your buddies have lights and you always have backup systems. You may have a temporary problem, but it is usually solved when you gather your thoughts and start back to the surface.

At this point another dubious stress factor may come into the picture due to the directional requirements associated with cave diving. When your light fails, you cannot ascend directly to the surface; you must go back the way you came. Upon entering the cave, it is assumed that you are close to the line and are wall referencing; however, you are accomplishing both of these with the use of your primary light. When you go to your backup light, the beam is often not as bright, and because of that, things look different on the way out than they did with the stronger light coming in. It is just another form of stress.

A silt out is not so subtle, however. This kind of darkness, which can be created by the diver or by some natural phenomenon, can be extremely stressful. Combined with the directional requirements of cave diving, a total loss of visibility can be one of the most stressful phenomena you will ever encounter. As indicated later in this chapter, this type of stress can be managed effectively. However, the majority of silt-outs are created by the divers themselves and fall within the category of *things to avoid.*

Confinement, Restrictions, and Distance

When an individual first considers cave diving as an avocation, the words *confinement* and *claustrophobia* are likely to be part of the conversation. People who have obvious or severe claustrophobia should not cave dive. The individual who tries to kick her claustrophobia by going "cold turkey" in a cave does not need any stress; she has already lost her marbles. The real concern with regard to the stress of confinement associated with cave diving is the person with latent claustrophobia. This person has herself pretty well un-

Figure 15-2 Cave diving can bring out latent claustrophobia.

der control in most situations but requires just a little something special to push her over the edge. Needless to say, the confinement associated with cave diving has a number of special considerations.

One is the possibility of physical restriction. Negotiating a restriction in a cave to get to "paradise" on the other side can add dimension to latent claustrophobia, which makes a brief stay in a stalled elevator pale into insignificance.

Another is the phenomenon of distance. Distance is the rather hard-to-describe awareness that when a problem occurs in a cave you cannot go up; you have to go back. The door out of the crowded room is open; only it will take you a long time to get there. This particular phenomenon occasionally creates a rather bizarre stress reaction in divers who successfully negotiate a restriction, and then as they continue their dive, become increasingly concerned about the return trip.

Loss of Body Control

A person is much less susceptible to panic and other stress reactions when she feels that she "has everything under control." For this reason, loss of body control on the part of a diver in a cave or even in openwater can be disconcerting. In cave diving this loss of control usually occurs as a result of one of two factors: either strong current or a buoyancy problem. In both cases, the diver may end up moving in a direction in which she does not intend to move. In a cave this can be particularly stressful since small passages do not allow bouncing room; there are more obstacles to strike, more equipment to damage, and certain directions in which the diver definitely does not want to go. When added to other stress factors such as loss of visibility, this loss of control can be quite distracting to a diver who is already "using mental blinders," otherwise known as *perceptual narrowing.*

Cumulative Factors

The previous paragraph alluded to the impact of multiple factors as building stress within the diver. Two consequential facts are: multiple problems are more stressful than single problems, and in cave diving (or any other undertaking in a challenging environment) problems tend to multiply once the first one occurs. It is therefore appropriate to consider what has just been said in this chapter in the context of possible multiple occurrences, such as time pressure, overexertion, lack of visibility, and confinement, rather than optimistically thinking that problems only happen one at a time.

Physical Threat

The stress of physical threat, of course, overlays all of the stress factors that have been discussed thus far. A well adjusted person is, most likely, not afraid of the dark. Darkness or poor visibility are stressful to the cave diver because they make navigation more difficult and confront her with the physical threat of entrapment and drowning. Task loading and time pressure may be mildly annoying as issues in themselves to a cave diver, or to a tennis player, but the cave diver realizes that errors made as a result of these factors can threaten her physically. The non-claustrophobic diver is still stressed by confinement; not simply because there are walls around her, but because those walls lie between her and a permanent air supply. This kind of physical threat lies at the core of much of the stress in cave diving and must be recognized as a general stress related to the sport.

Ego Threat

Physical threat is not the only form of stress in the world. An individual can be effectively destroyed by tearing down her self esteem, her pride, or as we sometimes call it, her ego. It is no secret that some insecure people may attempt to build or strengthen their egos through participation in such "heroic" sports as sky diving, mountain climbing, and scuba diving. Because of its technical complexity and environmental challenge, cave diving must be viewed by many as the ultimate ego trip. For those who are so motivated, it is often a one-way trip.

In the first place, the challenge of cave diving has no limits within the capability of our current technology. In this respect, every cave diver alive can and will encounter situations which, if pursued, would extend the individual and her equipment beyond the limits of her capability. An emotionally mature person with true *ego strength* can walk or swim away from such situations with no damage to her ego. The truly mature person can do this even when others may extend themselves further into the situation, either because of their superior capability or their own foolishness. The threat to her ego when she must back away from a challenge can be quite stressful, and tolerance to this stress is important in cave diving.

Figure 15-3 It takes maturity and true ego strength to turn the dive when your partner wants to go "just a little more."

If this tolerance does not exist, one encounters the second problem related to ego threat. The individual, either through challenge from within herself or because of social pressure from her peers, overextends herself thereby endangering herself and her companions. When this happens, a diver has demonstrated her inability to withstand the stress of ego threat and has become a prime candidate for a diving accident.

This leads to the final and somewhat ironic source of stress in cave diving: the divers themselves. Divers may be stressful to themselves if they are incompetent and know it. Finally, a diver may stress her companions into a catastrophic situation simply by threatening their egos. This occurs when they are constantly challenged to test their limits in order to save their pride.

EFFECT OF STRESS

Introduction

Now that we have established that the sources of stress in cave diving are almost unlimited, we will go on to find that the effects of stress are equally numerous. Please do not despair. In the final section of this chapter, you will learn ways to neutralize the effects of stress or, better yet, eliminate the source. First, you need to understand the problem.

Behavioral Mechanics of Stress — Mental Narrowing

As an individual is subjected to increasingly greater stress, more and more interference is created with the mental processes which stand between the environment and her reaction to that environment. A mental narrowing occurs which reduces the diver's sensitivity to her environment, hampers her ability to intelligently analyze the situation, and limits the number of skills and the amount of knowledge which she will bring to bear on a problem.

Perceptual Narrowing

Under stress, a diver may fail to notice the more subtle aspects of her situation ("My tank valve is caught on the safety line") and perceive only the more obvious factors ("I cannot move"). Termination of your air supply can be stressful in any situation, even a swimming pool training session. It produces more stress as depth increases, but it becomes especially stressful on a cave dive. In this situation, the diver's sensitivity to certain clues in her environment may be somewhat limited. She may not notice she is pulling water through her regulator. Bubbles being expelled from a major air leak somewhere in your breathing system is a dramatic experience easily detected in a swimming pool, but sometimes not even noticeable to a diver under stress.

Cognitive or Analytic Narrowing

Your ability to analyze a situation may also be hampered under stress. When your underwater pressure gauge indicates 1200 psig and you cannot breathe, it would seem to indicate a problem in the second stage of your regulator. Under enough stress a diver may not recognize this and may attempt to get out of a cave on her buddy's air without ever thinking to try the backup regulator. This kind of narrow thinking can extend to wall referencing, other navigation requirements, or to decompression problems.

Response Narrowing

The number of skills and bits of knowledge that a diver draws upon to cope with her environment also begins to diminish under stress. The first things to go are behaviors that have been poorly learned or insufficiently reinforced. The last skills to fail her are those which are so well learned that they have become virtually reflexive in nature. Unfortunately, this last category of behavior is not always the best way to solve the problem. A classic example of this in scuba diving is breath holding while on scuba. Years of experience prior to our diving training tells us to hold our breath when we are out of air. But this, of course, is not the appropriate thing to do when one is ascending following termination of the air supply while scuba diving. Breath holding during an ascent is something that we know is dangerous to do, yet some divers continue to revert to this more primitive behavior when they are under stress.

Divers have been known to buddy breathe during an emergency by passing a regulator back and forth between themselves when the diver supplying the air was wearing a backup regulator. Their subsequent explanation that they "liked the old method better" seems less credible than the possibility that they ***knew*** the old method better and simply overlooked the other possibilities while under stress. As a last resort, it occurs to most divers that breathing off their buoyancy compensator when their air supply is dangerously low has a lifesaving potential. Nevertheless, there is considerable evidence that this unique and seldom rehearsed alternative is usually overlooked by a diver under the stress of a last-ditch situation.

Panic

Panic, put simply, is the ultimate in mental narrowing. It marks a point at which there is no longer a relationship between what is happening to a diver and what she is doing about it.

We have seen that as stress increases, the diver's ability to diagnose problems and respond to them properly may diminish accordingly. It is predictable that more mistakes will be made. As more mistakes occur, stress increases for two reasons.

1) Mistakes usually do not fix a problem. Because of this, the possibility of physical threat tends to increase.

2) As the divers begin to realize that they are making mistakes, ego threat comes into the picture as an additional stress factor.

In any stressful situation, it is critical for the individual to break out of this escalating cycle as quickly as possible. As in any pathological condition, early detection is important. Thus, it is desirable to recognize the early symptoms of stress, in your own behavior and in the behavior of others, before these symptoms reach panic proportions. Panic is the end of the line. It is usually both terminal and contagious. It is very hard to control, as far as remedial actions are concerned. Fortunately, the behavior which we refer to as panic is preceded by a long string of other behaviors which, if properly recognized, can be used as a barometer by the intelligent diver both to determine her level of tension and her own individual sources of stress.

Physiological Effects of Stress

We are designed with a physiological adaption mechanism for contending with stress, unlike the other animals whom we competed with for existence. This adaption mechanism pumps adrenaline into the system and does other things to prepare us for battle when we are confronted with a stressful event. Unfortunately, these mechanisms were not all designed with scuba diving in mind. They include, among other things, a marked increase in heart rate and level of respiration. This can be detrimental to the diver in many situations, but it usually occurs whether desired or not. In many dire situations, it is unnecessary to check one's pulse, however, in other situations it provides essential information. Perhaps you can remember a time, either when diving or under other circumstances, when you were suddenly surprised to realize that your heart was "beating out of control." Along with that, your air consumption was twice that which you considered normal. Although many interesting things may happen to your body as part of a stress reaction while diving, increased air consumption is by far the most significant. You must always assume that this is happening under stress unless you are capable of making a deliberate and successful attempt to control it.

BEHAVIORAL EFFECTS OF STRESS

General Stress Reactions

When an individual succumbs to stress, she may exhibit certain strange behavior patterns, which while falling short of panic, are clearly identifiable as something other than normal. The *wild-eyed look* is not just a figure of speech; it actually occurs with some people in tight situations. The diver who exhibits this is unmistakably and clearly in trouble.

Rapid, jerky, and unrhythmic movement is another obvious sign of a diver under stress, as is trembling when the water is not that cold. Be alert for these warning signals in your own behavior. Another general sign of anxiety is muscle tension. The "white-knuckle look" is worth looking for in yourself and others during a dive. You may notice a heightened sense of fatigue in your hand when holding your spare light after the main one has failed: more tiring than holding the larger, heavier light on the way into the cave. Continuing to hold on to something after your mind tells you to let it go is another general sign of tension. It may be particularly embarrassing when you see you are holding a purge or filler valve on your buoyancy compensator.

Irritability or other extremes in mood can be a stress reaction which you should be alert to prior to, as well as during a dive. Knowing yourself and your buddy is very useful in detecting the more subtle signs of stress.

Perhaps the most subtle form of a general stress reaction is fixation or repetitive behavior. Preoccupation with a depth gauge or watch, as opposed to a general vigilance, is a common sign of stress in a diver. When your buddy begins to methodically wipe off a pressure gauge that is not dirty, repair a piece of gear that is not broken, or repeatedly clear a mask that is not flooded, it is definitely time to lead her gently out of the cave.

Human Error

By far the most significant effect of stress on the diver's performance is the commission of errors. People, including divers, make mistakes for a number of reasons. One of these is stress; yet it is the one we are less likely to admit. We can blame our instructors, the environment, and our equipment, but the fact remains that all kinds of errors occur with a greater frequency under conditions which have previously been described in the chapter as stressful. Certain kinds of errors occur under these conditions which rarely occur in other situations.

***Figure 15-4* Depth, distance and CAS can greatly add to the stress of unanticipated problems.**

The performance of basic skills often deteriorates under stress. A diver who can clear a mask any day of the week under normal conditions may experience difficulty performing the same task after having her mask kicked off. Similarly, disentanglement from a line is usually fraught with more errors 300 feet back in a cave than it is in the middle of a swimming pool during a training session. The diver who can perform admirably in a cave with the same proficiency as in other situations has taken the first major step in coping effectively with stress.

The second class of behavioral miscues which occur under stress is errors in judgment. We are all known to occasionally do things a little differently "in the heat of battle" than we would during a formal training session. However, if in retrospect a diver cannot explain a decision she made in a cave on a rational basis, she should look closely at the stressful aspects of that situation and how she arrived at her decision. Use of poor judgment in tieing off a line too frequently on the way into a cave may reflect a reaction to physical threat stress. Poor judgment in tying off the line too infrequently could be a reaction to ego threat. In either case, stress induces poor judgment. You may, of course, tie a line off too frequently simply as an honest mistake. The question to ask yourself following a dive is: *Knowing what I knew then, would I do things the same way in a similar situation?* If the answer is yes, blame your mistakes on inadequate skills; if the answer is no, look for the stress elements involved.

The final category of errors includes those for which there are no excuses. We usually label them as *careless mistakes.* Stories of such errors, when we admit to them, are usually preceded by the phrase, "it was silly of me, but...." These stories are usually told with a sheepish grin, if we are still alive to tell them at all. Quite often they are, in fact, little things which do not present a real hazard to us as divers. If you make careless mistakes all of the time when you dive, you should not be diving. If you make them some of the time, or rarely, then you are probably making them because something in the situation is stressful. Locate your source of stress and read on to see how you can contend with it.

COMBATING STRESS

Introduction

Folklore has it that tolerance to stress is an inherent trait that an individual either has or does not have. It may be true that certain individuals have such a low stress tolerance that diving, particularly cave diving, is an ill-advised activity for them. On the other hand, each one of us has the capacity to develop our stress tolerance by learning and practicing specific techniques for battling stress. While previous sections of this chapter may have presented a rather discouraging picture with regard to the sources of stress in cave diving and the possible effects on a diver's behavior, their purpose is really a positive one. The reader is now aware that stress is not a mystical phenomenon, but rather an affliction that can be tied to specific events within a diver's environment and to specific behaviors the diver may exhibit. Hopefully, the following pages will make you as confident of your ability to cope with stress as you are with your ability to avoid decompression sickness, air embolism, and other diving hazards.

Anticipation

An interesting discovery made some years ago by psychologists who were studying stress in human behavior was that it was not so much what you did to people that made them succumb to stressful situations, but rather what you did to them in relation to what they expected to happen. That is, people generally exhibit greater tolerance to stress when it is the type and intensity of stress that they expect. It is only when they encounter something which they had not anticipated that people tend to succumb to stress.

This means that it is very important for a diver to anticipate those aspects of a diving situation which may be stressful to her. Minimizing the surprise is half the battle. The more familiar divers are with an incident which could occur during a cave dive, the more capable they are in solving it, and the less stress it generates.

There are several ways to reduce stress related to the unknown in cave diving. Once you and your instructor have identified all of the potential problems which could occur during a cave dive in both routine and emergency conditions, experience then becomes the best teacher. That is why the cave diving curriculum requires a certain skill level and a specific number of open-water dives. The more experience you have in a multitude of situations, the less likely you are to be stressed by an "unexpected occurrence." When you first venture into a new situation, you should be accompanied by an individual who is trained and competent in that skill.

Some of the more stressful aspects of cave diving and particularly those which occur in an emergency situation should, if at all possible, be experienced in open water. In these situations simulation in a pool or other controlled environments is an excellent way of preparing yourself for the stress involved. Moving on a safety line in zero visibility while buddy breathing is an experience which we go to great lengths to avoid in a cave, but which can be effectively simulated during training.

In some cases, neither experience nor simulation can help because the situation is simply too dangerous to practice or too difficult to simulate. Studies have shown that mental rehearsal in itself is an effective way of combating stress and enhancing human performance in emergency situations. It involves three steps:

1) Information Gathering,

2) Group Planning,

3) Individual Planning.

The first step has to do with the collection of every piece of information that is available regarding the dive environment which you are about to enter. You obtain this information from people who have dived at that site before or from notes you have gathered from previous dives. You have ample opportunity to review this information while traveling to the dive site or from discussions with other divers prior to entering the water. When you and your buddies discuss the dive plan, consider not only the directional aspects of the dive, but special conditions which will affect your performance during the dive, such as current, silt, restrictions, etc. Remember, the reason for dive planning and discussion is to avoid surprises that may be just around the corner.

Dive planning as a group is a common practice, particularly among cave divers. Everyone agrees on where they are going, what they are going to do, who handles the line, and other pertinent information. If you want to avoid stress during a cave dive, the emphasis during group planning should be upon flexibility, not rigidity. Consider possible alternatives so as to avoid undue stress in case changes have to be made.

Individual dive planning is something that many of us fail to adequately do, and it may be the most important factor in dive planning, as far as stress tolerance is concerned. Following the group planning session while gearing up, you, as a diver, should consider what the dive plan means to you personally. Is it compatible with your air consumption? Does it involve the use of skills with which you are not generally familiar or something that you haven't practiced in a long time? Is there a new condition such as mud walls which you have never encountered in a cave before? If so, how do you personally plan to handle yourself in that situation? Are you properly equipped to do the job that you are supposed to do, both in terms of the hardware you have to carry and your ability to use it? Do not let time pressure deter you from this planning task. Indeed, individual dive planning is good insurance. It is a way to ensure that you have not allowed something to slip by because you are rushing into the dive.

Once in the water, your planning should continue. Wall referencing is a good example of dive planning *en route*; it is designed to minimize the stress of getting lost on your way out. Other factors can also be anticipated, however. Why be surprised at the strength of a current on the way out, when you swam against it all the way in? If you try three different ways through a restriction on the way into a cave, you should only have to try one on the way out. Always think ahead during your dive and eliminate the time pressure, ego threat, and perhaps the physical threat of having to plan a response well into a situation which you could have anticipated.

You may notice that a horror movie loses some of its impact after its third rerun on the late show. The reason? By the third rerun you know what all the monsters look like and what to expect when the hero turns the corner or the heroine backs into a closet. There are too many good things about cave diving to worry about turning it into a horror show. Anticipation through experience, simulation, and good dive planning can do much to maximize the pleasure and minimize the stress.

Over-Learning and Maintenance

As mentioned earlier, one effect of stress is to cause you to make mistakes even in basic skills if they are not particularly well learned. The skills required for emergency performance can be even more vulnerable to stress since less time is spent practicing emergency skills than other diving behaviors.

The United States Air Force and other agencies engaged in the training of personnel for duties which may involve stress long ago adopted the principle of ***over-learning*** as a means for assuring effective performance in tense situations. The principle is easy to understand but somewhat frustrating to implement. Each one of us has had the experience of trying repeat-

Figure 15-5 Reel handling is a basic skill in cave diving; however, the ultimate perfection of this skill is difficult to achieve.

edly to master a particular skill and finally, after many failures, performing it correctly. There is then a strong tendency to "quit while you are ahead." The difference between learning and over-learning is the contrast between having done something correctly once and being able to demonstrate that you can do something correctly every time, then continuing to practice. Over-learning takes all of the doubt out of performance under stress with regard to that particular skill. This not only greatly reduces the probability of human error while accomplishing certain tasks, but also frees the diver's mind to solve, confidently, more complex aspects of the problem.[1]

Reel handling is a basic skill in cave diving; however, the ultimate perfection of this skill is difficult to achieve. Practicing reel handling can be a pain in the neck, wrist, ankle, pressure gauge, or any other place that the line can be potentially entangled. At the same time, sloppy reel handling can cost you time, energy, or even your life in a stressful situation. Poor performance in this skill can snowball to a point that will actually impede your exit. Over-learning can eliminate this anxiety.

We must then consider the human frailty known as *forgetting.* Everybody forgets, and by doing it, you throw the benefits of over-learning right out the window. ***The maintenance of skills is going to be a critical factor in your ability to confront the stressful aspect of cave diving.*** Once they have passed their basic course, some open-water divers can go for several years without ever needing to clear their mask. This is an unfortunate occurrence because even openwater divers have certain skills they should practice before each dive such as mask clearing, switching to backup regulators, signals, etc. Some diving organizations require regular checkouts of even their most seasoned divers, interspersed with opportunities to drill in various procedures.

If this appears "Mickey Mouse," try teaching. If you feel that you do not need to practice knot tying, mask clearing, reel handling, or any easily-forgotten-if-not-practiced skill once in a while to stay sharp, make it a habit on a regular basis to demonstrate these skills to your students. Good old *ego threat* will come to your aid and make sure you stay sharp. Making a fool of yourself in front of a class after a year's layoff in the performance of some skill is not as bad as finding out 600 feet back in a cave.

Familiarization with Equipment

When viewing a photograph of a well equipped cave diver, one occasionally has difficulty identifying the diver. All they see is a pile of equipment bouncing through the woods. It is better to have jokes made about the equipment than to desperately need an item which you do not have with you, or worse yet, not able to use an item you lugged along. Everyone nods their head when we talk about being familiar with their equipment. Yet, a diver under stress may open the valve on her buoyancy compensator when she means to close it, break the switch off her emergency light while trying to move it in the wrong direction, or otherwise foul things up unless she knows what the term *equipment familiarization* really means.

Equipment familiarization does not mean, *"I am using a new buoyancy compensator today."* It means *"My new buoyancy compensator has a self-contained air supply. The red valve on the right side of the vest turns counter-clockwise, back toward me, to fill the vest and clockwise, away from me, to stop filling. Venting is accomplished by pushing a button near my right shoulder. Being new, the button is rather stiff right now. When the vest fills, it tends to raise my shoulder and my feet drop"* and so on.

Under the behavioral narrowing of stress, a diver does not have time to remind herself where her equipment is located and how it works. Fixation can cause her to continue to grope for her spare light on the left side of her belt when for some reason she relocated it on the right just before the dive.

Know your equipment intimately. Practice with a new piece of gear before you take it in the water, even if you are embarrassed about it and have to lock yourself in the garage to do it. When you are in the water catching your breath before descent, try the new equipment out along with any old equipment you have not used lately. As in the case of your basic skills, total familiarity with your equipment keeps you out of many stressful situations and helps you get out of others with a minimum of fuss and bother.

Physiological Control

Some very exciting research is currently being con-

[1]Studies have shown that the average person must repeat a correctly performed skill between 16 and 20 times to become comfortable performing it. — Ed.

ducted on people's ability to self regulate certain physiological functions with an eye toward enhancing their performance under stress. The research involves biofeedback training. Remarkable results have been obtained in certain individuals' ability to control such things as heart rate, blood pressure, and even brain waves; the most popular of which has been alpha rhythm. Direct links have yet to be established between behavioral control and physiological self-regulation techniques suitable for field use in an environment such as diving. This approach of combatting stress, as with other innovative techniques, presents a potential for both benefit and harm. The benefits of a slowed heart rate and lower level of respiration to a diver are obvious; the dangers lie in our relative ignorance of diving physiology and the possible interaction between physiological self-regulation and other physical reactions to diving such as bradycardia.

Until more research is done, the diver under stress is advised to adhere to the more traditional approach of physiological control commonly known as *get a hold of yourself* or *cool it.* It is still good advice. While we still cannot be sure what impact the calming of the body will do to the functioning of the mind, we definitely know that increased air consumption is not something that the diver under stress wants to confront. The stressed diver is well advised to keep a channel open to her heart rate, particularly her breathing rate, and if possible, take a minute to slow herself down if it appears that her body is over-reacting to her psychological problems.

Thinking Under Stress

Anticipation, over-learning basic skills, familiarization with equipment, and physiological control will take a diver only so far. In a stressful situation there is always the need to think clearly. There is also plenty of evidence, some of it tragic, that in many cases divers have simply stopped thinking under stress. Two mental techniques can be brought to bear on this problem.

Observation and Analysis

The first critical step in thinking clearly under stress is observation and analysis: These are not "action words." Someone might say, *Look buddy, when I am in the dark, 120 feet down, and 500 feet back with no air, that is no time for observation and analysis; that is the time for action.* ***THINK AGAIN!*** Such a situation is, very clearly, the time to stop and decide if you are indeed out of air, why you do not have air, and how you can go about getting air in the most efficient manner possible.

This is not to suggest that a diver should sit down and draw out a flow chart if this happens. Observation and analysis may only take a split second, but it may be the most important split second in a diver's life. Taking the wrong action, no matter how fast you do it, could kill you. There is ample evidence that you, the diver, have strong tendencies to take the wrong action when under real stress. Many people who act before they think and find themselves in a crucial situation can get out of it on the third try. Only one problem, though: often they will have only one or two chances available to them.

When a diver finds hersef in trouble — for example, when she is caught in a strong current, starts tumbling and loses her mouthpiece — there is a sequence of events she can follow which will help solve the problem efficiently and also eliminate stress.

1. ***STOP*** To act immediately often leads to panic.
2. ***GET CONTROL*** Take command of your built-in problem-solver, your brain. Look around you, take inventory to see if you have air and reference where you are in relation to your environment.
3. ***THINK*** This is the main step in the sequence and executing it is the most effective way of eliminating panic and solving the problem. Ask yourself, *Where am I, what is wrong, and what should I do?* By taking a few seconds to evaluate the problem, you can determine which action is appropriate.
4. ***ACT*** Your actions should be appropriate and performed in a calm and deliberate manner. While tumbling, your regulator moves within your grasp. You reach for it, purge it and cautiously take a breath. If you do not take the time to think before acting, an inappropriate maneuver could produce a fatal outcome.
5. ***EVALUATE*** Is the solution you have chosen yielding effective results? You have your regulator and now you can proceed to stop your tumbling. Do not continue executing a maneuver if it is not eliminating the problem. If you find after evaluating the situation that you have not solved your problem, repeat steps 3-5: THINK...ACT...RE-EVALUATE. Remember, when you find yourself in a stressful situation:

STOP
GET CONTROL
THINK
ACT
EVALUATE

This will help you solve problems, eliminate stress, and do away with the need for a rescue.

Let us look at a potential problem that could occur while training in the cavern: not having control of your buoyancy, then bumping the ceiling extremely hard with your first stage, causing a violent free flow which has left you choking. If this occurs, you are left there gagging with a feeling of air hunger. Do you rip through hoses looking for your backup, sending pieces of equipment in all directions? If you do, you may find your submersible pressure gauge in your mouth and you trying to breathe off it. The *thinking diver,* even if she is hurting just as much for air, takes a split second to make sure that the thing in her mouth is a regulator, that it is right side up, and that she is turning off the air on the bad regulator rather than removing it

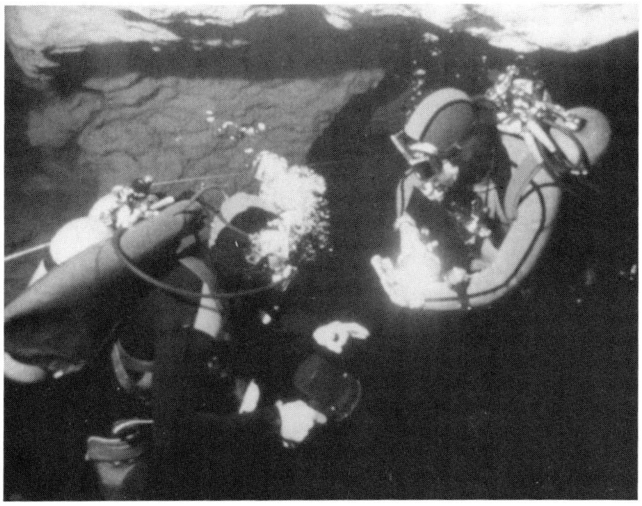

Figure 15-6 An attentive dive partner can ease the stress of entanglement.

from the tank valve. Put your basic skills and knowledge of equipment to use, but stop to think about it first. If you watch people practicing this kind of drill, you can actually see a split second hesitation when a good diver is confronted with a problem and reacts initially with observation and analysis.

Another example of good and bad behavior occurs when somebody gets pulled up short by a line caught in her tank valve. Divers who succumb easily to stress may initially lunge against the line until they finally admit that they are caught and perhaps even succeed in putting another loop or two around the valve. The desired behavior, or course, is to put on the brakes, back off a little, and start feeling around for the problem. There is nothing wrong with moving quickly in an emergency. That is what all the training in basic skills is for, but a good cave diver should know that it is well worth while to think before she acts.[2]

Disciplined Thinking-Concentration

The type of thinking described above obviously requires self-discipline. While this characteristic may to a great extent be inherent within the individual, some self-control can be instilled within your own behavior through training. In order to accomplish this, you must recognize the need to concentrate upon solving a problem rather than worrying about it. This is a very narrow distinction, but it is important. Let us assume, for example, that your buddy's regulator begins to free flow just before you reach your turn around point and that she runs out of air while you are still well back into the cave. The dive team should be expediently exiting the cave, buddy breathing from your air supply. To make it more exciting, we will add more stress factors. First let's assume that you must negotiate a restriction which contains silt and requires an individual swim-through. Second, a question now exists as to whether your air supply will be adequate for the required decompression slated for this dive.[3]

In a situation such as this, there are a great many things that you can worry about: getting stuck in the restriction, getting lost, drowning, getting the bends, wondering what it feels like to drown or get bent, trying to remember whether your life insurance is paid up, and wondering if your children will ever get through college.

None of these are appropriate thoughts for a diver under stress. In this particular situation, you and your buddy should both be thinking about how you will get through the restriction which lies ahead and what alternatives you have for augmenting your air supply for decompression. Thinking about anything but how to solve your problem is very inefficient behavior under this type of intense stress. You should try at every opportunity to instill, within yourself, the self-discipline required to behave appropriately.

Concentration is the answer to this form of self-discipline. Your objective is to concentrate on those aspects of the problem that matter and to ignore the other often emotional issues which are involved in this situation. You can examine your own capacity for this pattern of concentration in a number of ways Set up several mathematic problems of equivalent difficulty and time yourself in answering half of them while sitting in a living room chair. Then, see if you can answer the other half just as quickly while sitting on the bottom of a pool or standing in a cold shower. Problem solving while breath holding is another excellent way to test and develop your ability to concentrate under stress. In these situations, you will note a distinct tendency to concentrate upon your need to breathe rather than the problem before you. Passing out from hypoxia

[2]When performing any physical skill, proficiency is measured in terms of four elements: accuracy, coordination, efficiency and speed. The truly proficient diver always manifests these four ACES of technique. — Ed.

[3]When planning your D/C gas supply, you should have placed adequate gas not only for the planned maximum depth and time, but also including a safety factor in case either or both of these parameters increased unavoidably during the dive. — Ed.

while working math problems at the kitchen table is not a recommended procedure. However, the practice of drills such as those just described under controlled conditions may serve to develop a self discipline and concentration which will enable you to cope effectively with high stress in real diving situations.

PHILOSOPHY OF SURVIVAL

All of the techniques for coping with stress which have been presented in this chapter should be tied together with a philosophy. You may have heard that some people cave dive to fulfill a death wish. If you know of anyone who you feel honestly believes this, keep her out of caves, automobiles, airplanes, high buildings, or any other "daredevil" situations. Hopefully, our reason to cave dive is because it is challenging and fun. All normal people begin a cave dive with the idea that they are going to survive. In coping with stress, it is important to maintain this philosophy throughout the course of your dive, no matter how difficult or stressful the situation becomes. What this philosophy amounts to is when you get into a tight spot, no matter how hopeless it looks, it does no good to have a breakdown. As a matter of fact, even if you are going to die, you might as well die doing the right thing, which is doing your best to get out of the situation. Behaving in any other way does not make sense. Concentrating on solving the problem, no matter how desperate the circumstances, is the best and probably the only way to get of trouble. The person who gets out of the impossible situation is the person who believes in trying all the way.

This philosophy is exemplified in the motto: *When faced with dying or achieving the impossible, some people choose to live.* Adherence to such a philosophy provides an excellent basis for coping with stress.

Chapter 16

CAVE DECOMPRESSION PROCEDURES

by Charles Vallance

INTRODUCTION

This chapter discusses decompression procedures as they are applied to cave diving. The information and suggestions which follow are not intended to recommend or endorse the practice of decompression diving by cave divers, but to recognize that it exists. Current national training agency standards dictate that recreational divers practice no-decompression diving.

Cave divers must bear a large measure of responsibility for their own safety and well-being and must be able to gauge what is acceptable risk. When assessing risk, the following concepts should be considered. Decompression in cave diving enhances the danger of what is already widely held, by the general public, to be the most dangerous of all sport diving endeavors. Risk is increased in several ways.

(1) Additional planning and special equipment are required over and above the normal burden borne by a cave diver.

(2) A dive profile obligating a dive to decompression further delays safe access to the surface.

(3) Decompression following a cave dive implies that the dive has been long and/or deep.

In each case, the risk factor is increased. Finally, no matter how carefully and conservatively the planning and execution of a decompression dive is carried out, there is still the possibility that serious decompression sickness may occur. The odds for an incident of decompression sickness mount against divers who habitually practice decompression diving.

How do divers justify the risk? While most agree that personal choice is an important factor, they will also agree that there is a responsibility owed to the rest of the sport diving community. At the least, this responsibility dictates that those who exceed accepted limits make every effort to minimize the risk incurred by applying generous safety margins based on sound knowledge and mature judgment.

PRACTICAL CONSIDERATIONS

Cave divers realized long ago that making the most efficient use of their bottom time requires not only repetitive diving, but decompression diving as well. To many divers, it was not a question of whether or not to do it, but to what degree. Did viewing a particular section of cave make the extra 20 minutes at ten feet worthwhile? Was it still worthwhile when the discomfort and added risk of decompression sickness were considered? These are the types of questions cave divers must ask and, more importantly, answer honestly. Every diver should consider the following.

- Decompression diving complicates an already complicated endeavor.
- Decompression diving adds risk to an already risky endeavor.
- Decompression diving requires an additional investment in equipment.
- Decompression is often uncomfortable.
- Decompression stops can be extremely boring.
- Decompression diving may result in an incident of decompression sickness even with the most conservative dive plan.
- Decompression diving invites censure from the general sport diving community and may help to further an unfavorable image of cave diving.

DECOMPRESSION SICKNESS

Cave divers must be aware of risk factors which may predispose an individual to decompression sickness. These factors are often difficult to quantify but are, nonetheless, necessary considerations. They must be taken into account in any dive plan which places the divers close to or in excess of the no decompression limits.

Differences in physiological tolerances to decompression sickness have been observed to vary from individual to individual and even in the same individual from day to day. Virtually any physiological variable which alters the way the body absorbs or eliminates inert gases affects the incidence of decompression sickness.

CONTRIBUTING FACTORS

Physiological

General health and fitness, especially cardiovascular and respiratory fitness which help lower the stress factor of diving, are important considerations. Lifestyle and personal habits affect general fitness and, therefore, individual decompression sickness risk. Divers who smoke, are overweight, overindulge in alcohol, are dehydrated, abuse drugs, do not get enough rest, are ill, or fail to stay physically fit are apt to be at greater risk. Previous bone or joint injuries are also a concern even though long-since healed. A yearly medical examination should be part of every diver's general fitness program.

Environmental and Equipment Related

There are several physical and environmental factors which affect physiological functions and are known to randomly produce decompression sickness in divers who follow acceptable ascent profiles.

- Reduced water temperature which causes a drop in body temperature during the dive.
- Increased water temperature immediately following a dive which elevates body temperature; e.g., a hot shower.
- Excessive exercise during the dive, while decompressing, or immediately following the dive.
- Equipment that restricts circulation.

Divers should appreciate how the above factors might be influenced by long bottom times, cold water, deep diving, strong currents, warm water at decompression stops, difficult egress from the water, or ill-fitting equipment.

Psychological

Divers should remain aware of certain traits that are serious pitfalls when they involve decompression diving.

- The human tendency to look for shortcuts or apply personal modifications to the tables based on experience.
- The sometimes overwhelming urge to "push" the tables because of cold, fatigue, hunger, boredom, physical discomfort, or sense of invulnerability.

DECOMPRESSION TABLE SELECTION

The *U.S. Navy Standard Air Decompression Tables and Repetitive Dive Tables* have long been the accepted standard in the United States. Although their validity has been debated, they remain the choice of most American sport divers. Used properly and conservatively, they are capable of providing relatively safe guidelines for repetitive and decompression diving.

In order for divers to use the U.S. Navy tables safely, they must recognize their limitations. Certain limits are built-in. For example, the maximum depth found on the Standard Air Table is 190 feet sea water (fsw). However, to believe that this figure is the safe working limit for these tables would be similar to thinking that it is automatically safe to drive as fast as the highest number on a car's speedometer. In general, as exposures become longer and deeper, the risk of decompression sickness (DCS) becomes greater. There is no universally agreed upon magic number that reduces the risk. It is not uncommon for DCS to occur even with the most conservative use of the Standard Air Tables.

Exceptional Exposure Tables

For long bottom times and/or dives deeper than 190 fsw while breathing air, the Navy developed the *Exceptional Exposure Tables*. These tables are a mathematical extrapolation of the Standard Air Tables. Because they are derived from very little empirical validation and the diver is exposed to arduous conditions, the diver accepts a greater measure of risk than while using the Standard Air Tables. The Navy authorizes their use only in extreme emergencies and when a recompression chamber is available at the dive site.

Altitude Tables

Diving at elevations above sea level requires special tables. If the altitude at the dive site exceeds 800 feet, the U.S. Navy Standard Air Tables no longer apply. Most high altitude tables in use were derived in much the same way as the Navy Exceptional Tables and without the benefit of extensive field testing.

Very little cave diving takes place at high altitude and, considering the questionable reliability of high altitude dive tables, any individual who wishes to embark on this activity is encouraged to seek further advice from a high altitude diving specialist.

Foreign Decompression Tables

Numerous examples of dive tables in use by foreign navies have gotten into the hands of American divers. Any such dive tables should be carefully researched before a team makes a dive based on its data. Two dive tables that cave divers may find worth examining are the Canadian (aka DCIEM tables) and British Royal Navy Tables.

Decompression Computers

There is constant change in the field of dive computers, and it is difficult to predict what may be available in the near future. In general, current models are aimed at recreational divers attempting to avoid decompression profiles. Their primary design function is to allow multilevel diving with credit given for shallower depth. Divers should research what decompression data is available in each model, and from what tables the program data was derived. Cave divers employing dive computers ordinarily use them as an adjunct to their tables.

PRACTICAL DECOMPRESSION TABLES USE

A cardinal rule for any diver in the use of dive tables is that the diver be able to quickly and accurately work any problem. Cave divers can practice working decompression problems during an exit to see if they are proficient. Experience should be gained *before* a diver plans to apply the skill in a cave diving situations.

Safety Margins

Two of the most important considerations in decompression diving are the correct use and application of adequate safety margins. Divers should consider the following suggestions.

• Using the next greater depth and bottom time to calculate decompression profiles when risk factors are present.

• Planning dives so that bottom times fall five to ten minutes short of the no decompression limit or decompression schedule in use. For example, if the depth is 60 feet and the limit 60 minutes, divers should plan a maximum of 50 to 55 minutes.

• Using a slower rate of ascent. Many experts are reexamining the old standard of 60 feet per minute (fpm). Divers are encouraged to use 30 fpm as an ascent rate because it gives them more time to off-gas, which reduces the risk of DCS.

• Counting ascent time as part of bottom time. It is particularly important to do this when slower ascent rates are used or if dictated by the configuration of the cave system near the exit.

• Remaining aware of any modifications of the dive plan during the dive, such as slow ascents that are not added to bottom time, deeper stops, or longer bottom times than anticipated. Awareness and accurate record keeping is essential.

• Familiarization with the decompression area. Divers should be comfortable in a new system before attempting decompression dives there.

• Maintaining a body position that is comfortable and places the chest region at the stop depth.

• Breathing continuously — the gas has to get out the same way it went in.

• Avoiding vigorous exercise during decompression, but maintaining circulation with some limb movements. A diver can loosen restrictive equipment as long as his gear remains in place.

• Counting the surface as the final decompression stop and avoiding strenuous exercise immediately after surfacing. Divers should move slowly and methodically on exit to avoid undue physical stress. Any diver who feels winded should slow down or stop until rested.

• Avoiding hot showers or hot tubs immediately after surfacing. Heat causes vasodilation, an enlargement in the size of the blood vessels, but may also cause bubbles in those vessels to increase in size.[1] Layers of warm clothes are recommended for restoring any loss of body temperature.

• Avoiding ascent to an altitude greater than 800 feet above sea level for at least 24 hours. Ascents greater than this height reduce the partial pressure on the body, thus allowing nitrogen to come out of solution and form bubbles. The last dive at a location should be scheduled in accordance with the return flight of any members of the team.

• Refraining from the use of alcohol, drugs, or any other substances that might adversely affect the body's ability to react to inert gas in solution, or would interfere with the recognition of the symptoms of decompression sickness.

One final item that must be mentioned while discussing safety margins is the use of oxygen during decompression. A common practice among some cave divers, it is used because it helps speed the elimination of nitrogen and thereby reduces the risk of DCS. However, oxygen creates some complications of its own. There is a danger of fire or explosion if the equipment used to deliver the oxygen is not certified for oxygen service, or if it is handled incorrectly. The gas supply can become contaminated if oxygen decompression bottles are filled with industrial grade oxygen. Finally, individual tolerance for breathing oxygen underwater is variable: one diver may advocate the use of oxygen at a depth that he can tolerate but which could cause oxygen poisoning in another diver.[2]

Oxygen can be breathed safely on the surface to further enhance safety margins if proper precautions regarding safe handling are taken, but this should not be considered a substitute for actual decompression stops. Likewise, oxygen used during in-water decompression in no way entitles the diver to shorten decompression stop times. Oxygen should only be considered an adjunct to the safe use of standard air tables.

DECOMPRESSION DIVE PLANNING AND PROCEDURES

The dive plan (and the execution of that plan) is an essential element of successful decompression dives. Failure to properly plan and execute a cave dive involving staged decompression stops causes accidents.

The first step in planning is a diagram of the dive profile to maximum penetration, including planned inspections of side passages. Log books, if properly kept, can provide much of the information needed to plan a dive. Experienced cave divers and good cave maps are also excellent sources of information. Dives in unfamiliar systems should be planned as no-decompression dives.

---

[1]The solubility of any gas in a liquid decreases as the temperature of the liquid increases. Since inert gas was dissolved in the body tissues during the cooler temperatures of the dive when the gas solubility was higher, raising the temperature of the tissues may immediately drive dissolved gas out of solution. — Ed.

[2]The generally accepted safe limit for breathing 100% oxygen is 25 fsw. Most divers can usually tolerate oxygen at greater depths. But susceptibility to oxygen poisoning is variable from person to person, and in the same individual from day to day. Although most individuals show some mild signs or symptoms of O_2 poisoning before the onset of unconsciousness and seizures, some do not. In addition, the early signs and symptoms of O_2 toxicity are easily misinterpreted as being related to some other less serious condition. Remember: there is no universal sign of O_2 toxicity, and the first sign may be unconsciousness with seizures. — Ed.

Throughout the dive, depth should be continually checked to ensure correct data. Past experience or secondhand information can be inaccurate. Water levels fluctuate and bottom sediment can shift to produce a change. Depth gauges should also be checked for accuracy. Dive team members should compare gauge readings often.

Cave configuration and environmental factors are also critical concerns during ascent and exit. The dive team may choose to exit by a different route which reaches a deeper level. A gradually sloping exit passage may impose severe constraints on ascent rates. In this scenario, it is best to continue clocking bottom time until the first decompression stop, or if it is a no-decompression dive, until the surface is reached. In high out-flow systems with a near vertical exit, divers may find it difficult to maintain a safe rate of ascent. In extreme cases, divers must move hand-over-hand or use a decompression weight rather than allow the current to control their ascent.

Selecting Sites for Decompression Stops

The cave entrance area must be carefully surveyed prior to planning a decompression dive in order to locate sites for decompression stops. The survey should extend to the depth of the deepest possible decompression stop. This inspection can be included as part of a no-decompression familiarization dive, or may require a separate dive specifically for this purpose.

Decompression stops should be selected with care. Because the dive team members cannot surface early, they should try to be as comfortable as possible. A crevice, ledge, log, or other stable object at the exact stop depth is ideal, but it should be remeasured for depth on return dives. Crevices allow for maximum dry suit inflation, but comfort should not be sacrificed for accurate depth. The sites selected must accommodate all divers and their gear at proper stop depths; this may be a crucial element in determining dive team sizes. The most desirable stops provide a convenient staging area for decompression bottles and weight.

Cave divers should be concerned about the possibility of "salvage" attempts when staging decompression gear within reach of recreational divers. In order to leave equipment unattended, it should be clearly marked indicating its purpose.[3]

Divers need to have access to one another even during decompression. If conditions of poor visibility or restrictions exist, emergency signals should be established. Strong currents may make it extremely difficult for divers to maintain position and can dramatically increase air consumption. This situation increases the chance of decompression sickness and it makes good hand holds or convenient crevices a necessity. Tag lines with quick-release shackles can be used to secure divers in place.

Large cave systems or sinkholes may offer no staging areas for decompression. Divers must be able to hover neutrally buoyant. An underweighted diver risks an unintentional surface ascent, while an overweighed diver must expend energy in order to maintain his position. Decompression weights should be strategically placed below the first planned stop and buoyancy control systems must be fail-safe. If possible, weighted decompression shot lines should be deployed and decompression gear attached to the decompression line or to divers with tag lines.

Divers should ensure adequate thermal protection if colder water is expected at decompression stops. While most cave divers abstain from using gloves during a dive, a pair stowed at a decompression stop provides added warmth. Safety margins (using the next greater depth or time) should be increased if cooler water is encountered.[4]

Decompression divers have the right of way in a cave system but should not block other divers who are entering or exiting the cave. Boat traffic or surface swimmers can be a hazard at some sites and divers are advised to check the surrounding trees for rope swings and dive platforms. If the topography of the area surrounding the surface pool makes exiting physically demanding, divers should consider removing their tanks and other heavy gear before climbing out.[5]

Calculations and Record Keeping Procedures

In the initial dive plan, decompression is calculated according to the maximum *planned* depth and bottom time. At this point, divers are advised to check schedules for the next greater depth and bottom time. The example in Table 16-1 illustrates the importance of this

[3]Often, it is better to stage the D/C bottles, drop weights, and other D/C equipment well beyond the first D/C stop location in order to keep them from being "borrowed." I often stage D/C bottles up to 200 feet into the cave system at popular dive sites to keep them out of the reach of misguided open water divers. Unfortunately, it now seems that some cave divers are losing D/C equipment placed well beyond the range of open water divers. This means that other cave divers, who should know better, are taking life support equipment. My advice is to hide it well (but be sure YOU can relocate it fairly easily). — Ed.

[4]As noted previously, as the tissues of the body become cooler, the solubility of gas in those tissues increases. Cooling of the body during D/C could slow off-gassing due to increased gas solubility. — Ed.

[5]If removing heavy gear such as tanks is not practical, divers should take a *surface D/C stop* of 15 to 30 minutes prior to performing any significant post-dive exertion. This also applies to no-decompression dives made near the no-decompression limits. Remember, there's no such thing as a true no-decompression dive, because on every dive your body tissues absorb inert gas which must be off-gassed at the surface. On some dives, the inert gas must also be off-gassed partially during the dive to permit safely ascending to the surface. No-decompression dives are really no-staged-decompression dives, where the first D/C stop is the surface. — Ed.

practice. In this scenario, the divers exceeded their planned maximum depth by only five feet and their planned bottom time by only four minutes. However, these seemingly minor changes in the dive plan resulted in a total ascent time of **more than three times** that required of the original plan. It should be obvious that any failure to consider such contingencies and to plan accordingly could lead to problems.

In order to ensure accuracy, each diver should compute profiles individually. Results are compared and corrections made if any discrepancies are found. These pre-dive calculations are recorded on the diver's slate, along with calculations which provide for variations in the dive plan. All team members should agree on maximum planned depth, bottom time, decompression schedules, and variables which might affect decompression.

At the start of the dive, each diver sets his timers/bezels (if they do not begin automatically). Regardless of the timing system a diver uses, the actual (clock) time is recorded so that bottom times can be computed if the bezel moves or the bottom timer stops. Dive teams often synchronize watches during planning in order to assemble on the surface and designate a start time. Customarily, this time is set two to three minutes past the point all team members have indicated they are ready to dive. This allows the divers to record clock time prior to beginning the dive and provides a few moments to relax and make final adjustments to equipment.

PLANNED DIVE	ACTUAL DIVE
Depth: 110′ Time: 30 min	Depth: 115′ Time: 34 min
Decompression: 10′ @ 7 min	Decompression: 20′ @ 5 min 10′ @ 25 min
Ascent w/ Travel Time: 10:40*	Ascent w/ Travel Time: 33:50*

**Using U.S. Navy Tables with 30 FPM ascent rate.*

Table 16-1

Toward the end of the return swim, each diver should recheck decompression calculations, taking into account any variations from planned calculations. If any variations cause a change in calculations, divers should pause prior to ascent. All team members should compare calculations and recalculate if they do not agree. These figures should be double-checked at the first decompression stop.[6]

A written record of decompression is necessary for accurate stops and it should include the time arriving and leaving each stop and the arrival time on the surface. At the surface, divers should calculate and record their repetitive group designation.

Decompression Etiquette

Divers on decompression stops have the right of way at decompression stops and when exiting. Divers should remain alert during decompression and practice proper buddy techniques, checking air and equipment as soon as possible after beginning decompression. This is a good time for team members to relax, mentally review the dive, and make notes. Naps are not recommended.

Figure 16-1 Cave diving etiquette dictates that divers entering the cave yield to divers who are exiting or decompressing.

Decompression etiquette dictates that divers continue to use the same common sense and good judgment practiced during the dive. Eating, drinking, reading, stationary games, and other sensible forms of entertainment are often practiced on long stops but they should never compromise safe decompression. Caution is necessary when eating or drinking as choking is a possibility, and excessive physical activity should be avoided.

[6]The practice of most cave divers is to routinely stop their ascent 10 to 20 feet below the deepest planned D/C stop to re-check time, depth and calculations. If D/C bottles etc. are staged beyond the deepest planned stop, D/C re-calculations are often done while the team stops to pick up their D/C equipment. On no-D/C dives, many divers stop 10 to 20 feet from the surface for a *safety stop* of 3 to 5 minutes. Conservative divers often add 3 to 5 minutes to their shallowest D/C stop, in addition to taking a 5 to 15 minute surface D/C stop before exiting the water. If significant post-dive exertion is anticipated on the trip from the water to the vehicles, the surface D/C stop should be 15 to 30 minutes in length. — Ed.

EQUIPMENT

A plastic slate, pencil and submersible decompression tables should always be carried by each diver. Divers should not leave their tables behind at a planned decompression stop, nor they should be dropped with decompression bottles or drop weights.

Timing Devices

There are a variety of reasonably priced underwater timers currently on the market and divers should consider the use of a primary and backup timing device, one of which should read in real time. Stop watch and countdown timer functions are useful, as well as pressure activated bottom timers.

Depth Gauges

There is a wide selection of depth gauges (with varying degrees of accuracy) available to divers. In general, expensive oil-filled diaphragm gauges or electronic digital read-out gauges tend to be the most accurate throughout the entire depth scale, while a good capillary gauge gives the most accurate readings at shallower depths. Divers should carry one gauge for use throughout the dive that incorporates a maximum depth indicator and have a capillary gauge to check depth at shallow (less than 30 fsw) decompression stops.

Depth gauge readings should be continually compared during the dive and the deepest reading noted on any diver's gauge used to compute the maximum depth for decompression. Taking the average between discrepancies in the readings is not recommended. Depth gauges should be calibrated in the water against a measured shot line and corrections noted for all appropriate stop depths.

Decompression Bottles

Air for decompression purposes should be carried in separate staged bottles (tanks), even if the team believes they are carrying enough air to complete the dive and decompression. A staged decompression bottle for each diver enhances comfort and safety at decompression. When environmental or equipment restraints do not permit separate setups, ample air and regulator second stages must be available for **each** diver. Long hoses make the use of staged decompression tanks more comfortable and are a necessity when two or more divers will use one cylinder.

The configuration of stage decompression bottles may vary, but the following are some basic considerations.

- The tank and regulator package should be compact and transportable.
- Large elastic bands can be used to secure hoses to the tank.
- Regulators should be protected against damage and the intrusion of foreign material.
- Second stages should not be left dangling at the end of their hoses.
- Decompression bottles should be secured at the deepest stop. A short piece of line fitted with a quick release shackle allows for quick detachment and re-attachment at the next stop.
- Submersible pressure gauges should be attached to decompression tanks.

Decompression bottles should be placed so that they do not block the path of divers but can be readily located even in poor visibility. Decompression bottles should be labeled in an effort to prevent other divers from "recovering" what might appear to be lost equipment. When placing the decompression bottles, the regulators are pressurized and tested for inhalation, exhalation and purge button function. The tank valve should then be closed to avoid accidental loss of air.

When the first decompression stop does not afford a good staging area, divers should secure their decompression gear at a convenient spot below their anticipated first stop. The equipment must be placed so that it is easily relocated during the exit. A quick fastening system is particularly important so that an exiting diver can clip on the decompression bottle, leaving both hands free for the remainder of the ascent. This will also be helpful if a diver has to hover at a decompression stop.

Weights

Good buoyancy technique usually requires that a diver be weighted as lightly as possible for the planned depth of the dive. Although this may be fine at depth, it can be totally inappropriate for decompression. Underweighted divers at the decompression stop are a hazard to themselves and team members. A diver that is overly buoyant can suffer from inaccurate depth control, overexertion, and uncontrolled ascent.

Drop weights, staged at a depth below the first anticipated decompression stops, allow divers to execute all of the dive except the final ascent with as little weight as possible. Where a diver clips on the drop weight is dependent on individual buoyancy, the type of exposure suit, and physical aspects of the cave entrance such as depth, current, visibility, and cave configuration.

Decompression weights can consist of an additional weight belt or can be fashioned as a clump weight and fitted with a snap shackle (used on sailboats). The amount of weight required is determined through experimentation but it should be adequate to anchor the diver securely at the shallowest stop even in current. If a dry suit is used, the diver should ensure that there is enough weight to allow at least partial inflation for comfort and warmth.

Logbook

A logbook has particular significance to cave divers. It is an invaluable planning aid for checking depths, line locations, and distances of previous dives in the same system. It also helps promote the professionalism and attention to detail required to practice safe cave diving. Many cave divers have found that logbooks aimed at sport divers are inadequate for their purposes and have created their own custom formats. Logbook entries should be made as soon as possible after the conclusion of a dive.

OXYGEN DECOMPRESSION

As previously discussed, the use of oxygen during in-water decompression creates additional risks but does reduce the likelihood of DCS. If the dive team has chosen to use oxygen, special precautions should be taken.

All components of the delivery system including tank, valve, pressure gauges, hoses, and regulator should be certified for oxygen service. This can be done only by a qualified technician. Cylinders containing oxygen should be painted solid green and stenciled with the wording: **WARNING, CONTAINS OXYGEN. DO NOT USE FOR SCUBA DIVING.**

Cylinders should be filled only with certified medical grade oxygen. The best resource for locating medical grade oxygen and equipment is a hospital.[7]

Petroleum-based products must never be allowed to come in contact with oxygen delivery equipment. This includes most lubricants as well as certain substances which may be present on the user's skin such as lip balm, suntan oil, sun screen, and makeup.

The greatest danger in the use of oxygen underwater is the risk of oxygen toxicity. A diver experiencing an oxygen-induced seizure while underwater will likely drown. Prevention is obviously a necessity.

Considerable research as been done by the military, commercial diving companies, and universities to determine the mechanism of acute oxygen poisoning and ways to prevent its occurrence. Any diver who contemplates using oxygen should avail himself of current information and seek the advice of a physiologist or physician trained in diving medicine. Oxygen is considered a drug and should be treated as such.

It is worth noting that the U.S. Navy prohibits the use of pure oxygen below 25 feet, except in certain circumstances, and requires all prospective divers to undergo an oxygen tolerance test. Oxygen toxicity has been reported at depths much shallower than 30 feet. According to the U.S. Navy Diving Manual, acute oxygen toxicity may occur when oxygen partial pressure reaches 1.6 atmospheres absolute. A diver encounters this if breathing 100 percent oxygen at about 20 feet.

An alternative to the underwater use of oxygen to lessen the chances of DCS is the prophylactic use of oxygen on the surface. A general rule of thumb would be for a diver resting after an extreme exposure dive to breathe oxygen for 15 minutes. This treatment can significantly reduce the saturation of nitrogen in the bloodstream and tissues. If the diver is using a non-demand system, such as seen in the medical field, a non-rebreather mask (with a reservior) at a flow of 10 to 15 liters per minute is suggested. For most decompression diving, cave divers would find it far simpler (and perhaps safer) to practice conservative use of the tables rather than resort to the use of oxygen.

EMERGENCY PROCEDURES

Omitted Decompression

Certain emergencies may prevent a diver from properly completing decompression. Buoyancy problems, exhausted air supply, equipment malfunction, extremely adverse environmental conditions, traumatic injury, and serious illness are examples. Any significant deviation from the prescribed decompression schedule should be considered omitted decompression.

Most of the examples cited can be avoided if divers are properly prepared. Occasionally, a diver must make a judgment call as to whether or not a situation warrants an emergency ascent.

A diver who omits a decompression stop and makes a premature ascent faces two options. He can leave the water immediately and proceed directly to the nearest recompression chamber. Or, ***if no symptoms of DCS are present,*** he can follow the procedure outlined in Volume I of the U.S. Navy Diving Manual, in the section entitled *Omitted Decompression — When No Chamber is Available.*

Option two is probably the riskier of the two choices and requires that the diver return to depth within five minutes. It should not be used if symptoms are present, as the schedule is designed to prevent DCS, not treat it. Any evaluation of a diver's symptoms during the brief surface interval may be inaccurate and symptoms may become much worse once the diver returns to the water. Another factor to consider is that if complications develop, the patient would be in much better hands at a medical facility.[8]

If a diver is headed to a hyperbaric chamber, first aid for decompression sickness should be applied while en route to the chamber, even if no symptoms are present.

---

[7]Oxygen and oxygen equipment is not usually available from hospitals. Check your local area for oxygen suppliers. Often dealers who handle industrial (welding) oxygen also handle medical grade oxygen. — Ed.

[8]There is also a concern with the USN recommendations for ommitted D/C, which are apparently more of an informed guess as to what might be helpful rather than a scientifically researched and tested set of procedures. — Ed.

SUMMARY

Cave diving is sometimes done under conditions not normally encountered by recreational divers. To maintain a proper perspective, cave divers should keep in mind that professional divers engage in decompression diving only when sophisticated backup systems and trained surface support personnel are on hand. They are also paid handsomely for the work they do.

A safe cave diving attitude is a prerequisite to benefiting from any information presented in this chapter. Divers must be aware of and respect the physiological consequences of long and/or deep dives. They must also recognize the connection between their personal habits/lifestyle and a predisposition to decompression sickness. Finally, conservative use of the dive tables can help ensure that a diver will be around to make the next dive.

Chapter 17

ALTERNATIVES TO STAGE DECOMPRESSION

by Milledge Murphey, Ph.D.

FACTORS INFLUENCING DCS

Numerous technical and scientific articles have appeared in periodicals and books during the past two decades regarding problems associated with stage decompression as practiced by divers. In the United States, the *U.S. Navy Dive Tables, Exceptional Exposure Tables, Surface Decompression Tables Using Oxygen, Surface Decompression Tables Using Air,* and other publications have provided guidelines for these procedures. Worldwide, a number of tables (which vary from the U.S. Navy tables) have been developed and are currently in use. Today, there remains no absolute international standard which may be applied when diving under conditions which require stage decompression.

The literature has produced conflicting information regarding procedures, problems, solutions, and techniques for diver implementation in an effort to mitigate injuries related to stage decompression. Factors related to those problems include but are not limited to: diver age, level of physical condition, diet, percentage of body fat, alcohol consumption, tobacco use, effect of drugs, effect of debilitating conditions including asthma, diabetes, arthritic joints, visual impairment, and numerous other conditions.

The variety of these factors is seemingly infinite and no effort can be mounted within the scope of this chapter to cover the total range of factors which impact stage decompression. Rather, consideration of selected factors is given with the specific purpose of acquainting the reader with a variety of such factors, and indicating a number of alternative and adjunctive procedures which may be used to render stage decompression either not needed or safer for all divers.

As most scuba divers and nearly all cave divers are aware, the U.S. Navy Tables were developed using a population of Navy divers as its base. Use of these subjects (all young men) who were rigidly screened, trained, and acclimated to diving by the U.S. Navy, resulted in tables that have a very specific use population.

To extrapolate that all divers, regardless of sex or age, can use these tables with equal safety is spurious. Further, when considering individual physical condition variance, differing diving equipment and conditions, and an infinite variety of other variables, one can understand why accidents do sometimes occur when the U.S. Navy tables are followed exactly by sport and cave divers while using scuba.

Pioneering research in the safety of the U.S. Navy tables was accomplished at the University of Michigan in 1976 using Doppler ultrasonic bubble detection equipment. The tables that resulted from this research, commonly referred to as the *Spencer Tables,* are designed to eliminate venous bubbles and offer another option to stage decompression. These tables are more conservative than the U.S. Navy tables. Cave divers who use them presumably will not form venous nitrogen bubbles, and will thus (theoretically) avoid decompression sickness.

During his studies using the Doppler ultrasonic bubble detector, Spencer clearly demonstrated that venous bubbles were produced in subjects diving within the limits of the U.S. Navy tables. While the effect of such bubble development is unclear at present, it appears reasonable to avoid bubble formation if possible. Tables 17-1, 17-2 and 17-3 exhibit Spencer's findings.

NO-DECOMPRESSION LIMITS

Depth (in fsw)	USN (in minutes)	Spencer (in minutes)
20	None	None
30	None	225
35	310	165
40	200	135
50	100	75
60	60	50
70	50	40
80	40	30
90	30	25
100	25	20
110	20	15
120	15	10
130	10	5

Table 17-1

It appears that alternatives to the use of stage decompression techniques are appropriate in view of the foregoing discussion. Such alternatives should be considered by cave divers, especially those who have experienced past episodes of decompression sickness, dive under exceptional exposure conditions, are beyond forty years of age, are in less than optimum physical condition, or with any age related or debilitating conditions(s). Beyond these factors, workload, depth, distance, temperature, and even psychological factors may exert a profound influence upon suitably of stage decompression techniques selected and used. Without question, every individual trait, condition, and environmental factor must be taken into account in developing alternatives to stage decompression.

Cave diving is not a sport limited to youth. Many of the pioneers of American cave diving who began in the 1950's and 60's are still active after 30 (or more) years in the field. Most cave divers can look forward to a lifetime of underwater exploration. Yet there are basic physiological changes that all humans undergo as they age and these must be considered by every cave diver.

COMPARISON OF TISSUE M-VALUES

Tissue Group	USN	Spencer	% of USN
5 min.	104	102	98%
10 min.	88	85	97%
20 min.	72	67.5	94%
40 min.	58	54.5	94%
80 min.	52	47.5	91%
120 min.	51	43	84%

Table 17-2

Several examples may convey the implications of the decrements of normal aging for the cave diver: a 50 year old person needs twice as much light to see as well as a person of 20; muscular bicep strength is greatest at age 27 and declines 50 percent by the time a person is 50; between age 30 and 80 breathing and kidney function will decline by one-half; vital capacity at 70 is 50 percent of what it was at age 30; hearing losses begin at age 20 and after age 55 are accelerated even more among men than in women; and cardiovascular efficiency and resilience reaches its peak at about 30 and declines thereafter.

These facts of normal aging, while profound, are virtually ignored by the general population, and especially by the cave diving population. Obviously, as persons age, alternatives to the rigors of stage decompression must be selected and adhered to if safe diving is to be accomplished.

No-D/C Limits. The most obvious method for avoiding stage decompression is for a diver to never approach or exceed the no-decompression limits as suggested by the U.S. Navy Dive Tables. However, this alternative is unacceptable to most cave divers because of cave systems which require depths and times (because of penetration distances) that exceed these limits.

Multi-Level Dive Tables. Open-water divers now enjoy the availability of multilevel dive tables, which allow a diver to stay within a no-decompression profile while having longer bottom times. Both manual and computer models are on the market. The computer models offer the advantage of automatically entering the necessary information, and do not require the diver to make note of depths and times in order to function. The commercial models of multilevel dive computers use various tables as their foundation, the majority of which are more conservative than the U. S. Navy tables at most depths. Most require ascent times slower than 60 feet per minute.

Dive Computers. While multilevel dive computers have received a very positive response from the open-water diving community, their usefulness for cave diving is more limited. During an open water dive, divers can ascend to a shallower depth at will. A cave diver's depth is dependent on the system she is diving. However, there are situations where these devices could be beneficial to the cave diver and used as an alternative to stage decompression. For example, a diver in a system where one small section is significantly deeper than the rest would get "credit" on a multilevel dive computer for spending only a short time at maximum depth. Any diver who chooses to use a computer should still carry dive tables and make note of maximum depth and bottom time.

Mixed Gas. Another possible alternative to stage decompression is the use of mixed gas. Various combinations of two to three gases have been employed by cave divers with success. Mixed gas diving offers the possibility of avoiding (or limiting) the amount of nitrogen absorbed into the tissues and eliminating nitrogen narcosis from deep dives. However, use of mixed gas is an **experimental** endeavor and cannot be recommended as a general alternative to stage decompression. The future looks bright for mixed gas diving and continued success will certainly bring about a wider application of this technique.

DPV's. New technology in diver propulsion vehicles also offers an alternative to stage decompression. DPV's enable cave divers to go deeper and penetrate greater distances with less exertion and air consumption, and at greater speed, than possible heretofore. By reducing exposure time, *scooters* can help divers accomplish no-decompression dives that previously required stage decompression. Specialized instruction is necessary (and available) in order to use DPV's safely.

Future Technology. Cave divers will undoubtedly continue to apply future technological advancements to their sport. A revolutionary device that might eliminate stage decompression diving altogether is the *hemosponge*, currently under development at the Duke Marine Laboratory in Beaufort, North Carolina. Scientists are working toward developing a viable prototype which will supply divers with an unlimited oxygen supply underwater. This device will eliminate compressed air in diving. Functioning as an artificial gill, the molecules of the hemosponge are capable of extracting oxygen from either air or water. Actual development of an artificial gill diver pack lies in the future, but it certainly offers exciting possible applications to cave diving.

Stage D/C Precautions.

For those cave divers who have chosen to participate in stage decompression diving, the following is a list of practices in common usage at this time. No suggestion is made that all or any of these practices have been proven to be helpful. Rather, they are mentioned simply as some of the steps taken by persons currently cave diving in exceptional exposure areas.

1) Be in good physical condition through a reasonable program of diet and exercise. Do not dive when mentally or physically tired.

2) Should not be obese or overweight.

3) Should not use recreational drugs, alcohol, or tobacco. Obtain physician's approval if taking prescription medication before or after diving.

4) Ascend and descend slowly.

5) Rest prior to and after a deep or long dive. No exercise or exertion before or after diving.When there are no non-diving assistants to haul gear for you, make a surface D/C stop of 15 to 30 minutes before exiting the water.

6) Hydrate with water before, during, and after exceptional exposure diving.

7) No hot bath or shower before or after diving.

8) Add 5 to 10 minutes extra to the required time at the shallowest stop on final dive.

9) Use the next deeper and the next longer table on repetitive dives.

10) No *bounce* dives.

11) No tea, coffee, or soda pop before or after dives.

12) Pause before ascending on physically demanding dives.

13) Avoid deep dives.

14) Avoid milk or milk products before and after diving.

15) Avoid exertion during dive, especially involving the shoulders.

16) Avoid restrictive exposure suits and similarly restrictive clothing before and after dive.

17) Prophylactic tablet of aspirin or ibuprofen before the first dive of the day.

18) Avoid flying after diving.

19) Avoid large, high fat meals before and after diving.

20) ***If any bends symptoms appear***, call ahead and then go to the nearest hyperbaric chamber immediately.

Cave divers should be aware of the potential dangers of decompression diving that face them as individuals and plan their dives accordingly. Viable alternatives to this type of diving do exist, and the future is bright for eliminating incidents of decompression sickness.

DEPTH (FSW)	N0 D/C LIMIT	↥ ↥ ↥ ↥ ↥ TO SURFACE INTERVAL OFF-GASSING TABLE ↥ ↥ ↥ ↥ ↥													
		A	B	C	D	E	F	G	H	I	J	K	L	M	N
20	None	10	25	40	60	85	110	135	170	215	275	325			
30	225	5	15	25	40	50	65	75	95	110	130	150	175	205	225
35	165	5	15	20	30	40	50	60	70	85	100	120	135	155	165
40	135	5	10	20	25	35	40	45	55	60	70	85	100	120	135
50	75		10	15	20	25	30	35	37	40	50	55	60	70	75
60	50		5	10	15	20	23	25	27	30	35	40	45	47	50
70	40		5	10	13	15	17	20	23	25	27	30	33	35	40
80	30		5	7	→	10	13	15	17	20	→	25	27	→	30
90	25			5	7	→	10	→	13	15	17	→	20	23	25
100	20				5	7	→	→	10	→	→	13	15	17	20
110	15					5	→	7	→	→	10	→	→	13	15
120	10						5	→	→	7	→	→	10		
130	5						5								
REP. GRP. FOR S.I.T.		A	B	C	D	E	F	G	H	I	J	K	L	M	N
BOTTOM TIME and REPETITIVE GROUP MATRIX															

Table 17-3A No-bubble no-decompression limits and repetitive dive groups.

12:00 0:10	12:00 2:31	12:00 3:42	12:00 4:43	12:00 5:23	12:00 5:57	12:00 6:21	12:00 6:49	12:00 7:09	12:00 7:30	12:00 7:46	12:00 8:01	12:00 8:18	12:00 8:27	➤ *A*
A	2:30 0:10	3:41 1:20	4:42 2:21	5:22 3:01	5:56 3:35	6:20 3:59	6:48 4:27	7:08 4:47	7:29 5:08	7:45 5:24	8:00 5:39	8:17 5:56	8:26 6:05	➤ *B*
	B	1:19 0:10	2:20 1:04	3:00 1:44	3:34 2:18	3:58 2:42	4:26 3:10	4:46 3:30	5:07 3:51	5:23 4:07	5:38 4:22	5:55 4:39	6:04 4:48	➤ *C*
		C	1:03 0:10	1:43 0:50	2:17 1:24	2:41 1:48	3:09 2:16	3:29 2:36	3:50 2:57	4:06 3:13	4:21 3:28	4:38 3:45	4:47 3:54	➤ *D*
			D	0:49 0:10	1:23 0:43	1:47 1:07	2:15 1:35	2:35 1:55	2:56 2:16	3:12 2:32	3:27 2:47	3:44 3:04	3:53 3:13	➤ *E*
				E	0:42 0:10	1:06 0:34	1:34 1:02	1:54 1:22	2:15 1:43	2:31 1:59	2:46 2:14	3:03 2:31	3:12 2:40	➤ *F*
					F	0:33 0:10	1:01 0:34	1:21 0:54	1:42 1:15	1:58 1:31	2:13 1:46	2:30 2:03	2:39 2:12	➤ *G*
						G	0:33 0:10	0:53 0:30	1:14 0:51	1:30 1:07	1:45 1:22	2:02 1:39	2:11 1:48	➤ *H*
							H	0:29 0:10	0:50 0:29	1:06 0:45	1:21 1:01	1:38 1:17	1:47 1:26	➤ *I*
								I	0:28 0:10	0:44 0:26	1:00 0:42	1:16 0:58	1:25 1:07	➤ *J*
									J	0:25 0:10	0:41 0:24	0:57 0:40	1:06 0:49	➤ *K*
										K	0:23 0:10	0:39 0:24	0:48 0:33	➤ *L*
											L	0:23 0:10	0:32 0:18	➤ *M*
												M	0:17 0:10	➤ *N*
													N	NEW REP. GRP.

Table 17-3B No-bubble surface interval off-gassing table.

NEW REP. GRP. AT START OF REP. DIVE	20	30	35	40	50	60	70	80	90	100	110	120	130
➤ A	12	8	7	6	5	4	4	3	3	3	3	2	2
➤ B	28	18	16	14	11	9	8	7	6	6	5	5	4
➤ C	45	29	25	21	17	14	12	9	8	6	6	5	5
➤ D	65	41	34	30	23	19	15	10	8	7	6	5	5
➤ E	86	53	44	37	28	22	17	12	9	8	7	6	5
➤ F	111	66	53	43	32	24	19	14	11	9	7	6	6
➤ G	140	80	62	49	36	27	22	17	12	10	8	7	6
➤ H	175	96	73	57	40	30	24	19	14	11	9	8	7
➤ I	219	113	86	65	45	34	26	21	16	12	10	8	7
➤ J	279	132	103	75	51	38	29	23	18	13	11	9	8
➤ K	369	154	122	88	57	43	32	26	20	15	12	10	8
➤ L		178	139	103	64	47	35	28	22	18	13	11	9
➤ M		207	158	124	71	52	40	30	25	20	15	12	10
➤ N		225	135	135	75	53	41	31	26	21	16	13	11
	DEPTH FOR REPETITIVE DIVE IN FSW												

Table 17-3C No-bubble residual nitrogen equivalency table

Chapter 18

USES AND ABUSES OF DIVE COMPUTERS

by Karl E. Huggins

INTRODUCTION

Since the introduction of dive computers (DC's) divers have been developing imaginative methods of use, not all of them very smart. This article will describe what a DC is, some of the misconceptions the general diving population has regarding them, and how they are being used. Examples of how dive computers are being used are presented along with recommendations adopted by the American Academy of Underwater Sciences (AAUS) for DC use in scientific diving programs.

Of major concern is the accuracy of the information passed on from instructors to students, salespersons to customers, and divers to other divers with regards to DC's. Too often in the diving community, we see hearsay and biased or inaccurate information presented on pieces of equipment instead of factual information. DC's look as if they will be around for awhile. They should not be condemned outright, nor should they be worshipped as a panacea for decompression sickness (DCS). They are only tools, and as such are no better or worse than the person using them.

WHAT IS A DIVE COMPUTER?

A DC is just that, a computer. It does not, as some people think, monitor the amount of nitrogen in a diver's body. All it does is compute decompression status. This is done by sensing depth and time during the dive and then, by using a table or model, the decompression status is read or computed. This decompression status information is displayed to the diver, who can use it as an additional source of information in the execution of a dive.

The basic design of a DC is presented as a block diagram in Figure 18-1. The general components are the:

Pressure Transducer, which converts the ambient pressure surrounding the diver to a signal which is fed into the input of the A/D Converter.

A/D (Analog to Digital) Converter, which changes the pressure transducer signal to a digital "word" which can be "read" by the microprocessor.

Microprocessor, the "brain" which controls the signal flow and performs the mathematical and logical operations.

ROM (Read Only Memory), a non-volatile memory which contains the program steps which "tell" the microprocessor what to do. The ROM also contains the constants used in the program which determines the diver's decompression status.

RAM (Random Access Memory), contains the storage registers in which variable data and results are stored during computations.

Display, which presents the diver's decompression status.

Clock, which synchronizes the operational steps of the microprocessor and is used as the time input.

Power Supply, which runs the device.

Device Housing, which protects the components from the environment.

Many people believe DC's just read established dive tables. This is not true. Only one of the DC's available is table based (Suunto SME-USN). All the rest use a decompression model (algorithm) to compute the decompression status.

The algorithms used in DC's are mathematical and logical formulas with variables of depth and time, which makes them much more flexible than tables. A pure mathematical model affords an infinite number of depth/time solutions. Dive tables are finite listings of some of the solutions produced from a mathematical model.

The implementation of a decompression model in a DC is not "pure." As with tables, the DC deals with depth and time increments, though on a much smaller scale, based on the update interval of the computer (how often it recalculates the diver's decompression status) and the resolution of the pressure transducer circuitry (the smallest change in depth it can detect). The US Navy no-decompression table has only 135 depth/time combinations for depths between 0 and 140 feet of sea water (fsw). A model-based computer that updates its status every 3 seconds and has a depth resolution of 0.5 fsw can distinguish 400 possible "square-wave" depth/time combinations in a one minute period over a 10 fsw depth range.

Tables also base decompression status on the assumption that the entire dive was spent at the maximum depth. Most recreational divers spend only a small fraction of their dive time at the deepest depth achieved during the dive. This means that during most of dive the diver is taking on less nitrogen than assumed by the tables. Model-based DC's that update the diver's status every few seconds will compensate for the changes in depth. This allows the diver to be presented with a decompression status based on the actual dive that was performed. The advantages of computing decompression status in this manner include:

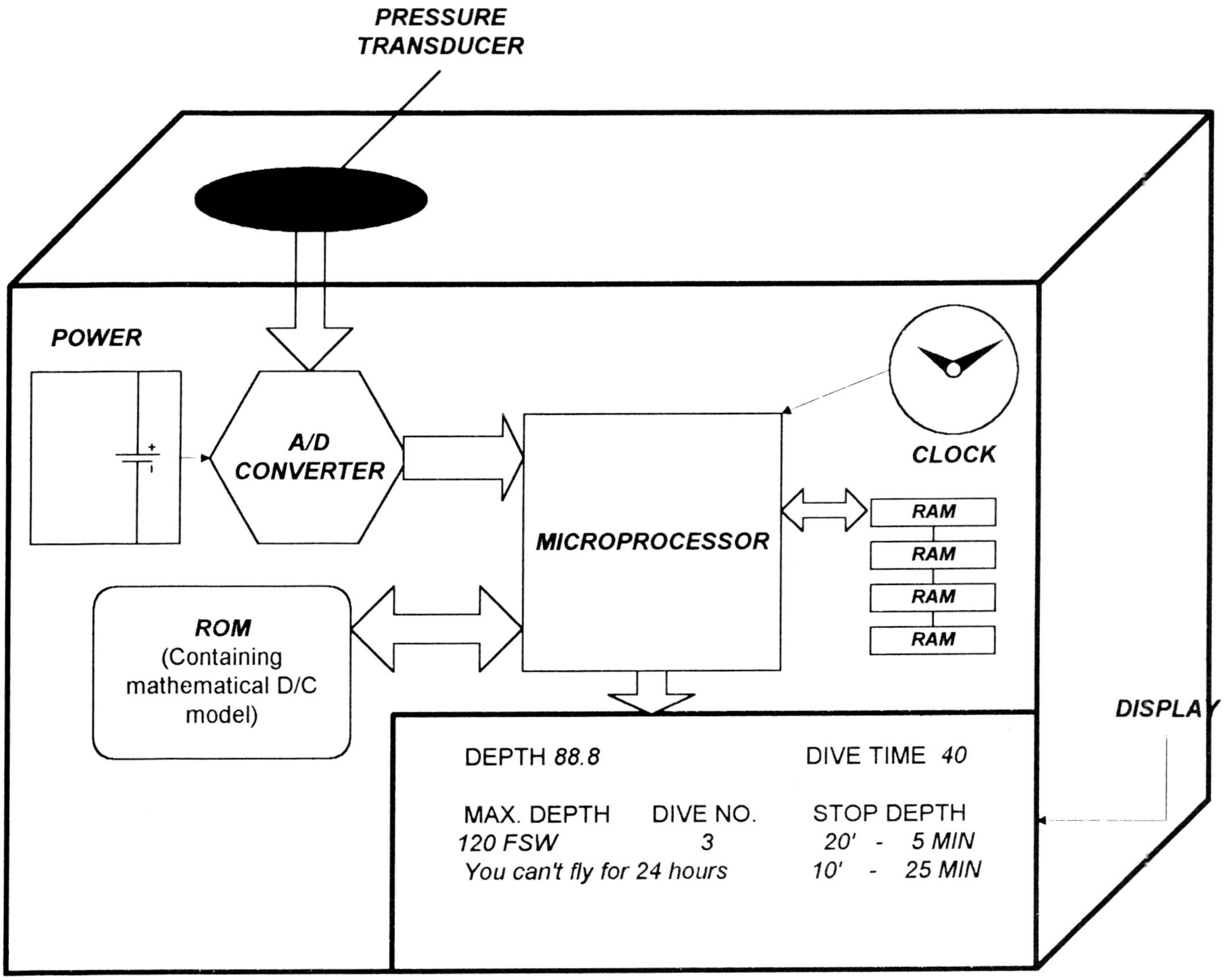

Figure 18-1 Schematic block diagram of dive computer.

(1) Profile Integration (no maximum depth-entire dive assumption).

(2) Shallow portions of dive are taken into account.

(3) Actual Depth used in calculation (51 fsw not 60 fsw).

(4) All compartments of the model are taken into account when calculating multi-level dive profiles (most table based techniques utilize the compartment representing their repetitive groups).

However, many of the advantages produce the disadvantages of DC's. If the device is pushed to its limit, the decompression model is pushed to its limit. There are no safety factors programmed into the units except for the models which are more conservative than the US Navy model. In using tables the maximum depth-entire dive rule adds a safety factor if the diver is at shallower depths during most of the dive. Another safety factor inherent in table use is the rounding up to a depth or time value greater than the actual depth and time of the dive. By using 60 fsw when the maximum depth is 51 fsw additional safety is added.

Other disadvantages present themselves. A diver needs to read the device, understand the information that is being presented, and act upon that information. There is also the possibility that the DC will become a crutch. Some divers might use it as an excuse to not teach, learn, or use tables (just like BC's are being used to circumvent the teaching of proper weighting). The major disadvantage, shared by tables and DC's alike, is the fact that all the DC or table knows about is depth and time.

Decompression Models vs Reality

Decompression models do not actually represent what is happening in the body. All the models do is attempt to produce depth/time combinations that are safe for most divers most of the time. Nearly all decompression models to date use these two variables, depth and time. These are used to compute the decompression status displayed to the diver. Many other factors can change the diver's susceptibility to DCS. These include ascent rate, physical exertion, water temperature, physical condition, hydration level, blood alcohol, age, gender, breathing mixture, etc.

If two divers perform the same depth/time dive profile, one being low exertion by a young, healthy diver in a warm Caribbean environment, and the other, performed in cold water by an older, out of shape, hung over diver who was working heavily, then the same decompression status will be computed by a DC (if the same DC model is used). All the DC "knows" is depth and time. A DC also has no memory of how it has reached its present decompression status. It does not keep track of the dive profiles that have been previously performed to modify decompression status calculations on subsequent dives. All it "knows" is the gas loading the model has calculated up to that point.

A mathematical equation does not a body make! Divers must be aware that they need to add safety factors based on their own physiological state, the diving environment, and their previous dive profiles, just as they have been taught do when using tables.

GENERAL MISUSES OF DIVE COMPUTERS

There seems to be some general techniques that have been developed by "clever" divers to squeeze every second they can out of a DC. The reasoning behind these abuses ranges from stupidity to blissful ignorance. Some of these misuses follow.

Regularly pushing unit to limits. There are many divers who run their DC's down to zero no-decompression time, ascend to a shallower depth, and then run the time back down to zero. This pushes the decompression model in the unit to its limit.

Ignoring ascent rate warning. Most of the DC's use ascent rates that are slower than the 60 fsw/min. US Navy standard. Using a faster ascent rate than suggested may place them outside the limits of the model. Following the slower ascent rates has the added benefit of requiring the diver to have good buoyancy control.

Not reading or ignoring the information. Some divers will just ignore the information provided by the computer if they do not like the information that is displayed.

Turning off unit to clear residual nitrogen. Some divers who do not like the repetitive dive information being shown by the DC will actually turn it off to clear the residual nitrogen from the computer's registers and give them more time on the repetitive dive. Clearing the residual nitrogen memory from the DC does not clear it from the diver's body!

Using outside operating range. About half of the DC's on the market are designed to be used at sea level or the first few thousand feet of altitude. The DC's based on the Swiss model generally adjust to altitude. However, some divers use the sea level DC's "as is" at altitudes outside the model's operating realm. Another problem in this category is diving to depths that exceed the maximum depth range of the DC. Why have a DC if it is being used on dives where it can't calculate properly or is placed in ERROR mode?

Abusing safety features. Some of the DC's have safety features that allow a diver to get out of situations outside the model or electrical limitations of the DC. Case in point: the *EDGE™* DC has a maximum depth resolution of approximately 165 fsw. At that point the depth register is storing the largest number it can. If the diver were to descend further the DC would not be able recognize the fact that the diver was at a deeper depth. However, a safety feature was added that assumes that the diver is at approximately 200 fsw any time the maximum depth has been exceeded. This assumption will only be "safe" (which is a questionable term for any dive to that depth) for a minute or so. After that time the compartment pressure registers will reach the maximum value they can store and they will not be able to distinguish any increase in compartment pressure, making the calculations and decompression information erroneous. There are divers who pervert this safety feature to make dives to 200 fsw with the *EDGE™* and some who use it to depths deeper than 200 fsw. Why? In most cases another diver has told them they could do it. Most of the time the divers don't really understand how the DC works, even though some think they do and they will believe what they want to believe.

Hanging the Dive Computer. One of the most ludicrous techniques observed. Some divers who violate the DC's ascent rate or have surfaced while the DC still indicates required decompression will tie a rope to the DC and hang it over the side of boat to clear the warnings and prevent the DC from going into ERROR mode. What can one say? The computer understands depth and time. It has no idea if it is attached to a diver or a rope.

Use with gas mixtures other than air. At this time all the DC models are based on the use of air as the breathing gas. Use of nitrox (enriched air) mixtures with less nitrogen content than air will theoretically add conservatism to the decompression calculations. However, the computers do not know anything about the increased potential of oxygen toxicity while using these mixtures. Other gas mixtures can actually increase the risk of DCS if decompression status is determined with an air based DC.

Blind trust in numbers. Many divers think that because the DC is telling them something that it is *TRUE*. The numbers produced by the DC are only a guide to a diver's decompression status, based on a decompression model using depth and time variables. The diver must be aware of the other factors that may influence susceptibility to DCS and add his own safety factors. As pointed out at the AAUS Dive Computer workshop in 1988, "They are like a small television,

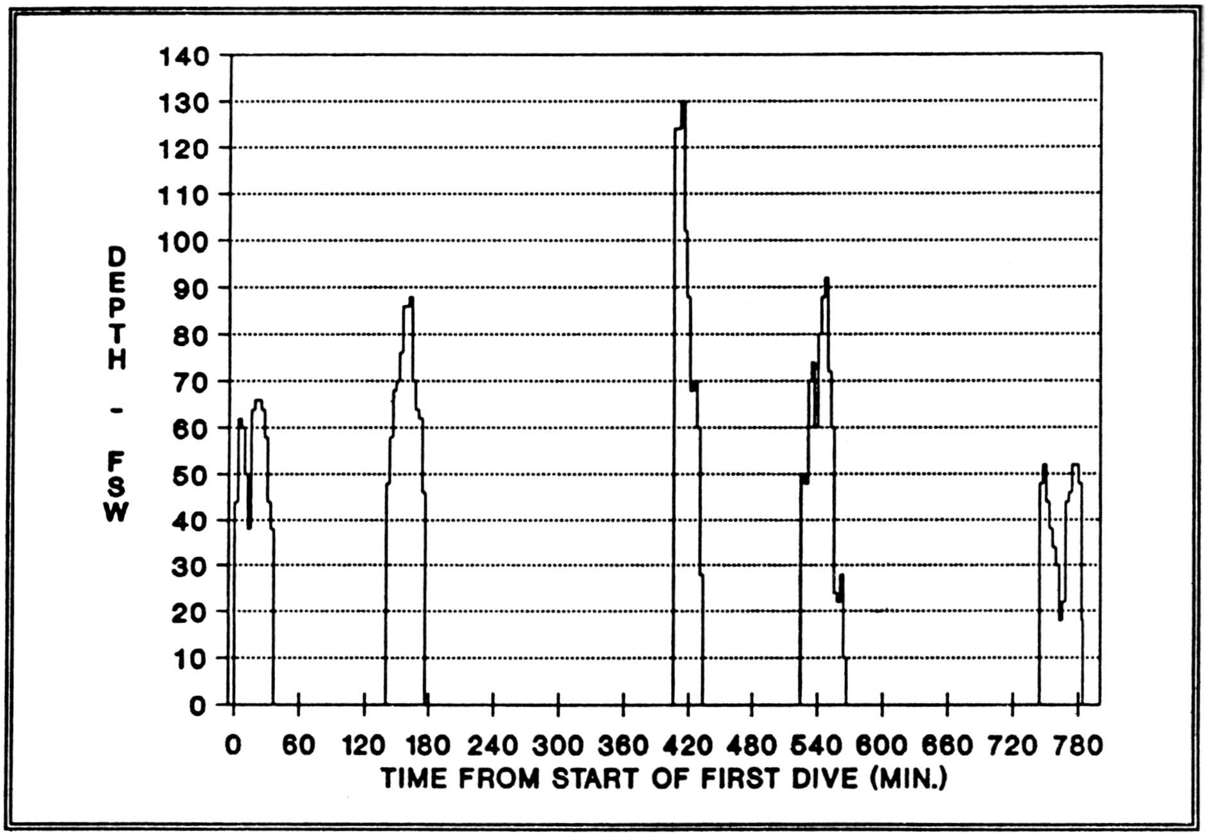

Figure 18-2 Dive profiles of single diver during one day of diving in the Galapagos Islands.

and people believe what they see on television."

Turn thinking over to a machine. Some divers do not want to worry, or think about their decompression status so they let a little box made out of silicon, metal, and plastic take over their thinking requirements. As stated before, the DC information is only a guide, not the gospel! Divers need to be able to think for themselves and understand the risks they are taking.

How Dive Computers are Being Used

This section deals with actual dive profiles that were performed using dive computers and the results of the dives.

Galapagos Trip. In 1987 a group of ten sport divers were monitored during a 14 day dive trip. All the divers, except one, used a DC. Following 76 of the dives the divers were monitored using Doppler ultrasonic bubble detector to check for "silent bubbles." On 65 dives the actual dive profile was recorded (maximum depth every 3 minutes).

When compared to the US Navy Tables 52 of the dives indicated omitted decompression. The maximum omitted decompression for a single dive was 71 minutes. The average was 23.0 minutes. For an entire day the maximum omitted decompression was 145 minutes and the average was 46.2 minutes. The maximum time extended past the US Navy No Decompression limits was 55 minutes on a single dive (average of 23.8 minutes).

The profile data indicated that 48.5% of the dive time was spent at depths which were 75-100% of the maximum depth range, 26.2% of the dive time was spent at 50-75% of the maximum depth range, 16.3% of the time was in 25-50% of the maximum depth range, and only 9.0% was spent in the shallowest quarter of the dive. This indicates that, for this group of divers, the DC's were not being used to make a short excursion to a deep depth followed by the remainder of the dive in shallower water. Also, the repetitive dive profiles did not follow the deep-to-shallow rule as can be seen in the graph of one day's dive profiles by one diver, shown in Figure 18-2.

The results of the Doppler monitoring indicated one definite and three possible cases of Grade I bubbles. No symptoms of DCS were observed in the divers.

Andrea Doria. Mike Emmerman reported dive profiles used on the *Andrea Doria* (1). What he observed was frightening. Divers would do a 210 fsw dive, wait 4 to 6 hours, and then do the same diver over again. Some did two dives a day and others did three! This was done three days in a row. Over 50% of the divers used DC's. Some used DC's that had maximum depth ranges that were shallower than the depths of the dives. Of the 16 divers on the trip six of them presented definite signs and symptoms of DCS. These six divers did express some concern for their condition, but none of them sought treatment!

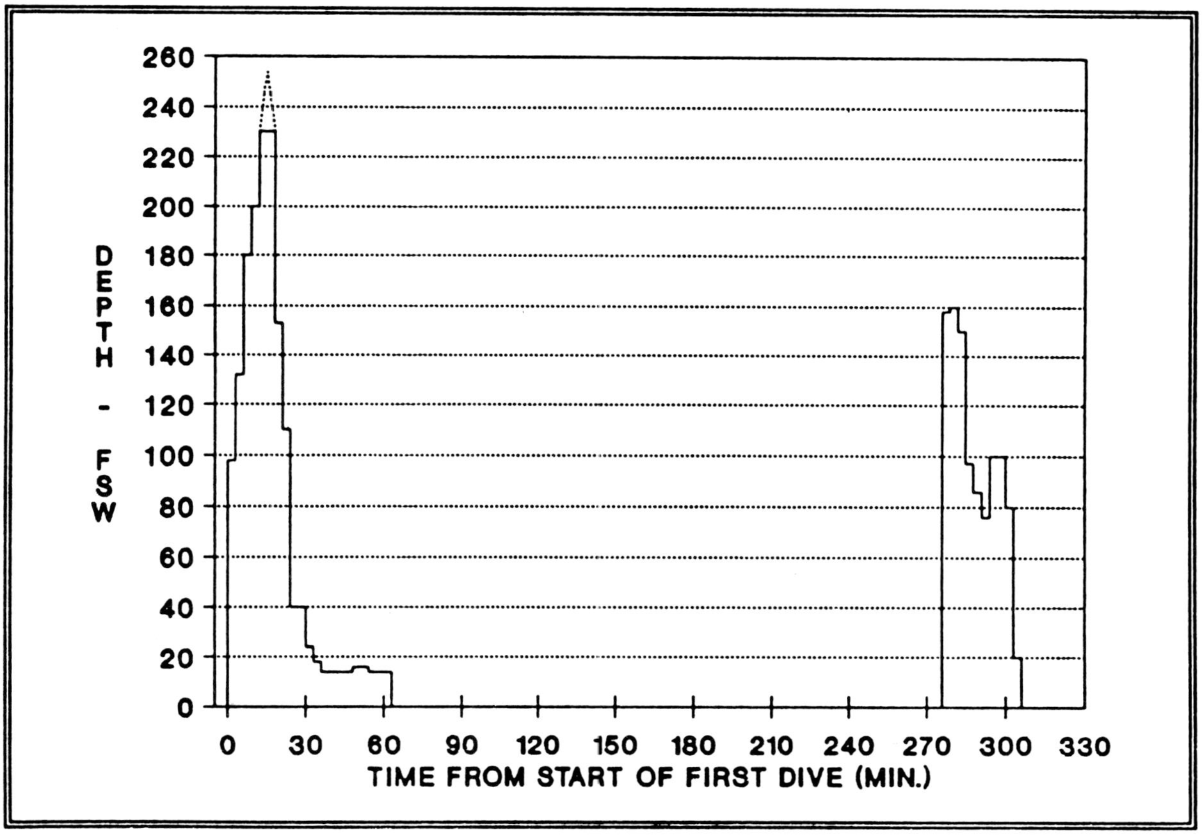

Figure 18-3 Deep repetitive dive series that produced DCS in one diver in a team. Dotted line represents where the diver's DC was taken past its depth range.

University of California at San Diego Bends Case. Dr. Tom Neuman at the University of California-San Diego related a case of DCS where a diver and his buddy had been diving with DC's (2). The dive history obtained from the diver was first a dive to 254 fsw followed by a dive to 160 fsw 3.5 hours later. Dr. Neuman found this hard to believe until it was discovered that the computer that diver wore also recorded the dive profile. The profile was recalled and the dives were confirmed, except for showing a maximum depth on the first dive of 230 fsw. This was due to the fact that the maximum depth limit for the computer was 230 fsw. However, when the dive log information was retrieved from the buddy's DC (one that has a depth limit of 300 fsw) a maximum depth of 254 fsw was obtained. Figure 18-3 shows the graph of this repetitive dive series.

Caribbean Vacation. This case involves a 26 year old male diver on vacation in the Caribbean using a DC. On the day the problem developed, the first dive was a multi-level dive to 140 fsw for a total dive time of 56 minutes. Four hours later a second dive was performed to a maximum depth of 160 fsw for a total bottom time of 47 minutes. The diver noticed an onset of fatigue 2 hours following the second dive, however he decided to perform a third dive following a 3 hour surface interval. This third dive was a night dive to 47 fsw for 67 minutes. That night he had a restless sleep, cold sweats, and minor pain in the elbow. In the morning the fatigue and pain remained so he proceeded to perform another dive. The dive was to 65 fsw for 40 minutes and during the dive he felt relief from pain. It was at this point that he concluded he probably was bent. The next morning the pain and fatigue remained along with a headache. That day he flew home to the states and sought treatment, four days after the dive series that produced the problem. After being treated with a USN Table 6 treatment schedule, the diver had no apparent residual problems. At all times the diver was within the no-decompression realm of his DC, but was pushing those limits.

Wreck of the *Regina*. Another case involves a 53 year old experienced female diver in excellent physical condition. She performed three dives to depths of 70-80 fsw using a DC. At no time was there less than 5 minutes of no-decompression time remaining on the DC. However, on the second dive the sleeve of her dry suit ripped exposing her arm to very cold water. Following the dive she had pain in her arm, but attributed it to the exposure to cold water. The suit was fixed and she performed the third dive. Later that evening, the pain in her arm became intolerable and she sought treatment. Besides the cold water another extenuating factor was that she had not had any hydration during the day (when she finally passed urine it was dark brown). There was no way for the DC to know that the

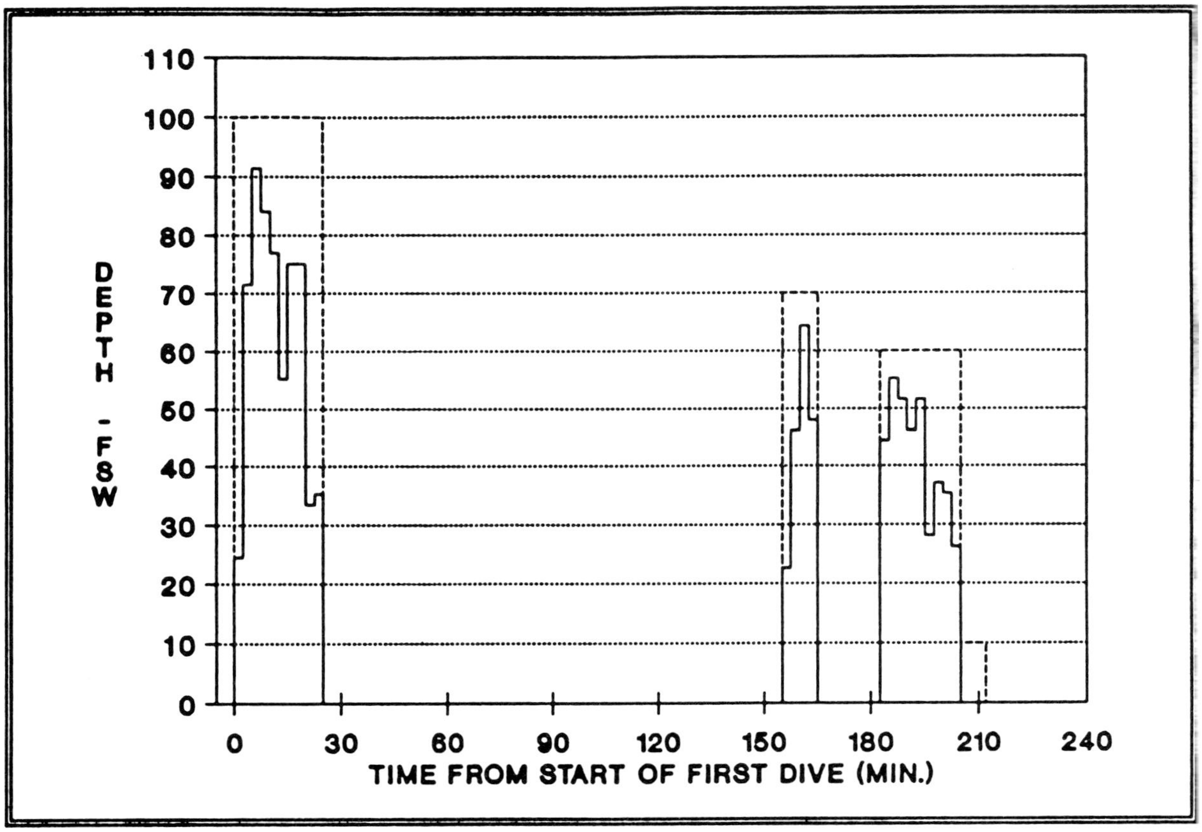

Figure 18-4 Dive profile that produced a "minor" bends case. Dashed line shows assumed table dive and US Navy D/C requirements (7 min. @ 10fsw).

dry suit had ripped or that the diver was dehydrated.

Northridge Chamber Treatment. The final case involves a diver who was treated for a "minor" bends case at the Northridge Hospital Chamber in California (4). The diver was suffering from elbow pain following a three dive series. The dive computer the diver was wearing recorded the dive series which consisted of an initial dive to 92 fsw followed a couple of hours later by two dives to 64 fsw and 56 fsw, in rapid succession. (See Figure 18-4 for a graphic representation of the dive profiles.) When these dives are run through the US Navy Tables a decompression requirement of 7 minutes at 10 fsw is obtained at the end of the third dive. The US Navy Table calculations assume that the diver spent the entire dive at the maximum depth for the entire dive, with that value rounded-up to the next depth available on the table. As can be seen from Figure 18-4, the actual dive profile is multi-level and the diver only went beyond 90 fsw for a brief time during the first dive. If the US Navy Table calculations were done using 90 fsw for the depth of the first dive, none of the dives would have required additional decompression. What does this tell us? Not much. No additional background information on the diver of the dive was communicated. The physiological and environmental factors of this dive series dealt the diver a diagnosed case of DCS. A series which was within the "safe" envelope of the dive computer's calculations. A series that would have been "safer" if calculated by a dive computer with the US Navy model programmed into it.

The Diver's Responsibility

Divers must realize that they need to take responsibility for their actions and safety. They must acknowledge the fact that every time they dive there is risk involved. One of these risks is the possibility of developing DCS. A diver needs to make a risk/benefit assessment as part of the dive plan. The goal of such an assessment is to maximize the benefit while minimizing the risk.

The operation and limitations of the DC's being used need to be understood. The more the diver understands about the equipment being used, the more educated and safe the decisions will become.

Dive computers should not be pushed to their limits. Divers should add safety factors just as they are added with table use. Remember, all a DC knows about is depth and time. DC's are not anti-DCS talismans. They will not ward off bubble formation or suck the nitrogen from the body. Most of all, a diver needs to employ common sense in all phases of diving.

CONCLUSIONS

It should be remembered that the advent of reliable DC's should not give the "train 'em fast and easy" people in diving an excuse not to teach tables and underlying decompression concepts, nor should they provide lazy divers an excuse not to learn and practice table use. I have talked to instructors who would have no qualms about having their students just strap on a little box that tells them their decompression status instead of teaching the use of dive tables. There are places where basic students are showing up to the first pool sessions wearing DC's. What incentive do they have for learning the concepts and use of dive tables? The introduction of DC's means that along with table instruction there is now the need to teach students how to use and understand computers.

No dive table or computer is 100% effective! Divers need to understand how and where the numbers are coming from, be it with tables or computers. They need to realize that all these devices understand are depth and time applied to a mathematical model. Common sense and understanding need to be part of the equation. Dive computers are good tools and as such can be used to enhance the diving experience, but they are only tools, not demigods to be worshipped and followed religiously. With hard work, training, and education we may be able to eliminate the event where a diver states, "I don't understand, my computer told me I could..."

AAUS RECOMMENDATIONS

In October 1988 the AAUS held a workshop on the use of DC's in scientific diving (3). The recommendations that were agreed upon that apply to recreational divers are listed below:

(1) ***Each*** diver relying on a DC to plan dives and indicate or determine decompression status must have his own unit.

(2) On any given dive, both divers in the buddy pair must follow the most conservative DC.

(3) If the DC fails at any time during the dive, the dive must be terminated and appropriate surfacing procedures should be initiated immediately.

(4) A diver should not dive for 18 hours before activating a DC to use it to control his diving.

(5) Once a DC is in use, it must **not** be switched off until it indicates complete outgassing has occurred or 18 hours have elapsed, whichever comes first.

(6) When using a DC, non-emergent ascents are to be at the rate(s) specified for the make and model of DC being used.

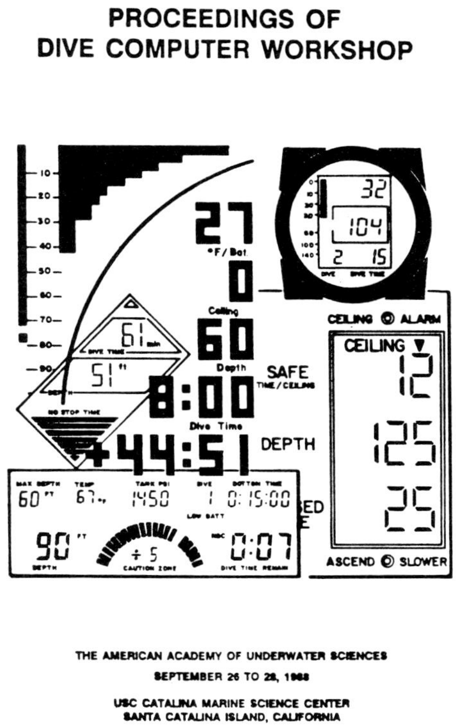

Figure 18-5 AAUS's Proceedings of the AAUS Dive Computer Workshop

(7) Ascent rates shall not exceed 40 fsw/min. in the shallowest 60 fsw.

(8) Whenever practical, divers using a DC should make a safety stop between 10-30 fsw for 5 min., especially for dives below 60 fsw.

(9) Repetitive and multi-level diving procedures should start the dive, or the series of dives, at the maximum planned depth, followed by subsequent dives of shallower exposures.

(10) Multiple deep dives should be avoided.

REFERENCES

1. Emmerman, Michael E. Personal communication, 1988.
2. Neuman, Tom. Personal communication, 1988.
3. Lang, Michael A. and R. W. Hamilton. *Proceedings of the American Academy of Underwater Science Dive Computer Workshop*, University of Southern California Sea Grant Program, 1989.
4. Heinmiller, Paul. Personal communication, 1990.

Chapter 19

LOW VISIBILITY CAVE DIVING

by Arthur Leithheuser

INTRODUCTION

A cave dive does not always mean a trip through crystal clear water with several powerful primary lights illuminating white limestone walls. For many reasons, cave divers can spend all or a portion of their dive traversing passages of limited visibility. On any dive, divers must be mentally prepared to deal with low visibility and be able to communicate with their dive partner(s) under such conditions.

There are two primary causes of low visibility: natural and incidental. *Natural low visibility* refers to pre-existing conditions where water visibility is reduced throughout the dive. For example, suspended silt in the water (which is typical of many sump diving localities), chemical characteristics of the water, such as pollution or tannic acid, haloclines, and even secondary sources of silting (such as runoff from rainfall into the cave system) may be considered natural low visibility conditions.

On the other hand, *incidental low visibility* refers to an alteration of visual conditions during the course of a dive. Examples of incidental low visibility would include: silting caused by divers, ceiling percolation, light failure, mask flooding, mask loss or breakage, loss of contact lenses, and physical irritation of the eyes.

PLANNING

Diving in conditions of naturally low visibility is more readily coped with by divers, since it is known prior to the dive that conditions are less than optimal and appropriate precautions can be taken. However, incidental low visibility often has an insidious onset because many dive teams do not mentally prepare for it in their pre-dive planning. In either case, the pre-dive plan may determine the success with which the team functions without the aid of sight.

In regard to low visibility diving, there are several areas of the pre-dive plan that a dive team can emphasize. If available, a map of the system should be examined and potential problem areas noted and discussed. This is especially useful for any member of the team who has not dived the system before. Guideline procedure and signals should be reviewed, to ensure consistency. Various communication systems available to divers during low visibility conditions are discussed later in this chapter. The dive team should review the chosen method of low visibility communication as part of pre-dive preparations.

The choice of lights should be discussed for a dive in natural low visibility conditions, with the team choosing primary lights that will provide optimal illumination. A more powerful lighting system does not always translate into greater visibility under these conditions. To reduce backscatter caused by suspended particles, the team may opt for lighting systems with lower output and a more diffuse beam. For example, a 30 watt sealed beam light may work better than a 55 watt quartz halogen light.

The dive team may decide that a more conservative (than usual) air plan is in order. An air plan more conservative than the "Thirds Rule" is advisable in known low visibility conditions because of the extra time that may be involved in solving problems. If a problem is encountered and the team knows that they have plenty of time to deal with it, then a source of stress is eliminated and the team can operate efficiently.

Finally, a short S-drill under simulated zero visibility conditions can reveal problems with communication or equipment that need to be worked out before the dive is begun. In order to share air in low visibility, each team member should be intimately aware of which regulator is available for her use, the location of that regulator, and its method of attachment.

During a certification course in cave diving, every diver undergoes several exercises that are related to low visibility conditions. These exercises should be periodically repeated to assure confidence in dealing with low visibility. For example, a diver who practices diving without a mask will probably have a calmer reaction to losing her mask during a dive than someone who has not experienced this since certification.

COMMUNICATION

Effective underwater communication among dive team members may easily make the difference between a safe dive and a life threatening one. In terms of communication, it is very helpful for a dive team to have had previous experience diving together under good conditions prior to engaging in a low visibility dive. Diving with the same buddy for a number of dives greatly enhances communication skills and any weaknesses in communication can be identified, discussed, and resolved.

Several publications describing underwater communication are available to divers. The first publication to address some of the specialized needs of communication in cave diving, *Hand Signals For Cave Diving* (Finley, *et al.*, 1977) attempted to standardize signals and offered a large repertoire of signals. This was later expanded, updated, and made available to the open-water diving community, as *Hand Signals For Diving.* (Finley, *et al.*, 1980) since most signals are applicable to any type of diving.

Many divers assume that hand signals must be seen to be used. However, hand signals may be used in low visibility conditions as well, through the medium of touch. This requires an intimate knowledge of hand signals and familiarity with any distinct method a dive partner might use to make signals. Using hand-to-hand contact for signalling is not difficult, but it requires practice, especially if the water is cold enough to warrant the use of gloves. A dive team can practice giving signals (both with and without gloves) under simulated blackout conditions. After the exercise is completed, team members can check on the accuracy of the signals that were exchanged.[1]

The *Rimbach* or *Touch-and-Go System* has been utilized by cave divers since the early 1970's and is an important communication resource for low visibility diving. Designed for increased team communication and efficiency during low visibility or emergency conditions, this techniques requires that team members maintain contact with both the guideline and each other.

Under the touch-and-go system, all divers stay on the same side of the guideline as the lead diver, in order to facilitate buddy breathing and decrease the chances of a line entanglement. The trailing divers grasp the calf, thigh, or upper arm of the diver in front of them. The configuration of the cave usually determines if the arm or leg is grasped.

Signalling is simple and straightforward. Once the team is in motion, the first signal a diver gives is one squeeze, which indicates *halt.* All members of the team stay in place until another signal is received. A push forward indicates *continue* or *move ahead.* A pull back indicates *come back* or that a diver needs assistance. The touch-and-go method may be used for a variety of purposes and is easily modified to suit the specific needs of any dive team.

The touch-and-go system requires constant contact between divers. However, there are situations where it is necessary for a diver to release contact from either the guideline or the preceding diver in order to solve a problem. Obviously, it is preferable to signal for a stop rather than to lose contact without giving the *stop* signal. Once the team has halted, the diver can solve the problem or indicate a need for assistance through hand-to-hand contact. If contact is lost between the members of a team, it is the duty of the lead diver to back up until contact is restored.

Special signals a team may want to employ, such as shifting to the other side of the guideline, should be covered in the predive plan. It is advisable for a team to practice the touch-and-go system under controlled conditions, simulating a variety of potential emergencies. This practice will give a dive team confidence in their ability to successfully exit a cave under these conditions.

Figure 19-1 Cave divers rehearsing low visibility communication procedures.

A variation of the touch-and-go system for low visibility diving is the *Wilson System* (1982). This system requires the divers to remain in contact with the guideline and each other and use the following squeeze signals for communication. 1) Two squeezes either asks whether the other diver is *OK*, or signals that the team should *proceed.* 2) Three squeezes signal that it is necessary to *exit* the cave. 3) Several quick squeezes indicate a problem and that *assistance is needed.* 4) Several quick squeezes, accompanied by tapping on a partner's second stage, indicate a *need to share air.*

In addition to these signals, if a dive team adopts one squeeze to indicate *halt*, most situations are covered under this system. However, a few problems remain. Most importantly, two squeezes has different meanings and could be misinterpreted. For example, while Diver B has stopped to fix an equipment problem, Diver A gives two squeezes to find out if B is *OK.* Diver B replies with two squeezes, which may or may not indicate that she is ready to continue the dive at this point. Diver B might only be thinking in terms of *OK* while her buddy thinks she is signalling *continue.* Because of this ambiguity, there is no clear signal to get the team moving again.

Another system available to divers is the *bump-and-go* method. Under this system, all dive team members maintain contact with the guideline but not with each other. Each diver swims an arbitrary distance, then stops to wait for the next team member to catch up. When the trailing diver bumps into the lead diver,

[1]Because of the need to be able to contact and follow the guideline in low or zero visibility conditions, use of gloves is not recommended except where imperative due to the water temperature. Cave divers who wish to wear gloves during the dive usually cut the fingers out of ordinary neoprene diving gloves. Some cave divers prefer to use gloves during long D/C, and leave a nice, warm, uncut pair of suitable gloves or mittens with their D/C equipment. — Ed.

the latter proceeds again. Several problems may be encountered using this system. Communication is at a minimum, resulting in numerous opportunities for confusion. For example, the trailing diver could inadvertently bump into the lead diver after losing contact with the guideline. The lead diver would interpret this as the signal to continue and leave the lost diver behind. Similar problems could arise if the trailing diver needed to share air. Finally, the stops and starts built into the system render it slow and inefficient.

Another system of communication for low visibility diving was developed by Jamie Stone in 1979. As with the touch-and-go system, the divers retain contact with both the guideline and each other. The signals developed by Stone may be communicated through any method devised by the team, including bangs, hits, tugs, squeezes, etc. It is the responsibility of the dive team to ensure that a standard system has been chosen. For example, the team might choose banging on their tanks, which is especially useful if divers become separated.

Stone's system consists of the following signals: 1) One signal asks whether the other diver is *OK* or serves as a reply meaning *OK*. This is used as the first signal because of the possibility of a diver giving an inadvertent signal. 2) Two occurrences of a signal indicate let's *move on*, let's *continue*, or *go ahead*. 3) Three occurrences of a signal indicate that the team should *stop* or *halt* immediately. 4) Four occurrences of a signal indicate the buddy should *come here* or that her partner *needs assistance*. This signal is generally reserved for emergencies and problems in which one team member requires the prompt assistance of another team member.

To be clear and effective, the signals should be performed rapidly and distinctly. The rate of signalling must be rapid enough to ensure their recognition as a related train of signals, but not so fast that they are confusing. Repeating the signal(s) after a short time may help avoid confusion.

The simplicity of Stone's system makes it especially useful for low visibility cave diving. Only signals that are absolutely necessary are utilized to prevent ambiguity and misunderstandings. There is no signal for sharing air, since part of the pre-dive planning effort should include emergency procedures for sharing air. A diver who needs to share air can signal by tapping on the second stage of the regulator her partner is using. The partner should then hand the regulator she gives away to the distressed diver.

In the event that team members become separated, an effective method of communicating can be established by repeated, gentle pulling on the guideline. It is unnecessary (and unwise) to violently jerk the guideline; most divers can detect moderate line movements with surprising ease.

The most appropriate communication system for low visibility diving relies on constant contact between members of the dive team. It is especially important that a team work together and constantly communicate as conditions worsen. The simple act of maintaining contact in very limited visibility offers assurance to team members and absolutely confirms a team member's presence.

LOST GUIDELINE

Losing contact with the guideline in low visibility conditions is a potentially disastrous scenario that must be dealt with logically and methodically. Cave divers need to address the problem of relocating a guideline before they are forced to deal with it in an actual low visibility situation. There are several techniques for finding a lost guideline, all of which may require considerably more practice than is readily apparent.

Depending on the condition of the line between two tie off points, lost guidelines may be in three different states: taut (tied off with little or no slack), loose (tied off with too much slack), or parted (broken line). If a taut or loose line is lost, it can be relocated with "relative" ease. However, if the line has parted, then the team has a more serious problem.

A parted or limp line lying on the floor of a passage is very difficult to feel. It may be necessary to retrace the route back to the last tie off point where a taut line can be located by one of the methods described below. The problems associated with attempting to relocate a lost parted line imply that more frequent tie off points and secure wraps may be desirable. This may become particularly important in areas where the line is wrapped over sharp projections.

It may be possible to relocate a lost line by ascending above the silty area and looking around. If the passage is small, it will be relatively simple to remain stationary and feel around for the line. Unfortunately, these techniques do not work for large passages with low visibility. In this case, a reference point must be established. A reference point is a fixed site from which a search pattern can be initiated using a safety reel.

The method of establishing a reference point depends largely upon the structure of the passage. If the bottom is silty or sandy, several feet of guideline from the safety reel can be bundled together and buried in the substrata. If the bottom sediment is not hard enough to hold the line, an object must be tied to the line to act as an anchor. A knife may be useful for this purpose or, if nothing else can be found, the diver's primary light can be attached to the line and dropped to the cave floor. At this point, the primary light is probably of little use and a diver's backup lights can be used once visibility improves.

On the other hand, if the cave passage is mostly hard rock with little soft bottom, a projection or large slab of breakdown can serve as a reference point. If the passage has no suitable features or projections for tying off the line, any piece of equipment which is negatively buoyant and sufficiently heavy can serve as an anchor.

Once a reference point has been established, the diver proceeds in the direction she thinks the line is located. If the line has not been parted, the diver can move along the floor to one wall, ascend up the wall, and start back along the ceiling in hopes of snagging the guideline while reeling in the line back to the reference point. This procedure can be used for taut or loose guidelines.

In the case of a parted line, the diver should follow the cave floor very slowly and (without gloves) feel for the line inch by inch. Most guidelines used in the United States are negatively buoyant and will usually fall to the floor if parted. However, there are situations where the line could be above the floor. The guideline could be tied off high, hanging from a projection, or suspended in the water in systems with a strong current. Buoyant guidelines, which are commonly used in Britain, will float and require a search pattern along the ceiling of the cave.

If more than one team member has lost the guideline and they are in contact with each other, it may be possible to use one diver as the reference point. While one diver rests on the bottom, holding on to a projection or whatever is available, the other diver initiates a search for the line. The "anchor point" diver should hold the end of the line from the safety reel. This allows more flexibility for the searching diver. Communication skills are obviously an important factor in the successful implementation of this method.

The same technique is useful under another set of conditions. There are dives where it is questionable for cave divers to place a guideline from the surface to the beginning of the permanent line, because of an abundance of open-water divers. Some cave divers consider it best to avoid placing a guideline in the basin of a popular dive site, because of the temptation of openwater divers to follow the line. However, this can cause problems for the cave diving team if other divers completely silt out the entrance or if heavy rainfall during the dive causes a drop in visibility.

When a continuous line to the surface is absent and a dive team encounters a low visibility situation between the permanent line and the surface, there are several possible solutions to the problem. One team member can be stationed at the tie-off point of the permanent line holding the end of a safety guideline, while the other diver searches for the route to the surface.

Another method is to clip the safety reel to the permanent line and have the entire dive team proceed out of the cave. On exit, the team can decide whether to leave the safety reel or retrieve it. In order to remove a line in low visibility conditions, one diver must unfasten the end of the line and be reeled in by the other diver.

CONCLUSION

Communication and planning are essential to all aspects of cave diving and especially important in any low visibility situation. Because it is not always possible to predict that a low visibility situation will arise, it seems reasonable to practice communication skills. As cave divers are well aware, stress is a skill narrowing experience. Therefore, practice of skills to the point of proficiency and making them second nature reduces the danger from an emergency situation. Through the implementation of good communication skills and techniques, low visibility cave diving can become a mere inconvenience and remain as safe as any other aspect of cave diving.

Chapter 20

RESCUE AND RECOVERY

by H. V. Grey

A TYPICAL CAVE DIVING ACCIDENT

On the morning of Saturday, March 29, 1986, Easter weekend, two certified cave diving instructors and one other, trained and highly experienced cave diver, arrived at a popular Florida spring to make a photo cave dive. Already gearing up at another site a short distance away were four certified open-water divers from Georgia, who had driven down to Florida for a weekend of photography and spring diving.

The open-water divers' gear (they were fully equipped for a pleasant day in the ocean) and the kinds of questions they asked immediately alerted the cave divers to their lack of cave or cavern diving training. The cave divers then tried to describe the potential hazards of the cave system, especially in view of the unusually bad visibility conditions, and the necessary equipment and techniques needed for a safe dive in the cavern of the spring. The cave divers even offered to forego their own planned dive in order to escort the open-water divers safely around the cavern area, but the four open-water divers were not interested in anything the cave divers had to say. Short of physical restraint, the cave divers tried every means of rational dissuasion. One of the cave diving instructors recalls his last words to the four open-water divers: "Stay in sight of the opening. We don't want to have to make a body recovery so early in the year."

After about thirty minutes, three of the open-water divers surfaced and reported that their fourth member was missing. One of the cave divers, already geared up for the photo cave dive, hit the water within minutes of the alert and began the search. The other two cave divers geared up as quickly as possible and joined in the search for the missing diver, and additional divers and surface support were called in. At this point, they were still hoping to make a rescue rather than a body recovery. (It was not until later that the cave divers found out that the three open-water divers were all very nearly out of air when they surfaced and at that point, in all likelihood, the missing diver was probably already dead.)

Splitting up to maximize their search potential, the three trained cave divers individually searched several different main passages and side tunnels. Approximately 45 minutes after the search effort began, the body of the missing diver was finally located off a siphon tunnel at the end of a meandering jump line.

The open-water diver's death was practically a standard textbook case. He had violated all established cavern and cave diving safety procedures: no cavern or cave training, no guideline, insufficient scuba equipment, air not planned according to the Third's Rule, poor buddymanship, only one light, diving deeper than the 70-foot limit prescribed for the minimum required cavern diving equipment (which he didn't have).

Figure 20-1 Truth in advertising.

This is the somber, tragic side of cave diving: rescue and recovery. It is particularly tragic in light of the fact that almost all of the victims fit the pattern of the above described fatality: they are ignorant of proper cavern and cave diving procedures and equipment; they willfully ignore verbal warnings, safety pamphlets, and warning signs posted on land and within the caves themselves; and upon occasion, even willfully violate their own signed and witnessed agreements to abide by the safety rules of a state park or dive resort. In several deaths there were clear indications that in addition to most of the above, the victims were also intoxicated and/or under the influence of illegal drugs. And yet, while thousands of extensive cave dives are made each year in relative safety by trained and certified cave divers, it is usually the "killer cave" or lack of government regulation of diving that is unjustly blamed for the drownings.

RESCUE AND RECOVERY PROCEDURES

General Information

Although a rescue is obviously the preferred activity, it is usually a recovery that is performed. There have been instances, particularly in dry-caving rescues, where dry cavers trapped by rising water have been rescued by cave divers who are specially skilled in the very advanced techniques of sump diving. However, the very limited time factor associated with single-tank air supplies makes the likelihood of a live underwater cave rescue extremely remote. Even when certified cave divers trained in rescue and recovery techniques are on hand and ready to go into the water, as in the above-described instance, rescue is still a relatively rare event.

It should be obvious that since it is generally an ignorance of proper cave diving procedures that causes the fatalities in the first place, attempts to search for and recover the victims should not be made by anyone who is also not trained and experienced in cave diving. Frequently, the victims severely silt out and completely destroy the visibility of large portions of a cave system, or even cut a permanent guideline, thus greatly increasing normal hazards. In this instance, even highly experienced cave divers are hard pressed to dive safely, much less to accomplish an exhaustive search for a dead body that may be wedged into a tight crevice or buoyed way up in a ceiling dome.

Just as no amount of previous open-water experience will prepare an open-water diver for the hazards of cave diving, no amount of open-water rescue/recovery training will prepare the rescue diver for the hazards that he will encounter trying to perform a rescue or recovery in a cave. Open-water rescue/recovery training cannot be considered an acceptable substitute for formal cave diving training and experience.

The lives of open-water rescue personnel should never be risked to recover a dead body — especially since an extensive network of trained and experienced cave diving recovery experts, which is capable of mobilizing on very short notice, has been established. These experts, certified by the National Cave Rescue Commission (NCRC) and NSS Cave Diving Section, are not only trained in safe cave diving procedures, but in specific underwater cave rescue/recovery techniques and in accident and criminal-evidence collection and preservation methods developed in cooperation with law enforcement agencies. In the interests not only of the safety of the rescue team, but of determining possible potential foul play underwater, it is very important that cave body recoveries be performed only by people who are well qualified in both areas.

When to Consider Divers Overdue

Ordinary cave dives planned within the limitations of the Third's Rule can vary in duration from 15 minutes to several hours, depending on the various depths encountered in the cave, the starting air supplies of the divers, and the length of required decompression. It may be difficult sometimes for friends or family waiting at the surface to judge when the cave divers are dangerously past due. Unpredictable problems which arise within the cave can extend the planned dive duration, causing the divers to be considerably delayed past any time limits they might have given their friends on the surface. The cave configuration may require that decompression stops be made out of sight of the entrance, and the lengthy decompression times needed for conservative, safe decompression may exceed predictions.

Traverses (trips made from one cave entrance to another) also present problems for surface personnel. The air rules require that the cave diving team turn the dive when they have reached their minimum exit air pressure. This may not permit them to complete the traverse as planned, causing them to return to their original entrance. And a dive may always be turned by any dive-team member for any reason at any time, thereby sending the team back to the starting point.

There are other possibilities with traverses as well. In a recent instance observed by this author, certified cave divers using drysuits and double 100's entered a Florida sinkhole intending to swim downstream to emerge approximately 40 minutes later at the headspring of the cave system, where their friends would be waiting with their vehicle. More than an hour later a rather astonished, bewildered, and hot cave diver came trudging down the road from a sinkhole quite a distance upstream. Never having dived this portion of the cave system before, they had taken the wrong tunnel and ended up a good mile from their intended destination.

Sump divers exploring wet portions of otherwise dry caves may discover additional dry passages beyond the sump and continue their explorations on foot for several hours before returning to their scuba gear and exiting back through the sump. There are numerous sump-diving instances where the sump divers curtailed their subsequent dry exploration only out of concern for the worry that their surface-support personnel might be experiencing on their behalf.

With open-water divers, usually diving only with single tanks, the time limits are much shorter. If the cave depths are known, it is a fairly simple matter to compute approximate air durations, and to judge when the divers can be considered to be seriously overdue. In the Easter-weekend accident case, one of the cave diving instructors had set the timer on his watch when the four open-water divers submerged and had actually walked back to the spring entrance to check to make sure that all the divers surfaced.

In general, friends on the surface should begin to become concerned when the divers fail to return within a reasonable time of their estimated return time. As the time grows longer, the surface personnel should begin to discuss contingency plans. If other cave entrances are a possibility, someone should be dispatched to check them out. Of course, if part of the dive team surfaces and reports a missing diver, then search and rescue/recovery procedures should be instituted immediately.

Initiating a Search

If qualified divers (i.e., certified cave divers with cave rescue training) are already at the site and able to gear up quickly, their aid can be enlisted to begin an immediate in-water search for the missing diver(s). Unqualified divers have no business in underwater caves under any circumstances, and run the risk of adding to the number of dead bodies that have to removed from the cave. Due to the emotional nature of such incidents, well-meaning but hazardous actions are sometimes proposed or undertaken. There can be no excuse for not observing all safety procedures and taking all proper precautions for the safety of the recovery divers.

If the missing diver's buddies surface with little or no air, and the missing diver started with approximately the same amount of air, then the chances are extremely remote of making an in-water rescue. By the time the missing diver's buddies could get switched to fresh tanks and try to go back in, the chances would be practically nonexistent. The surviving dive buddies should, therefore, be strongly discouraged from attempting an immediate body recovery themselves with the hope of still being able to effect a rescue.

Recovery Procedures

If the search fails to locate the lost divers within their probable air limits, or if qualified rescue personnel are not readily available at the scene, rescue efforts cease and recovery procedures are instituted. The proper law enforcement authorities must be contacted as quickly as possible. The local police or sheriff should be called and given the location of the accident and other particulars. When you call, you should be ready to provide your name, the number you are calling from, the name(s) of the missing diver(s), the location of the incident, and other pertinent information.

Figure 20-2 This applies to potential rescue divers, too!

The law enforcement agency puts in the official call for the Cave Diving Recovery Divers. They do this through the National Crime Information Center (NCIC) located in Jacksonville, Florida. When contacted, the NCIC provides the local law enforcement agency with the names(s) and phone number(s) of the nearest Cave Diving Recovery Team coordinator(s). In addition, they advise the NCIC cave diving coordinator that a rescue/recovery operation is underway.

Once it has been determined that rescue is unlikely due to lack of qualified personnel at the scene or length of time passed, no one should enter the cave system. This prevents further accidents and preserves the scene and visibility for the Cave Diving Recovery Team. While awaiting their arrival, gather all relevant information regarding the accident, such as dive plan, air supply, equipment, team members, route, experience, familiarity with dive site, etc.

In some instances the bodies are found very quickly and with minimum surface support. In other cases, surface logistics have required vertical rope techniques (rapelling, rachet-cam climbing systems, mechanical-advantage pulley systems, and mechanical removal of heavy equipment and remains). In a few cases, the bodies were never recovered (or only discovered by accident years later) because the diver worked his way into an extremely tight area of the cave and was missed during the search, or because the victim descended to depths that put the recovery team members in unacceptable danger. While it is usually important to the victim's surviving friends and relatives to have the victim's body recovered, it is never worth unduly risking the life of a rescuer/recoverer to bring back a dead body. There is an old US Navy saying: "Only risk a life to save a life."

Again, as with cave diving in general, reading a book is no substitute for actual certification training. Because of safety and accident/criminal-investigation considerations, recoveries should only be attempted by trained and qualified personnel. If someone who does not know the proper procedures attempts to make the recovery, valuable evidence may be damaged or disturbed making it impossible to clearly establish the true cause of death.

The NCRC Cave Diving Rescue/Recovery Team offers training seminars approximately once or twice a year and invites all certified and experienced cave divers to participate. Information on the time and location of the next course may be obtained by contacting the NACD or the NSS Cave Diving Section. Courses are usually held in conjunction with NACD Seminars and NSS-CDS Workshops and are conducted at springs in the north Florida area.

Chapter 21

CAVE DIVING EXPLORATION

by Paul Heinerth

INTRODUCTION

Cave divers worldwide continually seek out new systems to explore. To exploration divers who have logged hundreds or thousands of cave dives, a new system may mean a subaquatic cave that has never been visited by humans before. To other cave divers, a new system probably means one that they are diving for the first time and is only new to them. Regardless of whether a system has been explored by other divers or not, there are several procedures for divers to follow in seeking out new cave diving sites. They are:

(1) Research — books and other written material, old-timers' stories, topographical maps, word of mouth.

(2) Scouting — on land, by air, by water.

(3) Negotiations with property owners.

(4) Logistics of equipment transport.

(5) The first dive.

RESEARCH

The term *research*, as related to the subject at hand, is defined as the seeking out of information on potential cave diving sites. It does not pertain to scientific research methods concerning caves.

The most obvious source of information regarding dive sites are books on the subject. For Florida diving, Ned De Loach's *Guide to Underwater Florida* lists numerous cave diving sites and directions for finding them. Another book worth mentioning is *Florida Springs*, available from the Florida Department of Natural Resources. Past issues of the newsletters and journals of the NACD and the NSS-CDS are excellent sources of information on cave systems. Divers who attend cave diving seminars have an excellent chance of hearing about new systems.

For divers with a particular area in mind, topographical maps are indispensable. These maps are available from the United States Geological Survey Office and may possibly be found at a local library, store, or county building. Divers can study the contours of the area, paying particular attention to round ponds, especially when there is a decrease in elevation. These could be sinkholes. Sometimes topographic maps show bodies of water with names like *Blue Sink, Rock Sink, Round Sink*, etc., which can be checked out for cave systems.

Another good place to look on a topo map is along a river. Many Florida rivers are spring fed with numerous springs along the course of the river. A pond showing a creek leading to the river could be a spring, and there might be a diveable cave system at any spring. Anyone who uses this method to look for dive sites will obviously run across a fair number of shallow mudholes. It is helpful to mark ponds that have been visited, to avoid revisiting the mudholes. This can save divers time and trouble the next time they want to explore the same area.

The infamous old-timers stories or word of mouth are oftentimes very helpful, particularly when the person telling the story is willing to accompany the divers to the dive location. Although some stories will not pan out, divers should not be discouraged. Although the site could be a 20 foot deep mudhole, it could also be an excellent cave system waiting to be explored. Some of the best dive sites in the world have been discovered through local residents who had no interest in cave diving.

SCOUTING

Scouting is a proven method of finding new dive sites, and it can be done by air, land, and water. A high quality, recent topographical map is extremely helpful when scouting for dive sites.

By Air

Scouting by air works best in Florida during the winter. The temperature drops, cooling the surface water of ponds. Those connected to the aquifer turn a deep blue and maintain a fairly constant temperature. Sinkholes look very impressive from the air in winter and divers can mark any that look promising. By referencing the area, noting roads, clearings, etc., divers will be able to find the sinkhole more easily when they approach it by land. Over salt water, sinkholes and submarine springs are easily visible because their deep blue color contrasts sharply with the shallower water surrounding them.

By Land

Not everyone has access to airplanes and helicopters to search for new cave dives, especially in Mexico and the Caribbean. However, divers can scout for new dive sites by land. Armed with aerial photographs, a topo map, a day's supply of food and drink, a compass, and snorkeling gear, a team of two or more can tramp through remote areas looking for promising sites. Rather than starting from the nearest graded road, a four-wheel drive vehicle can often get a party much closer to the area they wish to explore.

To begin, divers should try to pick out landmarks from the aerial photographs and maps and determine the direction of the site from their starting point by using compass headings. Those who wish to explore for new sites should use common sense and take precautions. They should notify someone of where they will be searching and stay aware of property lines. Obtaining permission from property owners to search their land is discussed later in this chapter.

If a dive site is found that has fairly clear surface water, snorkeling the site may reveal whether or not it is worth bringing in cave diving equipment. However, the color or appearance of the surface water can be deceptive. For example, the famous Die Polder III sinkhole looks like a dirty green pond in the summer, giving no indication of the spectacular cave below.

By Water

Scouting by water can be even more challenging. To assist the exploration-oriented diver, offshore aerial photographs are available from the United States Geological Survey and a boat equipped with Loran C can find or return to a precise location on the ocean. Loran numbers of well-publicized sites are often listed in fishing books; however, the numbers of other sites can be closely guarded secrets.

NEGOTIATIONS WITH PROPERTY OWNERS

It is advisable for anyone interested in exploration to talk with the property owners before tramping around looking for new cave sites on their land. An open and honest approach is the best policy. Divers who are civilized, concerned, and courteous towards property owners are the ones who will most likely get a chance to explain what they want to do. With a little luck, a landowner will see no harm in their plans and will give permission for them to search and dive. It usually helps for an exploration team to promise to share any information they learn about the land: the owner may be just as curious about the system as the dive team is. Sometimes owners will not even realize the possibility of their pond being anything more than a pond, and cave divers can explain what might lie below.

Any final conditions that the property owner wishes to impose should be willingly accepted by the exploration team — at least diving is possible. Divers should question landowners to find out what their needs are and respect their privacy. If the owner wishes to limit access, cave divers may be able to set up a system of guides who have permission to dive there and share the responsibilities.

One such example is The Sand Hill Boy Scout Ranch in Central Florida which contains two diveable sinkholes. Twelve highly qualified cave divers act as director/guides, and no one can dive there unless escorted by a director. This reduces traffic and creates controls to minimize possible mishaps. It is up to each director to determine the qualifications and expertise of those requesting to dive. Such an agreement provides an opportunity for a positive cave diving experience to many divers who would otherwise be unable to dive there at all.

Cave divers need to be especially sensitive to keeping the site litter-free, and to avoid any degradation of the environment (such as erosion at the entry point). A professional approach speaks for itself. Divers must be prepared to keep the site clean, trash free, and as undisturbed as possible.

In other countries, divers will probably have to deal with a local or regional government. Courtesy, patience, and flexibility cannot be overemphasized. One area in which Americans are often found lacking is knowledge of the local language.

LOGISTICS OF EQUIPMENT TRANSPORT

If a discovery is made in a local cow pasture, the logistics of equipment transport can be as simple as keeping the gates closed so none of the cows escape. On the other extreme is a discovery in a Third World country where logistics can turn into a frustrating nightmare. Prior planning is the only answer, although there is no single formula that works for all trips and expeditions.

Ideally, when preparing for an exploratory dive, the dive team has sufficient time to make several dives if the site shows promise. Especially in remote tropical areas, it is extremely frustrating to carry full cave diving equipment (for any distance) to a site that may be extremely limited in depth and/or penetration. When diving an unknown site that is not easily accessible, divers do not have to take scooters, double steel 104 cubic foot tanks, and other equipment for an all out assault. Most exploration cave divers know that if they find a significant cave system, they will return for other, more ambitious dives.

An important part to transporting equipment is planning ahead. Once a site has been determined to be worth a serious effort, thorough preparations should be made for the dive. All diving equipment should be tested in advance, with the team taking a well-provisioned toolbox and extra equipment along with them. Divers who want to dive in more remote areas must be able to make minor repairs on their equipment. Also necessary for a successful effort is reliable transportation, although it is often difficult to find in more remote parts of the world. Equipment failures (of any type) can prevent a team from even starting an exploration dive, regardless of the time, money, and energy they have expended.

THE FIRST DIVE

All cave dives need to be planned, but special

preparations are necessary for exploring a new system because the team must plan for the unknown. Divers must be prepared to establish strict limits and follow those limits once the dive has begun.

The dive team should approach a new system cautiously and mentally prepare themselves for adverse conditions, such as low visibility, no sense of direction, tight passageways, strong currents, cold water, and encounters with marine life. Limits should be set on depth, penetration, and air supply.

For the first dive, a team must decide on the type of penetration technique they will use. A *narrow scope* penetration style is when the team concentrates on the main passage without studying the rest of the cave features. This style is chosen when the primary interest of the team is penetration. A *wide scope* technique means that the team proceeds slowly, absorbing all major features of the cave along with possible side tunnels. This method is especially helpful in drawing a map of the cave later. To enhance the accuracy of a preliminary map, compass heading and notes should be taken down on the diver's slate. Use of a line knotted every ten feet will also aid the team in drawing fairly accurate preliminary maps of the system.

Once a dive has begun, the team should remember the limits and purpose of the dive and strictly adhere to them. Divers should not be carried away with the wonder of exploration, which easily occurs if the dive is going well. If the system is a major find, the members of the team should maintain the attitude that they will be able to return and make many more dives at the site.

CONCLUSION

Information gathered about new sites should be shared with other certified cave divers. By opening up communication with other divers, a team will meet new dive buddies who are willing to assist with laying line, surveying, surface support, and negotiations for further access to the property.

Cave diving exploration is a multi-headed task. From researching sites in books, newsletters, and maps, to exploring from jeeps, boats, or airplanes, it is a time-consuming job that does not always pan out. However, the positive results always outweigh the dead ends. The spirit of exploration is strong in cave divers and, happily, many of those who have acted on their desire to explore have met with great success.

Chapter 22

SPECIALTY CAVE DIVING

by Milledge Murphey, Ph.D.

INTRODUCTION

Perhaps the most fascinating aspect of cave diving is the advanced exploration of the phreatic realm. Divers and non-divers alike are fascinated by accounts of world records which result from the application of advanced techniques. Revolutionary equipment and procedures, developed by those courageous few who go where no one has gone before, are not only the cutting edge of cave diving today, but also represent the future of recreational cave diving.

In the 1950's, the Peacock to Pothole sink traverse in North Florida was considered hazardous. Today, certified cave divers traverse this distance as a pleasure trip and most would consider the dive mundane. Thus, it can easily be imagined that future cave divers will routinely accomplish dives that are today considered extreme. Advances in techniques, equipment, and human conditioning will make previously unattempted assaults not only possible but plausible. Perhaps the eight kilometer penetration (from air space) will be accomplished during the life span of many present day cave divers.

As this chapter is being written, many new and exciting developments are taking place as international cave explorers continue to push into virgin passage. Suffice to say, this narrative is an attempt to relate advanced procedures which can reasonably be utilized by appropriately trained cave divers in presently known passages. Furthermore, it is fully recognized that the material included herein is dated as it is being written. The developments in cave diving since the 1950's are comparable to the developments in aviation and space travel during the same time frame. Arising from its beginnings as a potentially hazardous and (in some cases) daredevil activity, cave diving has become a science.

ELEMENTS IN ADVANCED CAVE DIVING

Advanced cave diving consists of many elements; however, there is a core group of factors which most considerations of the subject will include. Among these are diver conditioning and breathing techniques, equipment considerations, exploration, survey and cartography, scientific research activities, and technique-specific elements now being practiced in the sport. This last category includes the basic considerations regarding stage diving, safe use of diver propulsion vehicles (DPV's), and decompression techniques for use in extraordinary or exceptional exposure circumstances.

This chapter cannot cover every issue relevant to advanced cave diving. It is designed to provide information on the most pertinent (at present) areas. The reader is advised to seek training prior to attempting the activities described herein. Certification in cave diving should not mark the end of a diver's training. Specialized courses are available to help divers safely extend their cave diving parameters. These parameters should be extended slowly, with the diver always using reason, prudence, safe practices, and well-maintained and appropriate equipment.

WHY ADVANCED CAVE DIVING?

All cave divers should be aware of advanced cave diving simply because these procedures are presently in use. Advanced cave diving implies a level of participation in the sport beyond the ordinary. Even persons trained as cave divers who try such procedures in order to extend their depth or distance without training are putting themselves and others at risk. Every cave diver has responsibility to the cave diving community not to engage in activities beyond his capabilities. Training does exist to provide safe participation in events that go beyond what is covered in a full cave diving course. Active cave diving instructors are an excellent resource for specialized techniques.

Divers may desire to use such techniques for exploration, scientific study (hydrology, archaeology, geology, biology, cartography, etc.), to set world depth/distance records, photography, recreation, training, or a variety of other equally rational purposes. For any of these reasons, such divers should follow accepted practices used within the cave diving community regarding dives that involve exceptional exposure.[1]

---

[1]This form of cave diving is rapidly evolving; thus, those who choose to participate in it must make every effort to stay abreast of current knowledge. Full membership in both the National Association for Cave Diving (NACD) and the National Speleological Society-Cave Diving Section (NSS-CDS) will provide access to the most comprehensive and current printed material available containing cave diving information. Both of these organizations frequently conduct national and international workshops and seminars in specialty cave diving.

The cave divers who developed these practices certainly deserve recognition. It is impossible to name every individual, although I have previously chronicled many of them in articles for *Underwater Speleology*, the *N.S.S. News*, and *N.A.C.D. News*. I will, however, recognize the stellar and singular contributions of Wes Skiles, from whom much of the information contained herein was derived. Skiles has written and discussed this information and has been gracious in providing it for my use.

LINE USE

Everyone who cave dives is an explorer, as he ventures into areas where few (if any) persons have gone before. Some cave divers push beyond the zones previously visited and they are certainly explorers of the first order. One of the responsibilities which an explorer assumes is installation of a safe, permanent guideline for survey use and for future scientific and recreational purposes. The following is a list of practices currently being used by American cave explorers in regard to line use.

• 200 pound test nylon line, preferably white, woven, and non-floating.

• Knotted at ten foot intervals (an alternative is to knot the line at three meter intervals).

• Use of a large capacity reel and standard measure of 400 feet of line, the basic surveyable distance when laying line in previously unexplored subaquatic cave passages.

• Survey and safety are overriding considerations in initial line placement.

• Careful attention to placement, wraps, tie-offs, avoidanceof line traps, and appropriate marking of exit directions in all line laying activities.

• Extreme care must be exercised in developing additional lines in subaquatic caves; these should only be accomplished by exploration-oriented, advanced cave divers. This also includes off-shoot lines of any kind and installation of circuit lines.

Divers must follow-up survey work through documentation in writing (cartography and narrative) of all information of interest to explorers and other cave divers. This task must not be taken lightly and should be rigorously followed through to conclusion. This includes the unspoken mandate to write for publication all accounts of exploration(s) and the results. Finally, all incidents or accidents should be written and published for the mutual benefit and safety of the cave diving community. If the aforementioned elements are included in the planning schedules of advanced cave divers, a greater number will gain increased enjoyment through the careful execution of yet another safe dive.

STAGE DIVING

All advanced cave divers routinely participate in stage diving. In fact, to be considered an advanced cave diver one must effectively stage dive. It follows that penetration distance is a major factor in whether or not one is an advanced cave diver. There are a few advanced cave diving sites which do not require stage techniques: some which involve great depth and short penetration; some involving long penetration, small passage diameter; and a few shallow water caves. Except for these rare cases, however, extended penetration dives require stage diving.

To ask why persons stage dive is today a mundane question. There are a number of positive and appropriate motives for stage diving.

• A diver has extended the penetration of a system to the maximum limit of double cylinders and now desires to venture further into the system to explore passages not yet visited.

• As an explorer of a virgin system, a diver finds it necessary to have more air for extended exploration.

• A need is felt for additional safety air in a particular system (due to extreme depth, etc.).

• In order to extend previously impossible penetration limits.

Stage Diving Equipment

Commonly, 72 or 80 cubic foot cylinders in single configuration are selected as stage tanks. Either aluminum or steel may be selected although a slightly negative cylinder (when empty) is preferred. The cylinder is typically equipped with two clips (or more) for attachment to the diving harness rings, a nylon webbing carrying strap, and an elastic band (possibly an innertube ring from a tire, nylon shock cord, or surgical tubing).

The exact method(s) used to properly configure a stage bottle vary. This technique should be acquired by obtaining specialized instruction from a cave diving instructor. Although it is a relatively simple matter to attach clips, straps, bungee cord, and a regulator/pressure gauge to the tank, it is of paramount importance that an experienced instructor supervise the actual rigging.

The regulator and pressure gauge selected for use with a stage diving cylinder should have the following characteristics:

• Absolute dependability and current maintenance;

• Good operational performance in conditions of heavy silt;

• Specially designed short high pressure hose for the pressure gauge, in order to keep it from dangling.

Once configured, the cylinder is attached to the diver, usually at chest and waist, by snap rings. Specifics pertaining to the mounting procedure for one or more cylinders may be obtained directly from an instructor. Once attached, the diver should select a conservative air rule strategy; one-third's (or more conservative) due to the added time requirements for handling the additional stage diving equipment.

Safe Stage Diving

In stage diving, the diver starts the dive breathing from the stage cylinder(s). Once one-third of the cylinder contents have been expended, the cylinder is dropped. The dropping procedure is very explicit and must be followed precisely.

1. The diver shifts from the stage cylinder regulator to his primary regulator before detaching the

cylinder from the harness.

2. The stage cylinder being dropped is clipped to the line at a location where the cylinder can be placed (resting on the bottom) without undue silting or stress on the line.

3. The valve on the dropped bottle is closed; however, the regulator is not purged. Air purging while the cylinder is not open is a potential hazard. Furthermore, a purged regulator is not immediately breathable and presents a potential danger in case of emergency. Care must be taken to ensure that the cylinder is placed on a solid bottom, not on soft or silty surfaces. Additionally, the diver may experience a significant buoyancy change as the cylinder is dropped. The diver must be aware that this change will occur and make accommodations for it.

Following a cylinder drop, the dive is resumed, observing all standard safety procedures. Upon return to the previously dropped cylinder, the diver simultaneously unclips and lifts the stage cylinder as the BC is inflated to compensate for added negative buoyancy. (The cylinder should not be positively buoyant when two-third's full). The retrieved cylinder is then reattached to the diving harness with the diver monitoring his buoyancy to minimize silting.

After reattachment of the stage cylinder, the valve is opened and a check for free flow and/or leaks is made. The diver then replaces his primary regulator with the stage cylinder regulator. The diver can eliminate any water that has entered this second stage by exhalation or by light pressure on the purge button. Once the diver is comfortably breathing off the stage cylinder, the primary regulator should be clipped in a protected and secure location — it is never left dangling. The exit is then completed breathing from the stage cylinder.

Stage Diving Emergency Procedures

Emergency procedures remain absolute regardless of diver location within a cave, except in the case of air loss. All possible contingencies must be discussed prior to the dive so that the dive team will know the best action to take in case of emergency. While problems may arise at any time, diver Wes Skiles has grouped the potential occurrence of such incidents by whether the diver has stage cylinders attached to harness or whether the cylinders have been dropped. Obviously, problems which arise after the stage cylinder(s) have been dropped are of major importance, as the diver is deeper into the cave and has more tasks to accomplish in order to successfully exit.

During initial stage dives, one may discover that penetration is actually less than when diving with only large capacity double tanks. This occurs because of the increased task loading involved in stage diving and the additional drag imposed by one or more extra cylinders attached to the diver. As a diver's skill in stage diving increases, penetration will likewise increase.

DIVER PROPULSION VEHICLES (SCOOTERS)

A number of homemade and commercial diver propulsion vehicles (DPV's) have been used in cave diving for years. With the advent of efficient and small commercial DPV's available at low cost, scootering has become common in advanced cave diving. When used correctly, the DPV not only enhances safety but also improves decompression profiles and increases possible penetration limits.

Exertion is also reduced when scootering properly, thus lowering air consumption rates and enhancing all aspects of the cave dive. Another consideration is simply the enjoyment of moving quickly and effortlessly through the transparent waters of subaquatic caves. However, use of DPV's does entail additional special equipment and procedures.

- ***Helmet*** To scooter without a helmet is to court disaster.
- ***Harness*** A harness reduces fatigue in the shoulders, arms, and hands. With this apparatus the scooter is guided by arm action but pulls on the harness without undue fatigue to the diver.
- ***Primary light mounting bracket*** Use of this device enables the diver to mount the light head on the scooter or helmet, thereby freeing the hands for steering.
- ***Tow straps*** Enable a functioning DPV to tow out a disabled DPV and its rider.
- ***Seven (or nine) foot hose*** This is mandatory for use during emergency air sharing circumstances by a diving team riding DPV's.
- ***Additional air*** must be placed at the entrance to the cave system for use during decompression in the event of an incident during the dive requiring the diver to swim out, consequently consuming more air than planned.
- ***Full exposure suit protection*** is mandatory as longer dive times and less exertion, plus more contact with fast moving cold water, are a part of DPV diving. Further, during decompression the diver may become inordinately cold. Thus, hood, gloves, and dry suit with heavy under garment should be utilized.

DPV Safety Recommendations

Divers should follow all the aforementioned equipment requirements when DPV diving. In addition, divers should apply one of the three Flow/Diver/DPV air rules, which are based on the flow characteristics of the dive site.

1. High Out-Flow
    a. Provides best safety profile for dive teams exiting with DPV failure.
    b. Recommended air rule is one-fourth used at the turn. This means that the dive is turned

Figure 22-1 Cave divers scootering in Mexico.

when any diver on the team has reached one-fourth of his initial total air supply.

2. Medium Out-Flow
   a. Less flow to assist during an emergency exit, thus a more conservative air rule is necessary.
   b. Recommended air rule is one-fifth of initial air supply at turn.
3. Low to Zero Out-Flow
   a. Little or no outflow to assist exiting divers in an emergency.
   b. Recommended air rule is one-sixth of initial air supply at turn.

Without question, DPV's can convey divers beyond safe swim out distances. The aforementioned air rules may assist in safe DPV dive planning; however, personal swimming limits must be considered by all divers prior to participating in DPV assisted cave dives, as an emergency swim out is always a potential occurrence.

Not all caves are compatible with DPV's. Among the reasons for rejecting DPV's as the propulsion choice for a cave dive are:

• Cave system too small for appropriate scooter technique to be effective.

• Cave too silty for increased scooter speeds without silt disturbance.

• Cave too deep for depth limits of scooter. No scooter diving should be attempted in subaquatic caves below 130 feet[2].

• Cave features are too fragile to accommodate DPV wake.

• Cave water visibility at or near minimum for DPV use.

When utilizing DPV's in complex, maze-type caves, all continuous line rules must be strictly adhered to. The reason for this inflexible rule is that one may unknowingly motor past line gaps without seeing them. The results of such an error can produce a stressful high speed DPV search for a directional marker in order to locate a cave exit.

DPV riders should observe the continuous line mandate at all times while scootering. Any variation from this practice is questionable, given there are numerous possible silt-out scenarios unrelated to the activities of the cave diving team. For example, rain-

[2]Depth limits for scooters may vary from manufacturer to manufacturer. In addition, several advanced cave divers have successfully modified commercially available scooters for depths up to 360 fsw. Generally, a 130 fsw limit for air is advocated to limit narcotic effects of nitrogen and to minimize D/C exposure. — Ed.

fall can bring zero visibility water into the system during a dive. A large group of open-water divers visiting the entrance area presents this same hazard.

The future application of DPV's in cave diving is bright. They are now, and will continue to be, the major dive penetration extension apparatus in use. Divers without DPV experience should seek specialized training in order to fully enjoy DPV's and employ them safely.

Figure 22-2 Cave diver using side-mount rig.

SIDE MOUNT and ADVANCED CONFIGURATION DIVING

For many years European divers have chosen solo cave diving with their diving cylinders mounted on the side of the waist or under the arms. Diving conditions in Europe were the primary reason these configurations evolved on the continent, and especially in Great Britain.

More recently, American cave divers, having explored most of the presently known, larger-sized subaquatic cave passages located in Florida and adjacent locations, have begun experimenting with alternative cylinder mounting systems. The primary reason for this modification in cylinder configuration (away from the classic backmounted twin 103.5 steel cylinders) is the desire to explore smaller size passages, many of which remain uncharted territory at the time of this writing.

It is pointless to discuss in great detail the equipment used in a specialty that is undergoing rapid change, as inspired cave explorers/inventors search for more effective dive systems. Furthermore, specialized training is required before a diver can safely dive in a system that requires a side mounted or other advanced configuration.

Typically, 71.2 cubic foot or larger capacity steel cylinders are mounted via large diameter stainless steel radiator clamps, bungee cord, automotive innertube bands, and a variety of belt or boat snap clips. The configuration is sometimes stabilized using a hinged backplate/harness mounting. The exact placement of the cylinders is often dictated by the size of the passage to be explored. The present designs utilize free movement of cylinders in order to circumvent especially small passages and to enhance the safe removal and replacement of the cylinders as dictated by restricted diving conditions.

Cylinder valve selection is variable at present, with some divers choosing a single *K* valve in each cylinder and others utilizing a *K* valve in one cylinder and a *Y* valve in the other. Both cylinders require submersible pressure gauges and often the hoses and regulators exceed the number used when diving double backmounted cylinders. This requires extra careful equipment maintenance, as greater potential for equipment failure exists when more equipment is used.

Other alternative configurations are being tested at this time. Among these are smaller cylinders, multiple cylinder DPV sleds, hand-carried cylinders, modern rebreather units which are computerized and offer the potential for extremely long dive times with minimal decompression, and other equipment configurations.

DECOMPRESSION

The topic of decompression, despite the existence of considerable literature and research data, remains mysterious to many cave divers. One reason for this is the high number of advanced cave divers who have suffered decompression sickness while adhering to dive table schedules. Divers should examine the singular nature of advanced cave dives. Often these dives are deep, long, cold, and require high exertion. Methods for avoiding decompression sickness are discussed in the chapter *Alternatives to Stage Decompression*, and it is imperative that advanced cave divers be aware of this information.

Specialty cave diving frequently includes extended stage decompression schedules. For most sport divers, such schedules seem inappropriate and "not worth it." This is fortunate in the sense that it may prevent persons who are not psychologically or physically equipped for cave diving from entering the activity. Cave divers who make advanced dives, however, cite

Figure 22-3 Bill Gaven readying D/C habitat for Sullivan Sink Expedition.

a number of reasons for their willingness to undergo extended decompression schedules.

- Extended bottom times resulting from exploration and survey related cave dives.
- Incidents or near accidents that inadvertently result in extended bottom times.
- Accumulation of excessive inter-tissue nitrogen due to repetitive dive profiles.
- Participation in extremely long or deep cave dives.

Equipment Issues in Extended Decompression Cave Diving

Cave divers are generally aware of the need to maintain equipment in peak working order. In regard to decompression, the most essential item for a cave diver is to practice preventive maintenance on his own body. Although nearly all advanced cave divers recognize the need for and benefits from physical conditioning, too few are willing to pay the price in time and effort which is necessary to acquire optimum fitness. Put simply, a program of cardiovascular enhancing exercise is ***mandatory*** for those who expose their body to the rigors of extended decompression, especially for divers over 40. Divers who are grossly overweight should not engage in decompression diving.

Certain techniques and additional equipment can assist the body in withstanding extended decompression schedules. For example, divers can add time to scheduled stops to provide a greater safety margin. The following is a list of equipment considerations to make decompression diving safer and more comfortable.

- A decompression computer (in addition to watch, depth gauge, and bottom timer).
- An in-water oxygen cylinder for use from the 20 foot stop to the surface.
- A container tied off at the first decompression stop, holding squeeze tubes filled with either diluted fluid replacement drink or diluted fruit juice.
- Neoprene gloves or mittens.
- High sucrose/low fat candy or fruit.
- Submersible exceptional exposure decompression tables.
- Extra slate and pencils.
- An interesting book or other time consuming puzzle or game.
- A drop weight to compensate for added buoyancy from lower tank weight and air placed in drysuit for warmth.
- An accurate stopwatch for use in timing each stop on the schedule.

Procedures for Extended Decompression

In order to successfully engage in extended decompression one must consider several factors. Dives must be well-planned to avoid unnecessary decompression; e.g., one bounce to 200 feet during a dive can radically alter the decompression schedule.

Divers should take the time to prepare the decompression area with all the necessary equipment prior to the dive. It's nice to decompress in comfort as opposed to enduring three hours of decompression with a flooded drysuit and no food, drink, etc. Some dive sites now have underwater "habitats" established to ease the strain of decompression stops.

Aspirin can be taken prior to a long dive.[3] Divers

---

[3]Although some people regard this as controversial, it is not harmful to divers unless they are allergic to aspirin or sensitive to its side-effects. (Aspirin irritates the GI tract of some individuals.) To minimize the side-effects, buffered or enteric-coated aspirin may be used by most sensitive individuals. Aspirin should not be taken by persons with bleeding disorders or other blood abnormalities without a physician's approval, or by those who are allergic to aspirin.

The benefit that is theorized from the prophylactic use of aspirin is related to the formation of clots in the blood vessels. Doppler studies have shown that bottom times close to the USN no-decompression limits, as well as those requiring stage D/C, produce *silent bubbles* in the blood. With silent bubbles, the diver has no signs or symptoms of DCS. This indicates that the bubbles have probably not damaged his tissues.

When bubbles form, the natural tendency of the blood to clot may contribute to the extent of DCS suffered by the diver. In DCS, the bubbles are no longer silent and tissue damage occurs. If inert gas bubbles become lodged in the diver's blood vessels, clots may form at these sites, possibly increasing the amount of tissue damage. While it is not known if this occurs, it is possible. Because aspirin inhibits blood clotting, it is thought that it might be beneficial.

For the desired effects, one 325 mg (5 grain) aspirin tablet each 24 hours is sufficient. Begin taking the aspirin a few hours before your first dive, and continue through your last day of diving. Take it with food to help decrease GI tract irritation. Do not take a larger or more frequent dose. Taking more will not improve the anti-clotting action, but can increase side-effects. In addition, the analgesic and anti-inflammatory properties of aspirin may mask the symptoms of mild DCS, which could result in a delay in instituting appropriate first-aid measures or in seeking definitive medical care. — Ed.

should enter the water well rested and relaxed and then rest after a dive is completed. Relaxation helps prevent the bends. Divers should also try to stay in an uncramped position during decompression. Finally, those who engage in extended decompression should stay warm and well-hydrated before, during, and after a dive.

Stage Decompression Procedures

1. Calculate the decompression schedule prior to reaching the first stop depth.
2. Compare schedule calculations with dive partner and, if a discrepancy exists, decompress on the longer schedule.
3. At each stop, maintain exact depth constantly and relax — avoid exertion during decompression.
4. Use oxygen or nitrox at 20 fsw and 10 fsw stops.
5. Do not abbreviate a decompression schedule. Use of oxygen or nitrox does not enable one to safely modify the selected schedule.
6. Use food and fluids during decompression. Fluids should be taken whether the diver feels thirsty or not.
7. Avoid exertion upon surfacing. Consider the surface another decompression stop — relax for a reasonable period of time prior to the stress of exit. If possible, do not carry heavy gear to the vehicle for several hours, or have a non-diver carry it from the water for you.
8. Do not consume alcoholic beverages before, during or after dives. Similarly, smoking or recreational drug use is prohibited. Continue fluids, rest, and non-fat foods following exit from the water.

Extended decompression should be avoided when possible. When it is necessary, divers should carefully plan and equip themselves for stage decompression and make every reasonable effort to be comfortable throughout the procedure.

CONCLUSION

Specialty cave diving is the most advanced form of compressed air diving currently practiced. Hence, advanced cave diving requires technical skills, equipment, physical conditioning, and mental preparation far beyond the casual or ordinary approach to cave diving. The specialties discussed in this chapter, as well as such techniques as mixed gas diving, are not to be attempted by fledgling cave divers. The prudent cave diver will approach advanced cave diving with caution, seeking training, expert buddies and gradual experience. To get involved in specialty diving, a diver can contact a certified cave diving instructor who is active in the field that holds the diver's interest. Formal training courses in specialty cave diving are now becoming available from a number of active cave diving instructors.

Chapter 23

SUMP DIVING

by Tommy Cook

SUMPS AND SUMP DIVERS

In the United States, exploration of freshwater springs is the predominant cave diving activity. In scattered areas of the United States, as well as in many other regions of the world, exploration of sumps or siphons represents a second major form of cave diving. Sumps are water-filled passageways found within caves that are predominantly air-filled. They may take the form of subterranean lakes or fully flooded chambers. When an air-filled chamber sumps, the water level may reach the ceiling, or an air space of varying height may exist. A caver generally hopes to find more air-filled passage on the far side of the sump and recognizes the sump as an obstacle to exploration. Past the sumped region may lie a whole series of sumps with varying stretches of air-filled cave in between. Or, the sump may be terminal; that is to say, only underwater passage continues on as the cave dips deeper into the underground aquifer.

The nature of the sump will, of course, dictate the mode of passage of cavers. Thus, if possible, a caver may pass slowly through a sump with her head pushed close to the ceiling, breathing in a narrow air space. Attention must be paid to minimizing movements which might create waves, and special consideration should be given to weather conditions, lest cavers be trapped on the far side of a sump by rising flood waters. Twigs, debris, etc. lodged in cracks and crevices of the walls are signs of flooding and give reliable indications of the extent to which a cave passage floods during severe storms or snow melt. Cavers seeking to maximize their safety should cultivate an eye for such detail. Certainly, cavers should always heed weather conditions when traveling through river caves, but extreme caution should be exercised when passage through sumps is anticipated.

If a passageway is completely sumped, but the distance to the next air-chamber is short, a caver may elect to make a breath-hold dive to the far side. Clearly, this may entail considerable risk and requires exercising the utmost caution. A caver contemplating a breath-hold pass through a sump should consider her actions carefully.

If the distance to the next air chamber is too great for a breath-hold dive, or if the sump is terminal in nature, scuba must be utilized to pass through the sump or explore its depth. The perspective of the sump diver, therefore, is to pass through the water obstacle that has blocked the path of exploration. Thus, there is a fundamental difference between spring divers who are essentially scuba diving through water-filled caves for the sheer delight in their exploration, and sump divers, who are essentially cavers utilizing scuba as a tool to further their capabilities of exploration in air-filled caves.

This is not to say that the spring diver is a neophyte in the understanding and appreciation of the process or that the sump diver is a scuba diver of mediocre ability. Quite the contrary, spring divers are making continued contributions to speleology, and sump divers are steadily perfecting equipment and techniques that have application in both spring and open-water forms of diving.

One of the most notable aspects of sumps is that they exist as one component of a larger cave system. Interior cave travel to the sump may require the diver to negotiate a variety of dry cave passage configurations, often for considerable distances, before reaching the sumped area. It is therefore necessary for the diver to have some experience in dry caving techniques. Depending upon the nature of the cave, horizontal, vertical, hauling, or even subterranean mountaineering skills may be required. The diver, as a dry caver, should not depend heavily upon team members to get to the dive site within the cave. Rather, the diver should be self-sufficient and be able to safely travel underground. In general, sump divers are fine dry cavers in their own right. Spring divers, on the other hand, who may have little previous dry caving experience, must be careful when first developing their interest and skill in diving sumps.

In this regard, cavers should recognize the value of cave survey maps in the initial planning stages of a dive. The overall topography of the cave will be detailed in the map, providing team members with an appreciation of the type and magnitude of obstacles between the entrance and the sump. This is important in determining what special skills and equipment may be required, and whether or not the team members have the full complement of requisite skills and equipment for a safe and successful exploration. Maps, therefore, provide initial baseline information upon which a caver might judge whether or not traveling to the sump is within the team's capabilities. It will also provide the diver with some information about the sump itself, since the sumped passage often mirrors the dry passage preceding it. Traveling to the sump should be well within the capabilities of the diver. The diver who struggles through physical and psychological barriers to reach a sump may be in no condition to make a demanding dive.

Sump diving, by its very nature, requires a support

team not needed in spring diving. Thus, planning for a sump dive goes well beyond the actual dive. Although an estimation of obstacles can be gleaned from a survey map, a reconnaissance trip is necessary to get a full picture of the problems that will be encountered. In this way, the best route to the sump and the most efficient method of equipment transport can be determined. The trip can also provide some hard information relative to how many cavers will be needed to assist in hauling dive gear, how long the trip to the sump might take, where the diver may suit up for the dive, and where porters should best travel in order to minimize silting in water flowing into the sump.

Also important is the opportunity given the diver to closely inspect the sump. A common mistake among dry cavers is the assumption that a diver will dive anything with water in it. Only a diver can make the determination that a potential sump dive is worth the enormous expenditure of time and energy. When accomplished early in the planning sages, the reconnaissance trip can save a lot of time and aggravation later. As an example, flooded passageways sometimes exist well above the main passage. Although a sump is formed when a cave passage reaches the level of the local water table, perched water tables may be formed by overflow routes. While they may appear to be quite diveable, they are rarely passable.

An assemblage of cavers must be gathered, and appropriate means of protecting delicate dive gear must be found. They must put particular value on protecting tanks and tank valves from the abuses of transport.

If the sump is within easy reach of the entrance and no serious crawlways or vertical hazards must be negotiated, three cavers are generally sufficient to put one diver in the water. The number of porters required, of course, increases as the complexity of the cave system increases. Experience alone will dictate the number of porters that must be available for the expedition. It is best that the diver does not portage dive gear, as the journey to the sump and the dive itself will probably be demanding enough.

A wealth of information detailing the logistics of equipment transport from the cave entrance to the site of the sump can be found in the *NSS Cave Diving Manual* (1982). Local cavers are generally more than willing to help in the portaging of dive gear. Involving local cavers in a major sump diving expedition provides them with the opportunity to play a role in overcoming an obstacle that has thwarted their explorations. Organizations of dry cavers are liberally spread across the United States. They are usually affiliated with the National Speleological Society and nationwide listings of local chapters (called grottos) can be obtained from this organization.

EQUIPMENT AND TECHNIQUES

For a foray into the depths of a sump, much of the equipment is similar to that used in spring diving. As in all scuba activities, reliability of equipment is the

Figure 23-1 & 23-2 Vertical technique to reach sump.

hallmark of safety. In both sump and spring diving, safety through redundancy is they key-note of security. The sump diver merely needs to tailor the equipment to the characteristics of a particular dive site. Quality of conditions in sumps may differ markedly from those of the typical Florida spring. Some features to be considered include water clarity, water temperature, nature of sediment, current, depth, presence of obstructions, and passage size and configuration. With the possible exception of depth, these conditions, in most instances, are more adverse in sumps, thereby providing an added hindrance to the ease of exploration. Less favorable conditions always necessitate added caution and more meticulous dive planning.

Although exceptions certainly exist, sumped passageways are generally not as spacious and accommodating as the typical Florida spring may be. It is, therefore, much more common to find that sump divers often utilize single rather than double-tank rigs. An added concern, in this context, is the relative difficulty in handling a set of doubles through vast stretches of dry cave passage. Low weight, high capacity composite cylinders have proven useful in Mexican expeditions (Stone, 1982) and may, in the near future, prove to have widespread utility in sump diving. Indeed, they may prove highly serviceable in spring diving as well. Hopefully, continued testing will result in dissemination of more information on the potential of these relatively new cylinders.

Use of the Y-valve (slingshot valve), instead of the standard K-or J-valve, still provides the single-tank diver with the safety of a dual valve facility. This is an important consideration to the sump diver because regulator malfunctions are not uncommon in the often highly silted passageways.

Figure 23-3 Sump divers need dry caving skills and support.

A variety of methods for carrying single tanks have been employed by sump divers. Much of the rationale for individual selection relates directly to the nature of the passageways to be encountered. In very low ceiling tunnels, the diver may find it more practical to wear a side-mounted cylinder. The vertical clearance gained may be critical for the negotiation of very low tunnels. Use of the side-mounted tanks is, perhaps, more common in Europe than in the United States. As pointed out by Werner (1983), equipment configurations that produce a left-right asymmetry in the diver's profile may be of concern with regard to passage through one-way restrictions. This may be of greater concern in the narrow, low visibility conditions often encountered in sumps.

The numerous projections and debris that may be unexpectedly encountered in sumps have warranted mounting of the tank backwards by many sump divers. Thus, the valves point towards the feet rather than towards the head, affording both the valves and the regulator first stages greater protection. Additionally, many divers feel it is easier to reach their valves in case of an air leak when the tank is mounted in this fashion. This type of setup presents some obvious problems in terms of setting up regulator, inflator, and pressure-gauge hoses. With judicious use of appropriate-length hoses and some common sense, however, these difficulties are easily managed.

Figure 23-4 Divers preparing to enter sump.

As with all new diving rigs, it is important that the diver practice extensively in open water with this type of setup before venturing into a sump. Since the valve stems are in a reversed position, a diver not used to the switch may easily get confused with respect to which regulator is mounted to which valve stem and what kind of motion must be used to turn off a particular valve. For the diver who is accustomed to the more conventional positioning of tank valves, this is not an issue to be taken lightly. A regulator malfunction or a blown O-ring in a silty sump is not the time to realize that a previous ability to quickly shut down an improperly functioning system is no longer second nature.

Like the spring diver, the sump diver must provide adequate backup lights. While several lights are certainly important to the safety of the sump diver, they generally need not include the bright primaries which make up the backbone of the spring diver's lighting system. Very often gauges, safety line and perhaps a small segment of the passageway is all the sump diver will see. More often than not (especially on the way out), the passageway itself, befogged in silt, will melt into invisibility. In such circumstances, powerful underwater lights have little practical utility and, due to suspended sediment, may actually create a disturbing backscatter effect, diminishing visibility even further. The many small hand-held lights typically used as backup systems by spring divers are usually all that is necessary for the sump diver. Indeed, in many instances, the security of the warm, yellow glow is really all that the lights can hope to provide.

A very useful light is the helmet-mounted lamp. Many sump divers wear a hard hat over their diving hoods as added protection against unseen obstacles. The helmet-mounted light frees the hands for other tasks and is especially useful for surveying. If the sump is large enough to accommodate more than one diver, a chemical light stick worn by each will facilitate locating a buddy in low visibility tunnels.

The safety line is every bit as important to the sump diver as to the spring diver. In fact, given the generally poor visibility, the safety line probably plays a more prominent role in dive safety in the case of sump diving. Although sumps in more southern climates are warmer, northern sumps are very cold and require full exposure suits (wetsuits or drysuits). The need for gloves or mittens must be taken into consideration when selecting line since the gloves will considerably blunt the sense of touch. Many sump divers use 1/8″ or 1/4″ braided nylon line on fiberglass or metal reels. The 1/4″ line may also be used as a work line to pull along, if it is laid accordingly and adequately secured. Obviously, the thicker the line, the larger the reel required to contain a given amount. Large reels will increase the diver's drag in the water, which may lead to early fatigue. Each diver has to strike a balance, based on her own needs and the anticipated extent of exploration.

Some divers have found it useful to tether themselves to the guideline with nylon webbing and carabiners. A screw threaded into the frame of the carabiner will be a useful directional guide in case of disorientation. Wraps or obstacles can be accommodated by using two carabiners or two slings with separate carabiners. There is a higher probability of entanglement and *line swimming* when tethering oneself to the guideline, which may counter the potential for safety that the measure might offer. In fact, the low visibility of most sumps will, in all likelihood, increase the chances of entanglement of the guideline in logs and other debris that may be present in the system. The sump diver, therefore, should always proceed slowly and cautiously, especially in unfamiliar surroundings.

Swimming techniques employed by sump divers vary with the nature of the sump. In relatively large systems, typical diving techniques as practiced by Florida spring divers are effective. If, however, the passage is restricted and silty, then this style of diving may be abandoned in favor of a sump diving mode of travel which characteristically includes a degree of crawling about on the bottom, often without fins and with an apparent disregard for the extensive silt stirred up. In many systems, diver passage will result in massive silting, regardless of the diver's skill or caution. Use of shorter fins, modified swim techniques and pulling techniques may obviate silting to some degree. Silt technique, however, should not be particularly relied upon when planning or executing a sump dive.

Often, mud will be so thick that a diver will favor threading her way backwards into a tunnel. By this *worming* motion, a diver can increase the ease of retreat should the passage not pan out. Worming is most often done when the passageway is thought to be short, with a high probability of breaking into another air chamber. A small shovel may be useful for scooping through muck in mud-choked tunnels.

In some cases, it is possible to dive a sump without having to first travel through the dry section of the cave. This can be done by diving a resurging or insurging entrance. If the insurging current is particularly strong, use of a static caving rope, harness, and mechanical ascenders may be of value in moving safely through the inrushing waters. Practice can be obtained in swiftly flowing rivers prior to diving the insurging entrance. The inrushing water may carry an assortment of debris with it, and some prudent digging and hauling may be required to gain safe entry. Indeed, in all sections of a sump, the diver must be ever mindful of the great potential for encountering assorted debris, ranging from submerged logs and branches to dead and decomposing farm animals.

SOME AFTERTHOUGHTS

Sump diving is not a primitive form of cave diving. Although at first glance it appears to be less disciplined and refined than spring diving, it should be noted that this is most likely a reflection of the environment itself. A sump places different priorities on divers, forcing them to adapt their approach to the dive accordingly. The technology of sump diving, therefore, differs in many respects from that of spring diving. Thus, a seeming disregard for skills such as a finely developed silt technique, so important to the spring diver, is not a measure of the simplicity of sump diving. Indeed, the markedly adverse conditions found within most sumps may exert a more intense psychological strain on the explorer than the relatively benign and constant conditions found in most springs. This may be considerably accentuated by the environment

[1]That is, the diver should plan for extremely low visibility, regardless of her skill in silt control. — Ed.

of the air-filled cave, should the diver not be a particularly experienced dry caver. Sump diving is a specialized form of cave diving and should be approached with suitable caution. It is especially important for spring divers to recognize that the two environments present somewhat different extremes of hazard to exploration.

Sump diving is generally regarded as being a solo activity. While it is not uncommon to find solo diving practiced by a spring diver, such pursuit stems largely from a personal diving philosophy and it remains a controversial issue within the cave diving community. For the sump diver, however, solo diving is a matter of safety. In the limited confines of most sumps, more than one diver might severely compromise dive safety. Sump divers, therefore, depend largely upon self-reliance in their underwater problem solving. In many cases, however, a backup or safety diver is geared up and ready to enter the water, if needed. If the sump diver has not returned within an allotted time frame, the safety diver will begin a rescue dive. This system is a realistic compromise between absolute solo diving and a buddy team, and has proven effective over the years.

The generally adverse conditions existing within most sumps may be a psychological deterrent to some. Paradoxically, many cave divers who feel at home in submerged passageway are ill-at-ease in a dry cave, where more primal and deep-rooted fears may become manifest. In this same vein, many sump divers are uncomfortable with the greater depths and excessive penetrations that typify Florida spring diving.

These variations in attitude highlight the fact that just as all open-water divers are not well suited for cave diving, all cave divers are not equally at ease in moving freely between sump and spring. The environments are not completely equivalent, and each may evoke a distinctive reaction and tug at a slightly different fear.

It is in the light of these differences that this brief overview of sump diving has been presented. Although the membership of the NACD consists predominantly of Florida based spring divers, many are developing an interest in diving sumps. The NSS-CDS already has a large membership of sump divers, and as the members of these two cave diving organizations and the dry caving community mingle ever more frequently, it is only natural for interest in sump diving to increase steadily. In this regard, cavers are beginning to shed previous chauvinisms that have locked them into the exploration of specialized niches. The spread of involvement in different realms of cave exploration will serve to increase the awareness and appreciation that we all have for the underground environment. Concomitant with an increase in understanding will come an increase in safety and an ever widening array of talents that may be brought to bear on the frontiers of exploration.

REFERENCES

Rigg, R.H. and W.C. Stone (1982) "Logistics." In Exley, Sheck and I.F. Young (eds.) *NSS Cave Diving Manual.* NSS, Jacksonville, Florida.

Stone, B. (1982) "Composite diving gear. A critical appraisal." *Underwater Speleology.* vol. 9 (2):27.

Werner, R. (1983) "Every dangle is a potential tangle and cave destroyer." *Underwater Speleology.* vol. 9 (4):39.

Chapter 24

MIXED GAS DIVING

by Dan Orr

INTRODUCTION

In the early 1950's, divers ventured into the labyrinthine caves of Central Florida and California and called it sport. From these bold beginnings, sprang a version of recreational diving that is generally perceived as being advanced in technique and technology. Their quest to explore further and deeper into the subterranean passageways quickly surpassed the performance limits of the available technology. The ingenious spirit and creative energy of the avid cave diving enthusiast quickly solved most of the problems and reaped innovative benefits for the entire diving community. Cave divers have been responsible for the development of equipment which is considered indispensable in all aspects of contemporary diving: the submersible pressure gauge, the power inflator, and the octopus (long hose version), just to name a few. Alternative technology has always been on the horizon.

New ideas had to be based upon careful consideration and controlled application in order to prevent the process from being an exercise in natural selection. Prior to embracing any new ideas in diving, alternatives must be proven to be improvements over what is currently available. A proposed switch to a gas which is totally foreign to the average diver is bound to produce a certain level of skepticism, anxiety and, understandably, apprehension. Alternatives to air (i.e., a mixed breathing gas) also create a new set of challenges to safety which must be identified and completely understood to be widely accepted by the general diving community. These challenges to safety have even more potentially serious ramifications for the cave diver.

WHY NOT AIR?

Despite the fact that the exact physiological mechanisms of most diving medical problems are poorly or incompletely understood, a relatively substantial body of knowledge exists concerning air as a breathing medium and its general application to most diving situations. Air, however, due to its high fraction of nitrogen produces an intoxicating condition at depth known as nitrogen narcosis. The symptoms include deficits in reasoning, reaction time and dexterity. Nitrogen narcosis is considered the most significant limiting factor for the use of air as a breathing medium for deep excursions (>130 fsw) into underwater caves. Narcosis may effect the diver's behavior to the extent that he is no longer reliable nor effective as a buddy. The condition, known as behavioral toxicity, may be accentuated by a buildup of CO_2 from physical exertion, anxiety, or the influence of residual alcohol or other drugs. The depth (or pressure) at which narcosis symptoms first appear varies widely among individual divers and may vary from day to day or even dive to dive with the same person. The first observable signs and symptoms normally occur at a depth of 100 feet of seawater (fsw). Experimental evidence, however, has shown that certain susceptible individuals exhibit significant neurologic deficits even at depths as comparatively shallow as 60′. These symptoms involve significant decrements in conceptual reasoning, reaction time and dexterity, increasing markedly with depth. The effects are likely to compromise the safety of the cave diver and other members of the dive group.

An equally significant problem with the choice of air as the breathing medium is that the diver's decompression obligation is a function of the nitrogen in the breathing mixture. A nitrogen-oxygen mixture containing a lower fraction of nitrogen than air (e.g., 32% oxygen and 68% nitrogen), may significantly reduce or in some cases eliminate the need for staged decompression stops.

THE NITROX ALTERNATIVE

The common term used for gas mixtures with a greater fraction of oxygen than air is *Nitrox*. This term, however, has also been applied to mixtures with a reduced fraction of oxygen used in deep and/or saturation diving. Nitrox is sometimes confused with nitrous oxide or "laughing gas." Due to its anesthetic properties, nitrous oxide is obviously not compatible with safe open water diving, much less cave diving.[1] In order to avoid confusion, a more descriptive term, *enriched air nitrox* (*EANx*), may also be used. The term SafeAir™ has been recently applied to nitrox. It has, in fact, been stated that nitrox is not a mixed gas at all, but rather simply a safer form of atmospheric air. These statements are very misleading, and actually incorrect. Nitrox is, indeed, a mixed gas requiring a level of preparation and understanding to a degree far beyond that required of air.

The NOAA Diving Program commonly uses a standard mixture of 32% oxygen and 68% nitrogen known

---

[1]In addition, the oxygen in nitrous oxide is not available to the human body for respiration. Thus pure nitrous oxide (N_2O) is an asphyxiant which will suffocate anyone breathing it. When used medically, oxygen is mixed with N_2O so that normal respiration can be maintained. — Ed.

as NOAA Nitrox I (NNI). A second standard mixture, known as NOAA Nitrox II (NNII), has been proposed having 36% oxygen and 64% nitrogen.[2] Depending upon the mixing capabilities of the compressed gas source, any number of conceivable mixtures can be produced to give the desired extended bottom time or reduced decompression obligation. These mixes are commonly known as *optimal mixes.*

The Benefits of Nitrox

Greater *NO-STOP* Bottom Times — In order to take full advantage of nitrox and relate the reduced nitrogen fraction to a set of dive tables, the concept of *equivalent air depth* (EAD) has been developed. The EAD is a calculation method relating the depth of an equivalent air dive that has the same N_2 partial pressure as the dive to be made with the oxygen-enriched breathing mixture. The resultant shallower equivalent depth will, therefore, provide an extended no-decompression (no-stop) limit and, more importantly to avid cave divers, a reduced decompression obligation.

Definitions:

fO_2 = the fraction (%) of oxygen in the breathing mixture

fN_2 = the fraction of nitrogen in the mixture

fsw = feet of sea water

Depth = actual depth of the dive in fsw

The Formula:

$$EAD = \left(\frac{(1-FO_2)\ (Depth + 33fsw)}{0.79}\right) - 33\ fsw$$

Example: compute the equivalent air depth (EAD) for a dive to 100 fsw using NNI

$$EAD = \left(\frac{(1-0.32)\ (100 + 33)}{0.79}\right) - 33$$

$$EAD = \left(\frac{(0.68)\ (133)}{0.79}\right) - 33$$

$$EAD = \left(\frac{(90.44)}{0.79}\right) - 33$$

$$EAD = (114.48) - 33$$

$$EAD = 81.48\ fsw$$

$$EAD = 81.5\ fsw$$

Reduced Decompression Obligation — Contrary to popular myth and perpetuated misconception, every dive carries with it a decompression obligation. The decompression obligation for most dives conducted in open water is fulfilled during the controlled ascent and recommended safety stops. The lower nitrogen fraction of nitrox provides the opportunity to use a calculated shallower EAD depth representing a significant savings in all phases of the decompression obligation. For example: an air dive to 130 fsw for a bottom time of 30 minutes would result in a decompression obligation

USN DIVE TABLE COMPARISON*

Depth (fsw)	USN NDCL (AIR)	USN EAD (NNI)	Equivalent NDCL (NNI)	% Increase in NDCL Bottom Time
50	100	38	200	+100%
60	60	47	100	67%
70	50	56	60	20%
80	40	65	50	25%
90	30	73	40	33%
100	25	82	30	20
110	20	91	25	25%
120	15	99	25	67%
130	10	108	20	100%

*NOTE: It must be remembered that the EAD concept can be applied to any set of tables, but the cave diver must assume any and all inherent risks associated with that particular set of tables.

Table 1 Comparison of no-decompression limits using NNI vs. air.

[2]During the development of NNII, there was discussion of the NNII proportions and other mixtures (37.5% oxygen and 62.5% nitrogen) were considered.

requiring stops at 20 fsw for 3 minutes and 10 fsw for 18 minutes, with a total ascent of 23:10. The same dive using NNI (32% oxygen and 68% nitrogen) at an equivalent air depth of 107 fsw would result in a decompression obligation requiring only a single stop at 10 fsw for 7 minutes, with a total ascent time 8:50! It also appears from the theory and significant operational experience that any decompression obligations are likely to be more reliable and with a slightly lower risk of DCS when using a gas mix with a greater oxygen fraction. During the shallower parts of the dive, nitrogen elimination will increase significantly due to the higher fraction of oxygen in the mix. This is especially important during the ascent, and during any decompression stops, including safety stops. An added benefit from the lower nitrogen fraction comes in the form of reduced minimum surface intervals between dives. This largely depends upon the specific mix used. The calculated shallower equivalent air depth (EAD) would result in shorter required surface intervals.

Less Narcosis/Best Post-Dive Feeling — The choice of standard nitrox mixes (NNI & NNII) would result in a nitrogen reduction of 14% and 21%, respectively. Basically, this means a dive to 130 fsw on NNI would probably result in a level of narcosis similar to a dive to about 110 fsw. All things considered, the difference is probably operationally negligible. During training exercises with nitrox, reports of significant reductions in narcosis are generally attributed to divers being more attentive in anticipation of a difference. This fixation results in a level of concentration effectively neutralizing the deleterious effects of nitrogen narcosis. Similarly, some divers have reported a better "feeling" following the use of nitrox on a dive of the same duration as one made while breathing air. This is most probably due to a reduction in nitrogen load and accompanying reduction in decompression stress.

Use of Nitrox in Multi-Day/Multi-Dive Situations — There is currently some concern about divers doing multiple dives (3 or more) per day over a multi-day period. This would be true for professional divemasters, diving researchers and some hard core recreational enthusiasts. There is some reason, although the exact mechanism is unclear, to believe that extended diving activities and single dives with multiple ascents and descents (so called *Yo-Yo diving*) may predispose the diver to DCS. Using nitrox while following the dive tables for air creates a margin of safety that may do much to reduce the risks and the likelihood that the diver will become symptomatic. Using any nitrox blend in this way, the diver would reap the benefits of both the reduced nitrogen AND the increased oxygen fractions.[3]

Standard Equipment Can Be Used with Slight Modification — The use of nitrox does not require the use of advanced or exotic equipment. With oxygen fractions less than 40%, standard scuba can and is being used. (Higher oxygen fractions could create an explosive combination in the presence of petroleum or other combustible materials.) It is suggested that some scheme be used to identify tanks used for mixed gas. This prevents their use without the proper preparatory steps being taken.[4] A color scheme was developed by NOAA and is recommended for use by the general public.[5]

The bottom line, no pun intended, seems to be that the only significant benefit from the switch to a nitrox blend would be realized during the decompression phase of the dive. The increased oxygen fraction in the nitrox mix would increase nitrogen elimination during decompression. This would be an advantage on deeper, longer dives where 100% oxygen would not be feasible or prudent due to deeper decompression stops.

The Problems or Concerns

As with the uncompromising laws of physics, "every action results in an opposite but equal reaction." In other words, every innovation simply provides you with problem solving from a different point of view. A change in what we breathe, therefore, affects all of our body's reactions.

---

[3]Standard dive computers could also be used this way, since they assume that the diver is breathing compressed air. However, the safety margin will most likely be greater when using tables. — Ed.

[4]For example, before any bottle which contained a higher-than-normal O_2 fraction is used for air, it should be completely emptied. This prevents any leftover mix from unintentionally altering the gas fractions in a standard compressed air fill. — Ed.

[5]The color coding scheme recommended by the Compressed Gas Association is as follows.

Compressed Gas	**Cylinder Color**
Air	Yellow
Carbon dioxide	Gray
Helium	Brown
Nitrogen	Black
Oxygen	Green
Helium/Oxygen	Brown/Green
Oxygen/Nitrogen (other than Air)	Green/Black
Nitrous Oxide	Blue
Cyclopropane	Orange
Carbon dioxide/Oxygen	Gray/Green

Unless you will be dedicating a cylinder to a particular mix, it is probably just as effective to use duct tape and a waterproof marker to label each cylinder (even the ones containing air). In addition, to prevent error, an oxygen analyzer should be used to analyze each cylinder for % oxygen content immediately prior to using. — Ed.

Oxygen Toxicity (Hyperoxia) — Oxygen toxicity occurs when the diver is exposed to elevated partial pressures of oxygen for extended periods of time. The time/dose relationship is significant. Toxicity signs and symptoms occurring at partial pressures greater than one atmosphere differ, significantly, from those resulting from prolonged exposures to lower levels.

Central Nervous System (CNS) Toxicity — CNS Toxicity from exposure to elevated partial pressures of oxygen constitutes one of the most serious threats to the cave diver's safety. The most significant sign, a convulsion similar in appearance to a *grand mal* seizure, may manifest itself without warning. This type of reaction to high partial pressures of oxygen will, obviously, seriously compromise the diver's survivability. The signs and symptoms of CNS toxicity are unlikely to occur with exposures to pO_2's lower than 1.5 ata. Divers are, therefore, advised to choose 1.4 ata as the upper limit for O_2 exposure at depth. Recent developments suggest that pO_2's of 1.5 ata and even 1.6 ata could be safely tolerated at shallower decompression stops (<20 fsw) where little or no movement takes place. This is due to the fact that CO_2 build up from movement underwater lowers the diver's tolerance for hyperbaric oxygen.[6]

Open water divers showing signs and/or symptoms of CNS toxicity can abort the dive and initiate a direct, vertical ascent. As the ascent progresses, the pO_2 decreases and the effects diminish. Cave divers, on the other hand, very rarely have the same luxury. Most cave systems involve long distances of horizontal passageway, and, occasionally, a further descent must be made during exit from the system. Under these circumstances, the probability of a cave diver surviving an oxygen convulsion while in the system is highly unlikely. Divers are advised to **always** choose the most conservative approach where safety is concerned.

Pulmonary Toxicity — The pulmonary effects of oxygen toxicity come from longer exposures to lower partial pressures as compared to the CNS effects discussed previously. These problems are generally not encountered in normal recreational diving. But who ever considered cave diving a normal activity? One of the most recognized signs indicating the degree of pulmonary involvement is a reduction in vital capacity. Vital capacity, the amount of air that can be exhaled following a full breath, is reduced by the irritation of the lining of the lungs as a result of exposures to increased levels of oxygen over a period of hours or days. Other signs or symptoms include substernal burning, coughing, tingling and headache. The diver's susceptibility, as with CNS toxicity, may be significantly increased by increasing levels of CO_2.

For long duration or repeated exposures to elevated partial pressures of oxygen over hours or days, the concept of oxygen tolerance units (OTU) must be considered.[7] All of the information regarding the various forms and manifestations of oxygen toxicity are subject to a wide variety individual and operational variables. Since it is virtually impossible to predict an individual's unique susceptibility with any degree of certainty, the choice of oxygen enriched breathing mixtures must come under careful scrutiny. As stated previously, the safety of the diver is paramount and cannot be compromised regardless of the focus of the diving activity.

Shallower Depth Limits — In order to remain within the safe depth realm where CNS O_2 toxicity would not be a significant factor, depths must be limited to 100 fsw or shallower while using NNI (32% oxygen). With higher oxygen fractions, even more severe depth limitations must be imposed. This is based upon a suggested pO_2 limit of 1.4 ata. These depth restrictions would severely limit the application of nitrox in cave diving.

GAS MIXING

Since the purpose of this chapter is to provide sufficient objective information with which to make an informed decision as to the appropriate gas mixture for diving, the concept of gas mixing will only be addressed in very general terms. Additional training and/or information can be obtained from individuals with exceptional levels of practical experience. Errors in the calculations or in the actual gas mixing can have serious ramifications and ultimately compromise the safety of the cave diver and other members of the team. It is always advisable to secure pre-mixed gas from a reliable source.

Gas Analysis

All gas mixtures (other than those absolutely confirmed to be air) must be analyzed by the cave diver prior to being used. It is suggested that there be redundant analyzers in case a problem is suspected. The most likely problem being a suspected spurious analyzer reading. Since most analyzers have the same frailties and are subjected to the same abuse as other forms of instrumentation, it would be wise to have a backup. They are relatively expensive (in the range of

[6]CO_2 build-up (hypercapnia) also increases as the diver descends deeper in the water column. — Ed.

[7]Pulmonary oxygen toxicity occurs following exposure to pO_2 levels >0.55 ata for periods >24 hours. pO_2's high enough to cause pulmonary oxygen toxicity in less than 24 hours will cause CNS toxicity first. However, the higher the pO_2 and the longer the exposure, the greater the amount of pulmonary toxicity. For an explanation of OTU's, see the glossary. — Ed.

$300 to $1,000). There is a choice of digital or analog. It is more a matter of affordability and durability rather than accuracy. The solid state components of a digital analyzer would probably allow for more unintentional abuse than the analog variety. There is also less likelihood of perceptual error when looking at the digital readout. Analysis requires accurate record keeping. Each cylinder must be identified as to the specific analyzed mix, and that should be entered into the records for use in calculating EAD's. This information should also be added to the diver's emergency assistance plan so that if treatment is necessary, the medical emergency facility can make decisions based upon recent exposures to elevated partial pressures of oxygen.

In mixed gas diving, planning must be much more detailed and comprehensive. Consideration for a variety of previously discussed components must be made: maximum allowable partial pressures, exposure limits, oxygen fractions, EAD's and depth limitations.

Areas to consider in planning a mixed gas dive:

- Justification
- EAD
- Maximum allowable O_2 (should not exceed 1.4 ata except at decompression stops)
- Exposure limit at maximum pO_2
- Fraction of oxygen in mix

CONCLUSION

The intent of this chapter is to provide information and effective working knowledge so that the educated and qualified cave or cavern diver may, as an informed and educated consumer, choose the best gas to breathe.

Nitrox is a mixed gas and as such requires a much greater emphasis upon the concepts of risk management. A mixed gas dive requires comprehensive preparation, complete planning, and precise execution born of an understanding of the advanced concepts of mixed gas theory. The individual diver and surface support person must be satisfied that all areas which may compromise the safety of the diver are identified and neutralized prior to the beginning of any diving activity. The old adage, "when in doubt...stay out" should certainly apply to mixed gas diving. There is little room in the use of any mixed gases for bold divers with cavalier attitudes towards safety. You must choose and use all mixed gases wisely, with a wisdom born of knowledge and practice. After all, you do not want your next dive to be an exercise in natural selection.

Chapter 25

CONSERVATION OF CAVES

by Richard Franz

Figure 25-1 Cave diver in decorated subaquatic cave.

INTRODUCTION

Air tanks, weight belts, snorkels, masks, lights and other paraphernalia litter the shoreline in organized chaos. A man and woman, stripped to their bathing suits, towels, and dripping skins, talk excitedly, between bouts of shivers and chattering teeth. Two other men help each other out of their rubber suits. These divers just completed an early morning cave dive in a North Florida spring.

What is it about flooded caves that compels people to don garb straight out of a Jules Verne novel and dive into unlighted underground tubes and chambers? To place such trust in air carried in cylinders on their backs and swim with other technological marvels that light the way and limit the warmth-leaching cold water's access to the skin? Yet, more and more divers are attracted to this sport each year. Is it love of water, companionship, the physical act itself, or the challenge to go where few others have travelled? Maybe it is all of these.

For some, there is one more reason: a natural curiosity. A curiosity about these unique geological features and how they form. A curiosity about the environments associated with them and the biological entities that have managed, through evolution, to adapt to the rigors of life there. A curiosity about the paleontological and archaeological treasures that accumulate there.

There is still another aspect of which many divers are subtly aware. It is not difficult for a cave diver to picture a narrow path through magnificent oaks and hickories, a carpet of pale pink rain lilies stretching out across the forest floor, the smell of decaying wood, the feeling of space, and finally a woodland pool where turquoise blue water boils from rocky vents, collects for a short time, and then rushes over broken limestone rocks on its way to some distant shore.

My first cave diving experience occurred at the Jugg Spring on the Ichtucknee Springs Run, Columbia County, in northern Florida. On this occasion, my diving partner and I wanted to assess the vertical distribution of the spectacular river crawfish, *Procambarus spiculifer*. As we slipped below the pool surface, we immediately became part of an underwater world of waving tape grass, foul-smelling skunkgrass with its entourage of milling river snails, a bonanza of sunfishes, suckers, a bass, and struggling loggerhead musk turtles. A small flounder-like fish, affectionately known as a hogchoker, broke from its sandy hideout to quickly disappear in a sandy spot several feet away. A Suwannee cooter turtle paddled itself slowly across the surface of the pool until it perceived our presence and made a mad dash into the dense mats of vegetation on the bottom. Our search of the bottom rewarded us with several brown and olive banded river crayfishes with rust-colored abdomens, and menacing claws. We satisfied ourselves that our quarry was common in the spring pool. Eventually, we pushed through the rush of exiting ground water at the spring's main vent and entered the ghostly blue entrance chamber. After a careful search of this huge room, we exchanged the sunlit blue for the fluid blackness of the low winding tunnel ahead of us. Guidelines played out from mechanical reels as we advanced along the constricted path. Our air bubbles accumulated in silvery biscuits as they became entrapped against the pocked cave ceiling. For the moment, I was lost in thought. Minutes before, we were in a world full of color and life, and now there was only an occasional catfish poking its whiskered face from some crevice in the fossiliferous limestone, the stark white sand, and the dark tunnel ahead and behind us. There were no colorful crayfishes to distract us. Now, as we turned around and began our slow ascent toward the surface world again, I reflected on the splendid beauty of this alien place. It held a fascination for me and I knew that I would return again.

Awareness of the need to preserve natural resources has grown in recent years. Few natural environments remain that have not been touched by modern man, while many have been irreparably damaged. By conserving what remains, these resources will be available for not only our enjoyment, but for future generations as well.

Cave resources have not been exempt from the

Figure 25-2 Subaquatic speleothems.

impact of modern humans. Some problems are rooted in industrial sources, while others were caused by careless or unaware divers. It is the duty of every cave diver to ensure that she has a minimal effect on subaquatic caves and the surrounding surface habitat. This effort has become increasingly important as the cave diving community increases in numbers.

Cave divers can usually prevent damage to the system by simply using proper technique and refraining from vandalism. The cave diving community has demonstrated its environmental awareness and sense of responsibility by calling for diving moratoriums in extremely sensitive cave sites. Two such examples are the Room of Tears and The Car Wash cenote in Mexico; which are beautiful dive sites, but cannot be dived without negative effects. Other efforts have a positive effect on the environment, such as building a dive platform to stop erosion.

Inscriptions and other similar defacements are extremely unpleasant to encounter, but usually do not disrupt the functional processes of caves. This is not true for many other human activities, such as mining. This activity can bring about total destruction, or can so totally alter a cave that it loses its natural vitality.

Ground water pollution, particularly from industrial chemicals, radioactive waste, insecticides and herbicides, is a serious hazard facing modern humans, and caves can play a very ominous role in their dispersal. In a recent case in northern Florida, industrial chemicals stored in metal barrels at an old sanitary land fill years before began leaking into the local ground water, spreading through subterranean channels. This caused local residents to abandon wells for miles around, and to have drinking water piped in from uncontaminated areas. This and other such cases are becoming more common, not only in Florida but other places as well. In part, this is due to greater public awareness, particularly since the Love Canal incident.

Pollution and other factors stemming from deleterious land and water use practices can have a serious impact on the cave environment and the cave-adapted organisms that live there. In recent years, cave biologists and other members of the caving community have become very concerned over the environmental degradation occurring at a number of important sites and, as a consequence, are seeking protection for them. The NACD, the National Speleological Society, and other caving organizations have taken active roles in cave conservation. These groups, and individual members, have not only bought sites, but also have encouraged public and private conservation agencies to protect important cave sites. Interest on the part of non-caving organizations to conserve a particular cave usually stems form the need to protect certain cave-adapted species that are threatened with extinction. Many times, these species have been singled out by federal and state agencies for protection. In Florida alone, there are species of cave-adapted animals either listed, or proposed for listing.

Figure 25-3 Soda straws.

Mankind is unique among animals species in that we try to understand the world we live in. This is fortunate, indeed, because we are also its major despoiler. Through the cooperation of many different groups of people with many kinds of talents, we can preserve the viability and beauty of the natural world around us, including caves with their special and delicate ecosystems. Unfortunately, we may be losing untold natural systems and species because of our ignorance or thoughtless actions.

CAVES AS RESOURCES

Caves are unique geological features. They may form in many types of rocks: in limestone, marble, sandstone, lava, and even ice. Many of them are born from destructive weathering and erosional processes such as solutioning, while others result as by-products of mountain building processes. Caves may be water-filled or air-filled. They may be simple structures, or series of inter-connected spaces, chambers, and tunnels; barren, or delicately decorated with amazing crystal speleothems. Like other geological features, they are not static structures, but have beginnings, experience growth and maturity, become senescent, and finally collapse and die. Their lives may extend over millions of years, and as a result they can record important geological, biological, paleontological, and archaeological information. Many caves are presently, or have been in the past, part of local or regional ground water circulation systems. They receive runoff from the surface, and can carry flood waters away. Like surface streams, cave water can carry and deposit sediment along its course, and can support populations of aquatic animals. Dry portions of caves can also become homes for terrestrial species. Over time, these populations may change and become more finely-tuned for the challenges that energy-limited, unlighted cave environments offer.

Caves are part of our heritage. They have played important roles in the history of the human species: first as sources for water, landmarks, meeting places, and shelters; and then later as sources of raw materials for making gunpowder, fertilizer, and even moonshine. Historians tell us that many of our forebears settled along streams issuing from caves and springs, built lives there, died, and were buried nearby. Some of these pioneers constructed dams, weirs, and waterwheels to harness the water power to operate grist and lumber mills. In some cases, these supported concentrations of people, eventually leading to the founding of towns. Some sites were regarded as having special healing effects, became spas, and eventually tourist resorts. Artifacts reflecting these past uses still linger at many of these places, and tell the stories of people. Today, these crumbling edifices are our only link with this earlier tradition. In a few cases, these relics have been preserved, and are presided over by public or private managers.

Today, these same cave sites no longer witness the struggles of labor, but see people relaxing while picnicking, or swimming with the family, or exploring the spring pool or cave with a few comrades. Caves, and the water that emerges from them, are in great demand for recreation. Today, many state and federal agencies are in competition with private corporations for the development of these sites. Properties of this sort exchange hands for large sums of money. In some cases, this development can lead to new prosperity for certain economically-depressed areas.

In recent years, there has been another use found for caves, contributing to our knowledge of ourselves and our surroundings. Scientists are working to unlock the secrets about the nature of caves. Geologists are attempting to discover how caves form and the role they play in the development of karst landscapes. One example of an application of this type of research would be to gain a better understanding of ground water circulation and avert the serious impacts associated with the disposal of liquid and solid sewage and industrial waste in limestone regions.

Fossil specimens from the pleistocene era, or even earlier, are being retrieved from cave sites, and brought to museums to be cleaned and identified. They are

Figure 25-4 Fossilized sea urchins

Figure 25-5A Cave-adapted crayfish.

Figure 25-5B Cave-dwelling fresh water eel.

then accessioned into the collection and stored, so that they can be available for study, or for possible exhibition in the future. Each fossil is one of a kind, a piece of a once living thing, and irreplaceable. Such treasures belong to the world, and not to be shattered by some unthinking person, or collected to sit on someone's bookshelf where no one but the collector and her family or friends will ever see it. They belong in a museum that specializes in preserving important objects for future generations.

Caves are also homes to many unique living animals. These animals exist in a dark environment, devoid of green plants. Since nearly all biotic energy originates from sunlight, via green plants, how do these creatures find the energy to sustain life? Cave biologists are interested in such questions. But before they can even begin to adequately answer this question they first need to discover which animals are in each cave system. Then, they must investigate each species' role in the cave's ecosystem. These activities require the cooperation of many kinds of people. In this light, the entire caving community has contributed significantly to our knowledge of this unique world. Cave explorers possess the skills and desire to penetrate cave systems which many scientists would never see. In many regions, cave divers have been absolutely essential to research about aquatic cave fauna. Specimens

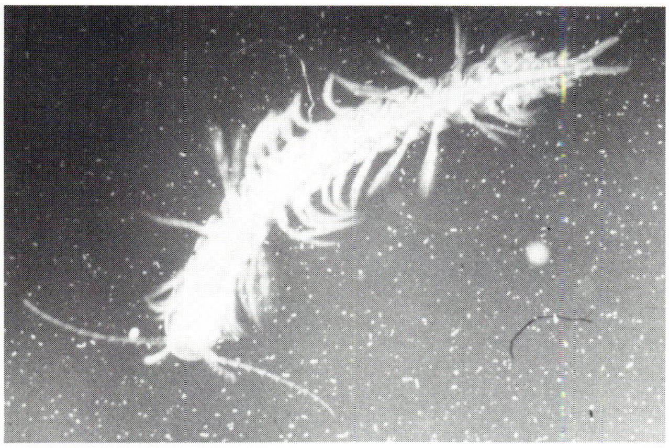

Figure 25-6 Remipede.

obtained by cavers and cave divers are identified by specialists and, like fossils, are placed in the care of museums. Many cave faunas are still poorly known and many undescribed species await discovery.

THE SENSITIVE ENVIRONMENT

For every action, there is a response. By our very presence, we helped to change the Jugg Spring. With increased use, the small winding path that leads through serene forests to the spring pool will, if not protected, become an ugly rutted road. Eventually, the luxuriant vegetation that gracefully leaned out over the glimmering sapphire-colored pool would become marred, cut, trampled, or in some cases completely removed. Trash would begin to accumulate along paths and on the shore, beer cans would get crammed into solution holes in the limestone, and the once special place would become an eyesore.

What of the spring basin itself, or the cave beyond? The greatest changes would occur in the spring pool and near the cave entrance. Damage would lessen with greater penetration into the dark. The greatest number of visitors will remain in the lighted pool. Heavy use in the pool causes a decrease in the amount of rooted aquatic plants, and with this, there will be a concomitant reduction in the number of animals that depend on this vegetation for food or shelter. If use is not limited, there is the possibility that in time the spring could become a sterile bowl, clouding with the slightest disturbance. Changes in the cave itself are much less dramatic, but nevertheless just as serious. It is usually only those divers who continually return to the site over the years that notice. It might be scrape marks on rock surfaces, or a reduction in the amount of silt present on rocks or in crevices away from the current. Or, the giant femur of the extinct mastodon that once was half buried in the sands but now lays shattered in hundreds of pieces. It is ironic that another diver seeing the same cave for the first time would not even be aware of these changes, seeing it with wonder and excitement. The oldtimers, however, only shake their heads and wonder what happened to Eden.

THE FUTURE

Many challenges face cave divers and other cavers in the future. There are four inter-related concerns that must be addressed.

1) **No Trespassing** — We all have been frustrated, and sometimes infuriated, by signs or fences that deny access to caving or diving sites. Unfortunately, posting of land is on the increase and there is little hope that this trend will change.

What has caused this condition, and is there anything that we can do about it? First, it is a sign of the times. Property owners have been "burned" by trespassers: cattle gates left open, stock animals killed, areas trashed, fences torn down, crops destroyed, etc. In some cases, cavers have been responsible for some of these acts. Even one thoughtless act can provoke entire communities to close important caving areas to everyone.

2) **Safety** — People are aware of caving accidents, including drownings. These incidents are considered newsworthy by the press and are widely publicized. Property owners in areas away from the site of the accident are frightened by this reporting. Even though there are thousands of cave divers safely enjoying this sport every day, one accident reported in a newspaper can cause landowners to close their holdings to outsiders, afraid they might be held liable for any accident on their property. Therefore, it is absolutely essential that divers be responsible guests and be safety conscious.

3) **Environmental Protection** — Cavers must become more environmentally aware, taking active roles through local, regional, and national organizations. Cave divers must function as watchdogs, because they are the ones who see changes occurring within these sensitive environments.

Sadly, divers can be responsible for certain kinds of environmental degradation which occur at some sites. Often resulting from ignorance, cavers have entered sites at times when cave species are particularly vulnerable. At other times of the year, there may not be a problem and the site can be entered freely.

In one example, visitors nearly destroyed a large maternity colony of southeastern bats residing in a small cave in Marion County, Florida, at the peak of that year's reproductive effort. As a result, there were hundreds of babies drowned and the females abandoned the site for two years. This cave was also one of only two sites where a species of cave crayfish was known to occur. This animal, dependent on bat guano for food, showed a marked decline in its population as a result of the bat decline.

Most cave divers are responsible people, and are conscientious in protecting caves. Unfortunately, they may be unaware of the consequences of their presence in a susceptible cave. Therefore, an important role of caving organizations is to disseminate information on sensitive subaquatic cave sites. Many divers have taken an active role in reporting such sites. Scientists who are familiar with the peculiarities of particular caves also need to relay their information to caving organizations for dissemination to their members.

Scientists are also finding that some caves and springs are depositories for fossils of creatures that once roamed over the area's landscape. On one occasion, paleontologists from the Florida State Museum excavated the skeleton of a baby mastodon from the sands at the bottom of the Jugg Spring. From this, and other finds, we will eventually be able to construct a picture of what Florida must have been like in the past.

4) **Education** — Divers must educate themselves about safety habits and sound environmental practices. They must also try to pass this knowledge on to new cavers and divers. The non-caving public needs to be provided with information about the role of cave divers in scientific discoveries, which in turn provides a positive reinforcement of the sport of cave diving. Furthermore, many people need to be educated about the professional, responsible attitude of certified cave divers.

Cave divers need to take time to talk with the general public, landowners, and park rangers. Permission should be sought to dive a site and safety regulations obeyed. Simple, informal activities can lead to a positive relationship between site owners and cave divers. A one-day dive site clean-up fosters good will with the landowners and the local community, and demonstrates that certified cave divers are mature individuals who care about the site and are not the ones responsible for any vandalism that has occurred. Positive activities such as this build strong ties which ensure that cave diving will be allowed at that site in the future.

A CONSERVATION MESSAGE

by Danny Brass

The wilderness environment, be it a forest, mountainside, or underwater cave, is a fragile system. Its survival is ever-threatened by the constant expansion of modern civilization. Despite this precarious existence, the preservation of these environments can be ensured if wilderness travelers and a conscientious public are willing to form an alliance for the continued protection of these natural resources.

It is, therefore, important that the wilderness traveler disrupts the environment as little as possible, striving to leave each ecosystem just as it was found. As the remaining patches of wilderness dwindle to mere vestiges, the explorer's impact on the environment increases considerably. This is especially relevant to the cave diving community, where a limited number of cave systems are repeatedly subjected to the stress imposed by diving parties. With successive closure of one dive site after another, the impact on remaining sites increases that much more. Ecological awareness must keep pace if the caves are to survive. The limited distribution of underwater caves, however, also suggests that the effects of diving upon the environment can be both rapidly assessed and continually monitored. This presents an opportunity for conservation not generally available in other wilderness areas.

Like other wilderness travelers, divers generally recognize a moral obligation to help preserve their underwater environment. For the cave diver, this means that the structural integrity of all cave formations must be left intact, trash (such as flashbulbs or nonfunctioning pieces of equipment) must not be abandoned in passageways, and acts of vandalism (defacing limestone walls) must be avoided. If we are to continue our safe exploration of this submerged wilderness and preserve a heritage for future generations of cave divers, ***a commitment to conservation is as important an outlook as is a philosophy of safe cave diving***. The impact of properly trained and equipped cave divers on the cave environment should be minimal. The diver should pass through the system with little or no contact with the ceiling, walls, and floor (where major disturbances to the cave are most likely to ensue). Fortunately, the majority of divers who penetrate deeply into the labyrinthine passageways of underwater caves are highly trained and conscientious individuals.

A meaningful approach to ecology and conservation must focus on the biotic as well as the abiotic components of the environment. Thus, divers should be particularly cognizant of the invertebrate life dwelling within the caves, being careful not to unduly disturb these animals. In fact, with the possible exception of valid, well-planned scientific studies (and then only when carried out under the supervision of a trained biologist with concern for the cave ecology), our interaction with fragile cave life should be solely of a visual nature. In this regard, the cave diver must come to recognize the fact that any diver-induced damage to the cave system (including overturning rocks, silt-outs, damage to formations, gouging handholds in the bottom, pollution, etc.) not only leaves permanent scars on an ancient and unique environment, but may wreak havoc with microhabitats essential for survival of the invertebrate population of the cave. It's a mistake to think that these creatures do not enrich our dives. The diver who has not yet observed them dancing in multitudes in the glow of a cave light, or who has yet to glimpse the circadian nature of their existence, has missed an intriguing dimension that the cave has to offer. That we express concern for these animals is a reflection of our humanity and a demonstration that we can, in fact, successfully exploit an environment and do it no harm.

The cave diving community is fortunate in having limited numbers of individuals who seriously and frequently explore beyond the range of surface light. It stands in marked contrast to the vast numbers of dry cavers, mountaineers, backpackers, and others who explore different portions of the wilderness environment. In the course of their explorations cave divers are continuing to adhere to the time-honored motto of the

Figure A-1

National Speleological Society, a maxim which should serve as an umbrella for explorations in all environments. ***Take nothing but pictures; leave nothing but footprints (bubbles); kill nothing but time***. In this context, disruptive influences upon the environment are kept to a minimum. In the long run, the small number of cave divers, their relative ease of intercommunication and their great capacity for camaraderie stack up favorably on the side of cave ecology.

Figure A-2

Appendix B

SPELEAN CODE OF CONDUCT

by Parker A. Turner

"Heritage is something we borrow from our children."

Every visit to a cave causes damage. Beyond the obvious damage that is visible to the naked eye, there is unseen impact. Even our bubbles can impact the cave and its ecology. It is our responsibility to minimize this impact in every way possible. In some cases the cave may be best served by our not entering it at all.

People and caves are both part of nature's reality and have frequently come in contact with each other throughout history. Civilization, overpopulation, pollution, and technology are parts of Mankind's reality and bring us into conflict with more and more cave ecosystems no matter how remote. Every cave contains precious secrets. Every cave deserves respect. These resources are most valuable in their natural state. They are most beautiful when undisturbed.

THE SPELEAN CODE OF CONDUCT

The speleology diver will always attempt to increase his/her swimming skills so as to cave softly and minimize physical contact with the rock, speleothems, and sediments that make up the cave. We touch the cave only when absolutely necessary. Even weightless divers can damage every inch of the cave, if they are careless. They can also demonstrate their skill by coming and going like ghosts touching nothing.

The scientific value of paleontological remains or early human sites can be destroyed by the haphazard removal of material of artifacts. In many countries it is illegal to remove artifacts or fossils without a permit. **The speleology diver will never remove anything from a cave unless he/she is part of a "permitted" study under the direction of a qualified scientist.**

Cave adapted animals are long-lived and sometimes sparse in population. Some are endangered. Countries may have laws requiring a permit to collect specimens of cave fauna. **The speleology diver will avoid disturbing all animals within the cave to the best of his/her ability, and will never capture specimens unless directed to do so by a qualified scientist as part of a permitted study.**

Caves may contain unusual minerals or deposits. **The speleology diver will always set the example by not removing speleothems or unusual minerals from the cave, unless as part of a legitimate scientific study. He/she will always oppose the sale of speleothems.**

The speleology diver will leave only those things that are absolutely necessary in the cave and will remove litter at every opportunity.

Many cave systems have restricted access. **As speleology divers, respect for landowners, for officials, and for native peoples and their rules or customs must be reflected in *all* our activities.** Caving is a privilege, not a "right."

Underwater caves are unforgiving. **The speleology diver must continually show maturity by a continuous willingness to follow safety rules.** A cavalier or casual attitude invites disaster.

Figure B-1

The speleology diver always maintains his/her physical and mental fitness. Smoking, drug or alcohol abuse, obesity, and poor physical condition are examples of a lack of discipline that is contrary to underwater speleology.

The speleology diver always regularly maintains his/her life support equipment and never begins a dive with equipment problems.

The speleology diver always strives to improve his/her skills, knowledge of diving and knowledge of speleology and related sciences.

The speleology diver strives to maintain an attitude of humility and always speaks publicly of the wonder of caves rather than of his/her own abilities.

The level of Advanced or Specialty Cave Diver[1] brings a burden of service to the community. **Having achieved such a high level of skill, the Advanced or Specialty Cave Diver should assist local officials with cave rescue or recovery as long as his/her own life is not in danger.** The speleology diver accepts no pay other than expenses for this service.

The speleology diver in no way will promote or recruit other individuals to dive in caves (beyond the cavern zone). If approached he/she will direct them to proper training.

The speleology diver will make every attempt to pass on his/her knowledge to novice cavers if requested to do so, whether through formal instruction or through writings in appropriate journals.

---

[1] In the original manuscript, Parker refers to the *CMAS 3 Star SC Class* diver. This is defined as "(a) diver who is competent in the use of the special techniques and equipment required to safely explore beyond zone two and is a living example of the CMAS Spelean Code of Conduct...." Basically, this means the 3 Star SC Class diver is trained in sidemount techniques, stage diving techniques, in diving below 130 fsw, in the use of DPV's, and in the use of O_2 dedicated equipment. There are additional requirements and abilities for the 3 Star SC Class rating. For the purposes of this appendix, I have chosen to replace all references to *CMAS 3 Star SC Class divers* with *Advanced or Specialty Cave Diver.* — Ed.

THE NACD PHILOSOPHY

by Dayton Saltsman

At the beginning of this book, Dale Malloy writes: "(t)he purpose ... is to stimulate consideration of each diver's need to develop a personal philosophy of cave diving. In some chapters ... the author explicitly states certain ideas related to philosophy. In other chapters, the philosophical statements of the author are only implied." It is appropriate for us, then, to consider the NACD's philosophy of cave diving.

The text for this chapter is taken from an NACD pamphlet entitled *Committment to Excellence.* It summarizes the NACD Philosophy clearly and succinctly.[1]

The NACD Philosophy

The goal of the NACD is **NOT** to encourage anyone to dive in the overhead environment. Our responsibility is to aid interested divers in becoming safe divers and to discourage those who may not qualify. Our philosophy of safe cave diving is based upon several basic principles.

• ***Cave Diving is NOT an Extension of Open Water Diving*** Cave diving is caving using scuba gear. No amount of open water training or experience can prepare you for safely diving in submerged caves. Yet it often looks deceptively easy. Many open water divers and instructors who believed that their open water expertise qualified them for cave diving drowned.

• ***A Strong Team Philosophy*** The NACD strongly believes that the team diving system provides the best approach to safe cave diving practices. A strong dive team is one that integrates two or three trained cave divers into an effective unit.

• ***Respect and Appreciate the Cave Diving Environment*** The NACD promotes a basic understanding of the unique cave environment so that it can be fully enjoyed. The geological, hydrological, archeological, biological, ecological, historical, social, economic and aesthetic values that exist to varying degrees at all cave diving sites represent an important aspect of the cave diving experience. To experience fully what cave diving is about, the diver must be aware of them. Conservation is a natural result of this awareness.

• ***Individual Responsibility*** Ultimately, the actions of each person who cave dives, whether trained or not, impact many other people. Respect and appreciation for the environment, and respect and appreciation for others, whether cave divers, open water divers, or non-divers, is an essential element of the NACD's philosophy. By accepting responsibility, each individual views his or her actions in terms of their effects on others and on the environment. This fosters a sense of *community* among cave divers.

Figure C-1 Speleothems

• ***Attention to Detail*** Submerged caves are complex, alien environments for humans where conditions can quickly and unexpectedly deteriorate. Survival is dependent on some unique and sometimes cumbersome equipment, its proper care and use, and on the skill and judgment of each diver. Only by giving adequate attention to all the details of the cave dive can the diver be safe. There is no substitute for thorough training and accumulated experience.

• ***Expect the Unexpected*** Dives should always be preplanned, but remain flexible and alert. Part of the dive plan should be devoted to solving several *"What If?"* scenarios, such as: *What If we get lost? What If we run out of air? What if our lights fail?* This "game" of *What If?* should continue throughout the dive, and in post-dive critiques.

• ***Avoid Stressful Situations*** As stress increases, judgment deteriorates producing mental narrowing. The individual is unaware of the full range of available options. When this process snowballs, panic results. Since there is no cure for panic, prevention is essential. The cave diver should anticipate potentially hazardous conditions, and must develop a safe diving philosophy. This demands the proper application of common sense, good judgment, techniques, skills and experience. Above all else, safe cave diving requires good judgment.

• ***Know Your Capabilities and Limits*** Build experience slowly, and be self-honest. Going beyond your "comfort zone" to impress others or to protect your ego is very unsafe. Don't be too goal-oriented during a dive: know when to call any dive, even if it's before you get in the water!

---

[1]A few years ago when I was President of the NACD, one of the duties the Board of Directors entrusted to me was updating several short NACD flyers. The result was an all-inclusive short pamphlet entitled *Committment to Excellence* with sections covering the information previously found in the older, separate flyers. In writing *Committment to Excellence*, I freely quoted and paraphrased information from the unknown authors of the older publications, adding current information to bring everything up-to-date. The sub-section title "The NACD Philosophy" came from one of the old flyers. The title *Committment to Excellence* refers to the following quote from Vince Lombardi: "The quality of a person's life is in direct proportion to their committment to excellence, regardless of their chosen field of endeavor."

Appendix D

GLOSSARY
by Dayton Saltsman

Abiotic - Not containing any life forms. Sterile, barren.

Accident Analysis - The rules for safe cave diving have been derived from an examination of data from drownings and near-drownings in submerged caves. This process is called *accident analysis*. Traditionally, there have been five key safety rules produced by the process of accident analysis. You will usually see these rules listed in the following way: (1) Be trained. (2) Maintain a continuous guideline back to the surface. (3) Reserve 2/3 of your air to exit. (4) Limit depth to 130 fsw or less. (5) Carry 3 sources of light. These rules address the problems usually affecting open water divers who attempt cave diving without proper training, and newly trained cavern and cave divers. Unfortunately, more and more experienced and trained cave divers are drowning. In order to cover the situations that are involved in the deaths of trained, experienced cave divers, each of the 5 basic rules of accident analysis must be more fully developed, and at least 2 additional rules must be added.

The expanded rules of accident analysis are: (1) Be properly trained and equipped for the type of dive you are planning. (2) Maintain a continuous guideline back to open water. (3) Reserve at least 2/3 of your gas supply to exit the cave. (4) Stay within the depth range of your breathing gas to limit narcosis, hypercapnia, toxicity and DCS exposure to acceptable levels. (5) Carry two or more back-up lights per diver. (6) Dive with a properly trained and equipped diving partner, maintaining dive team continuity throughout the dive. (7) Increase the complexity and competitive task loading of your dives slowly, as your experience increases. As you will notice, the two additional rules are also very applicable to all divers, regardless of their training or experience.

One last word of advice for experienced divers. Whenever diving with team members of varying levels of training, experience or expertise, always "dive down" to the level of the least experienced diver. And if you are the least experienced diver on such a team, insist on staying within your comfort zone.

ACES - An acronym for the four elements involved in developing proficiency in any physical skill: *A*ccuracy, *C*oordination, *E*fficiency and *S*peed. Sometimes called the Four ACES of skill development.

A/D Converter - An analog-to-digital converter, which changes an analog data signal to a digital signal. The signal can then be processed by a microprocessor or other digital device.

Aeration Zone - The subsurface zone that overlies the phreatic or saturation zone. Syn: *vadose zone*.

Aggressive Water - Water having the ability to dissolve rocks. For limestone, this means water that contains dissolved carbon dioxide (forming carbonic acid); or, rarely, other acids.

Air - According to the Compressed Gas Association, dry air is composed of the following gases (in percent by volume): nitrogen 78.084%, oxygen 20.946%, argon 0.934%, carbon dioxide 0.0335%, and rare gases 0.0025% (consisting of neon 0.001818%, helium 0.000524%, krypton 0.000114%, hydrogen 0.00005%, and xenon 0.0000085%). According to the *US Navy Dive Manual*, dry air may also contain trace amounts of radon and carbon monoxide (in amounts less than xenon). Air also contains some percentage of water vapor (which is also a gas). The composition of air can be represented as 78% nitrogen, 21% oxygen, and 1% other. For most practical purposes, including figuring nitrogen exposure during dives, 79% nitrogen and 21% oxygen is used.

Air Management - Refers to the planning and utilization of the breathing gas for any dive. It takes into account the divers' air consumption rates, total air supply, staged air supply, depth, current strength, current direction, configuration of the cave, dive objective, contingency plans, emergency plans, decompression requirements, additional equipment or techniques to be used, and safety margin.

Air Pocket - An enclosed gas-filled space between the water surface and the ceiling of a cave. The term *air pocket* is used, although the gas in the pocket may contain little or no air, and may be toxic or asphyxiating.

Air to Distance Ratio - The distance a diver can swim on a particular amount of breathing gas. Many factors influence this, including the diver's level of health and fitness, the diver's mental state, knowledge of the submerged cave environment, mastery of propulsion techniques, streamlining, properly functioning equipment, currents, and efficiency of effort.

Aisle - Another name for *cave passageway*.

Analog to Digital Converter - A device which changes

an analog data signal to a digital signal, which can then be processed by a microprocessor or other digital device.

Analytical Narrowing - A form of mental narrowing, analytical narrowing refers to the loss of the normal capabilities to analyze or understand. Syn: *cognitive narrowing.* Other forms of mental narrowing include *perceptual narrowing* and *response narrowing.*

Angle of Attack - The angle at which an object is oriented toward a moving fluid. The greater the angle of attack, the greater the force of the fluid on the object. A streamlined diver has a low or small angle of attack relative to the current.

Aquifer - An underground reservoir of water. In Florida, most cave diving is done in passage that has been dissolved out of one of the state's aquifers. Access to the aquifer occurs where the surface of the ground dips below the water table, creating a spring or siphon, or where the formation of a sinkhole has created a "window" into the aquifer.

Archimedes' Principle - This is the physical principle that explains why objects float or sink. It is usually stated: *A body immersed in a fluid is buoyed up by a force equal to the weight of the fluid that it displaces.* The amount of the fluid that is displaced is determined by the volume of the object. For example, a one-cubic-foot object displaces one cubic foot of water. If the object weighs more than a cubic foot of water does, it sinks. If it weighs less than a cubic foot of water, it floats.

ata - The standard acronym for Atmospheres Absolute. *Ata* is a measure of the total pressure in units of 14.7 psi (1 atmosphere = 14.7 psi).

Attitude - The position of an object's longitudinal axis in relation to some reference point. In this book, it usually refers to the position of a diver relative to the direction line in cave passageway, or relative to the direction of current flow.

Back Mount BC - A buoyancy compensator that attaches to the diver's tanks or tank harness and lies entirely on the diver's back. Syn: *wings.* This is the most popular type of BC among cave divers using back-mounted double cylinders.

Backup Light - A dive light that is carried for use in case of failure of the diver's primary light. Syn: *secondary light.* Backup lights are usually smaller and less powerful than primary lights, and are typically powered by disposable (non-rechargeable) batteries.

Backup Reel - A guidereel that is carried for use in unanticipated situations. It is usually smaller than the primary reel and typically holds much less line. Syn: *safety reel.* Some cave divers use 'backup reel' as a general term referring to all small reels (*jump reels, gap reels, and safety reels*).

Balcony - A projection above the floor of a cave that can support one or more persons.

Bare Karst - Karst terrain in which much of the limestone bedrock is exposed on the surface. Syn: *naked karst.*

Battery Pack - The power supply for primary lights consists of a battery assembly which is known as a *battery pack* or *power pack.* It is usually so large that it cannot be efficiently carried in the same case as the light head. The separate case which houses the primary light's power supply is also called a *battery pack, light pack, power pack,* or, more correctly, a *battery case.*

BC - An acronym for Buoyancy Compensator.

BCD - An acronym for Buoyancy Compensation Device, or Buoyancy Control Device.

Bed - A layer or stratum of sedimentary rock.

Bedding Plane - A plane or boundary-layer that separates two different rock beds.

Bedding Plane Cave - Cave passage formed along a bedding plane. This is often the result of different susceptibility to erosion between the two layers.

Bedrock - The consolidated rock which underlies the unconsolidated loose material, or *soil,* on the earth's surface.

Behavioral Toxicity - This term refers to the effects of narcosis on a diver's behavior to the extent that she is no longer a reliable, effective diver or buddy. The narcotic effect of the inert gas may be potentiated by hypercarbia, anxiety, or the influence of drugs.

Belly Bag - A type of buoyancy compensator which is worn over the front of the lower abdomen, usually in conjunction with a horse collar BC. It's purpose is to correct the slightly head-up attitude produced by the horse collar. It also functions as a backup BC. The use of belly bags has decreased as the use of back mount BC's has increased.

Belly Rub - A place where the ceiling of the cave passage is close to the floor, forcing the cave diver into contact with the bottom without being forced significantly deeper in the water column. Where the diver is briefly forced deeper in the water column, whether close to the bottom or not, is usually called a *duck under.*

Benjamin Manifold - A dual valve manifold for double cylinders. This name is due to Dr. George Benjamin, who built the first one. Syn: *ideal manifold, dual valve manifold.*

Biotic - Related to or containing living things.

Blue Hole - In the Bahamas and most of the Caribbean, it refers to a drowned solution sinkhole. Typically, these are submarine.

Boil - The point at which water emerging from a boiling spring reaches the surface.

Boiling Spring - A turbulent spring where the force of the emerging water pushes it above the surface. If there is a headpool or other surface water, the area of "raised" water is called a *boil* or, when it exhibits a smooth appearance, a *slick* .

Bottom Time - Ordinarily, the time during a scuba dive from the beginning of descent from the surface to the beginning of direct ascent back to the surface. This time indicates the diver's exposure to increased pN_2 (or pHe_2 when breathing trimix or heliox), which determines the diver's status for decompression and for repetitive diving. Since decompression tables are built on the assumption that ascent to the surface will be uninterrupted except for recommended D/C stops, calculating bottom time in the ordinary way would be potentially harmful to cave divers whose ascent must follow the contour of the cave. Most cave divers calculate bottom time as the time from the beginning of descent from the surface to arrival at the deepest decompression stop.

Boulder - Any particle greater than 256.0 mm in size.

Bounce Dive - A dive which involves rapid descent to depth, followed by a short time at depth, then a return to the surface. It is also sometimes used to refer to a part of a dive following the same pattern. For example, if your dive puts you near the ceiling at a depth of 90 fsw, with the floor below at 160 fsw, a rapid trip to briefly scout the 160 fsw area could be called a *bounce.*

Branch - A secondary passage, side tunnel, or fork.

Breakdown - Rock on the floor of a cave which has broken off the ceiling or walls after the cave passageway was formed.

Bridge - In a cave, a remaining rock span across a passage. Syn: *natural bridge.*

Bubble Check - Because a diver cannot check her own back-mounted equipment for small leaks, the divers perform this *bubble check* for each other prior to entering the overhead environment.

Bump-and-Go System - A system of communication for low visibility diving also known as the *touch-and-go* method. Under this system, all dive team members maintain contact with the guideline but not with each other. Each diver swims an arbitrary distance, then stops to wait for the next team member to catch up. When the trailing diver bumps into the lead diver, the latter proceeds again.

Buoyancy Compensator - Syn: *buoyancy compensation device.* This piece of diving equipment allows the diver to adjust for changes in her buoyancy as she moves up and down in the water column, or as she breathes gas from her scuba. Some types of BC's are also designed to function as surface floatation devices. Also see *Back Mount BC, Belly Bag, Horse Collar BC,* and *Jacket BC.*

Carbonic Acid - The acid formed by dissolving carbon dioxide (CO_2) in water or other liquid. It is important to cave divers for at least two reasons. First, water that precipitates out of the atmosphere absorbs CO_2 from the atmosphere. This makes rain water slightly acidic, and assists in dissolving limestone to form the characteristic features of karst terrain, including caves. Second, the scuba diver's body produces CO_2 as a by-product of cellular respiration. At the surface, the body's normal homeostatic mechanisms keep the amount of CO_2 within tolerable limits. For example, as the individual exercises, metabolic activity increases, producing increased CO_2. In response, her breathing rate increases, both to supply additional oxygen for cellular respiration and to eliminate the increasing levels of CO_2 she is experiencing. In fact, the primary stimulus for increasing her respiratory rate is the increasing amount of CO_2 in the blood. Both the addition of the scuba regulator for delivering air to the diver, and the effects of the increasing depths on the diver alter her body's ability to respire efficiently. These changes in the diver's respiration can decrease her ability to blow off the CO_2, which therefore increases in the diver's blood, lowering the pH of the blood and making it more acidotic. The condition of excess CO_2 in the body is termed ***hypercapnia*** or ***hypercarbia***. The normal pH of the blood is in the 7.35 - 7.45 range. If the diver's blood pH goes below 7.35, the ability of the red cells in the blood to efficiently transport oxygen to other cells and remove CO_2 from them is further impaired. The diver who wishes to go deep copes with these problems in several ways. First, the diver uses a high-performance, efficient and reliable regulator. Such a regulator has a low exhalation effort as well as a low inhalation effort and a low cracking pressure. Second, the diver limits exertion during the dive. This is done by swimming efficiently at a moderate pace, by streamlining her equipment and her body, and by avoiding fighting the current as much as possible. Third, for very deep dives, the diver uses a breathing gas containing helium, which greatly reduces the flow resistance of the gas compared to air, thereby increasing the efficiency of external respiration through the regulator and respiratory passages.

CAS - Critical Air Supply. This is the minimum amount of air needed by the dive team to safely exit the cave in case one diver experiences sudden catastrophic loss of the remainder of her air. The ***minimum*** CAS for a two-person dive team in a cave system with negligible flow is 2/3 of the air the dive team started with. This assumes that stage decompression is not required (or that additional D/C bottles have been placed and are secure) and that the dive team can anticipate no delay or hindrance to their exit due to dealing with the sudden unexpected loss of one diver's air supply, loss of visibility, disorientation, or restrictions.

Cave - A subsurface room or series of rooms and passages large enough to be entered by humans.

Cave Formation - A mineral deposit formed after the cave was formed. Syn: *speleothem.*

Cave Group - Several caves or cave systems that are not interconnected, but otherwise share some common geographical or geological feature.

Cave Series - A geographically-related cave group of similar morphology.

Cave System - The often complex network of tunnels, passageway, water flow and openings that connect to make up a cave. Sometimes caves which were originally thought to be separate are later shown to be parts of the same cave system.

Cave Void - The space within rock which creates the cave.

Cavern - See *cavern zone*, below.

Cavern Zone - Normally, a cavern is considered to be a large cave. *Cavern* is also sometimes used synonymously with *cave*. However, within the scuba diving community, *cavern* or *cavern zone* has come to refer to an area of a submerged cave that is illuminated by sunlight and offers ready access to open water or to the surface. It is an area of the cave which can be dived safely using standard open water scuba equipment with very little modification, provided that the diver has appropriate training and skills.

Caving Rope - A type of rock climbing rope designed especially for caving. Since air-filled caves often contain mud or flowing water, caving rope is most often of waterproof construction. Like most mountaineering rope, caving rope is typically kernmantle construction synthetic fiber, usually nylon.

Cenote - A term used for a steep-walled sinkhole that extends below the water table, usually formed by the collapse of a cave ceiling. It is applied only to such features in the Yucatan peninsula of Mexico.

Center of Buoyancy - Buoyancy is a force which acts on immersed objects. Although this force acts on the entire submerged portion of the object, it produces the same effect as if it were acting on one point within the object. The point where the buoyant force may be considered to be acting is the center of buoyancy.

Center of Gravity - Gravity is a force which acts on all objects. Although gravity acts on the entire object, it produces the same effect as if it were acting on one point within the object. The point where gravity may be considered to be acting is the center of gravity.

Central Nervous System - The brain and spinal cord.

Chamber - A room in a cave. *Chamber* is sometimes used to indicate a larger-than-usual room.

Chasm - A deep, somewhat narrow void in the earth, such as a canyon or gorge.

Chimney - A moderately small, usually tubular vertical shaft in the roof of a cave.

Circadian - Having a periodicity with cycles of roughly one day in length. Daily rhythms.

Clay - Any particle less than 1/256th mm in size.

Clips - Short for *line clips.* Most divers use modified outrigger clips as line clips. Line clips or line arrows are used to mark direction at any places where two or more lines intersect. Since placement of jump reels always creates a *T* or *Y* intersection, line clips (or arrows) are needed when making jumps.

Clock Time - The time shown on a clock. In diving, what is of greatest interest is the elapsed time. When dive watches are used, the elapsed time must be calculated from the clock time that is read off the watch.

CNS - The standard acronym for *Central Nervous System.* The CNS consists of the brain and spinal cord.

Cobble - Any particle between 64.0 mm and 256.0 mm in size.

Cognitive Narrowing - A form of mental narrowing, cognitive narrowing refers to a reduced capacity to comprehend or understand. Syn: *analytical narrowing.* Other forms of mental narrowing include *perceptual narrowing* and *response narrowing.*

Column - A vertically connected stalactite and stalagmite.

Compensator Jacket - A type of buoyancy compensator that can be put on in the same way as you would put on a jacket. The diver places each of her arms through arm holes, and secures the jacket BC with waist and chest straps to make it snug. Some types use a crotch strap. Most jacket BC's contain an integral backpack of some type for mounting scuba cylinders. Some have adjustable straps in the front parts of the arm holes. These are usually called *ADV-style BC's* after the first popular model that incorporated this feature.

Compensator Vest - A type of buoyancy compensator which is worn on the chest. The diver dons this type of BC by placing her head through an opening and securing the device with straps. One strap encircles the chest, while another runs between the legs to keep the BC from riding up. Syn: *front-mount BC, horse collar BC.*

Competitive Task Loading - Adding more tasks, or increasing the complexity of existing tasks that an individual must complete is *task loading.* When the tasks must be performed simultaneously, this is competitive task loading. (Because the tasks "compete" with each other for the diver's attention.) Cave diving often involves competitive task loading.

Conduit - A subsurface passage completely filled with flowing water. Such a passage is a conduit for water movement. Most of the diveable passage in submerged caves is conduit.

Contingency Plan - The part of the dive plan that deals with possible happenings. Some cave divers use the term to include both emergent and non-emergent events. Others use *contingency plan* only to refer to more or less routine events, preferring the term *emergency plan* for the emergent events. Examples of non-emergent events that one may want to formulate a contingency plan for include: exploration of a side tunnel, permanent line maintenance, adjusting new gear, etc.

Coral Caves - Coral caves are found in tropical marine environments. Corals are eroded by chemical, biological, and mechanical means to create cave passages. Mechanical erosion by wave and current action is the dominant method of creating coral caves.

Critical Air Supply - This is the minimum amount of air needed by the dive team to safely exit the cave in case one diver experiences sudden catastrophic loss of the remainder of her air. The ***minimum*** CAS for a two-person dive team in a cave system with negligible flow is 2/3 of the air the dive team started with. This assumes that stage decompression is not required (or that additional D/C bottles have been placed and are secure) and that the dive team can anticipate no delay or hindrance to their exit due to dealing with the sudden unexpected loss of one diver's air supply, loss of visibility, disorientation, or restrictions. It is abbreviated *CAS.*

Current Marking - Syn: *scallops.* These are shallow, asymmetrical hollows carved in limestone walls by turbulent water flow. The "scoops" are steeper on the upstream side.

D/C - An acronym for decompression. (It is abbreviated *D/C* instead of *DC* because *DC* is both an acronym for *dive computer,* and the standard medical abbreviation for *discontinue.*)

D/C Line - A rope or similar device placed to assist divers with maintaining appropriate depth at required decompression stops.

Danglies - The equipment that divers attach to themselves should be as streamlined as possible. This not only improves air-to-distance ratios, it also helps to prevent entanglement. Those items which are poorly streamlined or that hang off the diver are called danglies. Danglies are synergistic, rapidly interacting to form a critical mass. When a critical mass of danglies is achieved, the diver becomes a *cave diving junk pile.*

DC - An acronym for Dive Computer.

DCS - An acronym for decompression sickness.

Decompression Weight(s) - Weights not carried throughout the dive, but stowed with other D/C equipment for use at stage D/C stops. D/C weights compensate for the increasing buoyancy of emptying gas bottles at the end of a dive. They also permit the diver to over-inflate her dry suit, increasing warmth during D/C. Sometimes called *drop weights,* although drop weights may also be weights used to assist the slightly positive diver in descending at the start of the dive.

Decorations - Speleothems formed from different minerals than the cave walls and passages. (In solution caves, cave rock is predominantly calcium carbonate.)

Direction Line - The bearing of the path a diver is making through the water at any given time.

Display - The part of a dive computer which presents the diver's decompression status and other information.

Doline - A common geological term for *sink* or *sinkhole.*

Dolphin Kick - The dolphin kick is the kick used by swimmers doing the butterfly stroke. It is a method of kicking in which both legs perform exactly the same motion simultaneously. (For comparison, in the frog kick each leg performs a mirror image of the other leg; in the flutter kick each leg performs the same motion alternately; and in the scissors kick, each leg performs a similar but different motion.) This kick originates in the lower abdomen and hips, and requires good abdominal muscle tone. The pelvis is thrust downward, "whipping" the thighs downward with the knees slightly bent. In a smooth and continuous manner, the thigh muscles are used to "whip" the legs down. This is followed in a continuous motion with the knees extending and following through to the feet with the toes pointed away from the direction line. These actions result in the extension of the legs downward. From this position, the extended legs are kicked back up to the starting position using the muscles of the back and legs. This is one complete kick cycle. It is rather like doing a flutter kick with both legs simultaneously. When several kicks are performed, the swimmer's lower body movements have an undulating appearance. When using fins, the dolphin kick is most effective with a smaller range of motion. This kick is both very powerful and very tiring, but for short distances it can produce great speed. A regular fin dolphin kick is very difficult wearing full cave diving gear, and is probably a realistic kick only for cave divers with competitive swimming experience. Even then, the diver builds an oxygen debt very quickly. In cave diving, a modified version of the fin dolphin kick is used to minimize fin wash and maintain better control over body movements. The dolphin kick is appropriate only in fairly large tunnel, or in tunnel without loose sediments.

Dorff Markers - Triangular pieces of duct tape about 2 to 3 inches across the base, wrapped around permanent line for use as direction markers. The name comes from a shortening of the last name of their inventor, Lewis Holtzendorff. Holtzendorff later changed his last name.

Double 100's - A double tank configuration using any of several different gas cylinders of approximately 100 cubic foot capacity.

Double 104's - A double tank configuration using steel 104's. These were the first large-capacity gas cylinders readily available to cave divers. They are steel 3AA cylinders with a working capacity of 103.5 cubic feet when filled to a 10% overfill at 2640 psig. Pressed Steel Corp. manufactured them to the specifications of Sherwood Scuba, who distributed and sold them. These bottles, and any made to the same specifications by other manufacturers, are known both as *steel 104's* and *steel 100's*.

Drag - The resistance of a fluid to the movement of an object through it that occurs where inadequate streamlining disrupts laminar flow, creating turbulence. The turbulence interferes directly with the object's progress, and this is *drag*. We are especially interested in how it applies to the movement of a diver through water. Altogether, there are three components of resistance to motion through a fluid: drag, frontal area and skin friction.

Drag Force - A measurement of the amount of drag on diver.

Drop Weight(s) - Weights whose purpose is to assist the slightly positive diver in descending at the start of the dive. Since drop weights can also be used as D/C weights, the terms are essentially interchangeable. It is unclear whether the term *drop weights* is derived from their use to assist the diver in dropping down from the surface, or because the weights themselves are dropped shortly after starting the dive. Drop weights usually consist of the appropriate amount of lead weights on a short length of belt webbing, with some sort of spring-loaded clip or carabiner attached to facilitate fastening and unfastening the weights to the diver.

Dual Valve Manifold - A cylinder valve assembly which yokes two cylinders together through a common connection. The basic advantage of the dual valve manifold is that it permits the use of two independent regulators, each of which can access the total air supply independently. This allows either regulator to be shut down in the event of malfunction without restricting the supply of breathing gas available through the other regulator. Syn: *ideal manifold, Benjamin Manifold.*

Duck-Under - A place where the ceiling of the cave passage dips down for a short distance, briefly forcing the cave diver deeper in the water column, and perhaps close to the floor. When the diver is forced into contact with the bottom without being forced deeper in the water column, it is usually called a *belly rub.*

DVM - An acronym for Dual Valve Manifold.

Dynamic - Moving, energetic. The opposite of static.

EAD - An acronym for Equivalent Air Depth.

Elapsed Time - The length of time passed between any two (or more) reference points. It is distinguished from *clock time.* For example, a dive might begin at 9:05am and end at 11:34am, clock time. The elapsed time for this dive would be 2:29.

Emergence - The point where an underground river comes to the surface. Syn: *resurgence, rise.*

EANx - An acronym for Enriched Air Nitrox.

Enriched Air Nitrox - Nitrox which is made by "spiking" compressed air with oxygen. Nitrox made by blending oxygen and nitrogen will contain nothing else in the mix. Enriched Air Nitrox will contain the trace gases normally found in air, and in the same relative amounts, but in reduced concentration. (The added O_2 will dilute the trace gases just as it dilutes the nitrogen.)

Equipment Matching - Part of the normal safety check made prior to entering the water. Each member of the dive team compares (or matches) each item of her gear to the corresponding item of the other team members. When diving with a new partner, or with a familiar partner who has new gear, equipment matching should include hands-on practice by all team members not familiar with the operation of any particular item. When gear matching has been completed, each team member should know the location and operation of every other team member's primary light, backup lights, primary reel, safety reel, jump reels, BC autoinflator, BC deflator, BC quick-dump valve, dive computer, dive tables, etc. She should also know the hose configurations on the regulators, the appearance of line clips or arrows, whether the partner breathes the long hose or stores it, etc. It may seem like a tedious thing to get out your line markers for "show and tell," but it is necessary to avoid confusion should you encounter another dive team's markers (especially critical during a low visibility exit).

Equivalent Air Depth - A procedure used to determine nitrogen exposure and decompression obligation when breathing nitrox. It is based on equating the pN_2 of the particular mix and depth of the nitrox dive to the depth at which a diver breathing air would experience the same nitrogen exposure. This then enables the nitrox diver to calculate decompression obligation, repetitive dive groups, etc. from any standard air D/C tables.

Flutter Kick - It is a method of kicking in which both legs perform exactly the same motion alternately. (For comparison, in the frog kick each leg performs a mirror image of the other leg; in the dolphin kick each leg performs the same motion simultaneously; and in the scissors kick, each leg performs a similar but different motion.) This kick originates in the hips. The thigh is thrust downward, with the knee slightly bent. In a smooth and continuous manner, the thigh muscles are used to "whip" the leg down. This is followed in a continuous motion with the knee extending and following through to the foot. These actions result in the extension of the leg with the toes pointed opposite the direction line. From this position, the extended leg is kicked back up to the starting position using the muscles of the lower back and legs. This is one complete kick cycle. The legs are moved alternately, with one kicking downward while the other is kicking upward. When done without fins, the flutter kick contributes only a small amount to forward propulsion. For a skilled swimmer, the flutter kick serves mainly to balance and stabilize the body during the swimming stroke. When done with fins, however, the flutter kick can be very powerful. The depth range and frequency of kick cycles are both modified to take advantage of the power of the fins. The standard *fin flutter kick* must be modified by cave divers to minimize fin wash and avoid stirring up loose sediments. In very large tunnel where the diver can be well away from the silt, or in tunnel with high flow and no silt, the open-water fin flutter kick may be used.

fN_2 - An abbreviation for fraction of nitrogen in a gas mixture. For air, the $fN_2 = 0.79$

fO_2 - An abbreviation for fraction of oxygen in a gas mixture. For air, the $fO_2 = 0.21$

Force Couple - Two forces acting along parallel lines but in opposite directions in such a way that a twisting effect is created. For example, the cave diver's body is subjected to a force couple due to the downward force of her weight and the upward force of her buoyancy.

Formation - The basic unit of classification for naturally occurring rock, a *formation* is a distinct, mappable body of rock with similar properties.

Free End - When working with rope or line, the end of the line which is unencumbered and available for use is called the *free end.* Syn: *running end.*

Frog Kick - This is a method of kicking in which each leg performs a mirror image of the other leg. (For comparison, in the flutter kick both legs perform exactly the same motion alternately; in the dolphin kick each leg performs the same motion simultaneously; and in the scissors kick, each leg performs a similar but different motion.) The original frog kick is performed by turning the knees slightly outward and flexing them, which draws the feet up in line with the hips. During this, the feet are kept fairly close together with the soles facing each other. The legs are then extended to the sides and pressed backward and together. This completes a kick cycle. Because of the great negative action of drawing the thighs up and outward in this manner, the modern frog kick is a streamlined version of the original, and is called the *whip kick* rather than the frog kick. Due to the greatly increased power provided by fins, divers can make good progress using the original frog kick. However, the diver who has good flexibility, strength and coordination in her hips and legs can use the whip kick adapted for use with fins. This kick originates in the hips. The diver drops her knees while drawing her feet up towards her hips until her ankles are just about in the same vertical plane as her knees. Her fins should be in the same horizontal plane as her hips or tank. From this position, the diver slides the fin blades apart by separating her legs while keeping her knees close together. (The fin blades are kept flat in the water, and the knees are kept inside the diver's shoulder width.) If the diver has good mobility in the hip, knee and ankle joints, the fins can be separated a bit further by rotating the feet and ankles outward. Once the fins reach maximum separation, the diver turns the fin blades toward the perpendicular (about 60° - 75° is all that is possible) and pushes them backward against the water in a smooth, continuous motion. If the diver keeps the bottom surfaces of the fins pushing backwards as far as possible, the legs will naturally return to the starting position. This is one complete kick cycle. For divers who are uncomfortable doing the whip kick, the frog kick can be done most efficiently by de-emphasizing drawing the legs up (as this motion tends to slow forward progress), and emphasizing the propulsive phase. The frog kick and the whip kick are both powerful and efficient kicks which can be used as the diver's primary method of swimming.

Front Mount BC - A type of buoyancy compensator which is worn on the chest. The diver dons this type of BC by placing her head through an opening and securing the device with straps. One strap encircles the chest, while another runs between the legs to keep the BC from riding up. Syn: *horse collar BC.*

Frontal Area - In fluid dynamics, the total surface area which an object presents "against" the fluid. If you are looking at the object from the direction of motion of the fluid, the total surface area which you see is the frontal area. The greater the frontal area of an object (such as a cave diver with her equipment), the greater the resistance to movement through the fluid. Swimming in a streamlined position minimizes frontal area, thus reducing resistance to motion through the water. Altogether, there are three components of resistance to motion through a fluid: frontal area, drag and skin friction.

fsw - An acronym for Feet of Sea Water. All scuba depth gauges indicate depth by measuring pressure. They display the depth as the feet (or meters) of sea water at which that pressure is located. Also, all dive tables and computers are designed using pressures for sea water depths. Since these devices are all "calibrated" to the same standard (fsw), it makes no difference whether in fresh or salt water.

Gap - When running permanent lines in submerged cave systems, it is sometimes necessary or desirable to end one permanent line, then begin another further on into the cave system. The location where one line ends, then another line continues into the cave system is called a *gap.* Sometimes, where one line ends there will be gaps to two or more other lines. Gaps vary in length, depending upon the size and configuration of the cave tunnels, but they are usually less than 50 feet, and often less than 30 feet. Some gaps are as short as 1 to 3 feet. Gaps of this type are easy to overlook if you are not paying attention, or if you are using a DPV in unfamiliar tunnel (due to the speed of the DPV). You must be careful and practice good technique even in a system you have dived before, as the permanent lines are often moved for various reasons.

Gap Reel - Any smaller-capacity reel used to connect a gap in the permanent lines when cave diving. Typically, the reels used as gap reels hold 50 to 150 feet of line, though 30 to 50 feet of line is often sufficient. Since the only difference between gaps and jumps is how the permanent line is laid out in the cave system, the terms *jump reel* and *gap reel* are used interchangeably. Safety reels should contain more line. Many cave divers carry identical reels for use as either gap or safety reels. There are two differences between gap reels and safety reels. First, gap reels *may* contain less line (as explained above). Second, safety reels are not used during the normal course of the dive, but are reserved for use in handling emergencies such as a lost diver or lost permanent line. All team members must carry at least one safety reel. Usually, each team member carries one or two jump reels and a safety reel.

Gauge Error - There is no such thing in this world as perfection, though some things come close enough for all practical purposes. Diving gauges, unfortunately, do not. All mechanical and many electronic submersible gauges contain a small but sometimes significant error factor. At different depths in the water column, the same error may be more or less significant; or, the gauge may exhibit different amounts of error at different depths. For example, if your depth gauge reads 2 fsw shallower than your actual depth, it wouldn't matter much on an initial dive of 40 minutes to 53 fsw. But on a 90 minute dive to 91 fsw, your gauge would lead you to believe you had only been to 89 fsw. This would put you on the wrong D/C table schedule. Your errant depth gauge would then allow you to ascend 2 fsw above your recommended stop depth for decompression. Submersible pressure gauges, dive watches and timers, and compasses all are susceptible to error.

Geomorphology - The study of the evolution and configuration of land forms.

Glacier caves - Caves formed by the seasonal melting of ice near the leading edge and bottom of a glacier. Extreme exposure protection is often warranted before entering an ice cave.

Glaciokarst - A limestone region that has been glaciated. It possesses both glacial and karst characteristics.

Glaciospeleology - The study of glacial caves.

Goethite - A black-to-brown-colored mineral, $HFeO_2$. The dark surface deposits on limestone cave passages in north Florida were once thought to be goethite, which they more or less resemble. It is now doubted whether these deposits are goethite, but the name has kind of stuck among some Florida cave divers as a generic term for dark, iron-looking deposits on limestone cave walls.

Granule - Any particle between 2.0 mm and 4.0 mm in size.

Grotto - A small cave. Also, any modestly sized but highly decorated room in a cave system. Also, local chapters of the National Speleological Society (NSS) are called grottoes.

Groundwater - Subsurface water that is located in the saturation zone. Also, used loosely to refer any subsurface water. Syn: *phreatic water.*

Guideline - Any of the various sorts of twine or rope used in submerged caves as the primary navigational tool. Preferences in size, color and material for guidelines vary from region to region. Most commonly used by cave divers in the southeastern U.S. and Caribbean is 1/16th inch braided white nylon twine. However, conditions in other areas may require very different material for use as guidelines. In some areas, moderately large diameter rope is the most appropriate.

Head - Short for *light head.* Also, the thing on your shoulders that you are supposed to use when planning and executing every dive, no matter how good you are or how many dives you have made, even at this same site.

Headpool - The location where an underground source of water flows to the surface creates a spring. Usually, the water then flows along a surface channel, called the spring run, into a river or other body of water. If the spring emerges in a depression, or if rainfall or other factors temporarily cause the spring to flow faster than the run can handle, a pool will form at the spring. This is the *headpool.* The same phenomenon can occur at the point where a siphon enters the ground, and is likewise called a headpool. Some headpools contain both springs and siphons.

Heliox - To reduce the narcotic effects of nitrogen in breathing gases used for deep diving, the nitrogen is replaced with helium. The resulting mixture is *heliox.* Heliox can be mixed in several different concentrations. Because of the toxicity of oxygen at great depths, heliox mixtures often contain less oxygen than does air. Such mixtures may be too low in oxygen to support consciousness at the surface, or even at depths less than 100 fsw. Heliox diving requires special equipment, special training, and appropriate dive tables for the particular mixture(s) being used. It is a very advanced technique used only by the most dedicated (or the most fanatical) divers. Normal people with the desire, time, ability and money to go deep use trimix. Trimix is just about as complex as heliox, but it's a little bit safer — *safe* being a **relative** term in this context. Diving deep on air is foolhardy.

Horse Collar BC - A front-mount buoyancy compensator, which is worn on the chest. The diver dons this type of BC by placing her head through an opening and securing the device with straps. One strap encircles the chest, while another runs between the legs to keep the BC from riding up.

Hydraulic Conductivity - The capacity of rock to transport water under a set of specified conditions.

Hydrogen Sulfide - A gas formed by the decay of certain organic materials and characterized by a rotten egg odor, it dissolves readily in water. Hydrogen sulfide (H_2S) is colorless, flammable, and toxic to humans. Toxicity of water containing hydrogen sulfide depends on both the concentration of the solution and the length of the exposure. The dissolved hydrogen sulfide can be detected by various means. Some divers report that they can smell it in the water. Most divers can taste any hydrogen sulfide water that enters the mouth. Commonly, it produces a mild tingling sensation on fully exposed skin, especially mucous membranes such as the lips. Some divers report a moderate degree of numbness in the lips when exposed to hydrogen sulfide. H_2S is absorbed through exposed skin and mucous membranes. Exact limits of safe exposure are not known, but divers have successfully dived in hydrogen sulfide water for periods of 30 minutes or more. However, caution should be exercised! Dissolved hydrogen sulfide increases the density of the water to a level between that of freshwater and saltwater. Thus, H_2S-water will float on saltwater, while freshwater will float on H_2S-water. Because of the different densities, each type of water refracts light differently. In still, undisturbed water, a readily identified boundary-layer will form at the H_2S-water interface. When diving through freshwater, as this layer is reached it appears as a milky or murky bottom layer. If the diver carefully descends through the H_2S layer feet-first, when her face reaches the boundary-layer she will see an "horizon." Mixing of the waters will produce the same visual blurring effects observed at a halocline. Light that originates on either side of the H_2S layer will not penetrate it. Therefore, **all** surface light will be lost below the boundary-layer, and divers' lights will not be visible to others above it, even though visibility may be quite good on both sides. Therefore, cave-diving techniques are called for when diving below the H_2S layer, even in open water in the middle of the day.

Hypercapnia - An excessive concentration of CO_2 dissolved in the blood. Dissolved CO_2 forms a weak acid (called carbonic acid), causing the pH of the blood to fall. If the blood pH falls below normal limits, the individual becomes acidotic. Excessive CO_2 levels can cause drowsiness, lethargy and confusion. Because the human body is inefficient at respiration underwater, and because of the increasing inefficiency of all scuba regulators at increasing depths, hypercapnia occurs in all divers as they descend deeper. It has been implicated as a contributing factor in many diving drownings due to loss of consciousness at depths greater than 150 fsw.

Hypoxemia - A condition in which the amount of oxygen dissolved in the blood is below normal limits. It can occur when the breathing gas contains too little oxygen, when the lungs cannot properly transport oxygen across the air sacs into the blood, or when the individual stops breathing (either voluntarily, as in breath-hold diving, or involuntarily). When there is not enough oxygen in the blood, the tissues of the body cannot function properly. Because the tissues of the brain are very sensitive to lack of oxygen, the first signs and symptoms of hypoxemia are related to mental functioning. Initially, as the brain becomes *hypoxic*, the person may be restless, irritable or agitated, and may have a lowered capacity to solve problems or react appropriately to her surroundings. Later, she may become confused, lethargic, and eventually unconscious.

Hypoxia - A condition in which the amount of oxygen in the body is below normal limits. Hypoxic people are also hypoxemic, or become hypoxemic after a short period of hypoxia. The difference between these two terms is that *hypoxemia* refers only to low oxygen levels in the blood, while *hypoxia* refers to low oxygen levels anywhere in the body. Hypoxemia is hypoxia of the blood.

Ideal Manifold - A dual valve manifold for double cylinders. Because Dr. George Benjamin built the first DVM, it is also called the *Benjamin Manifold.* The basic advantage of the ideal manifold is that it permits the use of two independent regulators, each of which can access the total air supply independently. This allows either regulator to be shut down in the event of malfunction without restricting the supply of breathing gas available through the other regulator.

Image Referencing - Noting, while traveling into the cave, a particular reference feature the diver wishes to recall clearly during exit. The diver swims past the reference feature and then looks back to observe it from the exit point of view. The diver tries to form a lasting mental image of the cave passage at that point. It is very useful at branches in the passage; changes in direction; at jumps, gaps or intersections; just before and just after negotiating a squeeze, duck-under, or belly-rub; etc. Syn: *looking back, snapshotting, back seat driving.*

Incidental Low Visibility - Low visibility that is caused by some transitory condition in a cave system, such as poor silt technique, that clears up during the dive and doesn't become an emergency situation for the dive team.

Intake area - The area at the surface through which water is absorbed into an aquifer. Syn: *recharge area.*

Jacket BC - A type of buoyancy compensator that can be put on in the same way as you would put on a jacket. When worn, the diver places each of her arms through arm holes, and secures the jacket BC with waist and chest straps to make it snug. Some types use a crotch strap. Most jacket BC's contain an integral backpack of some type for mounting air cylinders. Some have adjustable straps in the front parts of the arm holes. These are called *ADV-style BC's* after the first popular model that incorporated this feature.

Jumars - Jumars are a brand-name of rope climbing or ascending devices. The generic name for these devices is *ascenders,* and other brands are available. Originally designed for use in mountaineering and rock climbing, Jumars permit the skilled user to climb up a free-hanging rope. This is done by use of a locking cam device which can be moved along the rope freely in one direction, but which ratchets down and grips the rope when moved in the opposite direction. Naturally, the cam must have a release mechanism so that the climber can come down. In cave diving, Jumars can be used to "swim" against heavy current. Of course, initial placement requires negotiating the current without using the ascenders. But use of Jumars on subsequent dives permits increasing penetration on the same gas supply by decreasing the time and effort involved in negotiating the heavy current.

Jump - To avoid confusion when running permanent lines in submerged cave systems, the lines placed in side tunnels are usually not connected to the line in the main tunnel. The location where the main line and the line in the side tunnel are closest together is called a *jump.* Sometimes, at one location on the main line there will be jumps to two or more other lines. Jumps vary in length, depending upon the size and configuration of the cave tunnels, but they are usually less than 50 feet, and often less than 30 feet. There is a difference between line jumps and line gaps. Line gaps occur where one line ends, then another line continues into the cave system. Line jumps occur where a continuous line nearly intersects another line, both of which continue into the cave system. If two permanent lines actually intersect, the intersection is called a *T* or a *Y.*

Jump Reel - Any smaller-capacity reel used to connect a jump in the permanent lines when cave diving. Typically, the reels used as jump reels hold 50 to 150 feet of line, though 30 to 50 feet of line is often sufficient. Since the only difference between jumps and gaps is how the permanent line is laid out in the cave system, the terms *jump reel* and *gap reel* are used interchangeably. Safety reels should contain more line. Many cave divers carry identical reels for use as either jump or safety reels. There are two differences between jump reels and safety reels. First, jump reels *may* contain less line (as explained above). Second, safety reels are not used during the normal course of the dive, but are reserved for use in handling emergencies such as a lost diver or lost permanent line. All team members must carry at least one safety reel. Usually, each team member carries one or two jump reels and a safety reel.

Karst - Surface terrain overlying limestone bedrock, characterized by solution channels where the limestone outcrops (*Karren*), closed depressions (*sinks*), few surface streams (because most drainage is subsurfacial), subterranean drainage, and caves.

Karst Bridge - A natural bridge or arch in limestone.

Karst Plain - A plain on which the general defining features of karst topography may be developed. Syn: *karst plateau.*

Karst Plateau - A plain on which the general defining features of karst topography may be developed. Syn: *karst plain.*

Karst River - A river whose headwaters originate at a karst spring.

Karst Spring - A spring emerging from karst limestone.

Karst Topography - Surfacial physical geography dominated by features of solutional origin. Karst on top means caves somewhere below.

Karst Window - A sink which extends down into the water table, revealing part of the subsurface river flowing beneath the soil. Also, any unroofed section of cave.

Keyhole - A small, usually oblong opening in a cave passage which resembles an old-fashioned keyhole in cross-section. In other words, roughly circular at the top and narrowed in the middle or bottom portion.

Labyrinth - A complex or confusing pattern of interconnecting passages in a cave system. Syn: *network, maze cave.*

Lake - Any body of standing water that is too deep to cross by walking.

Laminar Flow - Smooth, non-turbulent movement of a fluid. When tracers are observed in a laminar flow, they are more or less parallel and continuous, like layers. (*Lamina* is Latin for *layers.* It may help to visualize smoke tracers in a wind tunnel.) Objects projecting into the flowing fluid may disrupt laminar flow, creating eddies and counter-currents. Laminar flow is of interest to the cave diver in two ways. Perhaps the most important is the flow of gas through her breathing system. High quality regulators are designed to disrupt laminar flow as little as possible. Her second area of interest in laminar flow concerns the flow of water in the cave system. Here, she tries to be as streamlined as possible. Also, she can "hide" from the force of the flow by maneuvering behind projections or irregularities in the cave passage which create eddies and counter-currents to the main flow.

Lamp - The part of any lighting device which actually generates the light. On current battery powered diving lights, this usually refers to the bulb or bulb/reflector assembly.

Lateral Axis - An imaginary line running through the center of buoyancy of a diver (which is usually at or near the BC) at right angles to the her spine (thus, parallel to her shoulders). As the diver rotates around the lateral axis, she attains head-up trim, head-down trim, or neutral (horizontal) trim.

Lava tube caves - These are found throughout the world where igneous rock occurs. They are formed during the cooling and degassing phase of lava flows associated with volcanic activity. They exhibit mazes, pits, multiple levels, cave adapted animals, and wet zones very analogous to features exhibited by limestone caves.

Lead Diver - The member of a dive team who leads the team during the dive. This diver is the first in, running the reel and placing the line (with help from the second diver). She is also the last team member out, reeling in the line (except in emergencies, when the line is left in place). If the lead diver cannot ensure that all team members have exited in front of her, she must leave the line in place when she exits.

Lead Reel - A *primary* or *main reel.* A lead reel usually contains 400 to 500 feet of line. Typically, only one team member (the lead diver) carries a *primary reel.* All team members must carry at least one safety reel. Usually, each team member carries one or two jump reels and a safety reel.

Level - In a cave system, the development of passages within one horizontal plane. Some cave systems have tunnels at two or more levels.

Life Support System - The part of the diver's gear which must function properly to maintain her life. This is usually understood to be the breathing gas and its containers, valves, regulators, and any other components of the breathing gas delivery system such as submersible pressure gauges, hoses, tank harness or backplate. Some consider the BC as part of the life support system. In cold water the thermal protection system may truly be part of the life support system. For complex diving situations, the life support system may also consist of safety bottles, D/C bottles, habitats, and so on.

Lift - In diving, lift refers to buoyancy or buoyant force. Generally, it means any upward force.

Lift Force - The *buoyant force* of a submerged object. This can be calculated from the object's specific gravity and volume, or from its weight and volume. (The specific gravity of fresh water is 1.00, and it weighs 62.5 pounds per cubic foot. Salt water has a specific gravity of 1.03, and weighs 64.0 pounds per cubic foot.) A BC that weighs 2.5 pounds and is inflated to one cubic foot will exert a lift force of (62.5 - 2.5) lbs., or 60 lbs. in fresh water.

Light Head - The part of any lighting device where the light is generated and directed. This usually includes the lamp, reflector and protective case for these components, and the handle. Also, what the diver usually gets when diving deeper than 130 fsw on air.

Line - Short for *guideline*. Refers to any of the various sorts of twine or rope used in submerged caves as the primary navigational tool. Most commonly used by cave divers in the southeastern U.S. and Caribbean is 1/16th inch braided white nylon twine. However, conditions in other areas may require very different material for use as guidelines. In some areas, moderately large diameter rope is the most appropriate.

Line Arrows - Plastic triangles cut so that they can be easily secured to and removed from guidelines are called *line arrows*. Developed by Forrest Wilson, they are also known as *Wilson Markers*.

Line Markers - The generic name for line clips, line arrows, Dorff markers, etc. Syn: *direction marker*.

Line Person - The second member of the dive team is the *line person*, responsible to assist the lead diver with proper placement of the line during penetration. This includes such things as illuminating tie-off or wrap points while the lead diver is placing the line, looking for potential line traps and moving the line accordingly, taking up slack by placing extra wraps when and where appropriate, etc. She is also responsible to assist the lead diver when reeling out during exit by loosening wraps and taking up slack in the line, etc.

Line Swimming - A term used to describe a situation where the guideline wanders or "swims" out into the passage due to poor line technique, insufficient or improper tie-offs, excessive slack, being caught on a diver's gear, or other causes.

Line Trap - When placing line during a dive, current or other things which cause movement in the line (such as stretching the line around a corner without wrapping it first) can cause the line to move into small cracks in the rock. If it becomes necessary to exit in low visibility following the line by feel, such a situation will be experienced by the divers as following the line into impassable rock. An exit which has already been slowed by the necessity of navigating by touch is now further slowed while the *line trap* is negotiated. Line traps also tend to increase air consumption among all but the most cool-headed. Slack in a line can also lead to line traps.

Longitudinal Axis - The central line through the length of an object, around which it may rotate. On a person, the longitudinal axis runs through the center of the body from head to toe. In a normal swimming position, when you rotate around your longitudinal axis, you roll from stomach to back (or from back to stomach).

Lorraine/Smith Effect - Another term for pulmonary oxygen toxicity, derived from the two researchers who first described it.

Lost River - A surface river that assumes a subsurface course.

M & M Diving - A term used to refer to making multiple dives per day over multiple days. Researchers have noted that some instances of DCS have occurred after several days of this type of diving. While the explanation for this is not fully understood, it is believed by many that the standard US Navy Dive Table assumption that residual N_2 is cleared from the body fully in 12 hours is somewhat inaccurate. Some dive tables produced by other authorities increase the surface interval time to completely outgas N_2 to 24 hours. It is important to remember that even the US Navy Tables recommend that dives requiring stage D/C ***not*** be followed by a repetitive dive (which, according to the USN Tables, would be any dive made within 12 hours of surfacing from the stage D/C dive). This type of diving schedule is more likely for an instructor or tour guide. Cave Diving and other advanced diving instructional programs should be scheduled by the instructor to avoid M & M diving. This is especially important when teaching stage D/C.

Major Restriction - Any narrowing in a submerged

cave which cannot be negotiated while wearing standard back-mounted double cylinders. Negotiating a major restriction requires the use of alternate gear configurations (such as side-mount).

Maze Cave - A complex or confusing pattern of interconnecting passages in a cave system. Syn: *network, labyrinthine cave.*

Mental Narrowing - A phenomenon that occurs to people under stress in which they are unable to utilize their normal range of mental skills. Their attention can focus only on one, or a few, of the things going on around them. Mental narrowing can be broken down into its component elements. *Cognitive narrowing* refers to a reduced capacity to comprehend or understand, and is also called *analytical narrowing*. *Perceptual narrowing* occurs when the person is unaware of all that is going on around her. *Response narrowing* refers to limiting of the normal range of behavioral reactions to specific stimuli.

Microkarst - Karst terrain in which the typical surface features are very small.

Microprocessor - The "brain" which controls the signal flow and performs the mathematical and logical operations in any computer. Syn: *central processing unit, CPU.*

Minor Restriction - Any narrowing in a submerged cave which cannot be negotiated by two divers swimming side-by-side while wearing standard back-mounted double cylinders. Air sharing through a minor restriction requires the use of a long hose on the regulator second stage (at least 5 feet, though 7 feet is becoming the preferred length).

Mixed Gas - Any breathing mixture used for scuba diving other than compressed air. The most common mixed gases are nitrox, heliox and trimix. Specific blends of the different mixed gases are used for specific depth ranges and/or bottom times.

Modified Dolphin Kick - Like the modified flutter kick (see below), the modified dolphin kick is used to minimize downward fin wash. The main purpose of the modified dolphin kick is to provide the diver with a different muscle movement to prevent fatigue from using only one type of kick. To do this kick, the diver bends her knees, drawing her feet up until her ankles are just about directly over her knees. Her knees should be kept on the same plane as her hips. From this position, the kick is performed utilizing only the legs, ankles and feet; not the knees, thighs, hips or abdomen. It's similar to a modified flutter kick with the feet synchronized. Again, the legs only move from the knees down. In large tunnel where the diver can be well away from the silt, or in tunnel with high flow and no silt, it is possible to use the open water fin dolphin kick.

Modified Flutter Kick - When using swim fins, divers change the regular swimming flutter kick to take maximum advantage of the power of the fins. Cave and cavern divers use a modified version of the fin flutter kick to minimize downward fin wash. This is an important skill in silt control. To do this kick, the diver bends her knees, drawing her feet up until her ankles are just about directly over her knees. Her knees should be kept on the same plane as her hips. From this position, the kick is performed utilizing only the legs, ankles and feet; not the knees, thighs or hips. In areas with very low clearance, the motion can be further restricted to just the ankles and feet. If done with some snap, this variation is surprisingly effective. When using either variation of the modified flutter kick, most of the propulsion comes from the down stroke of the fins. In large tunnel where the diver can be well away from the silt, or in tunnel with high flow and no silt, the open water fin flutter kick may be used.

Modified Frog Kick - Cave and cavern divers use a modified version of the frog kick to minimize downward fin wash. As with the other modified kicks, it is an important part of silt technique. This kick is performed utilizing primarily the ankles and feet. The diver bends her knees, drawing her feet up until her ankles are just about in the same vertical plane as her knees. Her knees should be kept on the same horizontal plane as her hips. From this position, the diver slides the fin blades apart by separating her legs while keeping her knees close together. (The fin blades are kept flat in the water, and the knees are kept inside the diver's shoulder width.) If the diver has good mobility in the hip, knee and ankle joints, the fins can be separated a bit further by rotating the feet and ankles outward. Once the fins reach maximum separation, the diver turns the fin blades toward the perpendicular (about 60 - 75 degrees is all that is possible) and pushes them backward against the water in a smooth, continuous motion while keeping her knees and thighs in line with her hips. This is one complete kick cycle. The modified frog kick is a powerful and efficient kick which is used by some cave divers as their primary method of swimming.

Morphology - The study of form and structure. Geomorphology is of most interest to the cave diver.

Naked Karst - Karst terrain in which much of the limestone bedrock is exposed on the surface. Syn: *bare karst.*

Narrow Scope Penetration - When penetrating an unfamiliar cave system, a narrow scope penetration is one in which side tunnels and leads are ignored in order to concentrate on maximum penetration of the main passage.

Natural Arch - A rock arch over a tunnel or other relatively small erosional or dissolution feature.

Natural Bridge - A rock pathway spanning a relatively large erosional or dissolution feature, such as a chasm or ravine.

Natural Low Visibility - Low visibility due to some naturally occurring condition. This might be tannic acid dissolved in the water, lots of particulate suspended in the water, or transitory silting due to natural phenomena. Cave dives with natural low visibility are often among the most advanced.

Navigational System - The part of the diver's gear which enables her to know her position and find her way during the dive. This consists of the continuous guideline and all reels, line markers, clips and arrows, compass, maps or sketches, lights, etc.

Nested Sinkhole - A larger sinkhole formed by the coalescence of two or more sinkholes. This occurs when a new sink develops so close to an existing sink that part of the wall of the first sink collapses into the second sink.

Neutral Equilibrium - The state of a body in water such that when it is moved by a disturbing force from an original position, it remains in its new position after the disturbing force is removed.

Nitrous Oxide - A mild anesthetic gas, N_2O is also known as laughing gas. If inhaled without mixing in air or oxygen, nitrous oxide will cause asphyxiation. (The body cannot utilize the oxygen atoms that are bonded to the nitrogen atoms in this gas.)

Nitrox - Any breathing mixture of nitrogen and oxygen (with possible traces of other gases) other than air. (Air is roughly 21% oxygen, 78% nitrogen, and 1% other gases.) NOAA has two standard nitrox blends — Nitrox I and Nitrox II. There are several advantages when using standard blends, including standardized dive tables and a large base of research on the effects of the particular blend on a cross-section of divers. Most nitrox is blended by adding oxygen to air, so that the resulting blend contains the same trace gases as air, but in lower concentrations. This is Enriched Air Nitrox. Nitrox can also be blended by mixing nitrogen and oxygen directly. It has been said that air is just God's Own Nitrox.

Nitrox D/C - 1) Stage decompression using nitrox instead of air as the breathing gas during decompression. After a dive made on air, nitrox D/C is usually done by following a standard air D/C table (or computer), but breathing either Nitrox I or Nitrox II. Because the nitrox contains a lower concentration of nitrogen than air, out-gassing of nitrogen from the diver's body is enhanced. This decreases the diver's potential for DCS, but is much safer and easier to use than high concentrations of oxygen, especially when D/C stops deeper than 25 fsw are required. 2) *Nitrox decompression* can also refer to the stage decompression required following a dive made on nitrox. Even though the amount of nitrogen in nitrox is lower than in air, the body still accumulates excess nitrogen during nitrox dives If the nitrox no-decompression limits have been exceeded, decompression will be required.

Nitrox I - A breathing mixture consisting of 68% N_2 and 32% O_2. Developed by NOAA, it is also called NOAA Nitrox I. Established D/C tables for Nitrox I are available from NOAA.

Nitrox II - A breathing mixture consisting of 64% N_2 and 36% O_2. Developed by NOAA, it is also called NOAA Nitrox II. Established D/C tables for Nitrox II are available from NOAA.

NNI - An acronym for NOAA Nitrox I.

NNII - An acronym for NOAA Nitrox II.

NOAA - An acronym for the National Oceanic and Atmospheric Administration. NOAA oversees, directly or indirectly, all non-military diving and diving research activities of the U.S. government.

NOAA Nitrox I - The same as Nitrox I. The research demonstrating it's usefulness and safety was primarily done through NOAA, which also developed the D/C tables for it; hence the name NOAA Nitrox I.

NOAA Nitrox II - The same as Nitrox II. The research demonstrating it's usefulness and safety was primarily done through NOAA, which also developed the D/C tables for it; hence the name NOAA Nitrox II.

No-Bubble Tables - Dive tables with more conservative no-decompression limits than the standard USN dive tables, designed to prevent the occurrence of *silent bubbles*. At present, the technology does not exist, or is not known, to develop no-bubble stage decompression tables. (In other words, you always bubble when you stage decompress.)

Optimal Mix - For any particular dive profile and conditions, there will be an optimal mix for the breathing gas. For example, although most cave divers use air when diving between 90 and 130 fsw, NNI at these depths is within the limits to prevent O_2 toxicity for bottom times up to 45 minutes (at 130 fsw). It lessens the narcotic effects and decompression exposure compared to air.

OTU - An acronym for *Oxygen Tolerance Units.*

Outcrop - An exposed part of an underlying rock formation. A place where an underlying rock formation comes to the surface.

Outrigger Clips - Sort-of oversized clothespins that are used in trolling and deep sea fishing. Many cave divers use outrigger clips as line markers. To adapt them for this use, you should first cut the wire "keeper" that runs through the two springs that make the outrigger clip operable. The clips should then be marked in some way that enables you to **readily** identify them as your own. (Your Wilson Markers should be similarly labeled.) Some divers also mark them in some way so that you can tell the direction out by feel in zero visibility. For example, a friend of mine used to cut an arrow into the surface of his clips with a router. Other divers notch one side of their clips with a file or saw in some distinctive way. If you're not up to all that, then stick to Wilson Markers. They're inexpensive and also easy to make.

Oxygen D/C - Stage decompression using oxygen as the breathing gas during decompression. After a dive made on air, oxygen D/C is usually done by following a standard air D/C table (or computer), but breathing oxygen. Because oxygen contains no nitrogen, out-gassing of nitrogen from the diver's body is greatly enhanced. This decreases the diver's potential for DCS. However, oxygen is much more dangerous than other gases, such as nitrox. Handling oxygen requires care and specially prepared equipment to lessen the very greatly increased fire and explosion hazard it presents. There is also an oxygen toxicity potential when using it for D/C stops deeper than 25 fsw. When oxygen D/C tables are available for the relevant dive profile and breathing gas, decompressing on O_2 can dramatically shorten D/C stop times. In very cold water and other special circumstances, oxygen decompression may be essential for safely managing the operation.

Oxygen Tolerance Units - A system for keeping track of exposures to increased pO_2 for the purpose of determining the additive effects of different exposures on the development of pulmonary oxygen toxicity. It was developed by Wright in 1972 and reported in Charles Shilling *et al.*, eds. *The Underwater Handbook: A Guide to Physiology and Performance for the Engineer.* Plenum Press; New York. 1976. The toxic effects of oxygen on the CNS don't usually occur until the pO_2 exceeds 1.6 ata, and are of rapid onset. The toxic effects of oxygen on the pulmonary system occur with exposure to a pO_2 of 0.55 ata or greater for a period of 24 hours or more, and are of slow or insidious onset. For commercial or research divers, M & M diving is not uncommon. Wright's *OTU* system permits divers to quantify the pulmonary effects of the increased pO_2's experienced on dives to different depths for different bottom times. Nitrox diving increases the exposure to elevated pO_2's

p - The lowercase *p* is an abbreviation for *partial pressure.*

Panic - When anxiety in the presence of stress (physiological or psychological) increases, the individual can experience agitation and mental narrowing, compromising her ability to respond rationally. This in turn can increase the stress, which can increase the agitation and mental narrowing further, and so on in a self-reinforcing positive feedback loop. When this process continues to the point where the individual's ability to respond rationally is lost, only instinctive, infantile responses are possible. This is panic. The chief feature of panic is its unreasoning character. High levels of anxiety (near-panic), as well as genuine panic, usually lead to hyperventilation, which reinforces the vicious circle. If the individual hyperventilates long enough, she will stop breathing (because hyperventilation dramatically lowers blood levels of CO_2, which is the primary breathing stimulus) and pass out. This most likely explains the phenomenon of scuba divers who are found drowned in water shallower than 150 fsw with air in their tanks and fully functioning regulators. (Below 150 fsw, hypercapnia and narcosis play increasingly significant roles in altering the diver's mental state and level of consciousness as depth increases. Even at depth, however, if the deep diver experiences increasing anxiety, the same vicious feedback loop causing hyperventilation can occur.)

Particulate - Small particles of solid matter that are lightweight enough to remain suspended in the water column, often for long periods. Particulate decreases visibility and increases backscatter from lights. Particulate is usually of irregular dimensions — it often looks like little tiny flakes. This differentiates it from clay and silt, which can also remain suspended for long periods. Particles of clay or silt are of an essentially uniform size in all dimensions (at least to the naked eye).

Passage - In caves, the interconnections between rooms or chambers are *passages.* Sometimes also used to refer generally to the cave void.

Passageway - Syn. for *passage.*

Paul/Bert Effect - Another term for CNS oxygen toxicity, derived from the researchers who first described it.

Pebble - Any particle between 4.0 mm and 64.0 mm in size.

Perceptual Narrowing - A phenomenon that occurs to people under stress in which they are unaware of all that is going on around them. It is a form of mental narrowing. Other forms of mental narrowing include *cognitive narrowing* and *response narrowing.*

Percolation - The relatively slow vertical movement of water down through the soil due to gravity. Also, by extension, the relatively slow vertical movement of particulate matter down through the water column. This can occur in caves from the material being dislodged by the diver's air bubbles or the water currents generated by her body moving through the cave passageway.

Permeability - The capacity of rock for transmitting liquids through it.

Personal Hygiene - Cave divers who get clips or gauges or hoses or lights or D-rings or whatever tangled in lines, who drag gauges or reels or lights through the silt, or who in general have danglies, have a problem with *personal hygiene.* They need to clean up their gear. Very long dives made wearing a dry suit are also known to create problems of personal hygiene.

Phreatic - Referring to the subsurface saturation zone: i.e., the zone which is below the water table and which is constantly wet. This contrasts with the subsurface region that water percolates down through, but which does not stay completely wet, called the *aeration zone* or *vadose zone.*

Phreatic Water - Water in the saturation zone.

Phreatic Zone - The region below the water table where the rock is saturated with water, like a sponge. Syn: *saturation zone.*

Physical Stress - A stress which has a material basis. Examples include: extremes of temperature, too much CO_2 in the body, too little CO_2 in the body, too little O_2 in the body, too much O_2 in the body, fatigue, etc. When a person experiences physical stress, her awareness of it usually creates additional psychological stress.

Pillar - A vertical section of rock, resembling a column, that is left after erosion or dissolution of the surrounding rock. Also called a *rock pillar.* It differs from a column in that a *column* is formed by the convergence of a stalagmite and a stalactite.

Pinnacle - A tall, sharp projection rising from the cave floor. Also called a *rock pinnacle.*

Pit - A deep, more or less circular hole with very steep walls.

pN_2 - An abbreviation for the partial pressure of nitrogen.

pO_2 - An abbreviation for the partial pressure of oxygen.

Pocket - A roughly bowl-shaped cavity in cave floor, walls or ceiling, which has been "scooped out" of the rock unrelated to joints, fissures, bedding planes, or other weak areas.

Porosity - The ratio of the void space within a rock to its total volume. It is usually stated as a percentage. For example, some limestones exhibit porosities of 23-25%: that is, nearly one quarter of these rocks' volumes are made of airspace.

Porthole - A small, roughly circular natural opening through a cave wall which opens to an adjoining cave void.

Post-Dive Exertion - A contributing factor in DCS, post-dive exertion refers to exertion that occurs in the period immediately following a dive. For cave divers, climbing out of the water wearing double cylinders while carrying all the appropriate cave diving gear creates significant post-dive exertion. The surface D/C stop of 15 to 30 minutes practiced by cave divers not only continues out-gassing prior to post-dive exertion, it rests the diver while delaying the post-dive exertion. On dives with significant D/C exposure, it is also advisable to delay going back down to the water to haul up D/C bottles, DPV's, stage bottles, etc. until all the gear you hauled up initially is put away. It also helps to wait until you've changed into your dry clothes. On major exploration or research dives, gear porters are essential for these tasks to minimize D/C risks.

pp - Partial pressure is sometimes abbreviated as *pp,* though the usual abbreviation is just *p* followed by the symbol indicating what it is the partial pressure of, is in pO_2 or pN_2.

Pre-Dive Check - Before making any dive, the dive team should perform a *pre-dive check* consisting at least of equipment matching, dive plan review CAS review, bubble check, timing device synchronization and check, and S-drill. Is it tedious? Yes. Is it boring? Usually. Is it necessary? Absolutely! Are there any short-cuts? None. Can we get away with skipping some or all of it? Most of the time. In fact, all the cave divers I know of who didn't get away with fudging the pre-dive check only had that happen to them once. Fudging the pre-dive check is an excellent preparatory step for making a terminal cave dive.

Pressure Transducer - A device which converts a mechanical pressure measurement to a signal which is fed into the input of an A/D converter. It permits an electronic processing or display readout of the pressure. This can be used to measure and display the diver's depth in the water column, or the remaining pressure in a gas bottle.

Primary Light - Due to the absolute darkness of submerged caves, the cave diver usually needs a fairly powerful light. Due to the high failure rate of lights, the cave diver needs a minimum of three light sources. Because of the bulky size and significant dry weight of the battery packs needed to drive powerful lights, the diver usually carries only one such light. This light should drive at least a 30 watt bulb for the anticipated length of the dive, including exit. Increased bulb wattage means increased brightness but decreased burn time. Lamps in the 35 to 50 watt range usually represent a reasonable trade-off of brightness versus burn time. Higher wattage lamps demand shorter dives and/or bigger (or multiple) battery packs.

Primary Reel - A primary reel usually contains 400 to 500 feet of line. Typically, only one team member (the lead diver) carries a *primary reel*. All team members must carry at least one safety reel. Usually, each team member carries one or two jump reels and a safety reel. Syn: *lead reel* or *main reel*.

Pseudokarst - Karst-like surface features that were not produced by dissolution of rock. For example, this can occur when the ceilings of lava tubes in a lava field collapse.

psi - An acronym for Pounds per Square Inch. It is a basic unit of pressure measurement. When not specified, *psi* usually means *psig*.

psia - An acronym for Pounds per Square Inch Absolute. It is a measurement of the total pressure, including the pressure of the atmosphere. *Psia* is equal to (psig + 14.7).

psig - An acronym for Pounds per Square Inch Gauge. It is a measurement of the pressure a gauge calibrated to read "0" at sea level would show. *Psig* is equal to (psia - 14.7).

Psychological Stress - A stress which has a mental basis. Such a stress could be primarily emotional or intellectual. Examples include: claustrophobia, fear in low visibility conditions, loss of guideline, disorientation, sudden realization that a major dive planning error was made, etc. When a person experiences physical stress, her awareness of it usually creates psychological stress.

RAM - An acronym for Random Access Memory.

Random Access Memory - In a computer, *RAM* is volatile memory that can be erased or updated. The amount of available RAM determines how much data the computer can accommodate at any given time.

Read Only Memory - It is the memory in a computer which cannot be altered unless it is physically removed and replaced. For example, in a Dive Computer, the mathematical formulas for computing nitrogen exposure are stored in *ROM*.

Recharge area - The area at the surface through which water is absorbed into an aquifer. Syn: *intake area*.

Redundancy - Kind of like this glossary, where key terms that are explained in the text are re-explained in case the first version has been lost, misplaced, misunderstood, forgotten or jammed. When cave diving, the diver should only carry the equipment she really needs. If any of the equipment fails or is broken, as happens to all mechanical things from time to time, it is significant because the diver is carrying only necessary equipment. The most critical equipment the cave diver carries is her life-support and navigational equipment. For safety, she carries back-ups for key components of this critical equipment. Is there such a thing as too much redundancy? You bet! The choice of what back-ups to carry and where to carry them is a key element in streamlined, efficient cave diving.

Reel Person - The lead diver on a cave diving team. This diver is the first in, running the reel and placing the line (with help from the second diver). She is also the last diver out, reeling in the line (except in emergencies, when the line is left in place). If the lead diver cannot ensure that all team members have exited in front of her, she must leave the line in place when she exits.

Referencing - The cave diver needs to maintain a general awareness of her position in the cave at all times. By employing deliberate techniques throughout the dive, she is able to do this. She also needs to form mental notes (or sometimes even make notes on her slate) relevant to dive conditions which affect her or her dive team. Since she accomplishes these tasks by establishing specific points of reference, the process is called *referencing*.

Referencing Techniques - The various techniques used by the cave diver to maintain a general awareness of her position and of conditions in the cave. For example, using a compass to determine the general heading of the main passageway is a specific referencing technique. Another is noting peculiarities about the tunnel or line.

Response Narrowing - A phenomenon that occurs to people under stress in which the normal range of behavioral responses to specific stimuli is limited. It is a form of mental narrowing. Other forms of mental narrowing include *cognitive narrowing* and *perceptual narrowing*.

Resurgence - The point where an underground river comes to the surface. Some cave divers reserve this term to refer only to an underground river which has previously sunk below the surface. Syn: *emergence, rise.*

Reversing spring - A spring which periodically reverses flow through the same outlet. Such a spring is alternately a spring, then a siphon.

Rimbach System - The oldest touch-contact communication signal system. In this system, the dive partner is grasped around the arm or leg with one hand, while maintaining contact with the guideline with the other hand. Divers should be positioned on the same side of the line, single-file. Pushing the partner's extremity means *go*, squeezing means *stop*, and pulling means *back up*. Some cave divers also use *Rimbach* as a general name for touch-contact communication systems.

Rise - The point where an underground river comes to the surface. Syn: *emergence, resurgence.*

Rock Pillar - Another name for *pillar.*

Rock Pinnacle - Another name for *pinnacle.*

ROM - An acronym for Read Only Memory.

Room - A section of a cave that is larger than tunnel. A location where the tunnel widens.

Routine Maintenance - All dive equipment requires regular maintenance for proper and efficient performance. Cleaning, lubrication, scheduled replacement of dynamic or disposable parts, and inspection for signs of excessive wear or weakness are some examples. Cave divers should be especially conscientious about routine maintenance, because their lives could well depend on it.

Run - The stream of flowing water created by a spring, it usually drains the spring's headpool into a larger stream or river. Syn: *spring run.*

Running End - When working with rope or line, the end of the line which is free and available for use is called the *running end.* Syn: *free end.*

S-Drill - Short for *Safety Drill.* Before each dive, in the open water at the cave entrance, or just inside the entrance if necessitated by configuration of the opening, the entire dive team should rehearse air sharing. This should involve actually signalling for air, handing off the long hose regulator, swimming a few yards sharing air, etc.

SafeAir™ - The term *SafeAir* has been recently applied to nitrox. It has, in fact, been stated that nitrox is not a mixed gas at all, but rather simply a safer form of atmospheric air. These statements are very misleading, and actually incorrect.

Safety Drill - Before each dive, in the open water at the cave entrance, or just inside the entrance if necessitated by configuration of the opening, the entire dive team should rehearse air sharing. This should involve actually signalling for air, handing off the long hose regulator, swimming a few yards sharing air, etc.

Safety Reel - Any smaller-capacity reel held in reserve throughout the dive for use in handling emergencies such as a lost diver or lost permanent line. Typically, the reels used as safety reels should hold at least 75 to 100 feet of line. Many cave divers carry identical reels for use as either jump or safety reels, provided that they hold the required amount of line. Some divers believe that safety reels should contain significantly more line than I have indicated here. For example, see Mike McCaskill's discussion of reels in Chapter 4.

Safety Stop - On a no-decompression dive, this is a pause in the ascent at 10 to 20 fsw for 3 to 5 minutes or longer, as an added safety margin. On stage decompression dives, most divers add a *safety cushion* of 3 to 5 minutes or longer to the time required at the shallowest D/C stop. Cave divers with their heavy, bulky gear, should also add a *surface decompression stop* in addition to the *safety stop* or *safety cushion.* The purpose of the safety stop or safety cushion is to get you to the surface without getting bent. The purpose of the surface decompression stop is to delay post dive exertion until more out-gassing of nitrogen has occurred, reducing your chances of DCS.

Sand - Any particle between 1/16th mm and 2.0 mm in size.

Sea caves - Caves in marine environments formed by erosion due to wave and current action. They are found along high energy coastlines. Depths are generally shallow.

Senescence - Old age. All geologic phenomena have a life cycle consisting of creation, youth, middle age, and old age (or *senescence*).

Shot Line - A weighted line. Usually the line is weighted to help hold it in a position, or to enable the weighted end to be heaved across an open space.

Shuffle Kick - A silt control technique in which one fin is placed directly beneath the other fin. The top fin is used to do a one-legged modified flutter kick, while the underneath fin remains stationary to deflect fin wash away from the bottom. It is used in low tunnel over silty bottom.

Silent Bubbles - Research using Doppler acoustic devices has confirmed that divers who show no signs or symptoms of DCS can have nitrogen bubble formation in their venous blood. This occurs following dives near the no-decompression limits and also following dives involving stage D/C. These asymptomatic bubbles are called *silent bubbles.* Dive tables with more conservative no-decompression limits designed to eliminate the formation of silent bubbles are often called *no-bubble tables.*

Silt - Any particle between 1/256th mm and 1/16th mm in size. Also used by cave divers to refer to any unconsolidated sediment, regardless of the actual size of the particles, that can be readily suspended in the water column. In this second sense, *silt* is used to refer to clay, silt, and sand, as well as to decomposing organic matter. It is usually found on the floor of the cave passage, but may also accumulate on the irregular surfaces of cave walls.

Silting - Disturbing or stirring up the loose, unconsolidated sediments often found in submerged caves.

Silt Control - The ability of the dive team or the individual cave diver to prevent or minimize silting.

Silt Technique - The general term for all the skills the dive team or the individual cave diver uses to prevent or minimize silting.

Sink - A localized depression in the surface of the ground with a somewhat significant gradient, which may or may not contain water. A cave entrance that shows no relative flow characteristics and has a general depression of ground relief leading to the water is called a *sink*. Syn: *sinkhole, doline.*

Sinkhole - A localized depression in the surface of the ground with a somewhat significant gradient. Sinkholes are created when the supporting subsurface rock falls or shifts. If the sinkhole extends down into the water table, it will contain water and may be diveable (depending on the size of the opening).

Sinking Creek - A small stream that disappears underground.

Siphon - Also spelled *syphon.* Most water goes into the ground by percolating down through the soil, forming groundwater. A location on the surface where water is drained below the surface through tunnel, into the earth, is a siphon. *Siphon* is also used to refer to any section of tunnel, including the entrance, in which water flows deeper into the earth, away from the entrance. A siphon is the opposite of a spring. Siphons present an additional hazard to cave divers, as the flow tends to pull the diver into the cave, away from the entrance. Exiting through a siphon requires more time and uses more gas and more energy than the penetration did. The well-known Third's Rule is woefully inadequate for safe cave diving in siphons.

Skin Friction - As a fluid flows around an object that is moving through it, the molecules of the fluid tend to either slide easily past the object's surface or to "stick" to that surface. The degree of "stickiness" that exists between the object's surface and the fluid molecules is called *skin friction.* For example, lycra-covered wet suits have less surface friction than nylon-covered wet suits. Altogether, there are three components of resistance to motion through a fluid: drag, frontal area and surface friction. Syn: *surface friction.*

Slough - This term is sometimes spelled *slue* or *slew.* It is a stagnant or very slow-moving swamp, bog or pond.

Snapshotting - Noting, while traveling into the cave, a particular reference feature the diver wishes to recall clearly during exit. The diver swims past the reference feature and then looks back to observe it from the exit point of view. The diver tries to form a lasting mental image or mental *snapshot* of the cave passage at that point. It is very useful at branches in the passage; changes in direction; at jumps, gaps or intersections; just before and just after negotiating a squeeze, duck-under, or belly-rub; etc. Syn: *image referencing, looking back,* and *back seat driving.*

Soda Straw - A thin, tubular stalactite usually less than one centimeter in diameter and of relatively great length. Syn: *straw stalactite.*

Solution - Changing the state of matter from gas or solid to liquid, by combination with a liquid.

Solution Caves - Caves formed by the dissolution of porous rock. This dissolution is facilitated by the circulation of freshwater within the rock, which can react chemically with cements that hold individual grains of the rock together. The rock gradually crumbles and is washed away by currents in underwater conduits that develop in the dissolving rock. Generally, *solution caves* are composed of limestone, and represent the type of cave most frequently visited by cave divers.

Spelean - Relating to caves.

Speleogen - A structure formed by dissolving rock, but occurring after the initial formation of the cave passageway. Scallops in the cave walls are speleogens.

Speleology - The scientific study, description and exploration of caves and related geological features.

Speleothem - A structure formed by mineral deposition

after the formation of the cave passageway. Formation of speleothems cannot occur while the cave passage is submerged. Thus, submerged caves with speleothems have been air-filled at some time since the passage was formed. Syn: *cave formation, decoration.*

Spring - The location where subsurface water flows out at the surface of the ground, usually forming a pool or run. Springs are usually safer to dive than siphons, because the current tends to push the diver back toward the entrance.

Spring Run - The stream of flowing water created by a spring, it usually drains the spring's headpool into a larger stream or river. Syn: *run.*

Spring/Siphon - A surface pool of water which is fed from subsurface groundwater at one point by a *spring,* and drained back below the surface at another point by a *siphon.*

Stabilizer Jacket - Another name for a jacket BC. When Scubapro first introduced this type BC, they called it a Buoyancy Stabilizer Jacket. Like Band-Aid, Xerox, Scotch Tape, and Q-Tip, the trade name gradually came to be synonymous with the generic name.

Stable Equilibrium - The state of a body in water such that when it is moved by a disturbing force from an original position, it returns to its original position after the disturbing force is removed.

Stalactite - A roughly cylindrical or conical speleothem which hangs down from the ceiling of a cave.

Stalagmite - A roughly cylindrical or conical speleothem which rises up from the floor of a cave.

Standing End - When working with rope or line, the end of the line which is not available is called the *standing end,* or *standing part.* The standing end of a line is usually tied or otherwise secured to something. In cave diving, that is usually a reel or some tie-off or wrap point in the cave.

Static - Stationary; not moving. The opposite of dynamic.

Static Rope - A stationary rope, it is usually secured at each end so that it is relatively stable. Syn: *static line.*

Static Line - A stationary rope or line. Syn: *static rope.*

Steel 100's - A term used to refer to several different gas cylinders of approximately 100 cubic foot capacity. Since the first such cylinders available were actually rated to hold 103.5 cubic feet of gas, they are often called *steel 100's,* or just *100's.*

Steel 104's - The first large-capacity gas cylinders readily available to cave divers were steel 3AA cylinders with a working capacity of 103.5 cubic feet when filled to a 10% overfill at 2640 psig. They were manufactured by the Pressed Steel Corp. to the specifications of Sherwood Scuba, who distributed and sold them. These bottles, and any made to the same specifications by other manufacturers, are known both as *steel 104's* and *steel 100's.*

Stone System - A system of communication for low visibility diving developed by Jamie Stone in 1979. The signals may be communicated through any method devised by the team, including bangs, hits, tugs, squeezes, etc. It consists of the following signals: 1) One signal asks whether the other diver is "OK" or serves as a reply meaning "OK". This is used as the first signal because of the possibility of a diver giving an inadvertent signal. 2) Two occurrences of a signal indicate "let's move on," "let's continue," or "go ahead." 3) Three occurrences of a signal indicate that the team should "stop" or "halt" immediately. 4) Four occurrences of a signal indicate the buddy should "come here" or that their partner needs assistance. There is no signal for sharing air.

Straw Stalactite - A thin, tubular stalactite usually less than one centimeter in diameter and of relatively great length. Syn: *soda straw.*

Streamlining - Arranging the diver's body and equipment in order to minimize resistance to movement through the water. The streamlined diver presents minimal frontal area to the water, and has arranged all equipment to achieve the least disruption to water flow around or through it. Common diver errors which interfere with streamlining include overweighting, use of poorly designed or poorly fitting gear, excessive redundant gear, and poorly organized or secured gear (*danglies*).

Stress - A physical or mental strain or burden which wears on the individual unless a timely and appropriate response can be made. All stresses require an expenditure of energy for a successful response. The greater the energy required for a successful response, the greater the stress.

Sub-clinical DCS - DCS which produces no signs or symptoms, or produces signs and symptoms which are not urgent enough to be recognized as indicating DCS. Unusual fatigue following a dive is a commonly overlooked symptom of DCS because the high expenditure of energy on deep or long penetration dives causes the diver to misinterpret its significance.

Sump - A water-filled section of otherwise air-filled cave passage. Sumps tend to be located at low points in cave tunnel, or at places where the ceiling drops close to the floor. Often, sumps that can be traversed will open into further air-filled cave passageway.

Sump Diving - Cave diving done in sumps. Sumps are often small, constricted passages with low visibility and cold water. Sump diving is a very specialized and advanced form of cave diving.

Surface Friction - As a fluid flows around an object that is moving through it, the molecules of the fluid tend to either slide easily past the object's surface or to "stick" to that surface. The degree of "stickiness" that exists between the object's surface and the fluid molecules is called *surface friction*. For example, lycra-covered wet suits have less surface friction than nylon-covered wet suits. Altogether, there are three components of resistance to motion through a fluid: drag, frontal area and surface friction. Syn: *skin friction*.

Surface Decompression - An older, more widely used term for *surface decompression stop*.

Surface Decompression Stop - Formerly, cave divers used to refer to a few extra minutes of rest at the surface prior to exiting the water as *surface decompression*. However, some divers complained that *surface decompression* was a term already used by the US Navy to refer specifically to their procedure to decompress divers at the surface in recompression chambers after dives made within certain parameters. *Surface decompression stop* is used in this book in place of *surface decompression*, to avoid any confusion with the USN procedure. The purpose of the surface decompression stop is to delay post dive exertion until more out-gassing of nitrogen has occurred, and to provide additional rest following long, arduous dives. All cave dives should include this rest due to the amount of post-dive exertion involved in getting out of the water and back to the vehicles wearing double cylinders and other additional gear.

Surface Stop - Another term for *surface decompression stop*.

Swallow Hole - A sinkhole where a surface stream or river leaves the surface to assume an underground course.

Tag Line - Generally, a secondary rope or line attached to another rope or line to control or secure the first rope. For example, when dry cavers haul their gear across a vertical drop, the gear is usually moved using a rope. A *tag line* attached to this rope allows the caver at the bottom of the drop to guide the gear around snags while the caver at the top raises or lowers the gear.

Tannic Water - Water which comes into contact with dead leaves or other vegetation will dissolve the tannin they contain, becoming tannic. Tannic water is tea-colored. (Tea, after all, is made from dead leaves.) It has reduced visibility due to the tannin, even if otherwise clear, and absorbs light readily. *Tannin* and *tannic acid* are synonymous terms. The approximate composition of tannic acid is $C_{76}H_{52}O_{46}$.

Task Loading - Adding more tasks, or increasing the complexity of existing tasks, is *task loading*. Tasks are stressors, requiring the expenditure of energy. Tasks which are new and unfamiliar require more energy and attention than familiar, practiced tasks. Mastery of new and more complex tasks occurs with repetition and learning. As tasks are mastered, more energy is available to deal with additional tasks, so that more tasks, or more complex tasks, may be successfully undertaken. If task loading increases too soon, performance generally deteriorates. (This is what kills most open water divers in caves.) Cave diving involves significant task loading for the diver. One of the main goals of cave diving instruction is for the student to be assisted in mastery of the tasks of cave diving by the instructor. It is the instructor's job to assess the readiness of the student to attempt new tasks, to provide guidance (in the form of suggestions and model behavior) for efficiently completing the tasks, and to provide repetition so that the tasks become familiar. As the student masters various tasks, she becomes more efficient in their performance, conserving energy. Energy thus becomes available for mastering new tasks. As skills are learned, task mastery usually accelerates. This happens because the skills learned are applicable, or transferable, to other new tasks.

Threshold - The part of a cave entrance where natural light penetrates to some degree.

Thrust - A propulsive force or pressure: a push.

Thrust Force - The amount of propulsive energy applied in a given situation.

Torque - A force that tends to cause rotation, it results from the application of a force couple.

Touch-and-Go System - A system of communication for low visibility diving also known as the *bump-and-go* method. Under this system, all dive team members maintain contact with the guideline but not with each other. Each diver swims an arbitrary distance, then stops to wait for the next team member to catch up. When the trailing diver bumps into the lead diver, the latter proceeds again. Several problems may be encountered using this system, and it is slow and inefficient.

Touch-Contact System - Any signalling system which involves communicating with the dive partners while maintaining physical contact. It is used in very low visibility situations, when communication is not possible using hand signals or slates.

Trap - Short for *water trap*. A siphon.

Traverse - Entering a cave at one opening, then travelling to and exiting from a different opening, is making a *traverse.*

Trim - The state of balance or equilibrium of the diver. The diver's trim may be head up, level, or head down.

TriMix - A compressed breathing gas consisting of helium, nitrogen and oxygen (with traces of other gases possible). It is often made by spiking air with helium. Trimix is useful on deep dives to limit nitrogen narcosis, to dilute oxygen concentrations to subtoxic levels, and to improve gas delivery through the breathing system. Use of trimix is a very advanced technique that is fraught with complexity, hazard and expense.

Troglobite - An animal living permanently underground in the dark zone of caves, and only accidentally leaving it.

Troglodyte - A human cave dweller.

Troglophile - An animal habitually entering the dark zone of a cave but necessarily spending part of its existence outside.

Troglophobe - An animal or person unable physically or psychologically to enter the dark zone of a cave. Troglophobes generally believe that cave divers have a death wish or some other bizarre psychological condition.

Trogloxene - An animal entering a cave for various reasons, but not living there throughout its entire life cycle.

Tube - A cave passage with fairly smooth walls and a more or less circular cross-section.

Tunnel - A cave passage that is roughly straight and level, with a relatively uniform cross-section, and open at the ends. (If it is only open at one end, it is more properly called a *dead-end*, or *cul-de-sac.*)

Turbulence - Agitation, commotion, disorganization, disturbance, chaos. Cave divers are most interested in turbulence in fluids, such as the air in their regulators or the water in the cave.

Turbulent Flow - The motion of a fluid in which various local pressures and velocities fluctuate chaotically. The opposite of laminar flow.

Turn-Around - The planned point to terminate penetration and begin exiting from the cave. All dive plans should include turn-around points for air, time, depth and distance.

Turn-Around Air Supply - Another name for *Critical Air Supply*. This is the minimum amount of air needed by the dive team to safely exit the cave in case one diver experiences sudden catastrophic loss of the remainder of her air. The ***minimum*** turn-around air supply for a two-person dive team in a cave system with negligible flow is 2/3 of the air the dive team started with. This assumes that stage decompression is not required (or that additional D/C bottles have been placed and are secure) and that the dive team can anticipate no delay or hindrance to their exit due to dealing with the sudden unexpected loss of one diver's air supply, loss of visibility, disorientation, or restrictions.

Unstable Equilibrium - The state of a body in water such that when it is moved by a disturbing force from its original position, it continues into a position of stable equilibrium after the disturbing force is removed.

Vadose - Relating to the subsurface aeration zone in permeable ground.

Vadose Water - Subsurface water in the vadose zone.

Vadose Zone - In permeable ground, the subsurface zone that overlies the phreatic or saturation zone. Syn: *aeration zone.*

Vital Capacity - The maximum amount of air that an individual can take into her lungs. It is determined by measuring the amount of air that can be exhaled following full inspiration. As the diver ages, vital capacity decreases. It also decreases in certain diseases and other chronic conditions.

Vulcanospeleology - The study of lava tube caves.

Water Table - The upper boundary-layer of the unconfined saturation or phreatic zone. The hydrostatic pressure along the water table is equal to the atmospheric pressure.

Water Trap - Another term for *siphon.*

Wide Scope Penetration - When penetrating an unfamiliar cave system, a wide scope penetration is one in which side tunnels are identified and explored, at least to see if they represent potential leads.

Wilderness - An area left in its original, authentic natural state, which humans are able to visit or live in only temporarily. Wilderness is the opposite of civilization, affording one of the few places individuals can go for renewal and respite from its tensions and pressures.

Submerged caves represent a potential wilderness that we cave divers have managed to civilize at least partly by installing permanent lines, directional markers, etc. Continual placement and removal of line creates additional wear and tear on the cave, so permanent line installation is also a conservation measure. Fortunately, there are still some fairly accessible sections of submerged caves which do not have permanent line installed. This provides cave divers the opportunity to see nearly-natural cave passage and to experience an appreciation of these caves as part of the Earth's majestic and vanishing wilderness.

Wilson Markers - Another name for line arrows, which were invented by Forrest Wilson.

Wilson System - A type of the touch-contact system for low visibility diving communication. The Wilson system contains at least one ambiguous signal. Because of this ambiguity, it is not often used.

Window - A natural opening above the cave floor which permits access to an adjoining cave void or to the surface. Similar but smaller, roughly circular openings are called *portholes*.

Wings - Another name for a *back-mount BC*.

Worming - Negotiating a small, constricting, low visibility passageway, usually done feet first in unfamiliar tunnel (so that, if the tunnel becomes impassable, the diver can exit more easily). Since worms have to crawl blindly through the dirt, any time the passage requires the diver to wriggle or crawl blindly through the bottom sediments, she is *worming*.

Yo-Yo Diving - Dives made involving multiple ascents and descents during the dive. There is some reason to believe that *Yo-Yo diving* may predispose the diver to DCS.

BIBLIOGRAPHY

Leitheuser, Terry. "Classification of Cave Faunas." *NACD News*, Vol VIII, No. 2 (February, 1981): 4-6.

Monroe, Watson H., ed. *A Glossary of Karst Terminology : Geological Survey Water-Supply Paper 1899-K.* Washington: United States Government Printing Office, 1970.

Mount, Tom, ed. *Safe Cave Diving.* High Springs, FL: National Association for Cave Diving, 1973.

Morris, William, ed. *The American Heritage Dictionary.* 2nd ed., Boston: The Houghton Mifflin Company, 1991.

Charles Shilling *et al.*, eds. *The Underwater Handbook: A Guide to Physiology and Performance for the Engineer.* New York: Plenum Press, 1976.